STUART FISHER

BRITISH RIVER NAVIGATIONS

INLAND CUTS, FENS, DIKES, CHANNELS AND NON-TIDAL RIVERS

ADLARD COLES NAUTICAL
BLOOMSBURY
LONDON • NEW DELHI • NEW YORK • SYDNEY

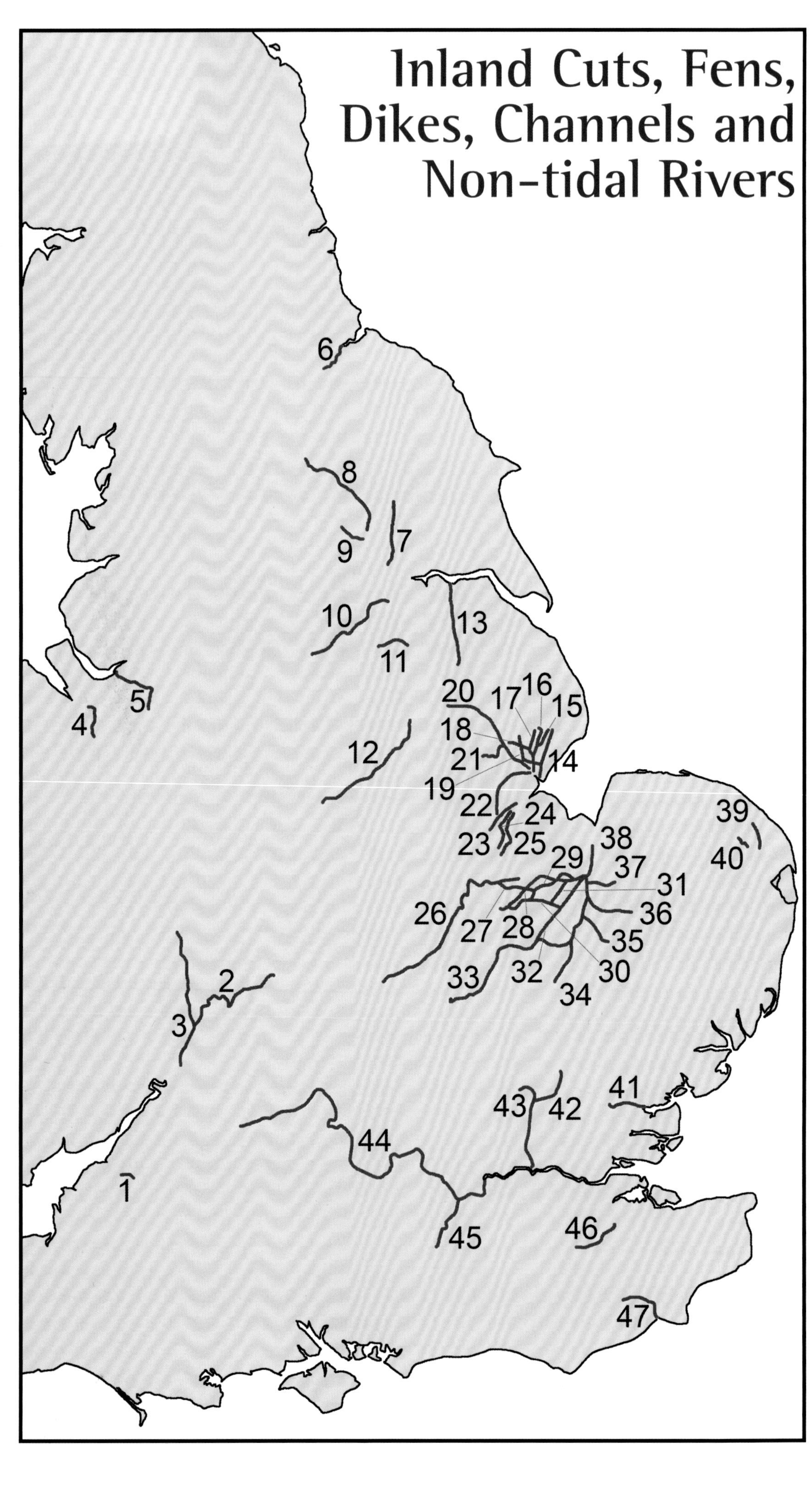
Inland Cuts, Fens, Dikes, Channels and Non-tidal Rivers
1
2
3
4
5
6
7
8
9
10
11
12
13
14
15
16
17
18
19
20
21
22
23
24
25
26
27
28
29
30
31
32
33
34
35
36
37
38
39
40
41
42
43
44
45
46
47

Contents

The Glory Hole, Lincoln, River Witham.

Cliveden is thought to be the best reach on the Thames.

Acknowledgements

P6 from *Little Billee* by William Makepeace Thackeray.
P12 from *Upon Eckington Bridge, River Avon* by Arthur Quiller-Couch.
P21 from *The South Country* by Hilaire Belloc reproduced by permission of Sharon Rubin, PFD.
P29 Anon.
P41 Anon.
P49 from *Rokeby* by Sir Walter Scott.
P59 from *Don & Rother* by Ebenezer Elliot.
P64 from *The River Idle* by Phoebe Hesketh reproduced by permission of Stephen Stuart-Smith, publisher of her *Netting the Sun: New & Collected Poems.*
P66 from *Clifton Grove* by Henry Kirke White.
P80 from *Boston* by Henry Wadsworth Longfellow.
P89 from *The Wytham* by Michael Drayton.
P109 from *Welland River* by William Morris.
P112 from *From Northampton Asylum* by John Clare.
P144 from *The Task* by William Cowper.
P156 from *The Prelude* by William Wordsworth.
P162 Anon.
P178 from *Essex* by Arthur Shearly Cripps.
P189 from *Prothalamion* by Edmund Spenser.
P198 from *The Glories of Our Thames* by William Cox Bennett.
P236 by John Pitt.
P244 Anon.
P249 from *Sussex* by Rudyard Kipling.

Every effort has been made to trace authors. Bloomsbury are happy to correct any error or omission in future editions.

Published by Adlard Coles Nautical
an imprint of Bloomsbury Publishing Plc
50 Bedford Square, London WC1B 3DP
www.adlardcoles.com

First edition published 2013

ISBN 978-1-4729-0084-5

A CIP catalogue record for this book is available from the British Library.

This book is produced using paper that is made from wood grown in managed, sustainable forests. It is natural, renewable and recyclable. The logging and manufacturing processes conform to the environmental regulations of the country of origin.

Typeset in 9pt Bembo

Printed and bound in China by C&C Offset Printing Co

Note: reference to waters do not necessarily imply that access and passage on those waters or their banks is legally permitted or that they are safe in all conditions. The author and publishers cannot be held responsible for any omissions of references to hazards on these waters. Circumstances can change without warning. The user should assess the situation using all information available at the time and act appropriately.

Introduction

Water transport for people has taken place for thousands of years on natural watercourses, rivers and the sea. Sometimes there was no dry land route between places of interest or it was blocked by vegetation. Increasingly, boats were used to move goods. People or horses could only carry limited loads on their backs. Wagons, perhaps pulled by oxen, on unsurfaced and poorly-drained roads, could quickly become bogged down or overturn in quagmires and were easy targets for the lawless.

Water allowed heavy loads to be moved but was not without its problems. Local difficulties on natural rivers could sometimes be removed by suitable excavation. Lock cuts past weirs and waterfalls became progressively longer until canals were being cut entirely free of rivers, such as the Nottingham Beeston Canal avoiding a difficult section of the River Trent.

Other interests conflicted with navigation, however. Where a weir could be built or a natural fall bypassed, the differential head of water could be used to drive a mill. Millers conserved their water. An obstruction such as this was bypassed by a flash lock, a single barrier to the flow which could be opened to let a boat shoot through on the resulting rapid when going downstream. Coming upstream involved hauling or winching a boat against the flow – even more wasteful of water. The introduction of pound locks, which released only one lockful of water with each passage, was thus a significant improvement.

Further obstructions to navigation resulted from fish traps placed in a river. Flood control required rivers to be drawn down ready for any spates, especially in the winter, often to levels too shallow for navigation. To this day there are people who think wildlife wants overgrown channels and no people or boats.

With the arrival of railways, able to move heavier loads more quickly, and the improvement of roads, so that factories did not need waterside locations, the use of boats for transport declined, especially on smaller rivers. In most places it was only the larger rivers which were still in use when recreational boating achieved widespread popularity in the twentieth century, not least by small portable boats.

This raised the question of navigation rights for those not used to seeing boats on rivers. In Scotland, as in most other countries, there is a confirmed public right of navigation on all rivers. The situation in England and Wales is less clear, with Defra, of which the Environment Agency is part, opposing the right. The Revd Dr Douglas Caffyn, whose research is supported by the law departments of two universities, has claimed (www.caffynonrivers.co.uk) that navigation rights have never been removed from rivers south of the border, either, but that confusion results from a series of errors in a law textbook of 1830, less significant at that time when river use was declining. Waterways Minister Richard Benyon has told me that the Government is unclear what the law says but is not prepared to spend time searching for evidence that the navigation right was removed from our rivers. Defra won't concede the right remains.

This book restricts itself to longer inland rivers on which there is an undisputed right of navigation, usually identified by a licence requirement. Tidal navigations, which include almost all river navigations in Scotland and Wales, have been featured in my *Rivers of Britain* published by Adlard Coles Nautical.

As well as natural rivers, this book includes fenland drains which were cut for drainage purposes across these low-lying areas but which included transport of agricultural produce as a secondary benefit. They are often drawn down in winter to handle potential floodwater, frequently do not have room to turn a long boat at their heads and suffer weed growth in summer because of low flows and the effects of fertilizers washed off the land. On these and the other navigations you will need to ascertain whether the depth and width are suitable for your boat, when you want to go, or that there is a right of way along the bank if travelling on land.

While some canals and major rivers can become congested because of their popularity, the more peripheral rivers, not least the rivers of the east of England, offer the freedom of light traffic and few locks for those who wish to get away from crowds. Several sections of the proposed Fens Waterways Link are described in this book. This scheme is unlikely to progress until the planned takeover of Environment Agency navigations by the Canal & River Trust takes place but should become accessible in the future, especially if the planned Bedford & Milton Keynes Waterway link is constructed, which will give further through route options to boaters. At present these waters offer more to those who boat with a pioneering spirit. Few who cruise down the Thames will reach the end of Popham's Eau but each has its attractions.

Whatever your preference, there is something in this book for you.

Stuart Fisher

Legend for maps

Featured river
Other canal or river
Motorway
Other road
Guided busway
Railway
Open water or sea
Inter-tidal zone
Built-up area
Woodland

Scale 1:200,000.
North is always at the top.

Photographs

Chris Blakey p200 inset
All other photographs by the author.

By same author

Canals of Britain
(abbreviated CoB in reference panels), 2009/2012
Rivers of Britain
(abbreviated RoB in reference panels), 2012
Inshore Britain, 2006
Visit www.adlardcoles.com for further information.

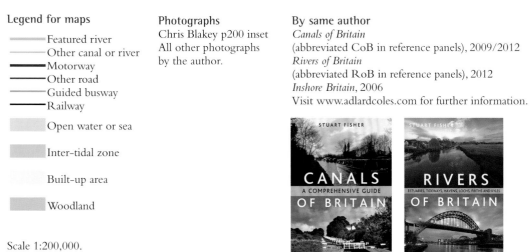

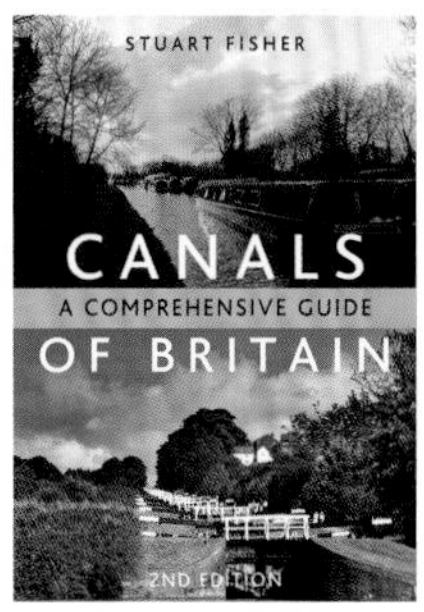

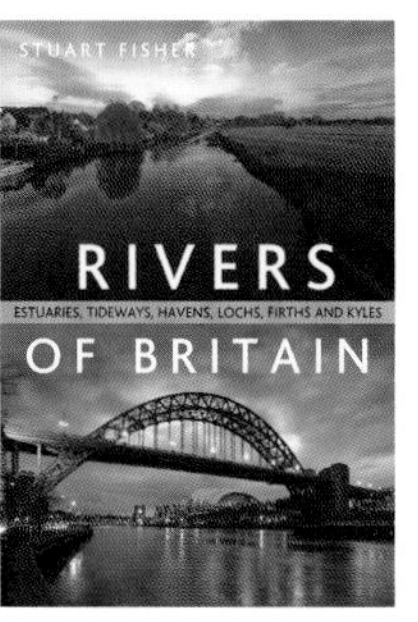

1 River Avon (Bristol)

The world's largest impounded harbour

There were three sailors in Bristol city
Who took a boat and went to sea.
But first with beef and captains biscuit
And pickled pork they loaded she.
William Makepeace Thackeray

Rising near Horton, the River Avon flows east, south then northwest to the Mouth of the Severn. Until the Bristol Channel was downthrown it may have flowed eastwards, fed by Welsh rivers and serving as headwaters for the Kennet. Normally tidal from the weir at Netham, it can be affected as far up as **Keynsham** on spring tides, to the extent that cruisers can float over **Hanham** Weir on the top of springs if the lock is not available. The flood is reduced by fresh easterly or northeasterly winds. Unusually, the river is in Bristol but the left bank is initially in Bath & NE Somerset and the right bank in S Gloucestershire.

The Chequers Inn and Old Lock & Weir Ale House above Hanham Lock make this a popular area for those arriving by car as well as by boat.

The wooded valley looking towards Conham.

The snaking cable-stayed Valentine Bridge.

By the time the river is crossed by the A4174 it is in a steep gorge of red Pennant sandstone although this is not often seen because of the covering of ash, sycamore, alder, oak, willow, hawthorn and Himalayan balsam. Fox's Wood was the site of some of the Great Western Railway's first water troughs for a couple of years until they were moved to Keynsham. The railway disappears into a tunnel for a while, leaving the muddy river to cormorants, mallards, herons, moorhens, swans, even seals, and significant amounts of flotsam at the top of a higher tide.

A large pipe follows the right bank for a while, made more conspicuous by the attentions of the spray can enthusiasts.

A deeply cut meander at Conham is one place where the orange cliff is clearly visible ahead. Bristol Ariel Rowing Club is located on the meander. Weeping willows and elms give way to what was an industrial reach of the river. Conham had copperworks, brassworks, a colliery, many furnaces, a tar distillery producing creosote for railway sleepers and an early pottery. Concrete staithes remain at St Anne's, which had huge board mills.

With the river in poor condition, approval was given in 1811 for a bypass canal from Bath to Bristol which was to have followed the developments in **Bristol**. In the Middle Ages Jessop closed off the river at Hotwells to create the Floating Harbour, a basin where ships would remain afloat, the world's largest impounded harbour and one of the only large floating harbours in Europe to become a good earner, and act as a flood reservoir to protect Bristol. Using French prisoners of war, a New Cut was made in 1804–9 to the south from Totterdown through solid rock to take the tidal river and a Feeder Canal was cut to the north from Netham. Beyond a concrete bowstring bridge is a large V weir which had its height raised in 1810 to deepen the Floating Harbour.

The Feeder Canal leaves to the right through Netham Lock, the gates of which are left open except when tides are high. When the gates are shut it is not an easy portage for small craft, even before all the silt is taken into consideration.

This canal, crossed by the railway and the A4320 Bristol Spine Road, is followed by an industrial estate with Fayes Café and by a road much used by commercial traffic yet it is also home to the kingfisher. A 17km/h speed limit applies and anglers are present.

The barge connection from Totterdown Basin to the tidal river was filled to prevent a potential Second World War bomb hit from draining the Floating Harbour. A former brass mill has also been closed and a former Royal Mail sorting office is seeing new use. The Motion night club and BMX park offer a confused mix of camouflage netting and garish fantasy artwork.

A pair of stone arches, extended each way in blue engineering brick like large tunnel bores, carry the railway back over the western end of what was referred to as Brunel's Billiard Table because of its smooth and level ride, his Great Western Railway from Paddington to Temple Meads. Brunel was chief engineer from 1833, when he was 27. The old Temple Meads station built next to the water by Brunel in 1840 was the world's first station to have a roof enclosing the platforms and track. The 22m span train shed has a mock hammerbeam roof, arches being formed by pairs of opposing cantilevers. The new station of 1876 bends away from it on a 300m radius curve, covered by a 38m span roof with a neo-

Castle Park with a ferry landing below St Peter's church ruin.

Gothic facade, it being unusual for the engineer to be the architect as well. This is the world's oldest railway station to preserve most of its original shape.

The oval Temple church, founded in the 12th century by the Knights Templars, was replaced in the 15th century by a Perpendicular design although the tower is no longer perpendicular because it was built on marsh but could have been much worse when wartime bombing delivered a shell.

A large fig tree grows from the bank between two modern footbridges, the first resembling a cheesegrater and the following Valentine Bridge cable-stayed design snaking across the river at Temple Quay.

Beyond the A4044 the Grade II 43m Lead Shot Tower replaces an earlier one demolished in 1968. Used for making recreational ammunition by allowing lead drips to solidify as they fell through the air, it has now become offices.

Opposite the former Courage's brewery site, redeveloped for housing, the River Frome joins on the right, having flowed for the last 700m in a medieval tunnel which can be used by a small boat. It has a further tunnel connection to the head of St Augustine's reach. A ferry landing below the derelict St Peter's church in Castle Park precedes the 13th century Bristol Bridge with pairs of columns beside each of its stone arches, too low to pass a sailing ship although five swing or bascule bridges cross the Floating Harbour downstream.

North of the park is John Wesley's chapel of 1739, the world's oldest Methodist building, rebuilt in 1748. Methodism was founded by Charles Wesley, the prolific hymn writer, whose house is a little further north. By the park is Christchurch, built in the late 18th century with a beautiful Georgian interior, a pair of 1728 quarterjacks, a gilded dragon weathervane and walls which resisted Second World War bombing. The Grade II façade of the 1900 Art Nouveau Edward Everard printing works has been retained, the largest decorated façade in Britain. A little further is St John's Gate, the city's last medieval gate with the effigies of the mythical kings Brennus and Belinus, who were said to have founded the city. St John the Baptist church is built into the wall. St Nicholas covered market of 1745 was rebuilt in 1850 to the same Palladian style. Lewins Mead Unitarian church in 1791 Classical style replaced an early non comformist chapel of 1694. The Rummer Hotel is on the site of the Green Lattis, the city's oldest inn. Corn Street has four nails or small, tall, round, brass tables used since the 16th century for completing business deals on the nail until the Grade I Corn Exchange was built in 1743.

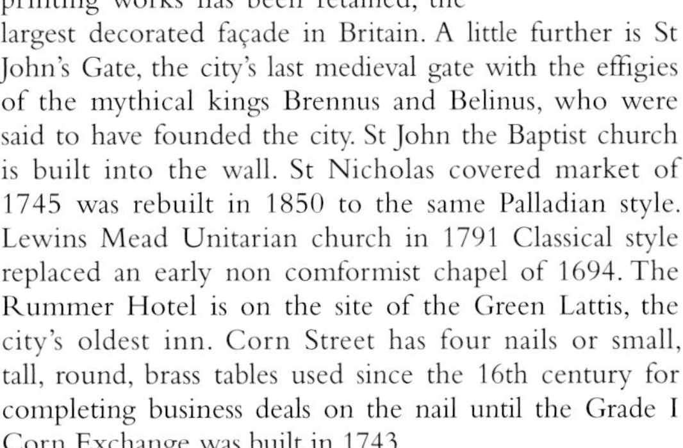

Bristol takes its name from the Saxon Bregstow or Old English brycg-stow, bridge meeting place. The harbour area was developed by Æthelred the Unready. The city was attacked in 1068 by three of Harold's sons with Irish support but was to become a leading port for seafaring, both exploration and commercial. There had been a Saxon mint and the first quay was built in 1247. Bristol ships were smart and efficient, leading to the expression

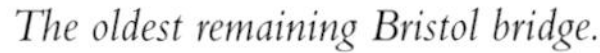

The oldest remaining Bristol bridge.

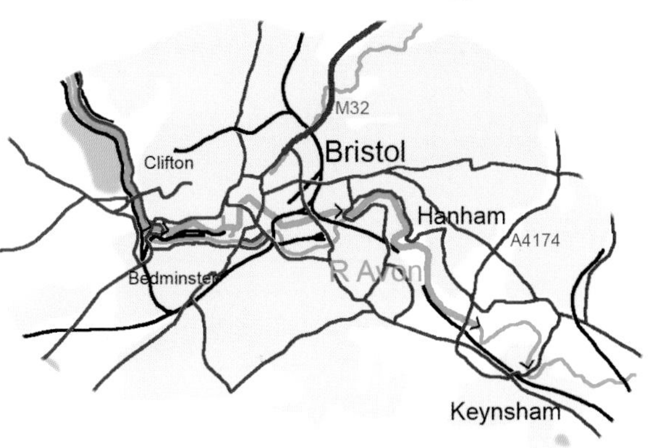

The Llandoger Trow off the Welsh Back.

'shipshape and Bristol fashion'. Cloth was exported in the Middle Ages and it was the second port and city to London in medieval times. Cabot helped fund the Merchant Venturers, incorporated in 1552, trading in wine, tobacco, sugar, rum and slaves as the colonies developed. By the early 19th century this had become the gateway to the Americas. Many of the buildings date from the Regency. Council plans to fill in much of the harbour were thwarted by the establishment of the annual Bristol Harbour Festival from 1971, which drew attention to the amenity potential.

The Glassboat restaurant and the Brigstow Hotel are on the Welsh Back, an area of waterfront which handled Welsh slate carried in trows. Robinson's Warehouse and the Granary, at one time a leading rock club, have coloured brick and Moorish arches in a style known as Bristol Byzantine. The half timbered Llandoger Trow inn of 1664 stands back from the right bank on the cobbled King Street, which had been laid outside the city wall the previous year. It featured as the Spyglass Inn in *Treasure Island*, the *Hispaniola* having sailed from here, and is where *Robinson Crusoe* was probably thought out after Defoe met Alexander Selkirk, this being described as the first true English novel. The inn has the ghost of a crippled boy who had to fetch water from a pump.

Queen Square, the largest square outside London, was named after Queen Anne's visit in 1702 and includes a statue of William III in Roman emperor dress. It was the centre of the action during the 1831 Bristol Riots opposed to official corruption. Brunel, as a special constable, made an arrest.

In use since 1766, the Grade I Theatre Royal was modelled on Wren's Drury Lane theatre in London and has had the longest run in Britain, its façade even older,

Bristol's M Shed with the Mayflower *and* Bee *moored in front and the Harbour Railway train about to pass the cranes.*

A replica of the Matthew *moored alongside the Arnolfini Centre. The Cabot Tower is just right of the crane.*

from the 1743 Hall of the Guild of Coopers. This is where Sarah Siddons started her career, her ghost being here. The Old Vic, Britain's longest continuously working theatre company, has been based here since 1946. The adjacent Merchant Venturers Almshouses of 1699 were for retired mariners.

St Mary Redcliffe is one of the best examples of medieval architecture in the country, partly 12th century, with an 89m spire restored in 1872 after being truncated by lightning in 1446, over a thousand carved roof bosses, a carved 13th century porch, 18th century ironwork, grotesque carvings, a notable organ, beautiful stained glass and a 200mm diameter copy of the Chartres cathedral labyrinth. It was where Thomas Chatterton claimed to have found the 15th century poems of a monk called Thomas Rowley although they were by himself in the 18th century. His forgeries and his death were the subject of paintings, poems and stories by some of the leading members of the arts of the day, the story being revived in Peter Ackroyd's *Chatterton* in 1987. There is a tombstone to Tom, the church cat living here for 13 years, leaving a legacy of three bath loads of fish bones and feathers hidden in the church.

Redcliffe Bridge opens. Although the barge connection to the tidal river was filled as a wartime measure, the Bathurst Basin is still used for moorings near Bristol General Hospital.

Prince Street swing bridge is followed by M Shed with four remaining travelling cranes, a museum featuring trains, ships, planes, buses, cars and slavery with a shunting engine, the world's oldest working tug in the 1861 *Mayflower*, the 1935 motor tug *John King*, the 1934 fire float *Pyronaut*, models of the *Great Western* and *Great Britain* and a replica of Brunel's *BD6* dredger, used as a cinema. There is a replica Concorde nose and an 1875 steam carriage which is probably the world's oldest operating self propelled vehicle. The 35t Fairbairn steam crane is an Ancient Monument but still works. M Shed is built over the dry dock used for Brunel's 2,300t PS *Great Western* in 1838, the world's longest ship with a 76m keel and an 11m beam. She was used to extend the GWR to New York and was the first to hold the Blue Riband.

Facing is the Arnolfini Arts Centre in the 1837 Grade II Bush tea warehouse, presenting contemporary arts, films, theatre, music, dance and exhibitions. This is the city where Cary Grant was born and began his career and where *The House of Eliott*, *Aquila*, *Casualty*, *Only Fools & Horses*, *Shoestring*, *Truly, Madly, Deeply*, *Animal Magic* and *Animal Ark* were filmed. Wildscreen is a wildlife film festival based here. Bellatrix is from Bristol. Another local artform is Bristol Blue glass, now made in Bedminster.

St Augustine's reach, a diversion of the River Frome, joins from the north, crossed by the 1999 Pero's Bridge, a bascule bridge balanced by horn shaped counterweights and named after an 18th century slave. The Architecture Centre and the Watershed multimedia centre are located on this reach which was previously busy with transit sheds. Harvey's Wine Museum in 13th century cellars includes antique bottles, corkscrews and 18th century drinking glasses. Science and rainforest centres, the All About Us exhibition and an Imax cinema are At-Bristol offerings.

Bristol Cathedral has a Norman chapter house and abbey gatehouse from the 1140 abbey of St Augustine,

The Amphitheatre at the entrance to St Augustine's Reach.

named after St Augustine's meeting Christians in the 7th century. It has been a cathedral since the 1542 Dissolution, restored in 1897. There are spectacular carvings, flying buttresses and an east end which is a leading example of a church hall. The 12th century Lady Chapel has a window with original glass from about 1340.

The Georgian House belonged to an 18th century sugar merchant, includes a plunge pool and was used by the BBC for filming *A Respectable Trade*. Opposite, the classical church of St George with excellent acoustics has become a concert hall.

The Red Lodge Museum of the former Tudor Great House of about 1590 is Bristol's only remaining Tudor interior, with magnificent plasterwork, oak panelling, a stone chimneypiece, 17/18th century paintings and an Elizabethan knot garden. Bristol Museum & Art Gallery includes ship models from 1780 to 1914, a Brunel dredger engine, a rope walk, anchors, tools, trade, industry, transport, a Bristol Boxkite, model locomotives and 14–17th century European paintings. The Victoria Rooms, now part of the university with a statue of Edward VII outside, are in classical style with Victorian portico, a 19th century public and political meeting hall. The city's oldest buildings are the 13th century almshouses which became the grammar school in 1532 and now belong to St Bartholomew's hospital.

An 18th century cylindrical crane base marks the entrance to the reach at Bordeaux Quay past the Amphitheatre. The Bank of England was in a Renaissance style building contemporary with the 1854 Lloyds Bank in a Venetian style with a notable frieze. Bristol University's 66m neo-Gothic Wills Memorial Tower recalls the tobacco magnates, whose business was developed in the city. Standing beyond the university is the 32m Cabot Tower of 1897, commemorating the 1497 expedition of Venetian John Cabot and his son, Sebastian, which discovered Newfoundland while seeking a route to the East Indies. John went to Greenland in 1498 without his son and maybe reached Delaware Bay. Sebastian claimed to have reached Hudson Bay in 1509.

Users of the water range from herring and blackbacked gulls, kayaks and offshore racing gigs to ferries and trip boats of all sizes plus some marine working vessels. Powerboat racing which took place from 1972 to 1991 was stopped as it was so dangerous that it had been called

Bridgwater trading ketch Irene.

the Widowmaker. Most conspicuous of the trip boats is a replica of John Cabot's *Matthew*.

Jacob's Wells date from at least 1042. Used by Jews to fill ritual baths, they have the oldest known Hebrew inscriptions in Britain.

The West Country trading ketch *Irene*, moored here, was used in the *Pirates of the Caribbean* and Blackbeard was a local pirate.

Brunel's SS *Great Britain* in 1843 was much bigger, the world's largest ship at 3,675t, capable of 22km/h and measuring 98m x 15m. The world's first ocean going, steam powered, iron screw driven ship but with six masts for extra power, this was the first large ship with a clipper bow, had a unique double bottom and had plates clinker-built for extra strength. It set a new record of 14 days for the Atlantic crossing. Because of excessive dock charges a relocation to Liverpool took place. She carried 15,000 emigrants to Australia and 45,000 troops to the Indian Mutiny and the Crimea but was damaged in a storm in 1886, used as a storage hulk in the Falklands before being recovered in 1970, brought back home and restored with a glass sea in the dry dock in which she was built. Bristol Marina is adjacent in the former Albion Dockyard.

Chicken Run and *Wallace & Gromit* were made in studios close by.

A modern footbridge over a small dock on the north side of the harbour appears to be a double bascule bridge but it is not what it seems. It leads to the Grade II Pump House, now a bar and restaurant, which looks like a church tower. It faces across to the Underfall Yard. The overfall was a weir to allow excess water to discharge to the tidal river but Brunel rebuilt it to flush silt out from the bottom of the harbour, where it was accumulating. As well as silt the harbour contains fool's gold, tipped in after being brought back from Canada by Frobisher. The yard is overlooked by two early 20th century bonded tobacco warehouses, now housing the Create eco centre and Bristol Record Office.

The Cumberland Basin Bridge and Junction Lock begin Cumberland Basin, built as a half tide basin, around which are four large anchors as features. Jessop's lock at the far end was modified significantly in 1845–9 by Brunel, following emergency changes by him in 1844 when the *Great Britain* wedged on leaving. The Howard Lock alongside is from 1873. This is the Floating Harbour exit to the tidal river, much of the time just a cleft through the silt. The fixed Avon Bridge and swinging Plimsoll Bridge of 1965 both carrying the A3029 across. A mark on the control cabin records a 12.4m tide experienced. Beneath the Plimsoll Bridge a wrought iron tubular swivel bridge by Brunel lies unused on the bank, this being his longest surviving tubular bridge and a precursor for his Chepstow and Saltash railway bridges. The bridge across Brunel's disused lock is a replica.

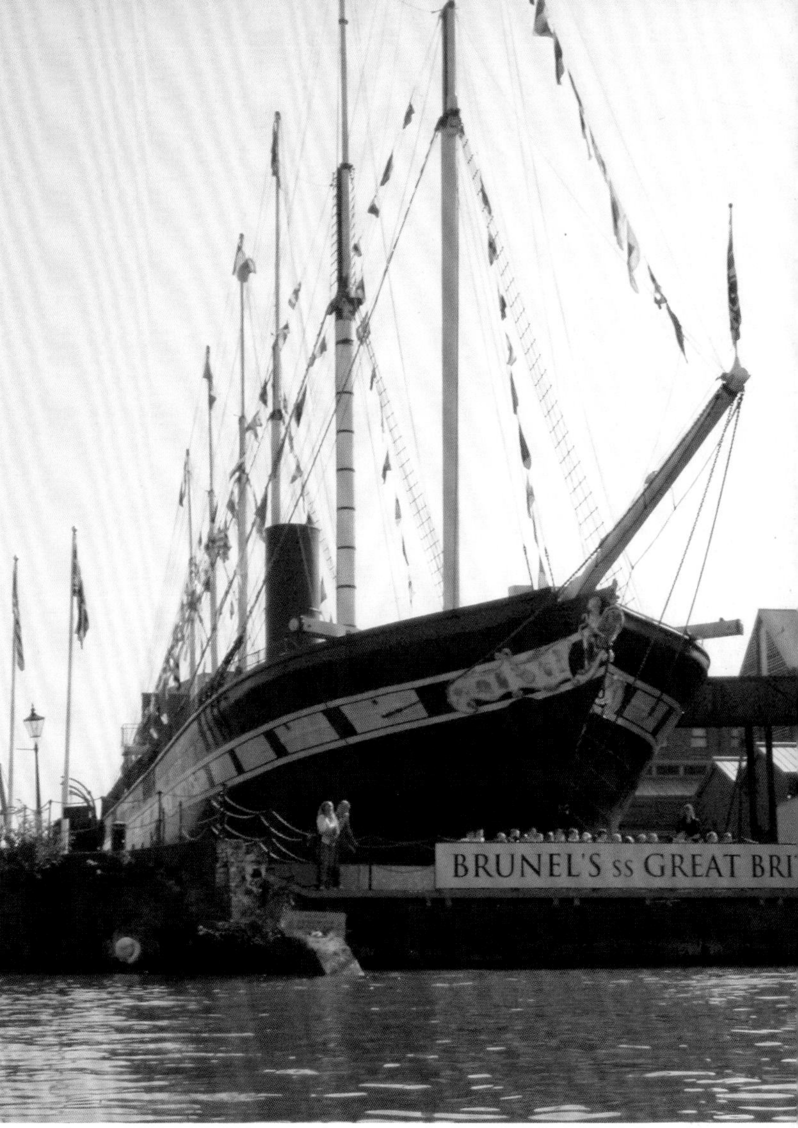

The SS Great Britain *back where she was built.*

Bridges can be finely balanced. Partway through resurfacing one, an engineer had to do some swift calculations on where to park a 10t dumper with contractors breathing over her shoulder as a ship approached in order to balance the material already laid to permit the bridge to be opened.

Plimsoll was born in the city, his legacy being lines on the side of every commercial ship to prevent overloading, having saved numerous lives at sea throughout the world.

Beyond the lock the harbour the tidal river heads away under the iconic Clifton suspension bridge, a route taken by so many explorers, emigrants and merchants over the centuries.

The last of Brunel's tubular girders below the Plimsoll Bridge at the mouth of the Cumberland Basin.

Distance
10km from Hanham to the Cumberland Basin

Navigation Authority
Bristol City Council

OS 1:50,000 Sheet
172 Bristol & Bath

Connections
Kennet & Avon Canal
– see CoB p125
Tidal River Avon
– see RoB p20

2 River Avon (Warwicks)

Literary and agrarian plums

Man shall outlast his battles. They have swept
Avon from Naseby Field to Severn Ham;
And Evesham's dedicated stones have stepp'd
Down to the dust with Montfort's oriflamme.
Nor the red tear nor the reflected tower
Abides; but yet these elegant grooves remain,
Worn in the sandstone parapet hour by hour
By labouring bargemen where they shifted ropes.
Arthur Quiller-Couch

The Warwickshire or Shakespeare's Avon has often been at the forefront of river navigation with improvements considered since the 15th century and it was the first river to have pound locks, installed from 1636 to 1665, by which time boats could reach Stratford. Defoe noted that boats could bring goods almost to Warwick by the early 18th century although the river was in poor condition by the 19th century. It became the first to be restored by volunteers and the first to use the Services to assist a civilian project, beginning in 1950, with the navigation being reopened below Evesham in 1964 and the section to Alveston a decade later, each time by the Queen Mother.

The technical problems were exacerbated by the opposition of landowners, repeated difficulties caused by the river authority and a lack of support from the authorities in Stratford. There is still plenty of opposition to boats, with many notices banning mooring even in open countryside. Attempts to restore the navigation upstream with a link to the Grand Union Canal at Warwick have been vigorously opposed with the only use permitted being canoeists allowed a charity trip for Guide Dogs for the Blind one day a year, the Doggy Paddle.

A house of the more substantial kind at Tiddington.

The sections above and below Evesham have been restored by separate trusts, both of which have had to adopt some unconventional solutions in the face of shortage of finances. Relations between them had been strained over the years and the merger to form the Avon Navigation Trust did not come until 2007.

The river rises on England's watershed near Naseby and flows southwest across Warwickshire to the River Severn. It floods quickly and, as seen at Tewkesbury in 2007, sometimes to extreme levels, these being the worst British floods in modern times. The line is into the prevailing wind. There is no towpath but footpaths frequently follow the banks.

Past users of the river have been Severn trows with their D shaped sterns, developed from square-rigged vessels. Regular users these days include coarse anglers with wooden platforms all down the banks and frequent estates of chalets on wheels near the river. Water extraction points for crops are also quite numerous.

The current head of navigation is Alveston where there is a steep weir at the site of a former mill, reached down a green lane from the village. Local farmers rear sheep in fields dotted with oaks, the river edged with occasional willows, ashes, sycamores, reedmace, teasels and marsh marigolds with mallards, herons, kingfishers, Canada geese, moorhens and pheasants on or near the river.

The Romans had a settlement at Tiddington where the Old Bathing Place is more recent and some very large properties currently back onto the river.

Until recently the only road crossing at Stratford has been the Clopton Bridge carrying the A3400, on the line of a Roman road and a ford. The bridge was funded in the 1480s by Sir Hugh Clopton, a Stratford merchant who became Lord Mayor of London in 1492. The 300m long structure with 19 arches was later reduced to 147m with 14 pointed arches of 5.6–5.8m, widened in 1814 with arches to 8.9m, an octagonal toll tower built at the north end and a footway added in 1827. The bridge's name has been used for a folk dance. The Tramway Bridge was built downstream of it in 1823 with nine semi-elliptical 9.1m brick arches extending it to 107m including two dry arches at the southern end. It was for the Stratford & Moreton Horse Tramway which it was planned to extend to London. Now the bridge carries only pedestrians but a replica wagon is in Bancroft Gardens. At the northern end of the bridges are a marina and Cox's Yard, Stratford Tales and a microbrewery.

Stratford-upon-Avon was first mentioned in 691 but is now so well known that it receives more overseas visitors than anywhere else in Britain except London. It has had a market since 1196 and retains its 14th century layout with more historic buildings for its size than any other English town. The visitors come because this

Stratford's Tramway Bridge and the Royal Shakespeare Theatre.

A replica tramway wagon in Bancroft Gardens.

was home to William Shakespeare, the world's greatest playwright, whose 1888 statue by Gower in the Bancroft Gardens is surrounded by some of his best known characters, Hamlet, Lady Macbeth, Falstaff and Henry V. Behind him the Stratford-upon-Avon Canal joins the river after a basin with floating facilities from fast food to the Barge Gallery with its art.

The 1769 David Garrick Jubilee was the first town festival in Britain, revived in 1983 as the Stratford on Avon Festival with music, poetry, jousting, street markets, open air theatre, river pageants, morris dancing and medieval banquets. Annual Shakespeare birthday celebrations take place about April 23rd. There are also a Stratford International Flute Festival, Stratford Regatta in June and Stratford River Festival while the Mop Fair in October has moved on from hiring domestic and farm workers.

The river is extremely busy with swans, despite problems which have been caused for them by boat propellers stirring up discarded lead angling weights. Canoes and rowing boats are hired out in profusion and it is where, in 1975, the Queen became the first reigning monarch to take a ride in a narrowboat.

The bard is everywhere. There is a Shakespeare Centre, the Shakespeare Express from Birmingham on summer Sundays is England's fastest scheduled steam railway service and Shakespearience is at the Waterside Theatre. Shakespeare's Birthplace of 1564 is half timbered, with a library, Shakespeare roses and more than a hundred trees, shrubs, plants and flowers mentioned by Shakespeare.

A lesser son was bicycle designer Alex Moulton.

Stratford-upon-Avon Butterfly Farm & Insect City is the largest in Europe with 1,500 butterflies, humming birds, koi carp, scorpions and Arachnoland.

The Royal Shakespeare Company, the world's largest classical theatre company, present high quality Shakespeare in the utilitarian 1932 red brick Royal Shakespeare Theatre, behind which is a nine men's morris pitch. There is the Courtyard Theatre and the RSC also perform in the Swan Theatre of 1986 with Elizabethan galleried style in the shell of a burnt out theatre of 1879.

The bard in Bancroft Gardens.

The Teddy Bear Museum is in a 16th century beamed house formerly owned by Henry VIII while the White Swan is a 15th century timber framed three storey hotel with a 16th century painted mural. Given by a Philadelphian at Victoria's jubilee are the American

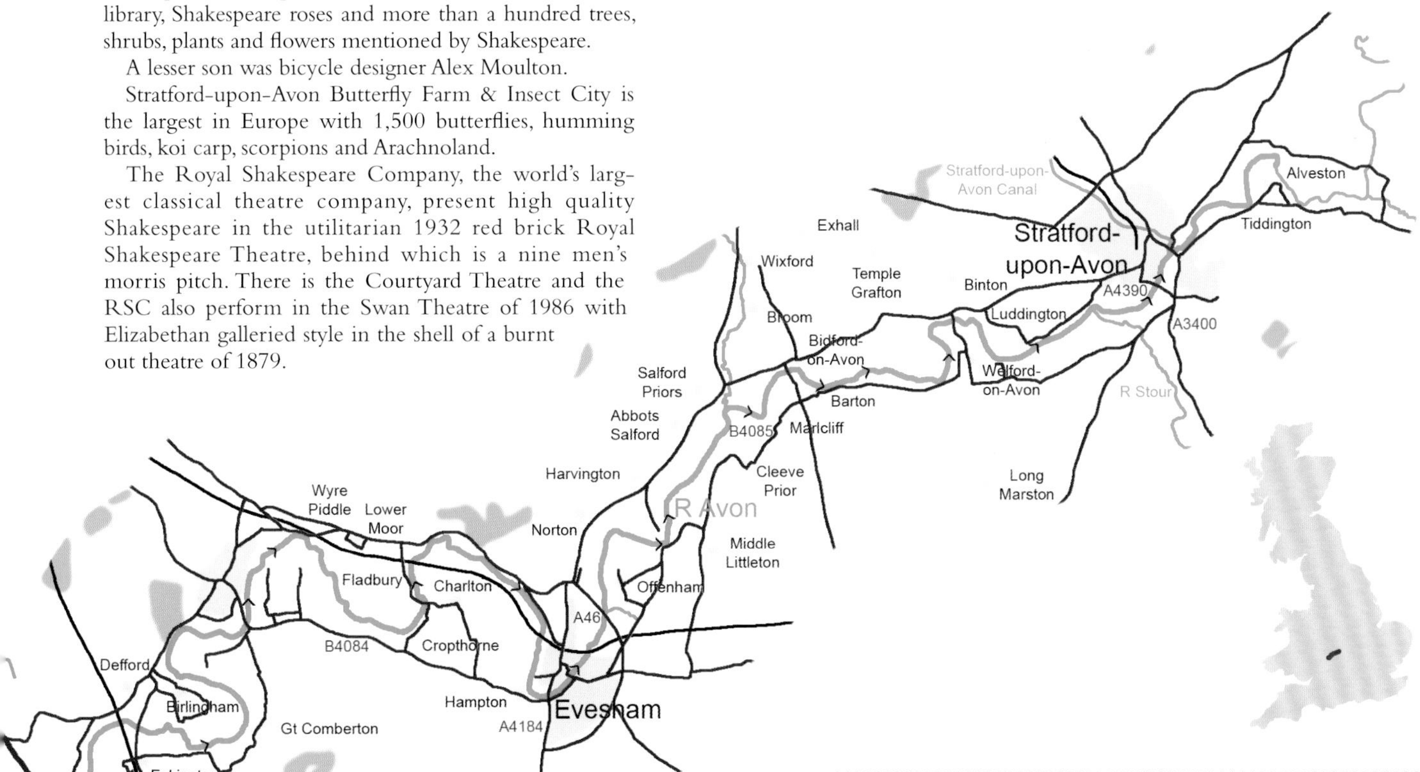

Fountain and Gothic clocktower. Harvard House, one of the town's best half-timbered buildings, rebuilt in 1596, was the childhood home of Katherine Rogers, mother of John Harvard, now donated to Harvard University and having the Museum of British Pewter from Roman times to the 19th century. The 16th century Shrieves House Barn houses the haunted Falstaff's Experience museum and the Witches Glade with its ducking stool.

The Town Hall of 1767 by Newman in Cotswold stone has a 1769 statue of Shakespeare presented by Garrick, restored after a 1946 fire. The Guildhall is part of King Edward VI Grammar School attended by Shakespeare, refounded in 1553 after more than 250 years. The Guild Chapel founded in 1269 and partly rebuilt in 1495 by Clopton contains the remains of a doom. Almshouses from the 15th century are still in use.

A variation on the acting theme comes with Ragdoll Productions, home of *Rosie & Jim* and the *Tellytubbies*. The Montpellier Gallery also gets away from the stage.

New Place is the site of Shakespeare's last home, knocked down in the 18th century by the owner in a dispute with the local council over rates and now home to an Elizabethan style of knot-garden but extensively excavated in 2011 in a search for Shakespearean clues. Panelling from the house has been used in the Falcon Hotel of about 1500. Nash's House was the home of Shakespeare's granddaughter, Elizabeth, with 17th century oak furniture and tapestries, local history, archaeology, Roman and Saxon finds, an Elizabethan style knot-garden, sweet peas and crabapple hedges. Hall's Croft, the 16th century Tudor House home with Jacobean additions which belonged to Shakespeare's elder daughter, Susanna, has Elizabethan and Jacobean furniture, paintings, medicine, growing herbal plants and a mulberry tree. The RSC also perform in the Other Place. Stratford Brass Rubbing Centre is in the conservatory of brewer Charles Flower.

Holy Trinity church is one of England's most beautiful parish churches, part 13th-century. It has 26 15th-century carved misericords, a spire rebuilt in 1763, a lime avenue representing the Apostles and tribes of Israel, a fugitive knocker on the north door giving 37 days of sanctuary and the graves of Shakespeare's family, resulting in its being England's most visited church.

Large linked buoys protect most of the weirs on the river, weirs which mostly have relatively gentle slopes, the buoys often positioned allowing white water canoeists to shoot them. The nine locks on the upper Avon have been resited as the locks and weirs could not be rebuilt. They have also been renamed to acknowledge their benefactors. The first, formerly Stratford New Lock, is now Colin P Witter Lock, reinforced with massive steel frames over the top to resist lateral movement, maybe the most prominently named lock in the country. Perhaps it is appropriate that someone responsible for so many towing brackets on cars should also have added protruding metalwork to this lock.

The A4390 crosses a bridge which was built to carry the former Stratford-upon-Avon & Midland Junction Railway. After it the old Weir Brake Lock has been renamed as Anonymous Lock, appropriately acknowledging a £100,000 donation and many smaller ones. It was restored in five weeks in the 1970s by Borstal volunteers.

Another railway bridge carried the line from Stratford on to Gloucester but now has only the Greenway for cyclists and Monarch's Way footpath. To its right is Stratford's horse racecourse and the River Stour follows

Colin P Witter Lock, one of England's most ugly.

Property at Luddington with a peacock and sculptures of a flamingo and a crocodile.

Holy Trinity church, one of England's most beautiful and the most visited.

on the left from Clifford Chambers and the Shirehorse Centre with over a score of horses including rare breeds. Poplars are grown by the river and water lilies float on it.

A church at Luddington is a replacement from one where Shakespeare may have been married. It overlooks the former Luddington Experimental Station for horticulture and what has become Stan Clover Lock.

From Weston-on-Avon the river makes a loop round Welford-on-Avon, approached over Binton Bridges with two sets of arches via an island. The arch next to the marked navigation arch has a rock slab right across just below water level. Adjacent is the Four Alls public house, alluding to the soldier, priest, king and yeoman who, respectively, fight, pray, rule and pay for all. The village acts as a dormitory but has half-timbered houses, one of England's tallest permanent maypoles, listed Grade II, and St Peter's church with Norman and Early English architecture. The location was on the edge of the glacial Lake Harrison, held back by the Severn valley ice.

W A Cadbury Lock is on the edge of the village, a rural position surrounded by a carpet of dandelions in the spring with orange tip and brimstone butterflies and tufted ducks, the setting only spoiled by the noise of shooting.

The haunted Hillborough Manor is where Charles II may have fled after the Battle of Worcester. A grey stone dovecote held 900 pigeons.

Pilgrim Lock was funded by the Pilgrim Trust and the next lock at Barton by Elsie & Hiram Billington, where the public house can be reached by walking across the weirface.

Shakespeare used to drink in the Falcon Inn in Bidford-on-Avon, now a private house, with Ben Johnson and Michael Drayton. Residents of this 16th century Cotswold stone village used to challenge other villages to drinking contests. They had little difficulty beating Shakespeare's team, who refused to continue next day because they claimed they had already drunk in Pebworth, Marston, Hillborough, Grafton, Exhall, Wixford and Broom, now known with Drunken Bidford as the Shakespeare villages.

St Lawrence's church of 1835 replaces one built in 1276. The Roman Ryknild Street crossed here but the ford was removed in 1970. The B4085 crosses Bidford Bridge at a Roman ford site, an eight arch packhorse bridge built in 1482 by the monks of Alcester, one arch each so the sizes vary from 3.6 to 5.2m and the road width is equally varied. It has a total length of 98m, 62m of it over the river. The navigation arch has been abandoned and the smaller southern arch used instead as it was easier for the restorers to reach and excavate. Work was completed by prisoners from Gloucester jail. The monks also built the White Lion. The Bridge Riverside Eaterie faces across to a field where local families park to enjoy this popular riverside venue, much of the rest of the river frequently being inaccessible to vehicles.

The river begins its transition from Warwickshire to Worcestershire at Marlcliff, where the wooded hillside rises steeply on the south side of the river. The approach channel for IWA Lock has been cut into the cliff and work on the lock involved blasting the marl, undertaken by the Royal Engineers.

Worcester Meadows follow the confluence with the River Arrow at Salford Priors, where St Matthew's church was rebuilt in the 19th century. Fruit farms and market gardening become more evident. Sandpipers and dabchicks might be seen around the abandoned diamond-shaped Cleeve Lock, the shape thought to have been to reduce paddle wash erosion. Cleeve Prior has the Norman and Early English St Andrew's church and a 16th century manor with clipped yews although these are hidden by wooded Cleeve Hill which rises like a cliff. It looks across to lower ground and a nature reserve on the west side where the Elizabethan Salford Hall nunnery at Abbots Salford has become a hotel and Harvington with its half-timbered houses is particularly attractive.

Robert Aickman Lock replaces one which was abandoned after only a decade. Change came even quicker at George Billington Lock which was built in six weeks so that it could be seen by its terminally ill benefactor who gave his life savings for the project. Below Middle Littleton with its tumulus the southern approach to the lock island is across a ford immediately above a low weir. The northern approach is usually used. The island ends with the Billington Tower, reminiscent of a squat lighthouse without the light.

Norton has apple orchards with springtime blossom while glasshouses appear on the other bank at Offenham, Offa's capital. Only the tower remains from Sts Mary & Milburgh's church, rebuilt in the 19th century, where there is also a maypole, another of England's tallest

The weir at Welford-on-Avon.

Bidford Bridge with the old navigation arch no longer used.

Woods rise up Marlcliff Hill.

IWA Lock at Marlcliff, about as tight a fit as is possible.

Cleeve Hill at Cleeve Prior.

George Billington Lock with its strange tower.

The house over the chamber at Evesham.

permanent ones at 20m. A country centre on the right bank has a helipad. Powerlines cross in the vicinity of the Broadway Brook confluence and the Bridge Inn. After the A46 Simon de Montfort Bridge crossing, the Riverside Hotel & Restaurant lives up to its name.

The Cotswold railway crossing starts **Evesham**, which has now spread across the river from its original site within a tight bend of the river. The half timbered market town is the capital of the Vale of Evesham, the Garden of England, and crops include gras, asparagus. The town developed on the manufacture of stockings and was the first place to have telephone STD.

Evesham Lock previously brought a change of river management, some of the locks now having canoe portages with clear signs indicating routes to locks, portages, weirs and moorings. Evesham has a triangular keeper's house built over an old sluice and eel trap adjacent to the lock chamber but it has been replaced with one 1.5m higher following 2007 flood damage. There are narrow gauge railway tracks behind the former gasworks wharf.

Workman Bridge of 1856 brings a different feel as the river enters parkland and a reach used by the rowing club and for the Evesham River Festival. The Benedictine abbey was founded in 714 and there are 14th century remains with a 34m pinnacled Perpendicular Abbey Bell Tower of 1539, the 12th century All Saints church, the 12th century timbered Abbot Reginald's gateway, the 15th century Booth Hall and the redundent 16th century St Lawrence's church. The half timbered and stone 14th century Almonry Heritage Centre has the oak Great Chair of Evesham Abbey, a Simon de Montfort room, Roman, Saxon and medieval remains and stocks, paddling and boating pools in the abbey fishponds and 3ha of park. Alistair McGowan was from here.

After the hospital the A4184 crosses and the river becomes less cultivated. The Hampton rope ferry crosses near Raphael's Restaurant, a sports field and Tesco. The Cotswold line recrosses just after the former line to Northway, of which the high bridge abutments remain, one with a tunnel running back into the abutment.

An obelisk on the next bend recalls the 1265 Battle of Evesham which ended the Barons' War. Henry III's son Edward was the victor with 4,000 killed including

Simon de Montfort, the 6th Earl of Leicester, who had effectively ruled the country for a year through the first English Parliament at which not only the church and the crown had been represented but also counties and boroughs. The Leicester Tower was added in 1840 beyond Abbey Manor House.

Powerlines precede one of the best laid out weirs in the country. The weir itself is long with a gentle sloping face, making it an easy shoot, accompanied by Chadbury Lock, a concrete canoe portage route, three fish ladders and a handsome mill.

Beyond Chadbury is Wood Norton, once the seat of the Duc d'Orléans and now home of a BBC engineering school below Tunnel Hill, topped by a mast.

The river curves round Charlton and, particularly, around Craycombe Turn near the 1791 Craycombe House. Highland cattle are reared here.

The Cotswold line makes a final crossing between Evesham golf course and Fladbury Canoe Club. When the vicar asked resident David Train whether he could do anything about the unoccupied youths in the village he got them canoeing, some going to Olympic level and the club taking national championships from the big London clubs. Despite the lack of a watersports history in the village he showed what could be done with enthusiasm alone. He also set up the Placid Water scheme to get people afloat in place of the usual white water introduction to canoeing, based on the fact that most people have better access to flat water than to the rough. He changed the national marathon racing scheme to divisions based on speed alone rather than on combinations of age, gender and type of boat. He also produced the Bell boat, a catamaran canoe particularly suited to getting groups of inexperienced children afloat and racing.

The village has half timbered houses and St John the Baptist's church which is partly Norman and has a 14th century porch and fine brasses. There was a mill here by 1085 and the current Fladbury Mill, used until 1930, is one of the best buildings on the navigation. Fladbury Lock is noted for the fact that its walls slope out, potentially embarrassing for those descending.

Jubilee Bridge, replacing a ford, is relatively recent but predates the removal of Britain's last flash lock in 1961. Fladbury Flood Bank, 1.2m high, joins the river at the bridge and provides protection for some 4km.

Cropthorne begins with a church containing a Saxon cross and finishes with a riot of spring blossom in orchards running up from the river. Alders, cow parsley, white dead nettles and feral oilseed rape add to the vegetation and birdlife includes cormorants and even a black swan.

The Coventry water main crosses the river as a double pipe bridge. Lower Moor stands back from the river but Wyre Piddle is right alongside with the Anchor Inn and Piesse of Piddle. The village, which

Fladbury Weir with its mills.

Fruit trees in bloom beside the river at Cropthorne.

takes its name from weir and a small area of land, finishes at a church with a Norman font and chancel and an Early English bellcote.

By the weir is Wyre Lock which is diamond shaped, perhaps having been turf sided and subject to scour by the flow. Pershore watergate was probably Europe's last working flash lock when demolished in 1955.

Pershore takes its name from pearshore or from perch, osier willow, but the pears have been replaced by plums, including the Pershore Purple and the Pershore Emblem, for which there is a plum festival. The half timbered Georgian market town was founded in the 7th century and was another manufacturing stockings.

Wyre Lock is diamond shaped.

Pershore Abbey, seen across the playing fields.

The initial view of Pershore is between horse chestnut trees, Pershore Town Football Club and Asda to Pershore Abbey church of the Holy Cross, bought by the locals for £400 at the Dissolution. The Benedictine abbey, one of the largest in England, was founded in 689 by King Oswald with the present building from 972, the eastern part with the 1350 lantern tower, a freestanding ringing platform and unique internal 13th century ploughshare vaulting, combined triforium and clerestory and some of the best Norman and Early English architecture in the country.

A large poplar tree laden with mistletoe stands by the Angel Inn. Gardens are large enough for the Grade II Brandy Cask brewery to have had a Wellington crash there in 1943 with the loss of the five crew. The Three Tuns has an elaborate iron veranda.

Below Pershore Lock, Pershore Great Bridge is met, a 14th century structure in stone and brick with six arches. The site of repeated Civil War clashes, it survived an attempt by the Royalists to demolish it in 1651 on their retreat from the Battle of Worcester but the largest arch has had to be restored and there is still damage visible. The B4084 is taken across a 1928 bridge, the first in concrete in Worcestershire. A Royal Horticultural Society Centre is based in the former College of Horticulture.

Bluebells form a sheet of blue at the foot of Tiddesley Wood but a more important find in 1827 was the Pershore Yellow Egg plum growing wild.

The river now makes a large loop around Birlingham, reaching out past pollarded willows to Great Comberton with its black and white houses and the pinnacles of its church tower showing above the trees. Larks and cuckoos are heard in season. Above all is 302m Bredon Hill, an outlier of the Cotswolds. On top is the 2nd century BC Iron Age Kemerton Camp with 4.5ha of inner ramparts and standing stones added to resist the Romans, unsuccessfully as there are also Roman earthworks. In the middle of it all is the 18th century Gothic Parson's Folly, built to bring the height up to 1,000 ft. There are gorse and Cotswold limestone flora, where Houseman's Shropshire Lad listened to the sound of church bells and many other poets, authors, painters and composers have featured it. It is necessary to pass between the King and Queen Stones to be cured of illness, if the climb up has not already resolved it one way or the other.

Nafford Lock has a bird sanctuary on the island, approached by a wooden swing bridge over the lock. The tightest corner on the river is at Swan's Neck where an owl box is attached to a tree.

The B4080 runs down from the dormitory village of Eckington to cross the 16th century sandstone Eckington Bridge with its arches where monks used a ford. A pillbox stands close below it rather than by the following Defford railway bridge which takes the line from Cheltenham to Birmingham. Moorings lead to Arden Sailing Club with its race control room by the water. Hives of bees are also located on this bank.

Strensham was the birthplace of Samuel Butler. Strensham Lock was the first postwar lock restoration and it has a Victorian lock cottage and a swing footbridge of angle iron.

Another Coventry water main pipe bridge takes water away from a waterworks on the west bank. The Severn Sailing Club is also on this reach, as if there was no suitable venue on the Severn.

Bredon has black and white houses, the 16th century Fox & Hounds, the 1761 Royal Oak Inn and a dovecote. Greylag geese may be on the river. Masefield mentioned the 55m spire on the 12th century Norman St Giles' church and it has a sanctuary with a 14th century coffin lid, heraldic tiles and stained glass from the same century and an Early English chapel. There are eight 1696 Reed Almshouses. The Elizabethan Rectory House was the summer residence of the Bishops of Worcester and it

Pershore Great Bridge resisted Royalist attemps to destroy it.

is said that the world will end when the silhouettes of Charles II and Cromwell on the roof meet. The 40m Bredon tithe or manorial barn of about 1350 was rebuilt after a fire in 1980. Bredon was Brensham in John Moore's *Brensham Village*, a gently humorous look at the people, the wildlife and the river between the wars. His *Portrait of Elmbury*, the best known of the Brensham trilogy, related to Tewkesbury.

The roar of traffic crossing on the M5 has died away by Twyning. The Fleet, reopened after a 2012 fire, has chipmunks in cages. Bredon's Hardwick has the Croft Farm Leisure & Water Park and racks of kayaks and other watersports equipment are located by the river, which eases its way into Gloucestershire.

Tewkesbury was named after the 8th century hermit Theoc, who lived at the confluence with the Severn. Approach is past another sailing club and then the

Bredon Hill rises behind Great Comberton.

Eckington Bridge survives from the 16th century.

Strensham Lock is crossed by a swing bridge.

extensive Tewkesbury Marina where there are plenty of moorings and rabbits at home on the land side. The blue brick viaduct of the former Tewkesbury & Malvern Junction Railway and a Carvery & Grill precede the five arched King John's Bridge of about 1200, rebuilt several times since and carrying the A38 on the line of a Roman road. The last bridge on the navigation, it was widened in 1964 but is difficult to pass as the arches are not parallel to the river. At night it is illuminated.

The town was used by the Romans and the Saxons and it became a port exporting wool and importing coal. Stocking making was the main trade in the 18th century and it is another asparagus growing area. Tewkesbury has many 16th and 17th century Elizabethan houses, often half timbered and overhanging. The Little Museum is presented as a medieval shop in a merchant's house, the half timbered Tewkesbury Museum has costumes, furniture, local history and a model of the Battle of Tewkesbury and there is a John Moore Countryside Museum.

The 1655 Old Baptist Chapel and Court is one of the oldest in England. The Bell Hotel is older with 13th century timbers and Benedictine monk wall paintings, appearing in Mrs Craik's *John Halifax, Gentleman* where the town was called Nortonbury. The half timbered Grade II Olde Black Bear of 1308 has some material from 1200 and a leather ceiling in the bar. It is claimed to be the fifth oldest public house in the country. It also has many ghostly goings on. May 5th brings distant screams of those dying in battle, a Cavalier searches the bedrooms, a boy looks for a tunnel to the abbey, a Victorian lady sits in the bar each evening, a horseshoe in the stable is found on the other side of the river every five years and 20–30 lightbulbs have to be changed every week. The 14th century Royal Hop Pole Hotel is mentioned in *The Pickwick Papers*. There is a priest hole in the 1540 Tudor House and Roses Theatre is where Eric Morecambe died while performing in 1984. By 1830 there were 22 public houses in the town.

The Mill Avon runs straight ahead for 2km to the River Severn, passing the seven storey Healings flour mill of 1865, disused but marked for redevelopment, approached by the 16m ornamental Quay Pit Bridge of about 1820. It is blocked by a weir near the abbey. Abbey Mill dates from about 1190 but has been rebuilt several times since, run by Samuel Healing in 1858 and by Abel Fletcher in *John Halifax, Gentleman*. An 1825 textile factory and 18th century stocking frame knitters' cottages are used for residential accommodation while the Tewkesbury mustard factory is now offices.

A Benedictine monastery from 715, the Norman Tewkesbury Abbey was completed about 1120, mostly from Bredon Hill stone, consecrated in 1239, reroofed in the 15th century after a monk's reading candle set it alight and, as St Mary's monastery church, was bought by the townspeople at the Dissolution for £453, the scrap value of the bells and roof lead. It has excellent 14th century vaulting and windows, combined triforium and clerestory and fine nave, west front, tombs and chantries and the tallest Norman pillars in England. The 1150 14m sq Romanesque tower is the best in the country and the highest remaining Norman tower at 45m. The high altar is a 4.1m slab of Purbeck marble and the organ pipework dates from 1610. The Abbey Cottages of 1450 were shops, the only ones of their kind remaining in the country, and the Abbey Gatehouse of about 1500 was restored in 1849.

Bloody Meadow is the site of the 1471 Battle of Tewkesbury where Edward IV and the Yorkists beat the Lancastrians under the Duke of Somerset, Edward Prince of Wales being killed after the battle. A group of passing Bewdley boatmen had decided to join the winning side and a grateful Edward IV granted them dispensation from paying river tolls. Battle reenactments are held.

Lighter entertainments are a Steam & Organ Festival in July and Barton Street Mop Fair in October, one of the oldest in the country.

The high Avon Lock feeds right to the Old Avon which soon connects with the River Severn.

Distance
73km from Alveston to the River Severn

Navigation Authority
Avon Navigation Trust

Navigation Society
Stratford upon Avon Canal Society www.stratfordcanalsociety.org.uk

OS 1:50,000 Sheets
150 Worcester & the Malverns
151 Stratford-upon-Avon

Connection
Stratford-upon-Avon Canal – see CoB p155

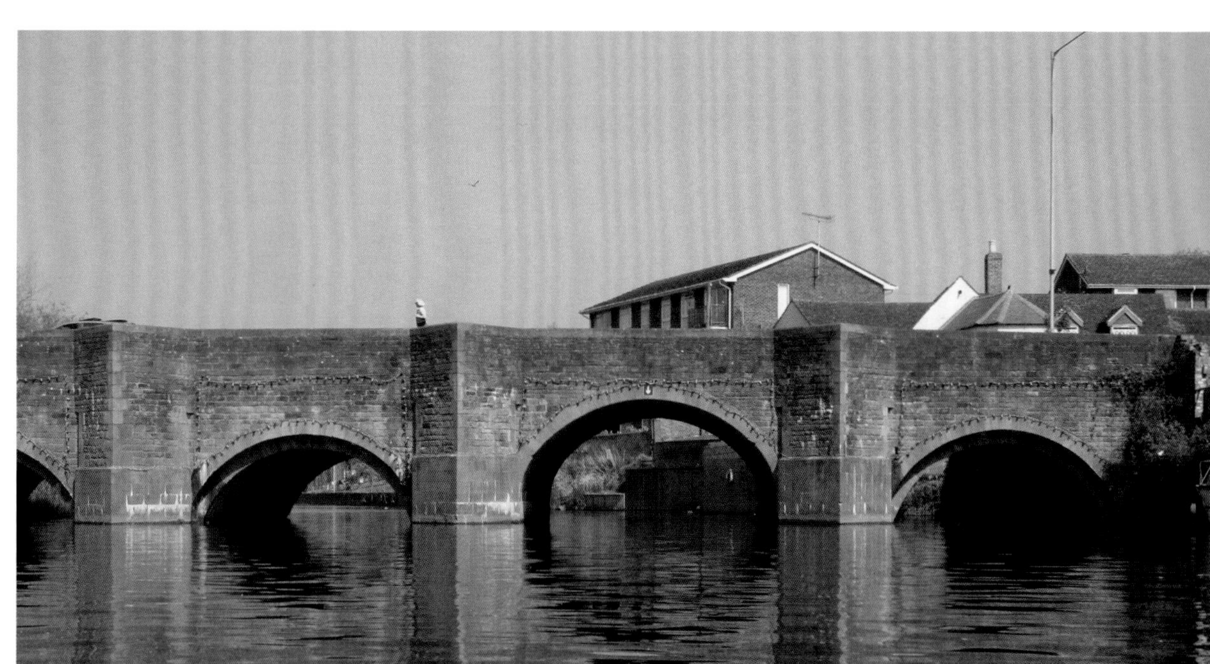

King John's Bridge in Tewkesbury, with poor approach lines.

3 River Severn

Red cliffs on Britain's longest river

The men that live in West England
They see the Severn strong,
A-rolling on rough water brown
Light aspen leaves along.
Hilaire Belloc

Named after the nymph Sabrina, who drowned in it, the Severn is Britain's longest river, followed by the 338km Severn Way. Improvements began in 1503 and it became Europe's second busiest river after the Meuse. In 1575 a court ordered the removal of fish weirs so barge gutters were cut round them. Trows were built with flat bottoms to traverse the shallows, 80t trows still being able to reach Pool Quay from Gloucester over winter floods until the 1820s. A further product of the river was the Severn punt. The route was part of Brindley's Grand Cross scheme, locks being built between Stourport and Gloucester from 1843 to 1958, the river having previously been tidal on springs to Bewdley. It is affected by rain in the Welsh mountains and can rise 6m in spate, as indicated by the tall poles for pontoons and moorings and the high banks which limit views and either funnel or block the prevailing headwinds.

The bridge over the River Stour.

The river has a quarter of all English hams with winter flooding, summer hay and then grazing. The IWA proposed closed-in variable weirs with locks round them to deal with low flows.

The current head of the deep navigation is just below the Gladder Brook, the target for a proposed extension of the Kington & Leominster Canal. The red soil is lined with willows and Himalayan balsam, moorings and angling platforms made from scaffolding and pallets.

Redstone Rock justifies its name.

Stourport Marina and a Clyde Puffer with a difference.

Woods enfold the Severn at Shrawley.

There are mallards on the water and pheasants and peacocks are heard from it.

The A451 passes over a blue and gold iron bridge of 1870 with spiral iron staircase between Areley Kings and **Stourport** with its funfair and Stourport Boat Club. Brindley had first bridged the river here in 1770 but his bridge and its successor were both lost to floods. The Staffordshire & Worcestershire Canal arrives at the red brick Georgian town of Stourport-on-Severn, built for it by Brindley at the village of Lower Mitton after Bewdley rejected the canal, 9m above the normal river level to clear floods. The town was built by the canal company, the only one in Britain built to serve canals, with what would become a 7ha complex of basins at the terminus, in use by 1771. The Venice of the Midlands, this is Britain's leading inland water centre with basins, wharves and warehouses. Now converted to residences is the Tontine Hotel, possibly designed by Brindley, a tontine being a funding arrangement whereby the last survivor becomes the sole owner. The Angel is still open for business, however. Regarded as the finest in the West Midlands is the Georgian Stourport Wesley Methodist church of 1788, extended in 1812 and 1896, with box pews, gallery and alabaster pulpit and screens.

Commercial craft may be met from here and there are also craft for hire below the town. Improvements to the river between Stourport and Worcester by the Staffordshire & Worcestershire Canal's promotors allowed it to remain competitive against the railways longer than in many other places. The River Stour joins under a brick bridge which appears to have a broken back but closer examination suggests it was built this way. The concrete bank beyond lined a former power station supplied with coal by barge from the Severn. The left bank has chalets and the right caravans, features to be met at intervals down the navigation.

Redstone Rock of red and grey Triassic sandstone has a 12th century hermitage and caves which Latimer told Cromwell could lodge 500 men, often thieves but also homeless monks after the Dissolution. Moored at Stourport Marina is the *VIC 99*, a Clyde Puffer fitted with two upper decks. Salmon leap from the river, coots and Canada geese are on the water and evening primroses grow here. Barbel are a non-native species put into the river in the 1950s for anglers.

Fulling mills at Hartlebury were a source of river traffic as cloth was brought in and then taken away again after treatment.

More red cliff brings Lincomb Lock. Astley Vineyard, once the world's most northerly, is not conspicuous but Hampstall Inn at the Burf welcomes boaters. There may be Jacob's sheep about but alders and other trees cloak the banks and the arrival of the Dick Brook is well hidden. Lenchford Inn is joined by more caravans and a well-sited half-timbered house near Holt Heath.

The navigation is not welcoming to those with portable craft, often steep banks or vertical sheet piling confronting the user, no guidance on the route to take or, as at Holt Lock, no passage across the lock for the shortest route. Crossing the river with a car is much easier, the A4133 passing over Telford's cast iron Holt Fleet Bridge of 1828 with a 46m main span and flood arches in the massive sandstone abutments. Caravan sites are found on both sides of the road. The Holt Fleet on the right faces across the river towards the Wharf Inn. Willows, oaks, hazels, hawthorns, mistletoe, toadflax and comfrey grow along the banks, tufted ducks are on the water, swallows swoop and the cuckoo is heard in spring as the Malvern Hills begin to be seen over the right bank.

Good carvings and ornaments are to be found in the Norman church at Holt. Holt Castle, built in 1283 against the Welsh, has a 14th century keep, 15th century hall and 1690 additions and has become a 19th century turreted mansion. Top Barn Activity Centre is based beyond around former gravel pits.

A church with some Norman work and outside stairs is found at Grimley and there are the remains of a Roman ford. Lucien, the brother of Napoleon, lived here after being captured in 1810. Across the river is Hawford with the Hawford Dovecote, quickly followed by the River Salwarpe confluence and the Droitwich Barge Canal, reopened in 2011 as a route through to the Worcester & Birmingham Canal.

Bevere Island, from beaver, with the Camp has twice been a refuge for the inhabitants of Worcester, the first time to avoid the Danes and again in the 17th century to avoid the plague. An iron footbridge leads from the island

A timber framed house near Holt Heath.

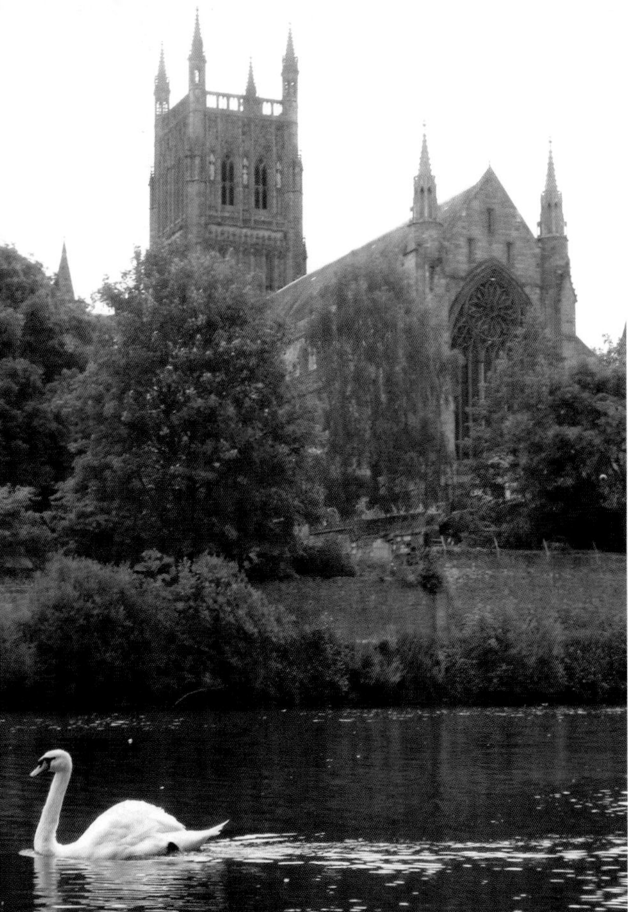

Worcester Cathedral rises above the river.

in the direction of the Bevere Vivis Gallery. For those not working through the lock the options are down the face of the weir or to the east side of it, both for the adventurous. The Camp House is a popular public house on the bank below the lock.

Hallow faces across to Northwick with the Northwick Marina.

Worcester had Stone Age inhabitants 5,000 years ago, had 3,000 year old Bronze Age settlements and has produced Iron Age finds. The Roman fort was named after the Weogorans and it became a half-timbered market town at the lowest non-tidal ford, as used by the Romans, a port and the Faithful City as far as royalty were concerned. Pitchcroft has a riverside walk and one of the country's oldest horse racecourses, in use since the 17th century. On the site of a Roman smelting slag tip which was later reworked on the Dick Brook for Royalist items, it was where the Royalist cavalry assembled in 1651, is where the Royal Engineers gave the world's first public radio broadcasts in the First World War, has hosted the National Waterways Festival, was the venue for canoeing's national marathon championships for a number of successive years, has an annual beer festival and is often badly flooded in winter. Behind is the site of the 11th century Worcester Castle. Balloon flights take off from here and Worcester Rowing Club and Worcester Canoe Club have their clubhouses next to each other on the riverbank so there is usually plenty of fast small craft activity but swans gather on the river in significant numbers.

The Glover's Needle is the slim spire which remains from the church of St Andrew, the city having made gloves since the 13th century. Worcester City Art Gallery & Museum recalls the history with Civil War relics and the Worcestershire Regiment and Worcestershire Yeomanry Cavalry (The Queen's Own Worcestershire Hussars) regimental collections including three Victoria Crosses.

From 1842 the Revd John Davies used the trow *Albion* as a waterman's chapel moored above the railway bridge. When it sank in the 1860s it was moved onto the bank where it served for many more years. The Sabrina Footbridge crosses the river, as do the iron bridge carrying the Foregate Street–Ross-on-Wye railway and the five arched brown sandstone Worcester Bridge of 1771–80 by John Gwynne carrying the A44 at the Roman ford site.

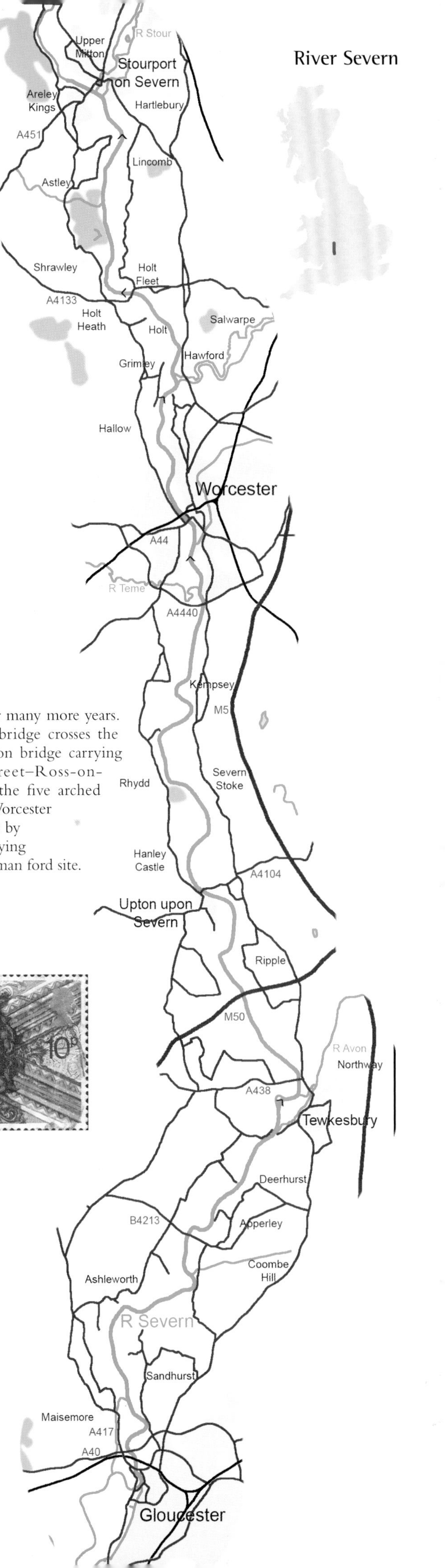

River Severn

The Methodist chapel has become the Grade II Huntingdon Hall Georgian concert venue. As Parliamentary troops entered the front of what has become the King Charles II Restaurant after the Battle of Worcester the king made his escape from the back door, on his way to France, the building having since suffered fire damage in the 18th century. Nash House is a four storey Elizabethan timbered building. The brick Guildhall of 1723, rebuilt in 1880 with an Italianate assembly room, one of the best Queen Anne rooms in the country, has statues of Charles I, Charles II and Cromwell with his ears nailed to a doorway and displays a cannon, Battle of Worcester armour, scold's bridle, leather fire buckets and paintings. Copenhagen Street was used to take witches and cuckolds for ducking.

Diglis Lock with a large ramp up onto the lock island.

The Malvern Hills rise to the west of the Severn.

Cliffey Wood at Rhydd.

Worcestershire County Cricket Ground has been used since 1899 and is claimed to be England's most beautiful.

Brass studs in a bus lane mark the line of a Roman road covered over. Greyfriars, a 1480 merchant's house with 17th and 18th century additions, an oak pannelled Great Hall and a walled garden, is one of the best half timbered houses in the country. The 15th century Tudor House folk museum is also half timbered and exhibits include a coracle. St Helen's church, founded in 680, was last rebuilt in 1880 and is now used for storing records. The Old Palace is another notable building. The city has many wine cellars dating from the Middle Ages, when it imported the king's wine.

Overlooking the river is Worcester Cathedral of Christ & St Mary, founded about 680, to which St Oswald added a Benedictine monastery in 983. St Wulstan was the only Saxon bishop to retain office after 1066. The present stone building was begun in 1084, the tower collapsed in 1175, there was a bad fire in 1203 and rebuilding began in 1395. There is an excellent 11th century Norman crypt with a pilgrim exhibition and an Early English quire and Lady Chapel. The circular 12th century Norman chapter house was one of the first of its kind and there are medieval cloisters and buildings, fine tracery, heraldry and sculpture. King John's Purbeck marble tomb of 1216 has England's oldest royal effigy although the king was buried in a monk's gown and cowl, perhaps in the hope that St Peter would not recognize this hoodie. There is also the tomb of Prince Arthur, the elder brother of Henry VIII. If he had lived he would have been king and Henry would have been Archbishop of Canterbury, which would have changed the course of world history. There is the tomb of former Prime Minister Stanley Baldwin and a monument to the Countess of Salisbury, the mistress whose garter was picked up by Edward III, leading to the creation of the Noble Order of the Garter. There are a 14th century Edgar Tower, Victorian stained glass, a library with 8th century Gospel fragments, the monks' herb garden and the flayed skin of a 12th century Danish invader caught stealing the Sanctus bell. The Three Choirs Festival, which is held here every third August, is the world's oldest choral festival, dating from 1715 or earlier. Turner painted it from the river. Sir Edward Elgar, who was born here, had a long involvement with it and has a memorial window. A bent arch is said to have gripped the neck of a 13th century Jew who had offered to trade 5,000 crowns for the week's alms after overhearing that 10,000 crowns would be donated to repair fire damage, being made to pay the whole sum himself. Charles II watched the Battle of Worcester from the tower. Birties of Worcester is a 15th century timber-framed art gallery.

Medieval carts became bogged down until 6d was paid to a witch. A wagoner with only a light load was affected like the rest, noticed a straw across his horse's back, cut it in half with his knife and escaped as the horse was freed. There was a shriek and the dead witch fell in the road in two pieces. Another witch turned a troop of tax collecting soldiers to stone.

Glasshouse Restaurant was a 16th century schoolhouse. The Commandery, founded in 1085 as a hospital and rebuilt in the 15th century, was Charles II's headquarters in 1651. It is timber framed with a galleried hall, hammerbeam roof and Elizabethan staircase and features Tudor and Stuart life and the Civil War. There is also a Royal Worcester Porcelain Museum. Royal Worcester is the oldest continuously produced British porcelain, founded in 1751 and noted for bone china but no longer produced here although there are factory tours. There is also a Dyson Perrins Museum. Lea & Perrins Worcestershire Sauce has perked up the world's taste

Facing Hanley Castle across the river.

Upton's Pepperpot church tower with cupola.

buds since 1838. Worcester has also produced the *Berrows Journal* since 1690, the world's oldest newspaper.

The Worcester & Birmingham Canal arrives, bringing the Avon Ring to Tewkesbury. The Severn was the country's major coal exporting river and Worcester was its main coal handling port. Of Britain's 18 river tax collectors, seven were based in Worcester. An old oil dock provides austere moorings while Diglis Hotel offers residents better surroundings. A large slipway up onto the island at Diglis Lock is served by a derrick crane, the name coming from the French d'église, a reference to the cathedral. Sited at a Roman port, the locks are twinned and are affected by the highest tides. A cable-stayed footbridge clears oilseed rape and stinging nettles lining the banks past a nature reserve, caravans and the Severn Motor Yacht Club.

The Battle of Worcester took place in 1651 on the west bank above the confluence with the River Teme, a site which had already been fought over in 1642. The Royalists were defeated after the Roundheads crossed the Severn on a pontoon of boats. The Teme was used by the Romans to transport much lead down from Velindre in coracles and this could have been the cause of significant ill health in the Roman empire. There is a battlefield observation point and the A4440 now crosses to bypass Worcester.

More caravans precede the large St Mary's church at Kempsey, a village with Iron Age and Roman settlements. The church has medieval glass and there is a Bishop's Palace nearby. Simon de Montfort and Henry III heard mass here in 1265 before the Battle of Evesham. Samuel Butler wrote part of *Hudibras* at the Ketch Inn, an indication that this was a place where craft would ketch or catch on the bottom and crews would need refreshment while waiting to get afloat again.

Red sandstone cliffs contain the river again and there is a notable viewpoint at Old Hills, to the west of the half-timbered hamlet of Pixham. Blackbacked gulls, kingfishers, herons, cormorants and buzzards might be seen while the roar of large jets intrudes in the distance. This used to be a popular area for salmon netting until stopped in 1929.

Rhydd formerly had a brickfield and has a 46m high marl cliff with trees which include Scots pines in Cliffey Wood. Standing back from 30m high red cliffs on the east bank is Severn Stoke with a half-timbered public house and a church with a 14th century side tower.

Hanley Castle recalls King John's 13th century castle which has gone, just the moat remaining. However, there remains the church in 14th century stone and 17th century brick, half-timbered houses, 17th century almshouses and the grammar school. The village made tiles and pottery. Much more conspicuous on the opposite bank is a tall cream house with turrets.

Poplar trees laden with mistletoe lead to the A4104 crossing at **Upton upon Severn**, a 1940 concrete bridge, Upton Old Bridge having been taken by floods in 1852, and caravans follow. The town was a ketch point and a port, used by the Bishop of Hereford to land wine from Bristol from 1289 with relatively good roads from Hereford and Leominster. The village's oldest remaining building is the Pepperpot, a 14th century red stone tower of a Norman church which had its steeple pulled down in 1745 by villagers using horses, to be replaced in 1769 by the present copper cupola. It now houses Upton Heritage Centre, about the Civil War. A local wreck was the ketch *CFH*, constructed at Calstock from trees blown down at Cothele in a gale in 1891, later playing a part at Scapa Flow in the First World War.

After few waterside buildings since Worcester, shoulder to shoulder along the waterfront are the Plough Inn, Kings Head, Boathouse café bar, Star Inn and Swan Hotel but not the 1510 stuccoed White Lion where Fielding's Tom Jones was seduced by Mrs Waters with more nocturnal disturbance than is met in most hotels. It seems to have been a riotous place generally. In 1690 butchers were ordered not to empty cow bellies in the street, dungheaps were not to remain for more than 16 days and there were sawpits in the main street and pigsties on the bridge. Not surprisingly there was plague in 1665, frequent smallpox and cholera which killed 50 people in a month in 1832, the same year in which the Scots Greys were called out to deal with bow hauliers protesting about the use of horses on the towpath. Large nets were taking so many salmon that few got through to others upstream. The 16th century rector John Dee proposed a royal navy of 60 ships, an idea ahead of its time. Timbered Tudor and Georgian buildings remain with the Tudor House Museum, the 17th century Olde Anchor Inn and

An active gravel terminal below the M50.

the 1878 church of Sts Peter & Paul. Upton hosts folk, jazz, blues and water festivals and has one of the best map shops in Britain. An independent lifeboat is based here. Kites, cormorants, curlews, great crested grebes, sedge warblers and wagtails might be seen.

A marina is sited in clay pits with tiled pagodas around. Cobbett claimed that the meadows at Ryall were some of the best anywhere. From here there are less trees and the scenery is more open. The banks are often edged with large stone blocks.

A railway from Great Malvern to Northway formerly crossed the river at Saxon's Lode. Gravel is shipped here from south of the M50, to disappear through the bank on a conveyor. Holdfast had a more gentle commerce, growing sweet peas.

Ripple has the Norman St Mary's church on a Saxon site. At the passenger ferry a Victorian cottage with dormer windows housed the ferryman.

The last Royalist victory of the Civil War was secured here when Prince Maurice beat Sir William Waller. Waterworks supply pipes and then pipes from a former underground oil depot have changed this reach but not as much as the Queenhill Bridge carrying the M50, also having its influence on Bredon School, 6km from Bredon itself, after which the left bank changes from Worcestershire to Gloucestershire.

A fan turbine on the right bank precedes the Mythe, from the Old English gemythe, meeting of waters, below a hill with pine trees. The red sandstone banks grow woad and the water can have a quarry, an unpredictable tide. Clay pits are the remains of the Mythe brickworks, started in 1634. Dominating the river is the 1825 cast iron lattice Mythe Bridge by Telford. The A438 crosses a 52m arch with a central sag and six 3.7m span Gothic arches in the abutments and a toll house at the east end. Beyond, in decorative brickwork, are the waterworks which supply Cheltenham but were inconvenienced by the 2007 floods. They were built with a roof to withstand Second World War bombs.

The River Avon joins from **Tewkesbury** above Upper Lode, a whirlpool forming at the confluence. A Victorian blue brick double-fronted lock house of 1858 faces Upper Lode Lock, the last to be built on the river. A large lock, it has a widening across its lower end to allow it to handle a tug with butties.

Severn Ham had a horse racecourse, closed off as an island by the Mill Avon.

Domestic geese guard the approach to the 15th century Lower Lode Hotel, which faces across the river to one of the most accessible pieces of bank on the river, used for the Cheltenham College boathouse. Care still needs to be taken, however, as a 500mm bore can reach this point below a golf course. The Vale of Gloucester follows the river which crosses a low wooded ridge several times from here.

St Mary's church at Deerhurst is partly Saxon from 804 and has one of the best Saxon fonts in England after its recovery from use as an animal water trough. The church has interesting brasses and stained glass, a memorial to St Catherine, martyred on her wheel, and the tomb of Sir

Mythe Water Treatment Works were affected by the 2007 floods.

Summer mist floats over the River Severn around Telford's Mythe Bridge.

John Cassy, Chief Baron of the Exchequer. Alphege was a novice monk in a priory here, later to be the Archbishop of Canterbury killed by the Danes. Cnut and Edmund Ironside signed a peace treaty here. The river was a ketch point here.

Odda's Chapel from 1056 was Anglo-Saxon, attached to a 16th century farmhouse and lost as a church building for two centuries until it was rediscovered. This is where one Smith, a labourer, killed a serpent by leaving it a trough of milk and then cutting off its head with an axe between the ruffled scales as it took a post-lunch nap. The king rewarded him with land on Walton Hill, held until the 16th century, and the axe was still in existence in the 18th century.

Water lilies are making their appearance by the Yew Tree Inn at Apperley. Perversely, Severn Sailing Club is on the Avon and Avon Sailing Club here on the Severn. The Coalhouse Inn is on the left bank, opposite caravans, and the Haw Bridge Inn is by the B4213 crossing of 1961, replacing one damaged by tanker *Darleydale H* during floods in 1958, the skipper being killed by falling bridge materials. The Haw has timber-framed cottages and a former malt house. Fresians and Herefords stand on the banks and house martins fly over the river, here available to water skiers despite the speed limit.

The Coombe Hill Canal of 1796 never reached Cheltenham and was abandoned in 1876 when the lock gates were lost to a flood. It has been partially restored but its use has been prevented by environmentalists who now claim it as a nature reserve. There are eels, rudd and trout in the river and teasels and ancient oaks on the banks.

Wainlode Hill, beyond the Red Lion, built to serve boatmen at a ketch point, brings the last of the red cliffs, 60m of Keuper marl rising to 86m Sandhurst Hill. The bank behind the river beach is reinforced with hulks and craft are warned to keep away. Stone wharves were built to unload coal for Cheltenham.

The stone Ashleworth Court dates from 1460 but the 38m tithe barn with its stone tiled roof is still in use. Ashleworth Manor is timber framed. The 1947 flood level was 1.2m above the pews in the church and there are 15th century buildings even closer to the river at Ashleworth Quay. Flood prevention management has stopped scouring of the river channel and the river is now subject to silting beyond Sandhurst. Pits for excavating brick clay were started in the 19th century, used until 1924, produced coppiced willow until the 1930s and are now a nature reserve.

The river divides at Upper Parting, the West Channel quickly reaching a weir which is the normal tidal limit above Maisemore. The East Channel suffers from turbulence when spring flows round the Isle of Alney meet at its northern end.

An explosion at a waste chemicals site in 2000 led to calls for its closure. A slipway feeds down near the start of the arm but this is the Severn at its least loved. Plastic bakery trays are trodden into the bank at intervals for anglers to stand on and shopping trolleys announce the arrival of civilization. Until the 13th century there was another arm which left at this point, flowed on the east side of the A417 St Oswald's Road and joined again at the Quay. This was the main channel of the Severn and the Roman Glevum fort at Kingsholm was built next to it in 97 to defend the lowest crossing point. It was deeped for shipping but then silted up. The river winds under the A40, the Gloucester–Newport railway and the A417 before arriving at Gloucester Quay, a difficult reach for craft waiting to negotiate Gloucester Lock, formerly a staircase pair. Celebrations at the original lock opening included firing a cannon which exploded, killing two people. This leads onto the Gloucester & Sharpness Canal, the only route downstream for larger craft although there are plans to install a lock at Llanthony Weir to give a route round the south of the island to reach the Herefordshire & Gloucestershire Canal, currently being restored. **Gloucester** has often been subject to floods, those of 1947 reaching 7.7m above the normal dry weather level.

By the quay is the prison on the site of a medieval castle while a Norman castle was a little further back

Upper Lode Lock is large and T shaped.

Coombe Hill Canal, now designated a nature reserve.

Wainlode Hill rising to Sandhurst Hill.

from the river. A timbered Tudor building of around 1500 houses Gloucester Folk Museum, one of the earliest museums featuring social history, including a dairy and wheelright's, ironmonger's and blacksmith's shops. Gloucester Cathedral was founded in 1089, ushering in the Perpendicular style in 1330 and seeing its last example in the 1483 Lady Chapel. The 24 x 12m east window was the world's largest, a memorial to Crécy victims, and there are memorials inside to Robert, the eldest son of William the Conqueror, and Edward II. The 9 year old Henry III was crowned here, the only coronation outside Westminster Abbey since the Conquest. Bishop John Hooper was martyred outside the cathedral under Queen Mary. The cloisters have been used in three Harry Potter films. The City Museum & Art Gallery has the 1st century bronze Celtic Birdlip mirror and part of the Roman wall in its basement. Arches remain from the former infirmary. Those born here included John Stafford Smith in 1750, writer of the tune that was later to be used as the American national anthem.

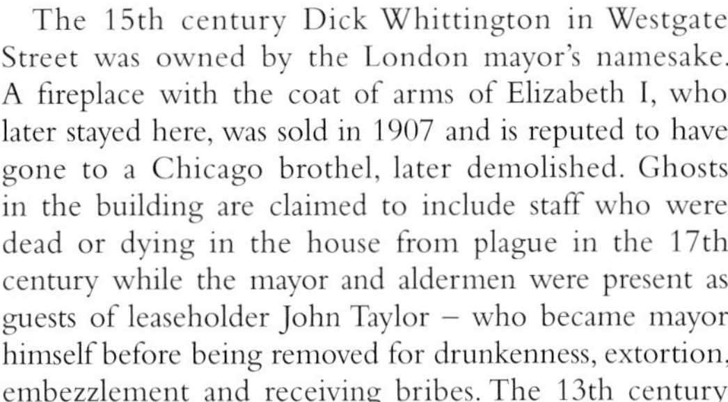

The 15th century Dick Whittington in Westgate Street was owned by the London mayor's namesake. A fireplace with the coat of arms of Elizabeth I, who later stayed here, was sold in 1907 and is reputed to have gone to a Chicago brothel, later demolished. Ghosts in the building are claimed to include staff who were dead or dying in the house from plague in the 17th century while the mayor and aldermen were present as guests of leaseholder John Taylor – who became mayor himself before being removed for drunkenness, extortion, embezzlement and receiving bribes. The 13th century Grade II Fountain Inn was to become a coaching inn but not before William III had interrupted a meeting of Jacobite rebels by riding his horse up the steps to their upstairs room. The Union was formerly the workshop of tailor John Pritchard, who came to fame through Beatrix Potter's *Tailor of Gloucester*. An uncompleted waistcoat was finished over a weekend not by the fairies but by employees who had been on a binge and let themselves in, completing the work to pass the time until they were in a fit state to go home. The former Monk's Retreat, closed in 2002, had a bar in what was said to be the finest 12th century vaulted undercroft in northern Europe, supported on Norman pillars. Now a pub, the 1622 Theatre Vaults began as a merchant's house and, in 1643, had a red hot Royalist cannon ball fired through the window from Llanthony during the seige of Gloucester.

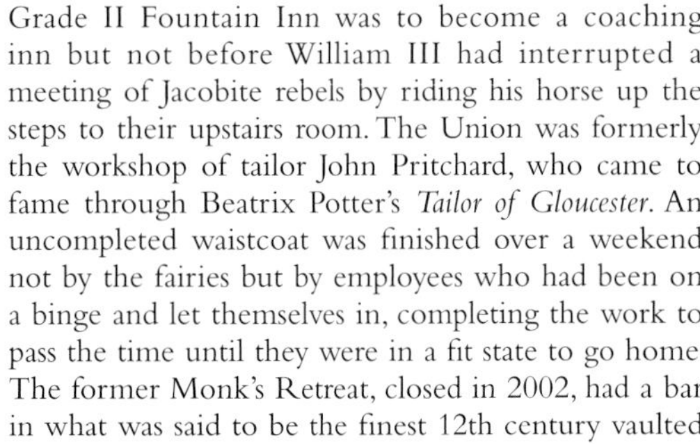

In Northgate Street the oak framed New Inn Hotel of 1430, on the site of an inn from about 1350, is the finest medieval galleried inn in Britain. Tunnels were said to run in various directions including to the cathedral as escape routes for the monks. This is one of the places Lady Jane Grey was claimed to be staying when proclaimed queen and her ghost is said to be here again.

Writer William Ernest Henley, born in Eastgate Street, provided Robert Louis Stevenson with the character for Long John Silver in *Treasure Island*.

A gap in Cromwell Street replaces the terraced house occupied by Fred and Rosemary West following their history of sadism and murders up to 1994.

The Bell in Southgate Street, featured in *Tom Jones*, was demolished in 1967. The adjacent Old Bell is reputed to have been made from timbers from the *Mayflower*, which was owned by a Gloucestershire family whose coat of arms is carved on a fireplace. It has windows of nautical design and salt was found on the beams during restoration in 2005. It also has several ghosts, including a cavalier who stabbed a landlady. In the same way, the Pelican is said to be built from the timbers of the *Golden Hind*, which was originally called the *Pelican*. The Café René has a Roman well in the centre of the bar, rumours of tunnels and ghosts of greyfriars. The speed at which the Home Office removed some documents discovered supported the claim that it had been used as a Second World War MI6 office. Robert Raikes' heavily timbered house of 1560 was used to publish the *Gloucester Journal*, the world's second oldest continuously published newspaper, since 1722, and from where the owner set up the Sunday School movement.

Gloucester has more seagulls than any other British city except Aberdeen. The city has traditionally supplied the sovereign with the first lamprey of the season and with a lamprey pie at Christmas from medieval times to 1836 despite the fact that it may have been a surfeit of local lampreys which killed Henry I. The Dr Foster of nursery rhyme fame was said to have been Edward I who ended up in a deep puddle and mud after his horse slipped, an event he chose not to risk repeating with a further visit.

At the southern end of the city Robins Wood Hill rises as an outlier of the Cotswold Edge.

Distance
82km from Areley Kings to Gloucester

Navigation Authority
Canal & River Trust

OS 1:50,000 Sheets
138 Kidderminster & Wyre Forest
150 Worcester & the Malverns
162 Gloucester & Forest of Dean

Connections
Tidal River Severn – see RoB p23
Gloucester & Sharpness Canal – see CoB p133

Gloucester Lock and the warehouses around Gloucester Dock.

4 River Dee

Extreme meanders and affluence

Belated travellers quake with fear,
And spur their starting horse;
For childish shrieks they say they hear,
As Farndon's bridge they cross.
Anon

The River Dee or Afon Dyfrdwy forms the border between the Welsh Wrexham and the English Cheshire West & Chester. Connecting the two is a 159m sandstone bridge of 1345. With a long approach on the west side, it has eight arches of about 7.3m span, Lady's Arch with an additional ring so it may have had a defensive position or a shrine above or could have had a Civil War drawbridge fitted. On stormy nights screams might be heard under the bridge from the ghosts of the two sons of Prince Madoc, drowned in the 14th century for their inheritance.

Holt, which is on the Welsh side, was the Roman Bovium and there was a Roman pottery and tile factory for Chester. Red Triassic sandstone cliffs were scoured not by the river but by sandblast under desert conditions when the climate was much warmer. A block of this sandstone was surrounded by a pentagonal 13th century castle with five corner towers by Earl Warenne by 1311, although it was destroyed by Cromwell in 1647 after a year's siege. Much of it was taken away by barge for the construction of Eaton Hall. Thomas Pennant said that Owain Glyndwr's 15th century insurrection had made the residents irascible.

Farndon, from the Anglo-Saxon Ferentone – fern covered hill – faces Holt from the English side in what was a strawberry growing area. King's Marsh provided sanctuary for criminals for 366 days in Norman times if the Earl of Chester's fines were paid.

The 15th century St Chad's church was used as stables by the Roundheads in 1643 and burnt down while they were pushing the Royalists back from the bridge into Wales, the Royalists regaining control two years later. The church was rebuilt in 1658 with a stained glass window dedicated to the Royalists and a steeplejack's prayer on the belfry wall but still has Civil War bullet marks.

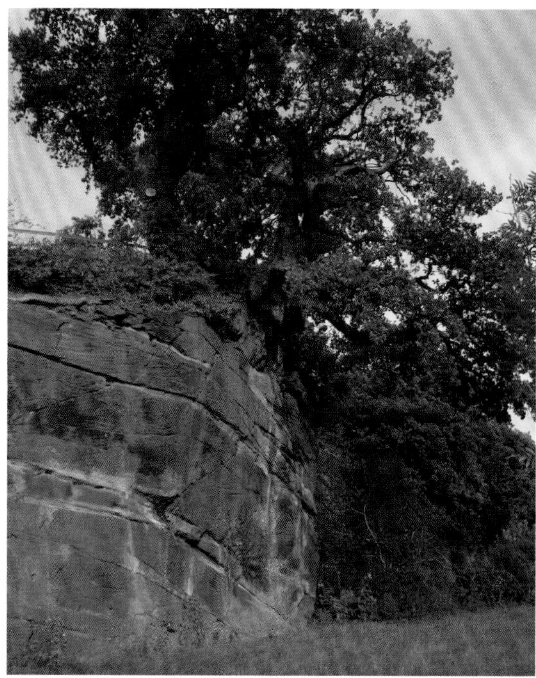

Weathered sandstone cliffs at Farndon.

Pioneering cartographer John Speed was born in the village in 1642.

Farndon Quay is at the official navigation head, a point which can be reached by some high tides.

The river carries water for Chester and there are five major water authority extraction points on this section of the river. There are many anglers as mallards and branches float past with the flow.

An obelisk to Major Roger Burnston in the Crimean War and the Indian Mutiny stands above an aerial. Welsh hills are seen to the west. Despite the

The border bridge between Holt and Farndon.

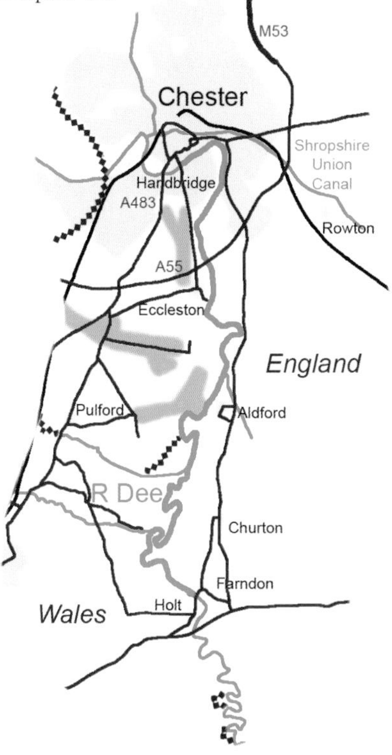

The Dee is often tree-lined, as at Aldford.

lining of oak trees, the river is scruffy at this point with shacks and caravans. Small cruisers are moored against tall scaffolding pole platforms which allow for large variations in the water level.

The River Alun joins at the start of one of the most extreme river meanders anywhere. After turning 270° to the right the river then unwinds again through nearly as tight a bend the other way with no obvious geological feature to account for such a convoluted layout.

Poplars, alders and purple loosestrife shelter the banks, visited by wood pigeons, rooks, kingfishers and cormorants. Gunfire may be heard in the distance near Churton. Pulford Brook is the last significant tributary from the west side before Wales is left behind and the river is entirely in England until beyond Chester.

Next to Norman castle earthworks and a 13th century church is the 19th century village estate of Aldford. It overlooks a reach which runs parallel to an old meander to reach a ford site used by the Roman Watling Street. Crossing here is Telford's magnificent Iron Bridge

Telford's Iron Bridge at Aldford.

Half-timbered buildings at Cheaveleyhall Farm.

of 1824. The 46m cast iron span with ornate lattice spandrels is based on his Craigellachie bridge. There is a gauging point here and Aldford Brook joins.

The bridge is privately owned, serving one of the estate roads of Eaton Hall, home of the Grosvenor family. The Duke of Westminster is Britain's richest person, valued at £7,000,000,000. Grosvenor Group assets include substantial properties in the most expensive parts of London.

Turning away, the river makes another conspicuous meander at the Crook of Dee to run past banks with red sandstone visible between the roots of beeches. Otters may be around.

A mound and a moat are hidden signs of former activity at Eccleston but the obvious action now is over the bridge carrying the A55 North Wales Expressway. An extraction point feeds a waterworks. Activity also begins to build up on the river. From the Roman settlement of Heronbridge there is a 1.4km long straight past Huntington and Handbridge where rowers can get up speed.

This part of the river reaches its widest where a passenger ferry crosses between Queen's Park and Boughton Heath with its sailing club, slipway and carpark. Blackheaded gulls are on the water with, perhaps, a kestrel watching from trees along the bank.

The river is deflected by a high ridge topped by the Mount Inn and the Grade II St Paul's church to double back round Earl's Eye. Canoe slalom gates hang over the river before it reaches a rowing area with Royal Chester, King's School and Grosvenor Rowing Clubs and the Boathouse and Blue Moon cafés, the latter run by the UK's first male civil partners, one of whom committed suicide in 2012. The Groves has had a rowing regatta since 1733, the oldest in the world. Boats are hired out to the public. A suspension footbridge crosses the river.

A Victorian water tower is a substantial structure above the river bank beside the Shropshire Union Canal. Water has been pumped from the River Dee 200m away, treated since 1853 and stored in the 3.7m deep 1,200m^3 cast iron tank on its 20m x 21m diameter tower. In 1889 the tank was jacked up 6m and more brickwork added to meet increased demand.

Steam Mill is home to the Artichoke café, bar and bistro and, like the Old Harker's Arms, is a trendy city base in an old industrial building at Boughton.

Chester, based on the Roman street pattern, was founded in 79 by the Roman 20th Legion, who named their Deva fortress after the River Dee although the Old English name came from ceaster, a Roman fort. The Roman amphitheatre, holding 7,000, was the largest in stone in Britain, half of it having been excavated. It had a shrine to the Greek goddess Nemesis and may have been used for gladiatorial combat. The Roman Gardens have stone and pillars from various sites and a reconstructed hypocaust. The Roman fortress houses the Dewa Roman Experience including a Roman galley and street. The Romans' legacy ranges from a cheese rolling contest and a Roman bath house below Spudulike to the red sandstone walls which run for 3km around the city, almost intact and the most complete Roman fortress walls in Europe, being broken only by the council offices. In what is the English city with more ghosts than any other, the footsteps of a Roman sentry are heard passing through the walls of the George & Dragon Inn and returning 20 minutes later at the site of a Roman cemetery.

There were Viking raids in the Dark Ages but Æthelflæd drove them back and had extended and strengthened the walls by the 10th century.

Grosvenor Park has a miniature railway while the Grosvenor Museum has exhibits from Roman times to the present day, including a Roman graveyard, a period house, a Victorian schoolroom, Chester silver, Anglo-Saxon coins and natural history.

The Saxon minster became the Benedictine

Several trip boats operate from Chester.

Boughton is built on a ridge high above the river.

Chester's waterfront with suspension bridge and bandstand.

abbey in 1092, part of the most complete medieval monastery complex in the country, replaced with Gothic construction in 1260–1537 and made Chester's St Werburgh Cathedral four years later. It has 11–18th century architecture of Keuper sandstone. The inside was restored in 1868–76 by Sir George Gilbert Scott but the west front is still 16th century. St Werburgh's tomb is inside with a shrine to this Mercian princess with miraculous healing powers. The 1380 carved choirstalls are the best in the UK, there is a Tree of Jesse and it has the most complete monastic cloisters in England with a notable 13th century chapter house and magnificent refectory. There is fine stained glass, the marked score of Handel's *Messiah*, first rehearsed here in 1742, a 19th century cobweb picture and a Renaissance-style font in black marble. A marble bust commemorates Brassey, perhaps the greatest railway contractor of all time. A weakness in the central tower resulted in construction of the separate Addleshaw Tower or Chester Space Rocket to hold the 13 bells in the 1960s. The cathedral is the most popular free entry destination in the UK. The Saxon minster of St John the Baptist, refounded in 1057 as a collegiate church, has Norman pillars and arcades although now in a Victorian exterior plus the ruins of the choir and collapsed tower of 1573. There is a 14th century anchorite's cell. The massive gateway to the square is the venue for Mystery Plays, the original texts being the most complete in existence. In 2002 the cathedral launched Chester Pilgrim Ale, made by J W Lees in Manchester.

Katie's Tea Rooms are the largest in England, contained in a 1,000 year old building with beams, wattle and daub. There has been a covered market since 1139. In a city of many half-timbered black and white buildings, the Rows are exceptional. These unique 13th century shop galleries on two levels through half-timbered Tudor buildings are like being on a galleon. The Three Old Arches of about 1200 is Britain's oldest shopfront. Stanley Palace is one of the city's finest timber buildings while Bishop Lloyd's timber framed town house from the early 17th century has ornately carved biblical scenes and fantastic animals. Chester Heritage Centre is in the old St Michael's church. St Mary's centre has exhibitions in the 14/15th century church of St Mary, an excellent example of Perpendicular styling with a Tudor nave roof, two 17th century effigies, medieval stained glass and a wall painting at the top of one of England's steepest streets. The Bear & Billet of 1664 was one of the last timber-framed houses in Britain for three centuries.

At the time of the Conquest, brewers of poor ale were fined four shillings or ducked in the town pond. At noon on summer Tuesdays–Saturdays there is a town crier at High Cross, where there were bear baiting, stocks, a whipping post and sedan chairs on hire at various times. After 1,600 years the changing of the Roman guard now takes place again at noon on summer Sundays.

The expression 'There's more than one yew-bow in Chester' made to jilted girls is a reference to the large number of local archers lost at Agincourt, Crécy and Poitiers, Chester archers being the best in the country. The Pepper Gate has been kept locked since a medieval mayor's daughter hit a ball away in a game, sent her English noble fiancé, Luke de Taney, to search for it and escaped through the gate to a waiting Welsh knight. Brawling Welshmen were an ongoing problem. Henry IV banned them after sunset and they were only allowed to have knives for meat.

The canal uses the moat at the foot of the city walls. Charles I watched his army being defeated at Rowton Moor in 1645 from what has become the King Charles Tower in the walls, now with a Civil War exhibition. The city was besieged for two years until starved out. To get the Wishing Steps to produce the required results it is necessary to walk the

Craft moored in the city centre.

walls, then run up, down and up again without drawing breath.

Queen's School of 1883 is on the site of a gaol where public executions took place from 1809 to 1866. More cheerful is the Victorian Diamond Jubilee Eastgate clock of 1897, the world's most photographed after Big Ben.

The Victorian Gothic style town hall of 1869 with its 49m sandstone clocktower has the Chester Tapestry inside. Chester Toy & Doll Museum has 5,000 items from 1830 on, including the biggest collection of Matchbox toys in Europe. Chester Visitor Centre, the biggest in Britain, is in a Grade II building with a history of Chester, including the Rows and a recreated 1850s Victorian street. The filming of the Channel 4 *Hollyoaks* series brought the city to a wider audience and it was the birthplace of the BBC's Barnaby Bear.

There are festivals for summer music, jazz, folk, literature, fringe, street processions and cheese rolling, an international horse show since 2002 and an international church music festival begun in 2003. In 1795 Chester produced an 8.3kg potato.

Above the weir is a Victorian bandstand. The Dee is normally tidal from Chester Weir. The stream is outgoing from twenty minutes after Dover high water and ingoing from an hour and a half before Dover high water although high water is not slack water. The 52m long weir is the oldest mill dam in Britain, built in 1071 by Hugh Lupus, the 1st Earl of Chester and cruel nephew of William the Conqueror. The mills were destroyed by floods in medieval times and by fire in 1895. The weir was raised in the 20th century. The 1,800km^2 catchment to here delivers an average natural runoff of 37m^3/s to the weir. A minimum compensation flow of 4.2m^3/s is taken down the Salmon Leap fish pass on the left, which has been used for canoe slaloms and by the Environment Agency to show that salmon are not affected by small boats. On the right is an unusual weir gate which can be opened to allow larger craft through but only when the water is high enough.

A rock rapid makes the river below the weir impassable by any craft at low water. It is crossed by the Old Dee Bridge, built in the 14th century by Henry de Snellston. Its seven red sandstone arches span from 7 to 15m on the line of a Roman road crossing. It has had various rebuilds but was the only bridge across the Dee in Chester until the 19th century.

In 973 King Edgar was rowed on the river by subservient kings. The mayor is still the Admiral of the Dee, a title first given to the Black Prince in 1354, and the Duke of Westminster is Sergeant of the Dee.

Chester Castle was built in 1069 on a Saxon fort site by William the Conqueror. It was rebuilt in 1788–1822 by Thomas Harrison as one of the best examples of Greek Revival style outside London and includes the Cheshire Military Museum with 300 years of Cheshire regiments plus an Ypres trench and the Victoria Cross of Todger Jones, who captured 120 Germans single-handed. The Agricola Tower is the oldest remaining part of the castle, dating from the 12th century with fragments of 13th century wall painting and the medieval vaulted St Mary de Castro chapel on the first floor, protected by the castle walls.

A large car park next to the river is unusual in allowing overnight parking, appreciated by visitors with campervans. Next to it is the Grosvenor Bridge taking the A483 over the river. Thomas Harrison designed it in 1802 but delays meant it was not opened by Princess Victoria until 1832, when its 61m span and 13m rise made it the world's longest single span in stone. It is still the world's fourth longest.

The Roodee became the horse racecourse in 1539, the oldest in the country. It is on the site of the Roman port, some of the Roman harbour walls still being visible. The Water Tower protected the harbour from 1322, built on the bank although it is now 200m away and accompanied by the Water Tower Gardens with their triple maze. By the Middle Ages Chester was the most important port in northern England, exporting cheese, candles and salt, but the river was silting badly by the 15th century, forcing trade to the village of Livpul.

Distance
19km from Farndon to Chester

Navigation Authority
Chester & W Cheshire Council

OS 1:50,000 Sheet
117 Chester & Wrexham

Connection
Tidal River Dee – *see RoB p61*

Chester's ancient weir stops most tides.

5 Weaver Navigation

A navigation founded on salt

The River Weaver drains the heart of the Cheshire Plain and its fortunes are closely tied to the deposits of salt which lie beneath. Even before the 18th century, sailing barges were working the river with difficulty to serve the salt trade. In 1732 the river was made navigable for 40t barges in a scheme which was unusual for being publicly financed. This boosted the salt industry. Coal was brought in and clay was taken on to the Potteries by pack horse, finished products being brought by the return trip.

There has been no regular traffic for years although a proposal was made for an inland port near the head of navigation at Winsford to serve the northwest of England.

The river is wide and deep with little current except after heavy rain. All bridges are high and the navigation is used by seagoing ships.

The head of navigation is at the A54 bridges in **Winsford**, just below the Bottom Flash, a large lake resulting from salt extraction subsidence. The two bridges form part of a large roundabout. There is parking available on the east side of the A54 roundabout where amenities include the Ark Inn, De Bees music bar, curries from the Hot Spot and the Red Lion.

The upper bridge is a modern structure but the lower one is built on sandstone blocks which have settled at an alarmingly steep angle, the tops being levelled with a few courses of bricks. Downstream of the bridges are the decaying wooden remains of old wharves with substantial metal securing points. The solidity is repeated in the large stone blocks which edge the navigation amongst all the landscaping.

The Whitegate Way at Meadowbank is a footpath based on a former railway line, ending on the left bank. Just before it is a sewage works but both are screened from the water by the tips from Britain's only salt mine. Standing beside the river, its rotting staithes, crumbling brickwork and remains of Newbridge Lock give it a derelict air but there is constant traffic of articulated lorries which now move the salt while a loading shovel clambers about the heaps.

A swing bridge near **Moulton** leads past a development of chalet houses and into the Valeroyal Cut, probably the most attractive reach on the river with watermeadows, protected in places by levées, patches of woodland and gently rising valley sides. Kingfishers, herons, magpies and jays are prominent parts of the wildlife. The beauty of the area impressed Edward I who, while Earl of Chester, named it the Vale Royal of England.

Edward founded the Vale Royal Abbey for the Cistercians although it was never to be completed. The 17th century sandstone mansion built on the site for the Cholmondley family is now an industrial firm's summer school and is built on the buried foundations of the largest abbey church in England. No less than 130m x 71m in plan, it was active from 1277 to 1360.

The cut passes to the right of the river as the first operational locks are approached. Like the others, the Vale Royal Locks are paired, one large and one small, with traffic being controlled by railway style semaphore signals. The locks frequently have additional gates halfway down their lengths for further flexibility of operation and the largest can hold four Weaver flats (or owner-operated Number One flats like the *Elizabeth* in Manchester Museum). The locks are powered with unusual capstan controls. They have limited opening for pleasure craft but are operated for commercial vessels at any time. Pleasure craft are only expected on the navigation at certain times. Vale Royal Locks have a Victorian steel and stone weir structure with guillotine sluice.

The lower end of the Bottom Flash at Winsford.

Two transport arteries follow, the Crewe–Liverpool railway line passing high overhead and the light blue steel arch of Hartford Bridge carrying the A556 dual carriageway.

Swans establish themselves in a backwater which was the river's original line. Alongside is a shipyard where tugs and other boats are built on sideslips.

The Manchester–Whitchurch railway viaduct crosses immediately below Hunt's Locks, the end of one of which collapsed in 2004, and trains of wagons might be seen leaving the nearby chemical works.

The Weaver Navigation has been designated as a canoe trail.

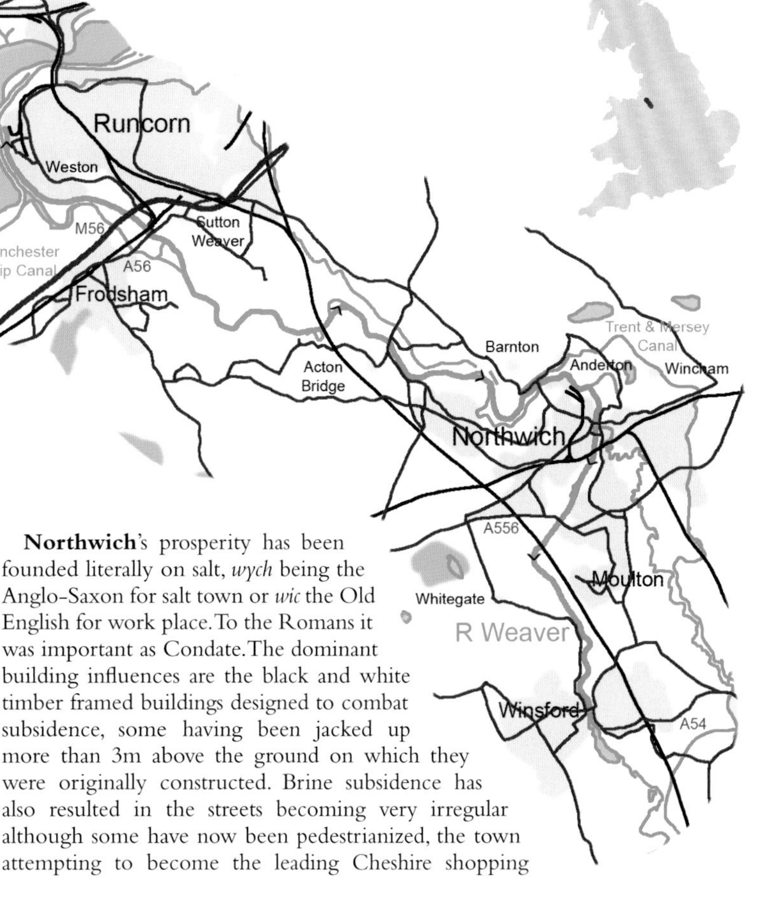

Northwich's prosperity has been founded literally on salt, *wych* being the Anglo-Saxon for salt town or *wic* the Old English for work place. To the Romans it was important as Condate. The dominant building influences are the black and white timber framed buildings designed to combat subsidence, some having been jacked up more than 3m above the ground on which they were originally constructed. Brine subsidence has also resulted in the streets becoming very irregular although some have now been pedestrianized, the town attempting to become the leading Cheshire shopping

Britain's only salt mine stands beside the Weaver.

The boatyard above Hunt's Locks has moderately large craft.

The old CRT clocktower at the trust's depot in Northwich.

The railway crosses over beyond Hunt's Locks.

centre. It houses the Weaver Hall Museum & Workhouse which covers salt and social history. Other prominent buildings include a parish church in Perpendicular style, dating from 1500, with a vast east window and splendid nave and chancel roof. The Canal & River Trust yard repairs quite large vessels, controls the Weaver Navigation, Trent & Mersey and other canals and accounts for the heavy Canal & River Trust traffic on the navigation, including the pusher tugs. The area engineer's office was formerly the Weaver Navigation Trust's office and the mellowed 18th century buildings include an office block with an elegant clocktower topped by a cupola next to the river.

Northwich has three swing bridges, a footbridge and two road bridges which were the first two electrically

The River Weaver leaves the Valeroyal Cut through sluices.

One of the swing bridges in Northwich.

The mighty Anderton Boat Lift, unique on the British canals.

Part of the Winnington chemical complex.

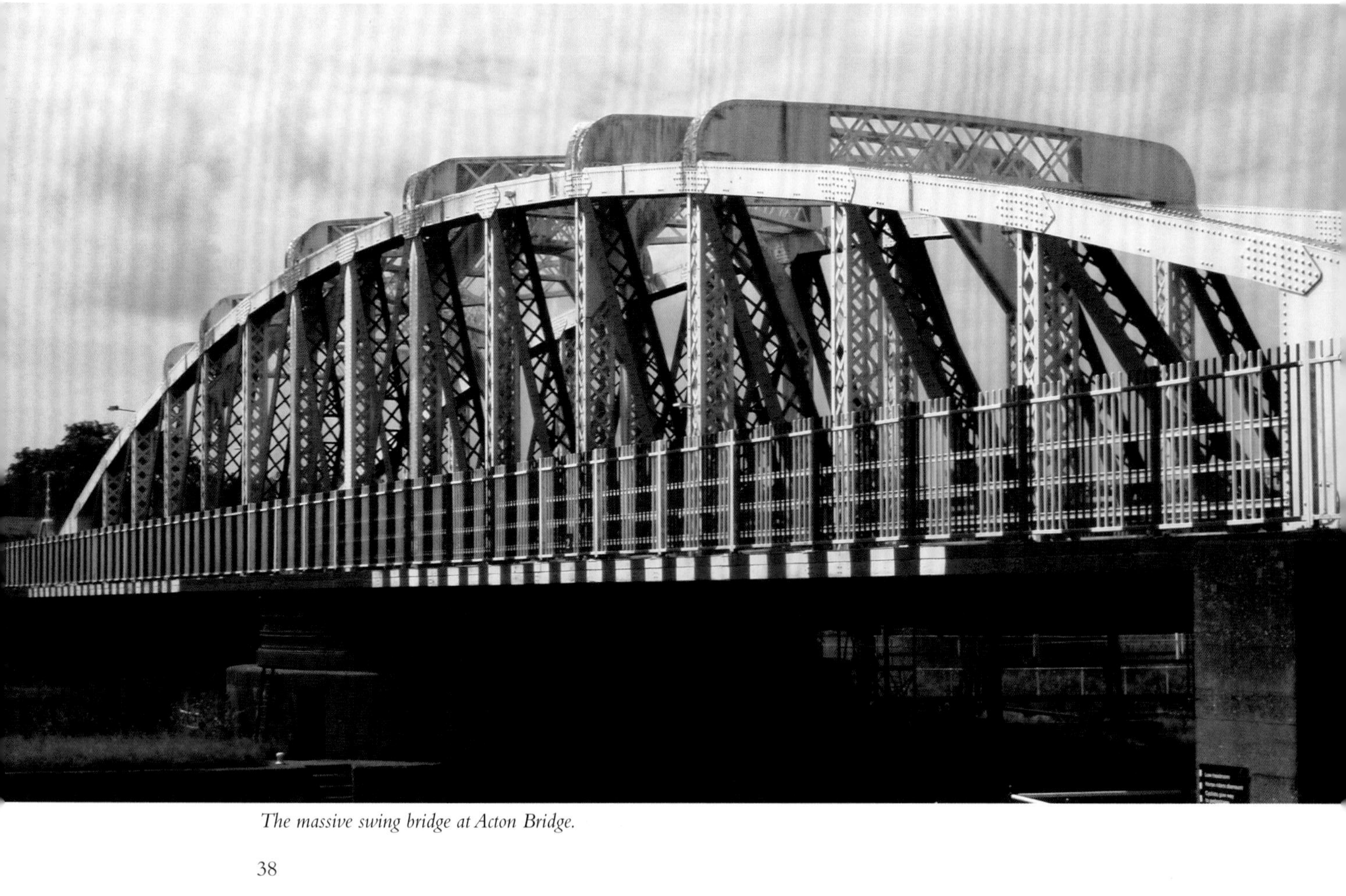

The massive swing bridge at Acton Bridge.

Determining who has priority at locks.

Assorted bridges below Dutton Locks.

powered bridges in Britain. Town Bridge was the first in Britain on floating pontoons because of salt subsidence. The River Dane joins the Weaver Navigation between the two swing road bridges, opposite a public house and next to a wharf building with rails running down diagonally into the water and cribs mounted horizontally on them for lifting out boats. Northwich has an annual rowing regatta on the navigation. After the last bridge there is a cafeteria and restaurant on the right bank.

The right edge of the river also seems to be a dumping ground for old lock gates with many of them standing along the bank. Gulls circle as household rubbish is spread on a tip on top of the hill.

The navigation widens and is joined by Wincham Brook, the river's widest tributary, before turning the corner to the site where Brunner and Ludwig Mond first established themselves in business, subsequently becoming Imperial Chemical Industries and now Tata Chemicals Europe. The vast chemical complex at Winnington still produces odours varying from sulphur to ammonia.

Opposite all the industry stands one of the wonders of the canal world, the Anderton Boat Lift to the Trent & Mersey Canal which is to follow the right bank of the navigation for some 7km. When the Trent & Mersey was opened, chutes down to the Weaver brought much new trade. In 1875 Sir Edward Leader-Williams erected the steel viaduct and pair of parallel tanks with guillotine gates to allow barges to be transferred the 15m between the two waterways. It was reopened in 2001 after being closed for 18 years awaiting repair.

The tanks were counterbalanced and operated by steam powered rams. Seven years after opening, a press burst but the boat on the lift at the time only fell slowly and little damage was sustained. In 1903 the locks were powered by electricity and allowed to operate separately, being individually counterbalanced in 1908. It was the inspiration for lifts in Belgium, France, Germany and Canada.

The 3km Barnton Cut begins almost immediately at Winnington Bridge, now marked by a swing bridge but more famous as the site of the last battle in the Civil War.

600t coasters load caustic soda, potassium and soda ash, the rabies warning notices and multilingual graffiti seeming strangely out of place in the middle of Cheshire.

The Saltersford Locks lie directly below the Trent & Mersey's Barnton Tunnel.

After a run through open country with the Trent & Mersey just visible from bridges over it, the Weaver Navigation passes a caravan site grouped around a tree house and slide. The Riverside Inn on the left bank is balanced by the Leigh Arms, the Horns and the Marco Marco restaurant by the swing bridge at Acton Bridge. The bridge, built in 1933, weighs 560t and is mostly carried on floats.

The MV *Chica*, sunk above Dutton Locks in 1993, remains there as being cheaper for British Waterways to leave than to remove. There is doubt as to whether she was a Liverpool fishing vessel or has had a more colourful history commandeered by the Nazis in Norway and then as a gun runner and smuggling vessel in the Mediterranean.

A grand footbridge with two laminated wood arches crosses the river channel as the navigation rejoins it below the locks. Beyond, Dutton Viaduct carries the Crewe–Liverpool railway back across. A marker post with the figure '200' in silhouette in its arm indicates the proximity of the lock. The first boat to reach this distance post had priority at the locks.

Grazing meadows near Crewood Hall.

A quad bike convoy near Crewood Hall.

The Victorian gabled lock keeper's house and the lock wall are all that remain of Pickering's Lock at what was once the tidal limit.

For the next 5km the river is again in countryside which is peaceful except for massed quad bikes, with regular pieces of woodland. Weed growth builds up at the edges. Below Catton Hall a section of towpath slip has been repaired with gabions. Blackamoor Wood has red sandstone cliffs and these are echoed further ahead by the ridge carrying **Frodsham** which is not particularly noticeable from the navigation except for an obelisk and a couple of aerials.

A fork to the left is the former Weaver Navigation cut, now abandoned, to be followed by another left fork which is the natural course of the river. The red sand of the dividing bank is being carved away by the river as wooden boat ribs rot in the mud nearby. The Weaver Navigation now takes the line of the 1810 Weston Canal and the scenery changes to that of Frodsham Marsh with its small silver birch trees.

The A56 crosses on a swing bridge at Sutton Weaver and the railway passes high overhead, as does the M56 which carries a high proportion of lorry traffic. To the right of the canal lies Junction 12 of the motorway and a railway spur crosses over this on one of two arched concrete bridges which are unusual in design. In the middle of this transport tangle lies a small marina with cruisers clipped to overhead wires.

As aircraft descend into John Lennon Airport at Speke the surroundings change dramatically with a vast and complex modern chemical plant which follows the rest of the canal. Such chemical works feature strongly around the upper Mersey estuary and at night the whole area is a dazzling blaze of lights. Hydrogen sulphide and other pungent scents waft past and the canal water is monitored regularly. Lights warn when ships are being loaded with toxic chemicals and vessels are instructed to pass slowly.

The River Weaver makes a last pass alongside the canal at Saltport before Weston Point Lock connects to the Manchester Ship Canal, Britain's largest canal, which runs next to the Weaver Navigation for the rest of its course, producing a multilane waterway for oceangoing ships.

The chemical complex ends abruptly with the spur of the abandoned **Runcorn** & Weston Canal going off right, the gates of the first lock being bound up with barbed wire.

Steel fabrication takes place on the left and the canal arrives at the Weston Point Docks, now owned by Eddie Stobart. Weston Mersey Lock guards Old Basin, Tollemache Dock and Delamere Dock which opens onto the Manchester Ship Canal. In the middle of the docks is the redundant, blackened, Grade II Christ church with its spire, built in 1841 for the dockworkers and barge people, as were churches and schools in Winsford and Northwich.

Traffic may only enter the dock with the permission of the dock manager after a fee has been paid. Two low bridges cross the docks. A public footpath leads out of the docks to the road where there is limited roadside parking.

Mechanism on the A56 swing bridge near Frodsham.

Rowers skylarking near the M56 crossing.

Distance
32km from Winsford to Weston Point

Navigation Authority
Canal & River Trust

Navigation Society
River Weaver Navigation Society
www.rwns.co.uk

OS 1:50,000 Sheets
108 Liverpool
117 Chester & Wrexham
118 Stoke-on-Trent & Macclesfield

Connection
Trent & Mersey Canal *– see CoB p205*

Start of the chemical complex at Weston Point.

6 River Tees

A polluted river comes clean

Yonder fair Yarm, extended in the vale,
Along the Tees as in a circle lies:
Ill fated spot by inundation torn.
Anon

Formed 18,000 years ago during the Ice Age, the River Tees rises on Cross Fell and flows east to Tees Bay, followed by the Teesdale Way footpath. The official public navigation begins at Holme Farm above Low Worsall, the tidal limit before the Tees Barrage was built, but this is difficult to reach except by coming up from downstream. By this point the river has slowed and is meandering across its flood plain.

Willows, hawthorns and Himalayan balsam overlook the peaty water, used by cormorants, swans, herons, moorhens, mallards and greylag and domestic geese. The river loops back towards Teesside International Airport, developed from the Second World War Goosepool Aerodrome, and passes the 14th century medieval Newsham Village site, probably deserted because of the Black Death.

Roach, chub, bream, rudd, dace, brook lampreys, stone loach, flounders and eels are in the river and an artificial retreat has been built for them on this reach.

In the mid 18th century Low Worsall had a quay with Low Town at the downstream end but the river is no longer accessed here.

The south bank ceases to be North Yorkshire and the river enters Stockton-on-Tees fully. Aislaby was Aislac's village, an early Viking settlement. Aislaby Green now has a walkway of carved railway sleepers across a marsh, the carving extending to a Sail to the Sea stile. However, it also has green huts for anglers, whose preferred locations on this river seem to be upturned plastic bakery trays trodden into the banks. There is a slipway.

Yarm Bridge and the railway viaduct.

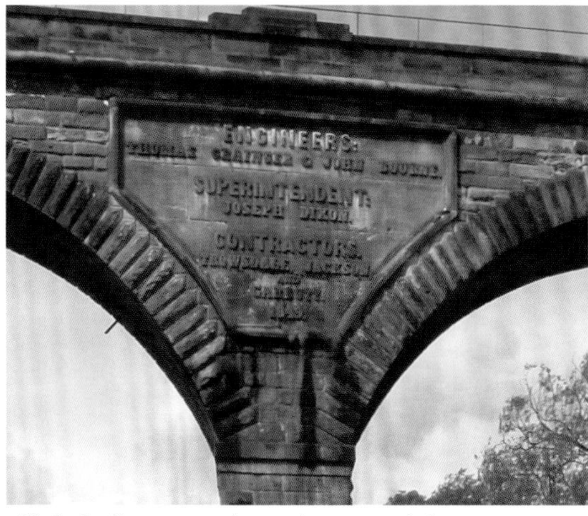

All the leading construction parties are recorded.

A well-butressed church tower in Yarm.

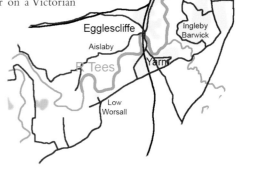

Two sets of powerlines cross before the large loop in which **Yarm** is located. The market town was built on a site in use since 600 BC. Its industry, brewing, nail making, rope making, clock making and boat building were aspects of this main medieval trading port on the Tees, one of the most important ports in Europe in the 14th century, Robert the Bruce sacking it five times because of its significance.

Apart from a church with a heavily buttressed tower, little is seen of Yarm at first except perhaps some activity on the railway on the top of the ridge. In 1820 the George & Dragon hosted the world's first meeting of railway promoters. The railway crosses the river on a Victorian

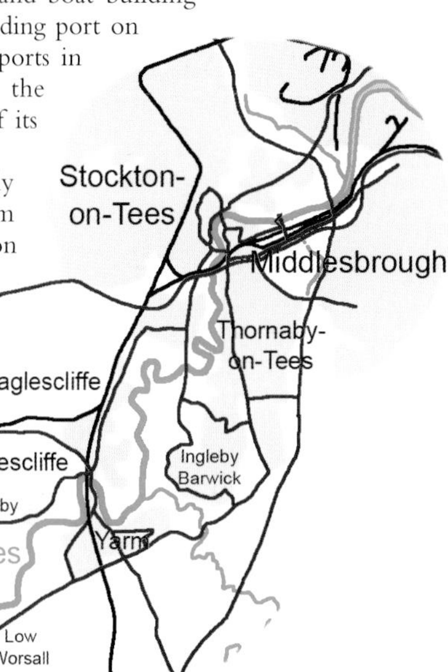

A field of giant hogweed beside the River Leven confluence.

A farm above flood level on the Ingleby Barwick side.

railway viaduct of 1852, one of the longest in Britain. The 43 arches, up to 20m high, used 7,500,000 bricks and are home to pipistrelle bats. A large panel listing those responsible for its construction faces the 15th century stone Yarm Bridge. By Bishop Skirlaw, the latter was fitted with a drawbridge at the northern end by the Royalists of **Eaglescliffe** during the Civil War. It now carries the A67.

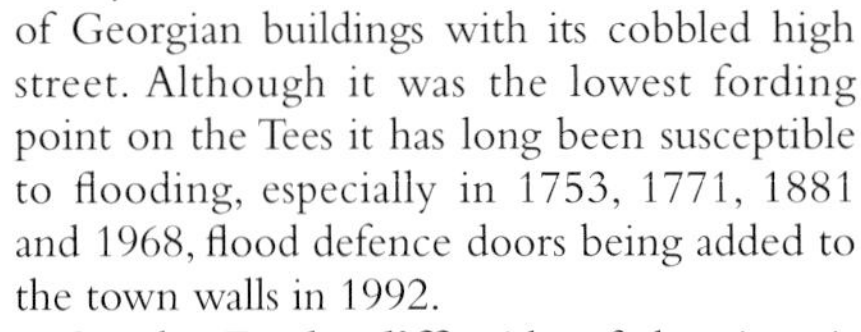

The Dutch style town hall looks small in this town of Georgian buildings with its cobbled high street. Although it was the lowest fording point on the Tees it has long been susceptible to flooding, especially in 1753, 1771, 1881 and 1968, flood defence doors being added to the town walls in 1992.

On the **Egglescliffe** side of the river is the Blue Bell, the landlord of which landed a 2.5m sturgeon of 92kg in 1890. The 18th century Ketton Ox is haunted. St John's church, in Norman style on a Saxon site, has a tunnel to Yarm School's Friarage.

Sycamores, alders and oaks grow on the banks and Yarm Rookery is an established wildlife site.

The River Leven joins just after powerlines cross. The Tees suffers from giant hogweed, which has escaped from Barnard Castle estate, but there is a whole field of it below the confluence. Reeds also appear along the banks.

Back out into open country, the river flows past farms sited well above the flood level. Golfing facilities appear on both banks, followed by a girls' school, near which is the world's oldest passenger railway, the Stockton & Darlington of 1825, operated by *Locomotion*. Preston Hall, the home of the Ropner shipping family, was built the same year. It is now the Preston Hall Museum with an 1890s Victorian street of shops, rooms from the 1880s to 1960s, Victorian industrial and domestic life, transport, some of the best arms and armour in the country, toys, John Walker, a children's zoo and Butterfly World. A domed aviary is seen from the river, where blackbacked gulls are unrestricted. All is set in the 48ha country park which hosted the 2001 canoe marathon world championships.

Beyond Preston-on-Tees the river almost completes a large loop, passing under pipe and road bridges to reach the ancient woodland of Bassleton Wood and the 1993 wetland of the Holmes with a fish retreat. Bowesfield Industrial Estate and a rubbish tip are prominent above the west bank, opposite the much larger **Thornaby-on-Tees**, rather better hidden, where St Peter's church is partly Norman.

Surtees Bridge takes the A66 next to the 1907 Darlington–Middlesbrough railway bridge on the site of Brown's Tees Suspension Bridge. With an 86m main span, this was built to extend the Stockton & Darlington Railway but deflected 230mm under an 18t load while a 66t load damaged the towers. It proved that suspension bridges were unsuitable for railways but the route did develop Middlesbrough from its population of 40 at the time.

As **Stockton-on-Tees** is reached the buildings take on bright colours and rowers appear on the water. The Victoria Bridge of 1887 replaces one which stopped shipping from reaching Yarm. Stockton had a market from the 14th century and claims the widest high street in the country. It is where Sheraton was born in 1751

The Teesside Princess *heads up the river with passengers.*

and made his first furniture and where John Walker invented the friction match in 1827, something he failed to patent.

Green Dragon Yard Museum features local history, railways, shipping, pottery and weights and measures. There are the remains of a Norman castle destroyed by Cromwell in the Civil War. A Georgian area includes the Georgian Theatre. Castlegate Quay has a watersports centre and a steel replica of Cook's HM Bark *Endeavour*.

A high fountain and a slipway accompany busy traffic along the riverside to the Princess of Wales Bridge. Inside the bend is the former Head Wrightson heavy engineering site, scene of Margaret Thatcher's walk in the wilderness, producing perhaps the most iconic picture of her premiership as she walked alone with her handbag across the derelict site. Teesdale is the largest urban regeneration scheme of its kind in Europe, covering 1km^2 and including University College and artificial canals. Teesside Retail & Leisure Park on the former Stockton horse racecourse covers 5.6ha and includes the country's largest 14 screen cinema. The steelworks of the Malleable Site have been replaced by gorse. Painted steel skeletons occupy Teesaurus Park.

Portrack Marshes were a turning area for a sewage works boat. Cutting off meanders shortened the line of the river by 5km from its old route south of the golf course, producing a 1km rowing course which is used for everything from water skiing to dragon boat racing. The Infinity double arched footbridge soars across the river between the River Tees Watersports Centre and offices occupied by such bodies as Barclaycard. At the end of the reach there is a slipway on the south side at Blue House Point.

This is where the Tees Barrage was built in 1995, when it was Britain's largest single engineering contract. The seven span tubular bridge is visually reminiscent of the Severn's Ironbridge and of Richmond Lock on the Thames. Four gates are 14m long and 8m high, holding upstream water at high water level and preventing polluted tidal water from coming up further, as a result of which 18km of water upstream has been cleaned up. Formerly, tar acids, cyanides and the untreated sewage from 250,000 people were free to pass to and fro. There is a lock, reached through a deep steel canyon, but the Port of Tees & Hartlepool discourage small boats, charge a fee, require third party insurance and want registration with them because this is one of England's busiest ports.

A fish pass was provided for salmon and sea trout. A white water canoe slalom and rafting course was installed as Britain's largest purpose built course, shallow at first but deepened in 2011. With a shorter course across the middle, the main course goes round in a loop to make it easier to get back to the start. Obstacles to the flow can be moved to change the course and there is floodlighting for use in the dark.

The skyline to the east is industrial but the Cleveland Hills stand to the southeast beyond the urban area.

A complex pipe bridge at Bowesfield Industrial Estate.

New building and the Victoria Bridge in Stockton.

The replica of Cook's Endeavour *at Castlegate Quay.*

Infinity Bridge with the North York Moors beyond.

The Tees Barrage has distinctive lines reminiscent of Ironbridge.

The slalom course without water, showing the design.

Distance
18km from Low Worsall to Tees Barrage

Navigation Authority
Canal & River Trust

OS 1:50,000 Sheet
93 Middlesbrough

7 River Derwent

A battlefield river

Two Roman roads crossed the Derwent at Stamford Bridge, the Bridlington–York road and the Newcastle–Brough road. The Battle of Stamford Bridge took place in 1066 when King Harold surprised Harald Hardrada. A single Norwegian held the bridge against the English until an English soldier used a bathtub as a boat, floating down the river to stab the Norwegian from below. Harald and Tostig were killed and the last Old English king had finally ended two centuries of Viking invasions, a victory still celebrated by residents who share a tub shaped pie on September 25th. However, the battle weakened the English army ahead of their march south to Hastings to face the Norman invasion of William the Conqueror.

The Derwent rises on Fylingdales Moor 6km from the coast but was blocked by glacial ice, the former Lake Pickering overflowing to the south. Although there is a Sea Cut to the coast above Scarborough it flows south to the River Ouse, draining a tenth of Yorkshire but enough water being extracted for the needs of a sixth of the Yorkshire population.

It was a navigation from 1701 with commercial craft from Yedingham but the upper section became disused after Melton weir was removed in 1846, the section above Stamford Bridge becoming unused from 1935. There is a 2.2m vertical weir here. Stamford Bridge Lock, now disused, passed this on a curved channel with a two rise staircase, unusual for the river, with extra gates for larger craft. This is now the head of navigation. There is a free carpark to the southeast of the bridge.

The Yorkshire Derwent Trust wanted to repair the locks, reopening Sutton Lock in 1972. However, this led to an acrimonious campaign by anglers to block restoration, eventually being supported by the Law Lords. The Worldwide Fund for Nature did not deny that they had given substantial funds to support the anglers. The anglers' objection was to powered craft but small unpowered craft were included in the blanket ban.

Use of the river from Stamford Bridge to Sutton upon Derwent requires Yorkshire Wildlife Trust permission. No licence is required but an Environment Agency certificate is needed to say that a boat will not pollute the river with fuel or waste. It is an attractive waterway with willows, alders and reeds growing into the river from the banks as far as the Pocklington Canal but these cause problems for larger craft as the channel is poorly maintained. The towpath is also in a poor state and there are few moorings.

The five storey Grade II watermill in **Stamford Bridge** has now become apartments. The A166 is taken over William Etty's three arched stone bridge of 1727, the single carriageway road climbing steeply over the central navigation arch.

Just downstream is Birkinshaw's 1846 red brick 16 span viaduct, now disused, its 27m cast iron river arch of 3.7m rise being the oldest remaining railway bridge of its kind.

The river forms the boundary between York on the west bank and the East Riding of Yorkshire to the east. It is all SSSI from here with very few buildings near the river. There are greylag geese, mallards, moorhens and wagtails on and around the river, which contains barbel, bream, chub, dace and roach.

Low Catton hides well from the river, as does Mill Mound in Scoreby Wood. On the other hand, the towpath, also serving as the

Stamford Bridge has long been a crossing point worth defending.

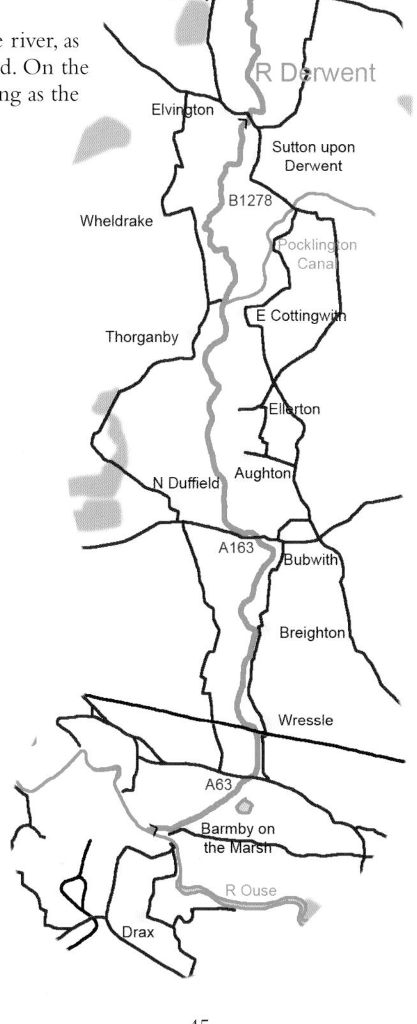

This disused railway arch at Stamford Bridge is the oldest remaining of its kind.

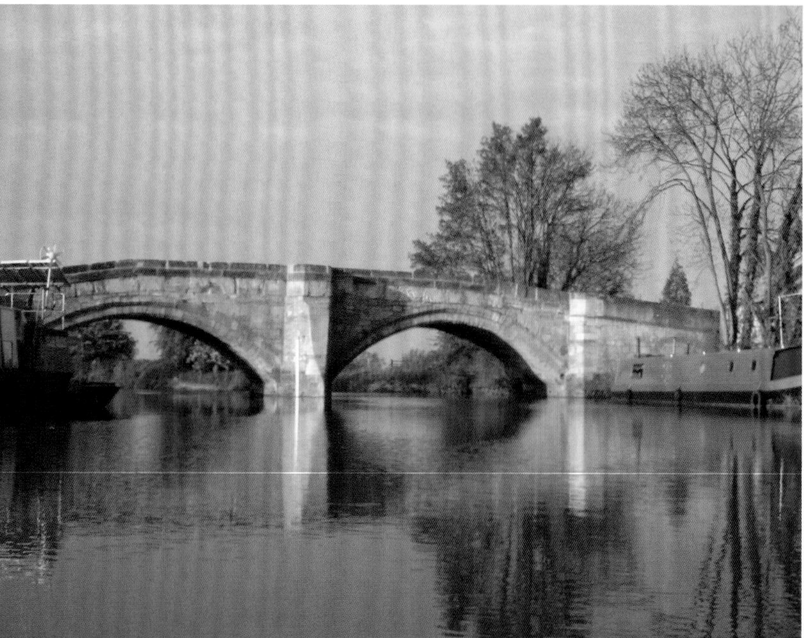

Boats moored by the old bridge at Elvington.

Sutton Lock, one of Britain's least user-friendly.

line of the Minster Way footpath, is signposted into a field with a large Beware of the Bull sign.

A concrete bridge takes the A1079 off the 17th century stone Kexby Bridge. Cuckoo Nest Farm comes before powerlines cross but a nesting box on a tree is owl sized. Yorkshire Air Museum is sited at a large airfield which is disused except for an annual airshow. Moats in the fields are unseen but deer may be spotted near the river. A line of reservoirs store water with an intake and an outlet on the right bank.

Moorings precede the old bridge carrying the B1228 from Elvington to Sutton upon Derwent and Sutton Lock, which has to be one of the least user friendly locks in the country. There is a guillotine gate at the top owned by the EA. Mitre gates at the bottom are owned by the Yorkshire Wildlife Trust. Permission to use them must be obtained in advance from both bodies. Operation is complicated and the instructions are often missing. The EA have to be given 24 hours' notice in order to send somebody from Barmby on the Marsh. There are boats moored in the area where crew members need to disembark. The lock is deep and there is fencing along both sides of the lock at the very brink so there is nowhere to stand and the handling of lines is obstructed. Those portaging small craft need to use a steep and complicated metal walkway before climbing past a gate which is usually kept locked. The lock cottage is privately owned and a vegetable garden prevents any portage route to the weir channel.

Small craft have a reasonable spot to relaunch round the corner once off the lock island but the water is shallow here, making it difficult for powered craft to approach, which they need to do because of the state of the official landing point. This has a locked gate with razor wire up the side. It leads to a short platform cantilevered over the river, a flight of steps secured in the vicinity on the end of a rope and a nearly capsized landing pontoon. There is work to be done here by the EA's successor as navigation authority.

An attractive wooden spire tops the church at Elvington, a village with a watermill and cottages with roses.

This was the tidal limit before the barrage was built and the level still fluctuates.

Gravel pits remain from mineral extraction. Gradually the trees drop away and the banks become lower and more open to the River Ouse. Wheldrake has a church of 1779 which replaced one from the 13th century. Former drawbridges over the river have gone although a substantial wooden pier narrows the channel at the Broken Bridge. Unearthly howls and growls emanate from a fan windpump which needs lubrication. A large wooden hide with some of its end missing overlooks the Wheldrake Ings nature reserve which floods in the winter, attracting Bewick's and mute swans, cormorants,

The landing pontoon has not been used for a while.

The river is frequently lined with trees.

oystercatchers, curlews and other waterfowl. In the river there are water lilies and eels and the west bank becomes North Yorkshire.

The Ferryboat Inn is followed by the junction with the Pocklington Canal. Levées begin and are to follow most of the rest of the river, initially hiding East Cottingwith and Thorganby. There is a priory site at Ellerton Landing and a motte at Aughton with an earthwork and a moat on the west bank, suggesting the river made this a more important area in the past than the nature reserve at North Duffield.

An arched toll bridge of 1793 carries the A163. In stone, it has settled badly, seen by a kink in the arch about a quarter of the way out from the east bank and a corresponding dip in the parapet line.

The large Norman All Saints church stands above the river at Bubwith. Also above the river are the abutments of a railway bridge which has been removed although the line to the east of the river is used as a cycleway and footpath.

A slipway leads down from a public house at Breighton to begin a long line of moorings. Lapwings, kingfishers, yellowhammers and swifts are not all that might be seen flying. Breighton Airfield was a bomber base. Although there are buildings on the old runway it is the home of the Real Aeroplane Club with over 40 planes including a Hurricane, biplanes, triplanes and microlights plus a museum. Gliders in the area are likely to be from the Wolds Gliding Club at Pocklington.

Breighton was a moated site and there are other

The A163 bridge at Bubwith has marked settlement of its main arch.

Bubwith's church tower overlooks the Derwent.

Remains of the castle at Wressle.

antiquities in the vicinity, such as Holmes House. At Wressle two short towers remain of the castle built in about 1380 for Sir Thomas Percy. The Selby–Kingston upon Hull railway crosses in the village and is quickly followed by a Georgian church and a windmill. There is another moat by the A63, which crosses on Loftsome Bridge. Large screens protect the extraction point for a reservoir but it is power which is intrusive; wind turbines stand across the area to the south and Drax power station is in the distance.

The river closes on Barmby on the Marsh, including the King's Head and the Barmby Barrage, built in the 1970s. With radial gates, it leads out onto the tidal River Ouse. The Trans Pennine Trail is taken across a bridge over the water at a sufficiently low level to prevent the lock from being used at high water, normally the preferred time for such a manoeuvre.

Drax power station dominates the bottom of the river.

Distance
35km from Stamford Bridge to the River Ouse

OS 1:50,000 Sheets
105 York & Selby (106 Market Weighton)

Connections
Pocklington Canal – see CoB p297
River Ouse – see RoB p154

Barmby Barrage where the Derwent discharges to the Ouse.

8 River Ouse (Yorks)

The only way is south

Where is that banner now?–its pride
Lies 'whelmed in Ouse's sullen tide!
Sir Walter Scott

Discounting Tewitfield on the Lancaster Canal via the Ribble estuary, the basin in **Ripon** is the most northerly point on the connected inland waterways network. The short Ripon Canal was built to avoid a rocky section of the River Ure, the navigation of which was opened in 1773 after being surveyed by Jessop with input from Smeaton. The New Bond Gate Green Basin is fed from the River Skell.

Ripon, named after the Anglo-Saxon Hrype tribe, is one of Britain's smallest cities. It was mostly under the ice sheet and has suffered from gypsum subsidence holes which may have inspired the hole in *Alice's Adventures in Wonderland* as Charles Dodson's father was a canon here. In his tirade against cars, E M Forster set one of his accidents in *Howards End* on the Great North Road here. Ripon Minster, St Peter's, was founded in 655 and enlarged in 672 to a monastery and church by St Wilfred, whose 670 crypt survives, the oldest outside Italy. The central tower collapsed in 1450 and the spire in 1660 so there is a mix of architectural styles, mostly Norman and 13th century with a 13th century west front which may be the best Early English in Britain, 14th century glass with a 15m high east window, carved choirstalls from about 1490, a 16th century Gothic nave, an 1896 Arts & Crafts pulpit and an ornate rood screen. The organist beat time for the choir with a wooden hand over the chancel entrance and the peal of a dozen bells plus a spare go at a fair lick.

The city is Georgian and Victorian. There is a Workhouse Museum, a Yorkshire Law & Order Museum, a Courthouse Museum and Ripon Prison & Police Museum in the 1815 Liberty Prison with police material from the 17th century onwards. The haunted 14th century half timbered Wakeman's House is now a restaurant. Setting the Watch is still undertaken at 9pm by the Ripon Hornblower or Wakeman in the marketplace, a ceremony which was started in 886 when Alfred the Great granted the charter and presented the Charter Horn, still present. It was a very advanced idea, the Wakeman being paid 2d per outside door by householders who were recompensed for any losses during curfew hours, an insurance and night security patrol scheme.

Defoe said the square was the best of its kind in England. A 27m obelisk of 1781 celebrates William Ailabie, who was the local Member of Parliament for 60 years.

The warehouse and wharf manager's house have been restored at the canal basin, accompanied by a fish and chip shop and the Navigation Inn. In the 19th century fly boats ran to Hull and the basin received 70t cargoes, making it a scene of much more activity than today. The water is clear and the canal slips out along a tree-lined boulevard, the B6265. The aroma of baking comes from beyond a screen of cypress trees and the canal is enclosed by greenery from sycamore trees to yellow flags with mallards dabbling along the way and trout and eels in the water.

Ripon Basin, the most northerly point on the connected canals.

The A61 Ripon bypass crosses on a concrete

The top winding hole on the Ripon Canal.

bridge faced with local stone from the bridge of the former Leeds & Thirsk Railway of which the A61 uses the line. The B6265 turns away near a sewage works and the navigation is free of following roads for the rest of its journey.

Rhode's Field Lock is accompanied by a caravan site while Bell Furrow's Lock has Ripon Racecourse Marina. Angling platforms and adjacent gravel pits are parts of the mix. A horse racecourse, Yorkshire's Garden Racecourse, threads through the pits and one is used as a marina at Littlethorpe.

Beyond Oxclose Lock the canal opens into what appears to be a large lake, actually the broad River Ure, forming the Boroughbridge & Ripon Navigation, at its most beautiful to Boroughbridge. The banks are grazed by sheep and the ribs of barges rise from the shallows in places. Grayling, barbel, chub, dace and salmon occupy the river. The Bishop Monkton Canal has been abandoned, like the Sugar Hill Landing.

The west and south aspects of Newby Hall face the river at opposite ends of a bend where tree flood debris is abandoned against the bank but largely hidden from one of the best gardens in England. A clearing in the vegetation secures the view from Newby Hall Landing although mooring is not permitted. The 10ha garden includes laburnums, old roses, the national dogwood collection, a rock garden, waterfalls, the longest herbaceous borders in Europe, a 260mm gauge miniature railway alongside the river, adventure gardens and classical statues including a 1675 Italian equestrian statue of the king of Poland altered to be Charles II. The 17th century Queen Anne hall was enlarged and now dates mostly from the 1760s with Robert Adam interiors, Zucchini ceilings, Gobelins tapestries and Chippendale furniture. An 1872 Victorian church in the grounds is richly decorated.

The river turns away from the estate to Westwick Lock, dividing round an island with alders, campanula, Jacob's ladder, meadowsweet, rosebay willowherb, valerian and yellow loostrife. Willows, rushes, giant hogweed and lilies follow past Brampton Landing and Brampton Hall, swallows swoop over the river and Canada geese offer more noise and less action. Beyond powerlines the

Rhode's Field Lock, the top lock.

Tunnel of trees at Littlethorpe.

Victorian church and Gothic almshouses at Roecliffe stand above a steep wooded hillside, to be followed by Green's Landing.

The A1M crosses with the A168 running alongside it for 20km. Langthorpe brings Langthorpe Landing, a slipway, Boroughbridge Marina and the Anchor Inn. To the south are the Devil's Arrows, three 36t standing stones from Knaresborough in a north–south line, said to have been fired by the Devil at a Bronze Age Christian missionary community.

Boroughbridge Wharf was an 18th century port serving Knaresborough's linen trade. The Boroughbridge Cut leads through a tunnel of trees towards Milby Lock. On the north side is the site of the 1322 Battle of Boroughbridge where Edward II defeated and executed the Earl of Lancaster.

Crossing the cut is the B6265, formerly the A1 Great North Road. The market town of **Boroughbridge** was an important staging post on the road with 22 coaching inns. The town had the Warwick brewery and a 78m deep well.

Dere Street also crossed the river from Aldborough, the Roman town of Isurium Brigantum and 22ha principal town of the Romanized Brigantes, the largest tribe in Britain. It was the headquarters of the 9th Legion and retains the Roman street layout with the forum, some 2nd century Roman walls and seven mosaic pavements found. More recent are the 14th century church and a tall maypole. Boroughbridge and Aldborough each had two Members of Parliament.

The River Swale joins at Swale Nab, downstream of an earlier battle site of 1319 and the Old Hall at Myton-on-Swale.

Lower Dunsforth stands back from the Ure, Aldwark with its moat and golf course being more brave. Aldwark Bridge, a lattice structure with a toll, cannot be missed because of the clattering as vehicles run across the planking. Downstream of the bridge is a Scout water activity centre before riverside woodland opposite Aldwark Wood. Oystercatchers, moorhens, herons and pheasants may be seen.

Newby Hall faces the river on two aspects.

The river doubles back on itself at Cuddy Shaw Reach where it joins the Ouse Gill Beck. While the latter is easily missed it provides the name as the river is known as the Ouse from here. First to use the title is Linton-on-Ouse Airfield with the main runway ending 1km away and some interesting aircraft doing bomb bursts over the river.

Beyond a sewage works is Linton Lock. The marina objects to small craft taking out on the slipway although it is not apparent from the river that this is not part of the

Trees beside the River Ure at Roecliffe.

The church at Newton-on-Ouse.

Shoals of fish below Milby Lock.

A dead narrowboat at the edge of the river.

lock facilities. Ownership of this section by Linton Lock Commissioners has caused problems in the past with the lock failing but a change to British Waterways resulted in restoration. The brick lock keeper's cottage has been adapted to have a café. The weir has a 3.7m vertical drop and a powerful fish ladder past it, used in the 1970s for a couple of experimental canoe slaloms which developed the rules towards those used today throughout the world.

A sandbank on the south side below the lock is now buoyed. Narrowboats have sat on it for up to three months, waiting for rain. The river suffers from clay huts – mounds caused by clay slips.

On the bank at Newton-on-Ouse are the Dawnay Arms and a church with a slender spire. Greylag and domestic geese patrol the river. The ribs of wrecks stand before a tower amongst the trees in decorative Victorian brickwork. Beningbrough Park contains the 1716 red brick Georgian Beningbrough Hall with its two storey Great Hall, baroque interiors, cantilevered oak stairs, notable carving and panelling, gilded Corinthian pilasters, over a hundred 18th century portraits, a walled garden, parterre, classical sculptures, Victorian laundry and potting shed. Until the late 19th century there was the ghost of the housekeeper of an earlier 1670 hall who was attracted to the gamekeeper but she was drowned by a poacher at the instigation of the jealous estate steward, the poacher being hanged and the steward committing suicide.

Nun Monkton has a 30m maypole with a weathervane. This is where the River Nidd finally joins after excessive meandering, bringing more water for bream and roach and finding poplars and a wall of horse chestnut trees.

Between Beningbrough and Overton the south bank changes from North Yorkshire to York.

A moat is unseen on the bank at Nether Poppleton but the crossing of the East Coast Main Line cannot be missed, to follow the river into York. The A1237 bypass leaves the river wooded and rural, fronting Rawcliffe Ings and Clifton Ings rather than Rawcliffe and Clifton villages themselves, rowers giving the first indication of the city ahead. York waterworks were built at Acomb Landing in 1846 by Hawksley, slow sand filters being added in 1853 by Simpson. Trip boats come up to the concrete Clifton Bridge. St Peter's School forbids bonfires, Guy Fawkes having been a pupil.

The National Railway Museum, the world's largest railway museum, is close to the river and exhibits include *Mallard*, the world's fastest steam engine, a replica of the *Rocket*, Eurostar and Shinkansen units, royal carriages and the 3.8m 1826 Gaunless Bridge by George Stephenson from the Stockton & Darlington Railway. The Scarborough–York railway crosses the river on a bridge by Andrews and carries steam trains on Tuesdays to Thursdays. The line leads into York station of 1877 by Prosser which allowed through running. The station is

The fish ladder and weir at Linton Lock.

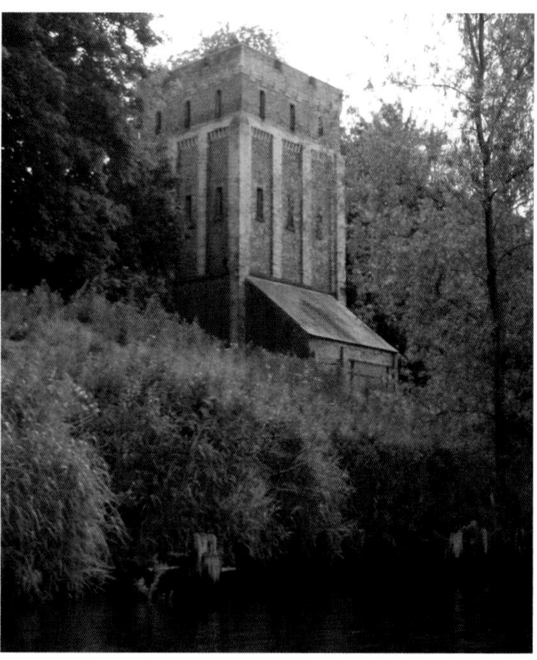

Victorian baronial engineering brickwork on the bank.

on a sharp curve, like Paddington but much later. George Hudson, the local Railway King, was an early promoter of this form of transport. York Old Station was one of the early stations, built through the city walls, similar to Euston with retained original features including offices, the train shed roof on cast iron columns, cast iron arches and wrought iron trusses. The locomotive water tank house is probably the earliest surviving, 9.1 x 6.1m.

York is sited where the north–south River Ouse crosses a west–east terminal moraine. Geoffrey of Monmouth claimed the city was founded in 980 BC by Ebrancus, from a fleet of Trojan galleys. It was certainly the British Celtic Eburacum, Eburos' estate, the name retained by the Romans in the 1st century for their base to conquer northern Britain after 70 AD and was probably the most important military and civil Roman settlement in Britain with a 20ha fort from 72. Britannia Inferior, meaning further from Rome, was governed from York with one legion. Caesars Septimius Severus and Constantius I died here and Constantine was proclaimed emperor here. It became the Anglo-Saxon Eoforwic then the Viking Jorvik from 867. In 1639 it was Charles I's northern headquarters.

Rowers warn of arrival in York.

The medieval street plan of what was Britain's second city has been retained. Only London and Norwich have more churches and 18 of these are medieval. It is Europe's

The Scarborough railway line crosses.

Lendal Tower and the Lendal Bridge.

most haunted city and was the world's first to have a ghost walk. York architect Aloysius Hansom designed the Hansom cab and the Quaker Rowntree and Terry families developed chocolate, together with Craven's confectionery. There is a Festival of the Rivers, a Viking Festival in February, a Comedy Festival in June, Britain's largest Festival of Food & Drink in September and a St Nicholas Christmas Fayre in November and December.

The Guildhall fronts the Ouse.

York has one of the best waterfronts in England. York City Art Gallery has outstanding European paintings, especially the large William Etty nudes. King's Manor was the 1270 abbot's house, now used by the university. The 11th century St Mary's abbey ruin is the stage for the York Mystery Plays, started in the 14th century and performed every three years, the full texts having survived in Fairfax's library. The Yorkshire Museum has some of the best Roman, Anglo-Saxon, Viking and medieval finds in Britain including the 15th century Middleham Jewel, local pottery and the hair of a girl from Roman times, set in 4ha of botanical gardens with peacocks and squirrels.

The Roman Multangular Tower became part of the 1220 medieval city walls for Henry VII, the longest in England at 4.5km, surrounding 1.1km^2 with four gateways and 39 towers. St Leonard's hospital was rebuilt in 1137 after a fire.

The 1863 Lendal Bridge by Thomas Page in heavily decorated Gothic cast iron has a 53m span Tudor arch and ornamental lights and was strengthened in 1910 to take tramcars. The Barker Tower on the station side and the Lendal Tower on the Minster side were connected by a chain across the river from 1380 to 1538 to complete

More of York's historic waterfront.

York's Millennium Bridge, its arch leaning downstream.

The Palace of the Archbishop of York.

the defences. The Lendal Tower has been a water tower with a Newcomen engine, used to distribute river water through wooden pipes.

The 1740 Theatre Royal is one of the oldest working theatres outside London and was one of the most important in Georgian times. Of similar vintage are the 1732 Assembly Rooms, 34m long with 52 marble Corinthian pillars.

York Minster was founded on the site of the Roman headquarters in 627 by Edwin, King of Deira. The fourth on the site, it is mostly from 1220 to 1470 and is the largest Gothic cathedral north of the Alps. Measuring 125 x 76 x 60m it has a 71m lantern tower, 30m limestone pillars, rib vaulted roof and the biggest bell in England, St Peter. The 15th century Central Tower was shored up in the 1970s because of 300mm of differential settlement. The 19m octagonal Chapter House has a 20m high unsupported timber roof. There is over half of Britain's medieval stained glass including the world's largest pre-Renaissance window at the east end, $160m^2$, and the oldest glass in England from about 1150. A stone choir screen has all the English rulers from William I to Henry VI, an astronomical clock memorial remembers 18,000 northeastern airmen lost in the Second World War and a decorative elephant drinking horn over 600mm long was given by 11th century Danish chieftain Ulph to confirm donation of his lands in western Yorkshire to the church. There is a window to St William, William Fitzherbert, the Archbishop of York in 1141.

The Treasurer's House was built over a Roman road in the cellar for the treasurer of York Minster with a 1620s exterior, remodelled inside from 1897 to 1930 with a half-timbered gallery, exquisite plasterwork and elaborate fireplaces, the first house to be given complete with its collection to the National Trust. A young plumber working in the basement in 1953 saw a Roman Legion of about 20 plus their horses marching on the road.

St William's College was the home of the minster clergy priests in 1453. The 14th century Bootham Bar with its two hanging turrets has been underpinned as it was tilting.

The Roman Stonegate became a notable medieval street. Monk Bar has two gun ports and the Silent Watchers, six stone figures with missiles. The Twelfth Century House was Norman while the Mansion House with its magnificent silver is from 1730.

Yorkboat have one of the largest inland fleets of passenger boats, joining plenty of swans on the river. One of the most notable buildings on the waterfront is the 1448 Guildhall, set on fire during a 1942 air raid and restored in 1960. It has oak tree columns, two secret doors in the panelling and grotesque carvings. All Saints church has 14/15th century stained glass and the Prykke of Conscience window predicting the world's last 15 days. St Martin-le-Grand, also rebuilt after the 1942 air raid, has one of England's finest 15th century windows. Holy Trinity church of 1250–1500 has box pews, a two tier pulpit, ancient glass, a nun ghost and the 15th century ghosts of a family of three with the mother fetching her child from a grave outside the city where it was buried because it had died of the plague. Our Lady's Row dates from 1316. Merchant Taylors' Hall is also 14th century with a fine timber roof. All Saints Pavement is 15th century with a 19th century west tower and there is an octagonal lantern as a guide to travellers. The Shambles has overhanging buildings and may be Europe's finest medieval street. The Archaeological Resource Centre allows hands on exploration. The two storey St Anthony's Hall was a 15th century workhouse, then a jail, a school, an armoury and a merchant guild meeting place.

York Brewery of 1996 is near the Micklegate Bar which has a Norman arch and two large turrets and was used to display the heads of traitors.

The 1820 three arch Gothic stone Ouse Bridge was by Peter Atkinson. In 1141 William Fitzherbert, Archbishop of York, had been deposed by the Pope. When he was restored in 1154 a bridge collapsed into the Ouse under the weight of his supporters but he made the sign of a cross and the water formed itself into a bridge, one of three dozen miracles he performed. The Roman bridge was just upstream. Beneath Church Street 46m of Roman sewer and its branches in sandstone and millstone grit have been found in good working order.

The Bar Convent Museum features the oldest active convent in the country. Jorvik Viking Centre presents Viking York in 975, Britain's first journey through time with visitors riding in time cars and experiencing the sights, sounds and smells of those days. The Merchant Adventurers' Hall of 1361 is the finest surviving British medieval guildhall and the Friargate Wax Museum is near the York Dungeon which includes the execution of Dick Turpin in York Gaol. Turpin was credited with a phenomenal ride to York but it was actually undertaken in 1676 by Swift Nicks who rode from Gad's Hill in Kent in a day to appear in a public game of bowls to establish an alibi.

By John Carr, the 1750 Fairfax House is one of the best 18th century town houses in England with one of the best collections of mid 18th century furniture, an outstanding clock collection, old masters paintings, Chinese porcelain and oriental rugs, having been converted back from a cinema and dance hall. The Impressions Gallery of Photography was the first contemporary photo gallery outside London. There is the Regimental Museum of the 4/7th Royal Dragoon Guards and the Prince of Wales Own Regiment of Yorkshire.

The Quatrefoil Clifford's Tower is on one of two mottes, one on each bank, for William the Conqueror's 1068 castles, part of his Harrying of the North, burnt down in 1190, when the Jewish community was massacred, and rebuilt in stone in 1245–59 as one of a pair for Henry III. Sir Robert Clifford, the first governor, was defeated in 1322 and his body hung in chains from the tower. York Castle Museum in two 18th century prisons includes Dick Turpin's cell, a gypsy caravan, Edwardian and Victorian streets and rescued buildings which have been imported. Scott mentioned an escape from the castle in *The Heart of Midlothian*.

The Selby–York Railway Path uses what was the East Coast Main Line.

The 1881 Skeldergate Bridge by Page is in wrought iron and heavily decorated Gothic cast iron on three arches with a lifting span, the decorative arches swinging aside. The three storey 1873 York City Bond warehouse has brick walls and 200mm cast iron columns while Raindale Watermill is an 18th century cornmill restored from a York Moors site. Walmgate Bar is the only gateway in England which still has a barbican.

The River Foss joins, carrying commercial traffic from York. There was a report of an iron boat being launched here in 1777, which would have made it the first.

The 150m Millennium Bridge has an 80m main span with hangers radiating from a stainless steel arch inclined at 40° from the vertical and supporting a box girder to carry cyclists and pedestrians. It is followed by York Motor Yacht Club.

Knavesmire horse racecourse is to the west of the river, referred to as the Ascot of the North. Nearer is Middlethorpe Hall & Spa, a 1699 William & Mary building in an 8ha walled garden and park, formerly the home of Lady Mary Wortley Montague.

Harald Hardrada beat Edwin and Morcar at the Battle of Fulford in 1066 and then made a treaty with them to join him in a march south in an attempt to conquer the whole of England.

Bishopthorpe Bridge with sinusoidal deck and elliptical piers takes the A64 York Ring Road. Below on a bend of the river is the Palace of the Archbishop of York, mostly 18th century but with a 13th century chapel.

Bishopthorpe ends opposite a sewage works with the bridge that used to carry the East Coast Main Line until it was diverted away from the Selby Coalfield and now takes the Selby–York Railway Path and has a flimsy sculpture balanced on top. York Marina follows and the Yorkshire Ouse Sailing Club have a slipway.

Opposite Naburn is the church at Acaster Malbis. Jews fleeing persecution in York in 1189 used it for worship so angry villagers set fire to it, killing all those inside. There are still bloodstains on a windowsill and it has been referred to as the Synagogue. Trees with mistletoe face across to one of various caravan sites around the village.

The Grade II duplicated Naburn Locks of 1757 and 1888 have a swing bridge over and unusual bellclough ground paddles. The weir has been modified with funding by RJB Mining to allow it to be raised after mining subsidence. From here the river is tidal.

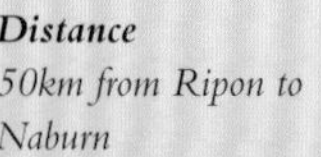

Distance
50km from Ripon to Naburn

Navigation Authority
Canal & River Trust

OS 1:50,000 Sheets
99 Northallerton & Ripon
100 Malton & Pickering
105 York & Selby

Connection
Tidal River Ouse – see RoB p153

Naburn Lock buildings at the tidal limit.

9 River Wharfe

As used by the English fleet

The substantial weir in Tadcaster.

Named from guerf, swift, the River Wharfe rises on Langstrothdale Chase by the source of the River Ribble, which flows westwards. The River Wharfe flows southeast across North Yorkshire to the River Ouse, draining a twentieth of Yorkshire in the process but never entirely forgetting its rapids. A large weir at **Tadcaster** provides an impassable head of navigation for any non portable boats which have managed to get this far.

Tadcaster was the Roman Calcaria, perhaps a reference to magnesian limestone quarrying, and the Romans had a wooden bridge over the river.

Tides can reach here and must have done so on the day in 1066 when the English fleet arrived, retreating from Harald Hardrada, who had ceased the chase at Riccall. King Harold came, set his boats in order and continued to York and Stamford Bridge.

The large Virgin Bridge upstream of the weir was for a Leeds–York railway but the project ran out of money before the track was laid. It passes a 13th century Norman motte and bailey castle built using Roman stone, the motte and ditch remaining.

The 1150 church of St Mary was burned by the Scots, rebuilt in 1380 as well as a century later and then dismantled in 1875 and moved to foundations 1.5m higher to avoid floods. The first stone bridge was built in about 1200 with the present Tadcaster Bridge, carrying the A659, being built in about 1700. The market was given its charter in 1270 by Henry III. The Ark, Tadcaster's oldest building, was reputed to have been used in the 15th century by the Pilgrim Fathers to plan their emigration to America. The town has three breweries, those of Samuel Smith, John Smith and Molson Coors.

Stakes in the river from former anti scour measures.

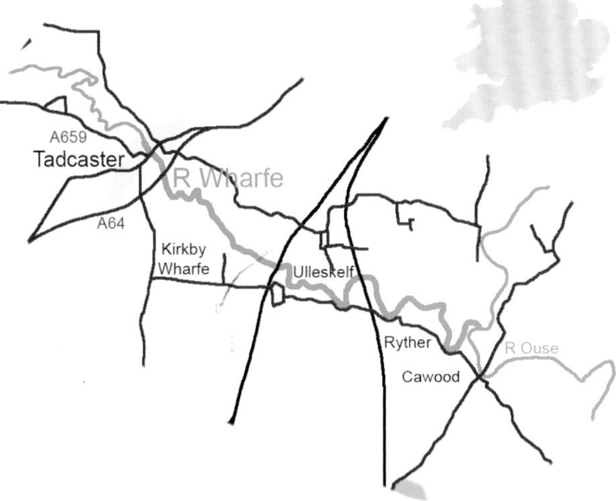

Riverbank trees near Ulleskelf.

Rapids at Ryther on the tidal river.

There is a free carpark between the bus station and the river but it may be closed in the evening for football games, any remaining cars being at risk of damage, so permission to use the Britannia Inn's carpark might be a safer bet if necessary.

Stone and gravel rapids occur from time to time, the one below the bridge being the shallowest. There are barbel, chub, dace, minnows, trout and eels in the river. Willows and other trees line the bank as the built up area is quickly left behind. The A64 draws a line under Tadcaster, except for the sewage works located across on Tadcaster Ings.

Pairs of wooden groynes have been angled out into the river, to be followed later by wooden protection along the banks. In each case any boarding has gone, leaving just lines of stakes. Sandy edges to the river are a luxury which will not last, being replaced by silt further downstream. There are water lilies while the banks have colour from cow parsley, oilseed rape, dandelions and trees which include some fine specimens of horse chestnut, especially around Grimston Park. There was a Roman villa sited at Kirkby Wharfe.

Herons, swans, moorhens, lapwings, mallards, Canada geese and oystercatchers might be seen around the river and there are mussels in the water.

The York–Leeds railway crosses above Ulleskelf, the normal tidal limit. It is followed across Ozendyke Ings by the East Coast Main Line, diverted to avoid the Selby coalfield. This was the first major railway for so long that it was necessary to return to 19th century contract documents to prepare the project.

The river has clay huts, sections of bank which fall into the water and provide obstructions, sometimes quite substantial ridges in the river. Even on the tidal section there are rapids at Ryther. Curlews and greylag geese are present.

Mote Hill is at the southern end of Nun Appleton Park. The river meanders past East Ings and Wharfe Ings, the gaps between the branches of trees on opposite banks sometimes less than 3m. The Wharfe nearly meets the Ouse flowing the opposite way at Cawood but continues for another 600m before finally joining the larger river at Wharfe's Mouth.

Prior to joining the Ouse above Cawood.

Distance
15km from Tadcaster to the River Ouse

OS 1:50,000 Sheets
105 York & Selby

Connection
Tidal River Ouse – *see RoB p153*

10 River Dun Navigation

Waiting for commercial traffic to return

Again we meet, where often we have met,
Dear Rother! native Don!
We meet again, to talk, with vain regret,
Of deedless aims! and years, remember'd yet –
The past and gone!
Ebenezer Elliot

The first attempt to make the River Don navigable for commercial craft in 1697 was a failure but the Cutlers' Co of Hallamshire and the Corporation of Doncaster completed the River Dun Navigation in 1751, a broad canal for Yorkshire keels. Running northeast, it replaced a toll road. In 1847 it was bought by the South Yorkshire, Doncaster & Goole Railway, who also bought the Sheffield Canal and the Stainforth & Keadby Canal in 1849, all parts of the Sheffield & South Yorkshire Navigation. They were all bought in 1864 by the Manchester, Sheffield & Lincolnshire Railway, later the Great Central, and a new Sheffield–Rotherham railway was built partly on the line four years later, the canal being diverted back to the River Don where it was subject to flooding and silting. In the early 1980s it was modernized and enlarged to take 700t barges up to Mexborough and 400t barges to Rotherham although this has not resulted in the business which was anticipated. Vic Waddington, the 92 year old prime mover and owner of the fleet located on the navigation, died in 1999 and the future of the canal is again open to question. British Waterways had already reduced the dredging profile.

The navigation has two significant problems for small boats. The fact that it is constructed for large craft means that portaging at locks often involves high sides. The Canal & River Trust sometimes have to use high security arrangements in vandal areas but even these have not been enough on this navigation and most locks have had to be surrounded by high security fences.

Sheffield basin was restored in the mid 1990s as Victoria Quays. The basin is dominated by three large warehouses, particularly the Straddle Warehouse which was built across the basin in 1895 for ease of loading. Between the warehouses can be seen the bowstring bridge carrying the Supertram over the roundabout next to the Ponds Forge International Sports Centre. Close by is Sheffield cathedral, noted for its fine monuments. It was founded in the 12th century with 19/20th century additions, but was a parish church until 1914. On the north side of the basin is a line of stone arches, overlooked by the Stakis Hotel, while a swing footbridge closes off the entrance by the Sheaf Quays public house in what was the first steam powered cutlery. The name comes from the River Sheaf, the Old English sceath meaning boundary. Life in the water includes a form of freshwater jellyfish up to 20mm in diameter. Much more conspicuous, though, are the large fish. Angling is not permitted in the basin and the full sized fish contrast dramatically with the tiny specimens out on the canal itself, which has a heavy angler presence.

Sheffield has been making knives since the 7th century and is famous for its cutlery, together with its leftwing views, sometimes causing it to be referred to derogatively as the capital of the People's Republic of South Yorkshire.

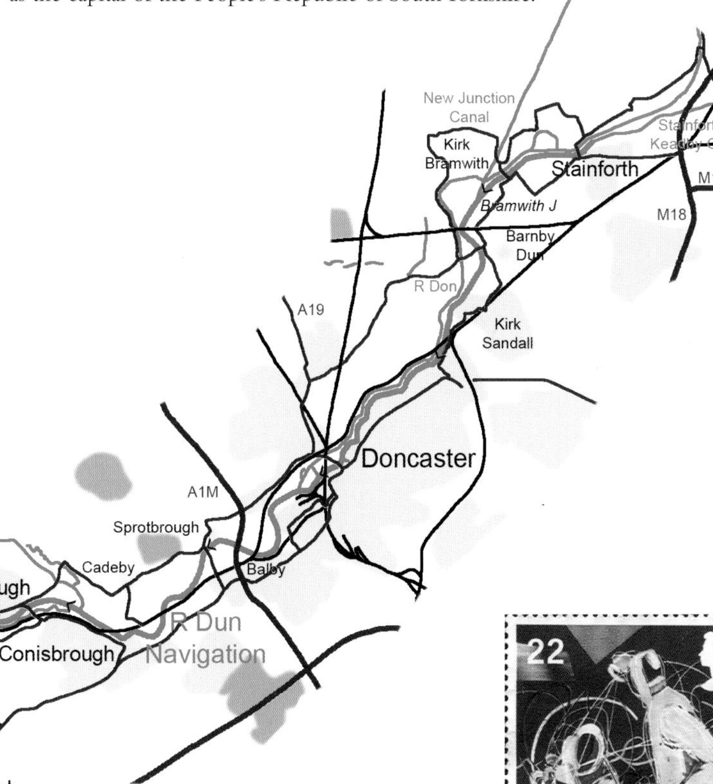

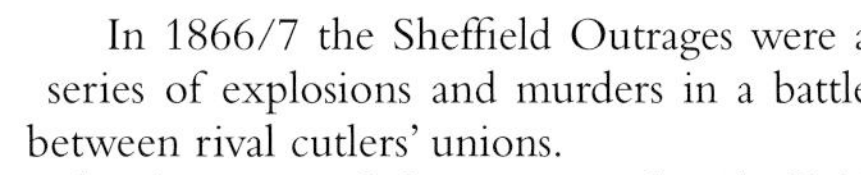

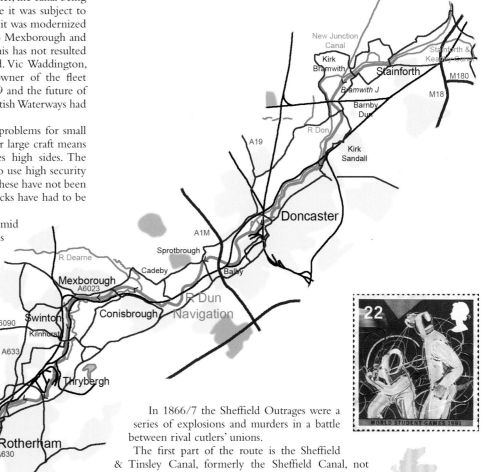

In 1866/7 the Sheffield Outrages were a series of explosions and murders in a battle between rival cutlers' unions.

The first part of the route is the Sheffield & Tinsley Canal, formerly the Sheffield Canal, not completed until 1819 because of arguments with millowners over water supply.

On leaving the basin the canal is crossed by the A61 and the Wicker Arches of 1845. Most of the 41 arches of the viaduct, carrying a railway line over the canal and the River Don, are not visible from the canal but it is probably the finest British railway bridge of its kind. A large gas holder stands beside the canal and steelworks have never been far away, the first Bessemer works being built here in 1859.

The magnificent Straddle Warehouse crosses Victoria Quays, the terminal basin in Sheffield.

Tinsley Viaduct, carrying the M1 above the A631.

Boat rally at Rotherham Lock.

Attercliffe cutting was said to have been dug by Napoleonic war prisoners. Today it is a wildlife haven in the city with greater reedmace, water lilies, blackberries, buddleia, sloes, peacock butterflies, dragonflies, damselflies, flatworms and sticklebacks. The canal was also used for the car in the water scene in *The Full Monty*.

The B6200 crosses over and then the Supertram does, too, following the canal to Tinsley, together with overhead powerlines. Several of the bridges are of imaginative modern steel designs featuring arches and tubes, all bridges being named and numbered. The single stone arch of the Darnall Road aqueduct carries the canal over the B6085 and under the flightpath of Sheffield City Airport. Modern styling also features with the Don Valley Stadium, built for the 1991 World Student Games, and the Sheffield Arena, from where there are extensive views over the industrial Don valley to the northwest.

Broughton Lane bridge is the largest so far, carrying the A6102 as the canal approaches the top of the Tinsley 12, accompanied by an oxygen pipe beside the towpath. There is solid stonework and heavy paddle gear on the locks. Only 11 locks are left, despite the name, not because of the one bombed in December 1940 instead of one of the surrounding steelworks but because two were rebuilt as a deep lock in the 1950s to allow clearance under a railway bridge serving the new Tinsley marshalling yard which is no more.

The massive Meadowhall Shopping Centre is to one side of the canal. The bridge by Turnpike Bridge Lock used to carry Sheffield–Rotherham trams which served the steelworks but, surprisingly, could not go in reverse and so had to turn round a large loop at each end of their journey. A brick building houses steam pumps to pump water to the summit level, later replaced with diesels.

The canal passes next to junction 34 of the M1, which is carried over the top deck of the massive Tinsley viaduct which runs for over a kilometre across the valley, also carrying the dual carriageway A631 at an intermediate level. Following problems with box girder bridges in the 1970s, the whole structure was strengthened internally with an arrangement like large coat hangers, being further strengthened in 2006. The Transport Research Laboratory established an exposure site beneath it to test the effect of the polluted atmosphere on samples of steel with different paint finishes.

Tinsley Low Locks drop away from Tinsley Low Wharf and the Templeborough works, formerly a Roman fort site. At Halfpenny Bridge the canal joins the River Don, much wider than the canal, which passes a sewage works and heads right across the top of a large unguarded weir where a heron may pick about on its sloping face. The navigation goes ahead and turns to follow the river, dropping through Jordan's, Holmes and Ickles Locks. The water weirs over these locks and it might be possible for a small craft to go with a significant flow. At normal levels the problem is more of heights of towpaths. At the third of these locks it is necessary to climb a fence on the left, cross a road and get back in beyond a railway bridge where the towpath is still quite high above the water.

Derrick cranes at Masbrough sift through piles of scrap. The A630 passes over and a section of towpath has been opened, cantilevered out from sheetpiling along the bank, the adjacent building heavily fortified against this potential intruder route.

The magistrates court at Rotherham Lock.

While the reaches upstream have such botanical rarities as wild liquorice and goat's rue, the navigation rejoins the River Don, now enlarged by the River Rother, the strong river, opposite a couple of full size fig trees growing from the towpath.

Rotherham United Football Club have managed to fit a new stadium onto the bank in the town centre and Tesco have managed to fit a store between the river and the navigation. Further development takes the form of a major rebuild of the railway station.

Rotherham magistrates court is a modern building making best use of its canal lockside location, except that railings obstruct the launch point, requiring small craft users of portable craft to move round the corner to get back on the water. The River Don has left before the lock and passed under a 15th century bridge with the Chapel of Our Lady over the original channel. After the Reformation this was used as a prison, almshouses and then a tobacconist's until being restored in 1924. Boys from the grammar school took part in an unsuccessful attempt to defend the bridge against the Royalists in 1643.

Heavy loss of life, mostly local boys, took place in 1841 when the billyboy *William & Mary* overturned on launching, drowning 57, it being the tradition to let them go down the slipway aboard on such occasions. They are remembered in the 15th century battlemented All Saints church, one of the finest of its kind in Yorkshire, with Jacobean pulpit and 18th century organ. The Clifton Park Museum in the 18th century house of Victorian ironmaster Joshua Walker has Rockingham porcelain, the Rotherham Art Gallery has Roman remains from Templeborough, local pottery and gemstones and there

Interesting garden ornaments by the navigation in Mexborough.

Waddington barge outside the former tram sheds in Rotherham.

is a Yorkshire & Lancashire Regimental Museum. Local industry is heavy, coal mining, iron, steel and glass. The Canal & River Trust have their depot in the former tram sheds.

Between the second A630 crossing and the A633 is a reach overlooked by a boatyard and electricity substation, beyond which the Greasbrough Canal remains lie to the north. Waddington's light blue topped barges wait for work in a spur above Eastwood or Sir Frank Price Lock with Eastwood Trading Estate and colliery waste. The River Don returns, perhaps a swan guarding her nest and a spur which is the end of an earlier line of the Don.

After Aldwarke Lock the steep sided valley is covered with weeping willows which make a brave attempt to beautify a reach which runs by Tata's **Thrybergh** bar mill. The church at Thrybergh has a Saxon cross.

The navigation has been realigned at Kilnhurst Flood Lock where the river leaves again, an old spur running next to the Sheffield–Doncaster railway which now crosses and follows the navigation. The navigation opens up after the B6090 crosses and there are fine views up the wooded hillside towards Conisbrough.

Vic Waddington had a fleet of over 70 steel barges, many of which are still here, particularly around **Swinton** Junction at the end of the remains of the Dearne & Dove Canal where Rockingham bone china was made from 1745 to 1842. A Rockingham desert set made for William IV in 1830 is still used in Buckingham Palace. Don Pottery was also made in Swinton until sold to Mexborough Pottery. More barges are moored below Waddington Lock where security fencing prevents getting back to the water and it may be best to launch off a Canal & River Trust barge, some of which have been growing a healthy crop of hay since they last went anywhere.

Security fencing is a greater problem at Mexborough Top Lock and it is necessary to portage on the right before the fence starts and get back in beyond. **Mexborough** was a town of coal mining, steel making, brick making and engineering but neat lawns now reach down to the navigation and there are numerous garden features. A half timbered house has such items as a pump, cartwheel and hayfeeder and, in the middle of the garden, what looks like the end wall of a chapel, topped by a cross.

After Mexborough Bottom Lock, set in an area of landscaped opencast spoil tips beyond the A6023, the River Don joins from the right and the River Dearne from the left. As with all these locks, the lock keeper operates from an enclosed control tower rather than a small hut as would usually be the case elsewhere. She warns that a pastime of the local youths downstream is dropping boulders off bridges onto narrowboats.

Conisbrough Castle beyond the Sheffield–Doncaster railway.

The Earth Centre was opened on two former slag heaps, the world's first environmental theme park including the first solar powered boat to cross the English Channel. Lack of vegetation made it look more like the Moon and it was shortlived.

The Sheffield–Doncaster railway crosses over and the red brick houses of **Conisbrough** appear, above which towers the white magnesian limestone bulk of the castle, one of the finest examples of Norman English castle architecture. It has an oval bailey with curtain wall but the main feature is the 20m diameter keep, its 30m height now reduced to 27m, with six massive buttresses. Built 1180–90, probably by Hamelin Plantaganet, half brother of Henry II, it featured as Athelstone in Sir Walter Scott's *Ivanhoe*, which notes a barrow close by as the possible tomb of Hengist.

Moving away from the town, another notable construction is the now disused Conisbrough viaduct, a brick structure which is both high and long. A much smaller structure carries the railway back over the river in front of Steetley's Cadeby limestone roadstone quarry with heaps of sand piled along the bank.

The river enters its most attractive reach for the next 2km, a wooded valley which is shared by the Sprotbrough Flash SSSI. In places the bank has been repaired with environmentally friendly bunches of withies staked in place, a contrast with the sheetpiling which lines so much of the navigation. Moorhens and coots are amongst the commoner wildlife.

Scott is believed to have written part of *Ivanhoe* in Sprotbrough in 1819, a village which includes a 14th century stone chair in the church chancel. By the water is the Boat Inn with a coat of arms built into its stonework. Taking out at the lock can be difficult because of the height of the towpath.

High above the navigation, traffic on the A1M roars across the valley, followed by low railway bridges, both disused and operational for freight at Balby.

Opposite the railway workshops in **Doncaster** the River Don leaves the navigation for the last time, flowing under a substantial wooden barrier in front of the large modern prison, referred to as Doncatraz, on what was a power station site. There is another cut to the left, the Gas House Bight, then comes Doncaster Lock, the most difficult on the navigation for small craft. The take out is a high wooden platform covered with chicken mesh for grip in front of a bramble covered bank. The boarding at the front stops well short of the water so there is nothing against which to hold a boat while standing up to get out. Trying to hold a boat steady and pointing in one direction while trying to climb onto a wire covered platform at chest height is not one of life's pleasures. The re-entry is not a lot easier, from a slot in the wharf which is still well above water level. Between the two it is necessary to portage over the lock, which is also crossed by the East Coast Main Line. Users have to duck down to get under the bridge girders and the rails are little above head height on an open structure so that rail wheels are close to eye level and plainly visible. The capstan lock apparatus remains a more appealing outdated piece of equipment. Also crossing the lock above the railway is the A19 on the line of a Roman road. Doncaster was Danum, a Roman fort site as the name suggests. It was also the fourth location for Agatha Christie in *The ABC Murders*.

The town is at the centre of the South Yorkshire coalfield. The Grade I Mansion House of 1748 houses the corporation's silver collection and the Museum & Art Gallery contains regional items and British paintings and sculptures. St George's neo-Gothic church of 1858 replaces a medieval one burnt down in 1833.

There are a couple of spurs on the right of the navigation and a couple of lengths of twisting cutoff channel. From here the route is much more open as the navigation cuts across the alluvial bed of the former glacial Lake Humber. Fields of oilseed rape add garish spring colour while birdlife varies from great crested grebes to the cuckoo.

Long Sandall Lock is now 66m long, lengthened from 19m in 1959 to take Tom Pudding trains – lines of coal carrying tub barges towed by tugs. It seems incongruous for such a commercial entity to be decorated by boats filled with flowers and a painted anchor gracing the lockside.

Just part of the enormous Conisbrough Viaduct, now disused.

The aqueduct carrying the New Junction Canal over the tidal River Don at Kirk Bramwith.

The Doncaster–Hull railway passes over at the tidal limit of the River Don which is still flowing alongside.

New Land Rovers have a storage yard in front of Pilkington's glass factory. Behind the factories of Sandall Grove is Kirk Sandall with its Grade II 12th century redundant Norman church of St Oswald, one wall possibly Saxon.

A recent low drawbridge at Barnby Dam is in front of the Bridge Stores, after which is the 14th century church of Sts Peter & Paul. A freight railway crosses over to complete this mixture of the old and the new.

An amazingly oblique junction gives access to the New Junction Canal. Straight and 9km long, it was the last major canal to be built in England and allowed trains of Tom Puddings through from Goole via the Aire & Calder Navigation, cutting off three sides of a square. As a consequence, the River Dun Navigation carries less traffic below this point. The New Junction Canal crosses the River Don on an aqueduct with water spilling over the flush sides and a large guillotine door at each end.

Lines of hawthorn bushes flank Bramwith Lock and are alive with the din of twittering birds. A swing bridge gives access from South Bramwith to Kirk Bramwith where the church dates from Norman times and has been owned by the Crown since 1311. Bulrushes line the navigation and the kingfisher streaks away down the water.

Another bridge crosses at **Stainforth**, a colliery village. The navigation originally rejoined the River Don but the lock was closed in 1939 and bulldozed over as part of a flood protection embankment. The spur serves as a private marina and the navigation continues as the Stainforth & Keadby Canal.

Windlasses are needed to open the heavy lock gates at Bramwith Lock.

Distance
45km from Sheffield to the Stainforth & Keadby Canal

Navigation Authority
Canal & River Trust

Navigation Society
Rotherham & Sheffield Canal Association
www.rasca.org.uk

OS 1:50,000 Sheets
(110 Sheffield & Huddersfield)
111 Sheffield & Doncaster
(120 Mansfield & Worksop)

Connection
Stainforth & Keadby Canal – see CoB p303

11 River Idle

A much diverted river

Here the River Idle sidles leisurely across the plain
Broad between the bending willows; grey beneath the tilting rain,
Like a looking-glass reflecting silent trees and whistling train.
Phoebe Hesketh

A single stunted tree stands on the bank of the Idle at Bawtry.

The River Maun and the River Meden both rise near Mansfield, joining and flowing northeast across Nottinghamshire to the River Trent as the River Idle. It used to run north to join the River Don to the east of Thorne but the Romans dug the 8km Bycarrsdyke to divert it eastwards. It was improved in the 1620s by Vermuyden as part of his plan for draining the Isle of Axholme and a section at **Bawtry** was straightened when the East Coast Main Line was built.

Bawtry has lost much of its former importance. A battle in 616 resulted in Æthelfrith being killed and Edwin accepted as king of Deira and Bernicia, leading to his becoming king of all the English south of the Humber.

In the 13th century it was an important port but was to lose its commercial trade to the Chesterfield Canal. Georgian houses remain. The river crosses fertile agricultural land and flows freely although the towpath

A rare wooded reach of the Idle near Misson.

Old stone bridge, Haxey Gate Inn and A161 near Misterton.

The steam pumping station at Misterton Soss.

is often in a poor condition. The banks are low, levées being usually some way back from the river. There are occasional willow and hawthorn trees with cow parsley and dandelions adding spring colour, to be replaced by reedmace in the river as the year progresses. Swans, mallards, coots, moorhens and lapwings are present. There is parking near the A631's stone arched bridge, easily accessible but rather secluded.

Austerfield was the home of some of the Pilgrim Fathers. The Austerfield Drain runs to the south of Newington, blocking easy access across the field to the popular Ship Inn with its petanque pitch, mini golf and swings. Because of private gardens it would need to be approached from an unmade track to the east of the village, passing works which throw out offensive smells.

A surprisingly long and high concrete weir feeds a relief channel running direct to Misson. The river itself meanders much more slowly, giving views to the south of the Barrow Hills and Cuckoo Hill.

Misson is met with weeping willows, poplars, some lawns to the river and approach down a green lane past a moat. The levée to the south is named Barrier Bank. There are few landmarks for a considerable distance. Horses in fields graze between stinging and white dead nettles and some gorse. Near North Carr Farm a Bailey Bridge gives access, accompanied by a gauge. Greylag geese paddle past a nature reserve as the north bank becomes the East Riding of Yorkshire briefly at the Idle Stop, a name as relaxed as they come.

After a long run across open country the river reaches a stone arch bridge next to the Haxey Gate Inn. The A161 has been moved to a new bridge downstream. Also removed have been an 18th century lock and sluice. A slipway and caravan field follow the bridges.

The Doncaster–Gainsborough railway crosses. Among the ashes and alders on the banks there is an owl box. Great crested grebes and cormorants may be seen and pheasants heard. At Misterton Soss, from the Dutch sas, meaning lock, there is a tall chimney and an 1823 steam pumping station on the adjacent Mother Drain. These days it is a private house.

Two sets of powerlines give notice of arrival at West Stockwith and, particularly, the Environment Agency's two sets of guillotine gates 320m apart. The first gate is alongside a large pumping station and the second passes out onto the tidal Trent. They may only be passed on the ebb when the tide makes a level. Although there is an undisputed right of public navigation the EA impose a punitive charge for opening the sluices such that cruising clubs tend to band together to share the cost but this is likely to happen only at infrequent intervals. A 300m connection with the Chesterfield Canal would solve this problem but the canal was built as a commercial rival to the river.

West Stockwith was a 17/18th century inland port with warehouses and boatbuilding, the church being founded in 1722 by William Huntington who described himself as a ship carpenter.

There is a carpark at the end, serving the White Hart Inn.

Distance
18km from Bawtry to the River Trent

OS 1:50,000 Sheets
111 Sheffield & Doncaster
112 Scunthorpe & Gainsborough

Connection
River Trent – see RoB p161

Sluice gate and pumping station at West Stockwith.

The second sluice gate controlling exit to the tidal Trent.

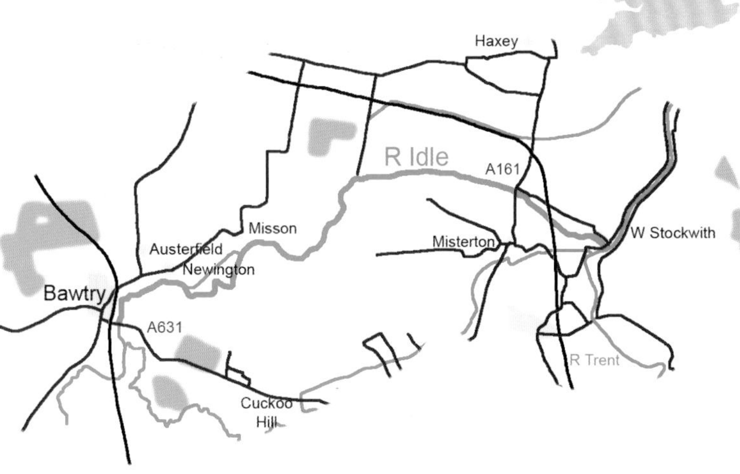

12 River Trent

Red cliffs and big holes in the ground

Still'd is the village hum - the woodland sounds
Have ceased to echo o'er the dewy grounds
And general silence reigns, save when below
The murmering Trent is scarcely heard to flow;
Henry Kirke White

Emerging from Knypersley Reservoir, the River Trent flows southeast and then northeast to the River Humber, forming part of Brindley's Grand Cross. It may have been the route of the River Severn until that was blocked by the Irish Sea ice sheet. It may also have been a Bronze Age trade route from Ireland to the Continent and was later to become an important export route for cheese. The British Celtic Trisanton, the flooding river, was to become the Roman Trisantona Fluvius. It was made navigable below Burton under a 1699 Act although the upper part was closed in 1805.

The level can change quickly and it has a faster flow than might be expected for a lowland river but there are usually shallows opposite the Navigation Inn at Shardlow. Maybe this is why the head of navigation is just a little downstream with anglers' paths cut through the riverbank vegetation the only features.

Sawley Marina at dawn with Ratcliffe on Soar power station.

Turning under the B5010, formerly the A6, the River Trent wanders between meadows edged with willows, cow parsley, reedmace, sedges and lilies and is used by coots, mallards, herons and swans. In 2011, eight years after its predecessor was demolished, Long Horse Bridge was reinstated as an arched bridge at Derwent Mouth where the Trent is joined by both the River Derwent and the Trent & Mersey Canal, less suited to tow horses but fine for everyone else. The canal brings boat traffic and forms part of the Pennine Circuit to the north and the East Midlands Circuit to the south as far as the River Soar.

A prominent arched pipe bridge crosses before the M1, after which powerlines cross both ways and large floating booms funnel boats into the Sawley Cut. Gone are the days when empty barges were released over unguarded weirs while tugs worked through the locks, collecting the loose barges downstream, a significant saving in time if all went to plan.

Sawley Flood Lock is usually left open. The B6540 crosses before it and passes Sawley's medieval church. Gravel working has been extensive in the valley and a pit here houses Sawley Marina, one of the largest inland marinas in the country. Ahead rise clouds from the cooling towers of Ratcliffe on Soar power station, which has been invaded by environmentalists.

Sawley Lock, at the end of the cut where a freight railway crosses, has two chambers. The users of small craft will find themselves faced with high sheet piling or steep banks above and below locks on the Trent. Even when safe routes exist there are often no route directions or, worse, erroneous instructions. Angelica grows near old earthworks with Sawley Golf Course standing back from the other bank downstream.

Trentlock brings a complex junction with the

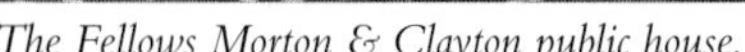
The Fellows Morton & Clayton public house.

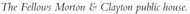

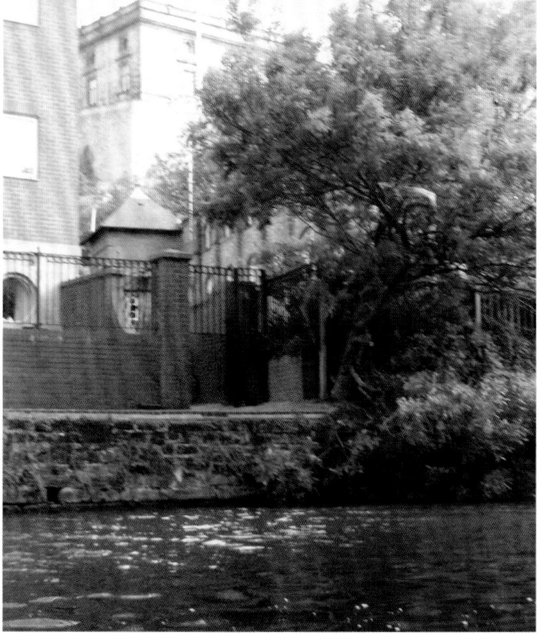

Nottingham Castle is glimpsed from the canal.

Erewash Canal emerging from the left. All craft are directed to the Cranfield Cut of 1797 except for those continuing on the Trent to ascend the River Soar which joins downstream and replaces Leicestershire with Nottinghamshire on the south side. The Trent Valley Sailing Club has a prime position at the junction with a Scout Activity Centre, followed by Nottingham Yacht Club. There are more floodgates by the St Pancras–Nottingham railway crossing. A rifle range is fitted in between the various transport routes, the cut finishing at Cranfield Lock.

Red marl cliffs with trees rise on the south side, as they are to do at intervals down the valley. The James I Thrumpton Hall has a Carolean oak staircase, a priest-hole, Byron relics, a secret garden, an arboretum with one of the first larches planted in England in the 17th century, cedar trees planted for the jubilee of George III and subsequent occasions and a lake which is a backwater of the river. Thrumpton's 13th century church was restored in 1872 by Street. A prehistoric trackway passes nearby.

Flooded gravel pits follow the left bank continuously for 5km and have been designated a nature reserve. The River Erewash discharges into them before Attenborough, where the Derbyshire/Nottinghamshire boundary is met. There are knots and greylag geese and common terns breed but the wildlife goes back a long way, the pits having produced mammoth's teeth and Ice Age trees as well as two 1000 BC dugout canoes and a Roman sword.

Barton in Fabis, or Barton in the Beans because of its crops, has a 14th century church and was a British and Roman fortified site. The 2nd Beeston Sea Scouts also have a suitably defended base on an island.

Moored craft, **Beeston** Marina, the Riverside Bar, a pirate in a fire basket and numerous chalets warn that things are to change at Rylands. The river goes ahead over Beeston Weir, where a hydroelectric power generating station has resulted in low water levels upstream, and heads towards **Clifton**, named after the Clifton family rather than the land overlooking Trent University. The Wilford shallows have always been a problem and since 1796 traffic has been diverted to the Beeston Canal, now the Nottingham Beeston Canal. The canal begins at Beeston Lock where a side lock formerly allowed access to the river below the weir for craft which wanted it. Amongst the early users were the Chester Canal Company, who ran excursions to Chester Races.

Rushes, poplars and blackberries cannot disguise what is now a built up environment, housing at first, giving way to a sewage works and other industrial premises as powerlines follow the canal yet Canada geese, moorhens and cormorants adapt to the surroundings. Nottinghamshire becomes Nottingham.

The St Pancras–Nottingham railway crosses the canal at Dunkirk and the A52 crosses both with the Nottingham University campus and an arts centre to the north.

An aerial marks where the Beeston Canal joined the 1796 Nottingham Canal by Jessop, the northern end of which has mostly been lost, especially in the city. Today the change is seamless but this was the location of the Lenton Chain which used to be placed across the canal to prevent weekend use. Nottingham had opposed making the Derwent navigable as it resulted in through traffic which had previously needed to unload in the city.

Among the red brick buildings the Sheffield–**Nottingham** railway crosses, there is a drydock and the White Hart has the remains of the 1113 Peveril Jail for debtors. The city was the home of chemists Boots, Players, who produced their ready rolled cigarettes in 1877, and Raleigh, who started making bikes a decade later. Arkwright's first spinning frame was introduced in

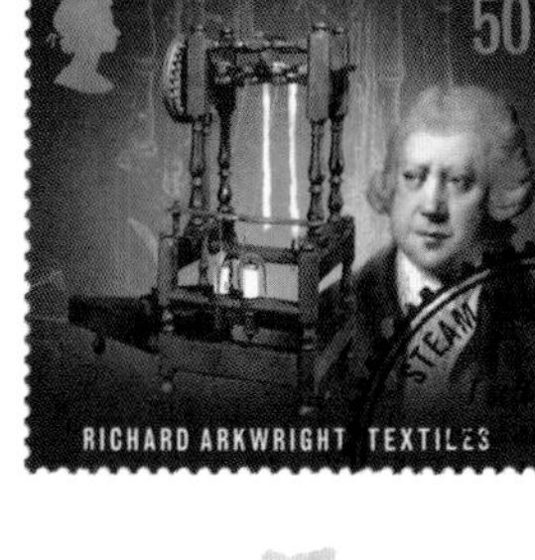

1767 but the Luddites destroyed new knitting machines in 1811 although leader Ned Ludd may have been fictitious.

Nottingham was Snota's people's village, given its charter in 1155 by Henry II, described by Defoe as one of the most pleasant and beautiful towns in England and promoted to a city in 1897. The capital of the East Midlands, it has been voted the fourth best shopping centre in the UK.

The A6005 runs alongside the canal. Nottingham Castle on red Bunter sandstone 40m above the city is also close but only glimpsed between buildings. First built as a motte and bailey for William the Conqueror, every king until Henry VIII stayed here. Rebuilt in stone in the 12th century, it was held in the Civil War by the Parliamentarians and then destroyed afterwards by them and replaced in 1674–1875 by a mansion for the Dukes of Newcastle. Richard the Lionheart ruled the country from here, Henry II burned the town, Edward III lived here, Edward IV proclaimed himself king here, Richard III set off from here for Bosworth in 1485 and Charles I started the Civil War by raising his standard here, although less than 300 rallied to him. In the 1831 Reform Bill riots it was burned by the mob as the Duke of Newcastle was opposed to reform and it stood as an empty shell for 44 years. The medieval outer bailey and gatehouse remain.

Robin Hood was one of England's great folk heroes, slightly awkward as his enemy, the Sheriff of Nottingham, was the baddie and did not come onto the scene until 1449 although Robin was a 13th century outlaw. There is a 2.1m bronze statue of Robin.

Nottingham Castle Museum & Art Gallery is in the mansion. Caves under the castle are among 400 below the city, some multi storey, including King David's Dungeon, the Duke of Newcastle's wine store and Mortimer's Hole where Edward III's men seized pretender Roger Mortimer. Mortimer's ghost still haunts the caves. The 1240 Olde Salutation Inn is the city's most haunted building with a Saxon cave below which served as a tanner's home and shop. Charles I and Cromwell both used it as a recruiting station and it was later used as an air raid shelter.

The Nottingham Castle Marina development includes the first Homebase store. Castle Lock has tables from the Navigation public house set out on the lockside, giving the potential for more spectator comment than usual for those working through the lock.

Nottingham was the lace capital of the world with a third of the Victorian population employed in the industry, the indoor work resulting in the girls having the fairest complexions in the country. A 1450 timber-framed medieval building is one of the oldest in the city and housed a lace centre. There are former lace warehouses and the Lace Market Theatre was a 17th century chapel. The Museum of Costume & Textiles from 1790 is in 17/18th century Georgian houses. The Brewhouse Yard's Museum of Nottingham Life is housed in five 17th century cottages. The Olde Trip to Jerusalem of 1189, possibly used by Crusaders, is claimed to be England's oldest public house.

Beyond the A453 a large new magistrates' court has a brick arched towpath bridge in front but the arm leading towards it is going nowhere, bricked off beneath the bridge. The Galleries of Justice are in the 19th century Grade II shire hall, Victorian courthouse and county gaol, outside which gallows were sited.

There are some large British Waterways warehouses and the Fellows Morton & Clayton public house in what was an FMC warehouse with a basin inside. This replaced one where 21 barrels of gunpowder blew up in 1818, having been a canal museum in recent years. Adjacent is the Canalhouse bar and restaurant.

The 13th century man-made caves under the Broad Marsh shopping centre occupy a Druid site, serving as dwellings, food and wine store, medieval tannery and then air raid shelters. Modern building has taken place alongside the canal near the station and trams were reintroduced in 2003.

Old Market Square is one of the largest in England and chimes ring out from the Little John Bell. St Mary's church was in existence by *Domesday*. There is a Nottingham Brass Rubbing Centre, a Nottingham Playhouse and the Victorian Malt Cross Music Hall as one of the last remaining. An annual Nottingham Festival, Nottdance Festival in May and Robin Hood Pageant in October spice up the arts and author Alan Sillitoe was a local resident.

A former railway bridge and the A60 each cross at Poplar Arm Corner where there is a spur as the canal turns south. Torville and Dean are associated with the ice stadium. An aerial and the five storey Green's Mill with its four operating sails rise above the skyline, the latter with a science centre because it was occupied by the 19th century mathematician and scientist George Green. The William Booth Birthplace Museum recalls the 1829 arrival of the founder of the Salvation Army.

Another survivor is a Victorian cast iron public urinal near where the Nottingham–Grimsby railway passes under the canal. The Meadows alluvial area was not built on until the 19th century and is protected by flood banks.

Meadow Lane Lock takes the navigation back onto the River Trent. There is commercial traffic from here. The Danes came up the river to this point and in

Training on the artificial slalom course at Holme Pierrepont.

The Cliffs at Radcliffe on Trent.

A seat carved from a log at Stoke Bardolph Lock.

Stoke Bardolph's lock keeper keeps his feet dry.

The secret boat rollers at Gunthorpe.

the 19th century there were regular boat services to Gainsborough. Locks from here to Newark were completed by 1926, navigation hazards removed including cows bathing in the river in hot weather. There are kilometre posts from here to keep track of progress.

Just above the junction is Trent Bridge, the site having been used since the 920s. The current one was built in 1871 with three 30m spans, cast iron arches, floral decoration facades, ashlar abutments and three flood arches, being widened and reinforced in 1926. Two flood arches from a 1683 bridge damaged by floods remain on a traffic island.

Trent Bridge Test Match cricket ground was founded in 1838. Notts County was founded in 1862, the oldest Football League club in England, and Nottingham Forest followed three years later. Nottingham Kayak Club is sited at the top of the stepped concrete banks of the river with Olympic gold medallist Tim Brabants a member.

Environment Agency offices overlook the bottom lock of the Grantham Canal, fully restored and restoration of the canal under way when a road scheme truncated it. The A6011 crosses Ladybay Bridge which formerly carried a railway.

The glacial Lake Humber lay to the southeast of the line of the Trent downstream of Nottingham, resulting in alluvial areas and a floodplain up to 3km wide. Defoe noted large salmon and there are great crested grebes, tufted ducks and banks with alders and yellow flags.

Beyond the TS Orion with its anti-aircraft gun are Nottingham's horse and greyhound racecourses. The 1km^2 Colwick Country Park has Colwick Marina, gravel pits, sailing, angling and rowing in a 26ha lake. Water skiing on the river has had the added risk of Trent Tum, reputed to require a day off work in the event of taking a ducking.

On the south side of the river is the 1.1km^2 Holme Pierrepont National Water Sports Centre in old gravel pits, a small one having a ski cable tow, a regatta course being used for rowing, canoeing and dragon boat racing regattas and a white water course bypassing Holme Sluices being used for canoe slalom and white water rafting. The site has been used by canoeists to run world championships in sprint, marathon and slalom but rather faster was Gina Campbell who set the first women's world water speed record of 198km/h here in 1984 in *Agfa Bluebird*. The 2.2km course does not give much acceleration or braking distance for a measured kilometre and the width gives little steering latitude. She smashed up the boat doing a backward flip on the validation run, reminiscent of her father's death on Coniston Water.

Holme Cut dates from 1800 and has the twin Holme Locks. The left bank returns from Nottingham to Nottinghamshire, where old factories have been demolished and old staithes serve no more purpose.

It is hoped that the Grantham Canal can be linked to the outside world by running across to the Trent at Holme Pierrepont. The hamlet has a 17th century church with a monument to Sir Henry Pierrepont. Holme Pierrepont Hall, by the Pierrepont family, is 17th century Tudor with an 1800 battlemented brick façade, regional oak furniture, two tables from Nelson's HMS *Nile*, a maritime display, an 1875 secret courtyard garden, 80ha of park and Jacob's sheep.

The Nottingham–Grantham railway crosses Radcliffe on Trent Viaduct, a 34m Victorian cast iron span of 1850 with 3.5m rise and three brick arches with stone voussoirs and abutments, converted to reinforced concrete with little visible change. On the other hand, the former timber viaduct on the eastern side is now 28 blue brick arches.

Gravel pits begin to appear again and a set of powerlines cross for the first of three times. Chalets nuzzle up to the wooded red sandstone cliff which gives **Radcliffe on Trent** its name, a nature reserve with woodpeckers, owls and bats. Stoke Bardolph Lock has unmarked rollers if the direction signs are ignored although it is possible to get out at a pontoon at this lock.

The Ferry Boat faces the river at Stoke Bardolph itself. Higher land at **Burton Joyce** turns the river back towards Shelford on its raised gravel patch. This village had a 12th century priory. It still has a church with a Perpendicular tower, the 13th century tomb of village

Trent Hills below Kneeton.

Remains of the windmill at Farndon.

The Bromley Arms by Fiskerton's heavily piled riverside.

Old and new building by the Trent in Newark.

The new Staythorpe C power station.

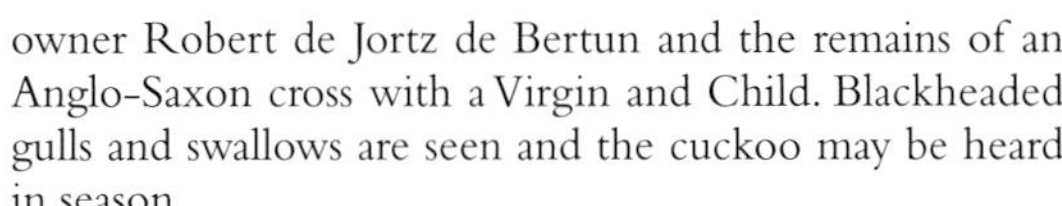

owner Robert de Jortz de Bertun and the remains of an Anglo-Saxon cross with a Virgin and Child. Blackheaded gulls and swallows are seen and the cuckoo may be heard in season.

Shelford Manor was burnt down in 1645 by 2,000 Roundheads after killing 140 Royalists inside, being rebuilt in 1676.

Beyond gravel pits on the other side of the river is the three arched reinforced concrete bridge of 1927, the first free bridge in Britain to replace a toll bridge, the remains of which are downstream. It carries the A6097 although there was a straighter line for the ford in Roman times. Gunthorpe, built on a raised gravel area, is fronted by the Unicorn Hotel, Tom Browns and the Biondio bistro.

It also has Gunthorpe Lock, one of the worst in the country for portable craft, unnecessarily so. A hoarding sized sign directs all craft to the left, where users find the pontoon and locked gate of Kingfisher Wharf boatyard on the site of an old port. Otherwise they are faced with shoulder-high sheet piling with recessed ladders, no safe place to take out. In fact, there are rollers at the foot of the red cliffs on the East Bridgford side for those who cross the top of the weir but even the local staff don't seem to know about them.

East Bridgford has Georgian houses and a church rebuilt in the 12th century with a Saxon cross and foundation found under a horse trough in a wall.

Unique clapper gates are found on the towpath as it runs opposite Old Hill.

Hoveringham, on raised gravel, has given its name to a major aggregates company. Large sandpits accompany the river, gravel having been exported by barge, for which loading staithes were built. A mammoth skeleton was found here. Facing are the Trent Hills which continue from Kneeton past Syerston Airfield, now with gliders but with Wellingtons and Lancasters during the Second World War. Beyond Gibsmere and Hazelford Ferry the river divides round a 1.2km island and Hazelford Lock again has no safe place for small craft to take out. Rollers have been removed although dredger buckets are used as flower tubs – little consolation. The best place now is amongst the reeds on the far side of the large weir.

Fiskerton with its red brick Georgian houses was a thriving port. It is now fronted by very high sheet piling but visitors are assisted and there is a pontoon and steps up to the Bromley Arms. The River Greet joins by Fiskerton Mill.

Sand martins and oystercatchers might be seen as Gawburn Nip leads to Stoke Hall where Henry VII won the final battle of the Wars of the Roses in 1487.

Beyond East Stoke Wharf four sets of powerlines cross as the Fosse Way, until recently the A46, runs to the Ad Pontem Roman city and fort. Large sandstone slabs are set into the bank in flights of steps for anglers to stand on.

Farndon has a 14th century church above Farndon Ferry and used to produce willow for baskets. Gravel pits are occupied by Farndon Marina, approached under a lifting towpath bridge.

The silver Staythorpe C power station, opened in 2011 after controversial construction with foreign labour, is the second largest combined cycle gas turbine power station in the UK. It has a sculpture of a turbine wrapped in boiler tubes and, inevitably, powerlines radiate out from it.

At Upper Water Mouth the Kelham Branch or original course of the River Trent heads north over Averham Weir, in two sections. Boat traffic turns southeast on the Newark Dyke, cut to the River Devon in 1773. As it passes gardens at Farndon one contains the stump of a windmill and Farndon Field Maltkiln was also built here. The A46 crosses to bypass the town.

The dyke joins the River Devon below Queen's Sconce, the Royalists having been ensconced in their hill earthworks here. In the 13th century Sir Guy Saucimer had killed his friend Sir Everard Bevercotes in a dispute over Isabell de Caldwell and fled abroad, after which she died from grief. He caught leprosy but was told in a dream by St Catherine to wash in a spring here. This cured him so he built a chapel round the spring, lived a holy life and was canonized as St Guthred. Newark Marina is sited here.

Newark developed around the new werk to oppose the Danes, a Saxon market town redesigned by Alexander, Bishop of Lincoln, in 1134. In 1787 John Wesley called it one of the most elegant towns in England. River features include Mill Bridge and a steam crane. The Grade II Kiln Warehouse of about 1857 was one of the first constructions in mass concrete, rebuilt as offices after the roof was destroyed by fire in 1992. The Navigation Company Brasserie occupies another warehouse leading onto the river. The Millgate Museum of Social & Folk Life has a warehouse location while half of Newark Museum with archaeology, history and the Civil War is in a 1529 schoolroom.

Goods were transshipped at the Town Wharf as upstream was shallow with a fall of up to 300mm/km. One chamber of Town Lock is roofed over as a drydock.

The Clinton Arms Hotel in the town is where Gladstone made his first election speech in 1832. The 17th century Saracen's Head was used in Scott's *The Heart of Midlothian* and there is a 1708 Moot Hall, now occupied by Curry's.

The Trent Navigation Wharf & Warehouse finding new life.

Newark Castle fronts the river below Newark Lock.

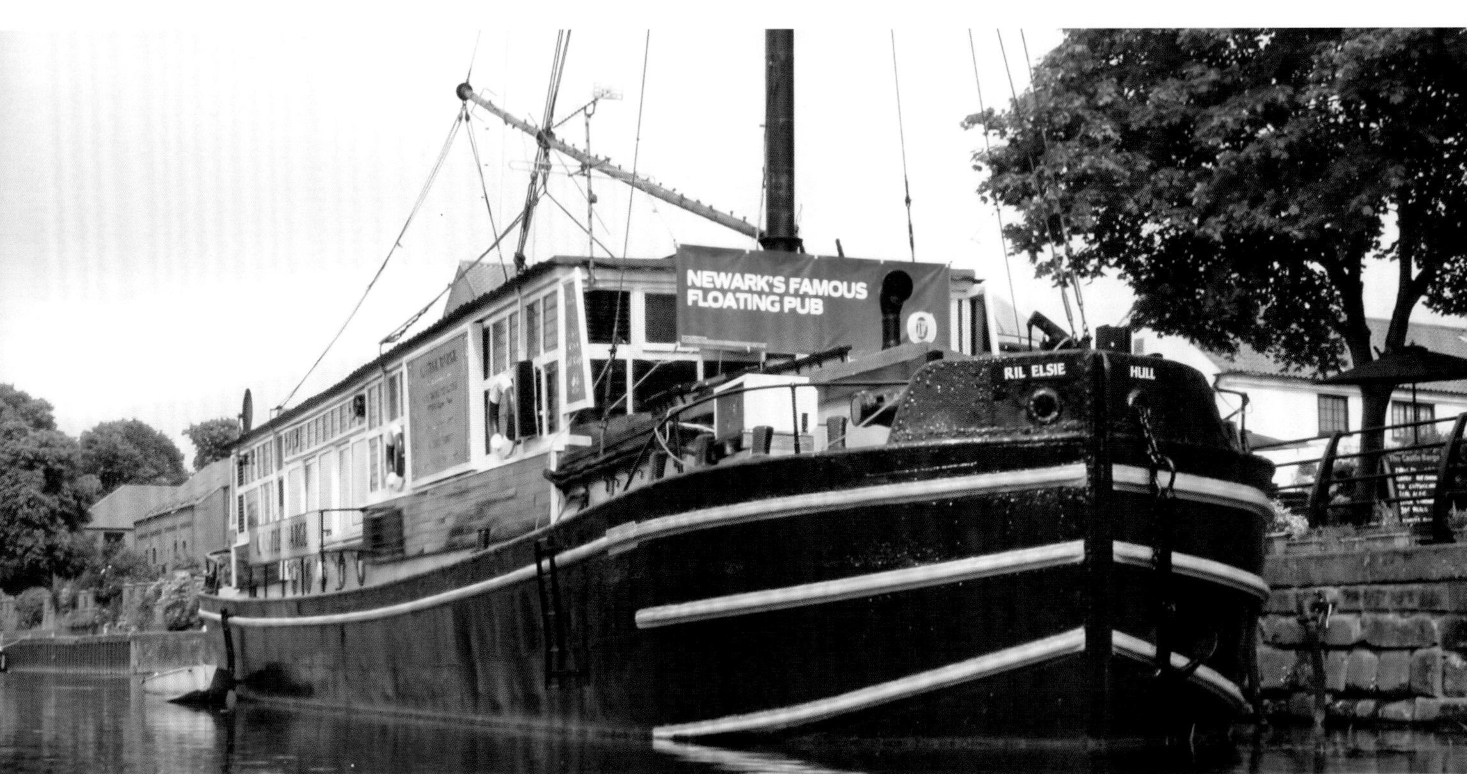

The Castle Barge speaks for itself.

The castle ruins are the 1133 work of Alexander at this important port. It became the Royalist Key to the North, resisting three Parliamentary sieges, to be slighted in 1646 by Cromwell. Only the grey stone west wall remains of the curtain wall rectangle built in the 14th century, together with the 1170 Norman three storey north gatehouse, one of the finest in the country and the largest of any English castle, the three storey rectangular corner tower and the remains of the 12th century crypt. King John died here in 1216 during a violent storm, Charles I gave himself up to the Scottish army here in 1645 and it was painted by Turner in 1796. In 1848 it became the first monument to be restored at Government expense. It has the Gilstrap Centre and the grounds act as a municipal park.

The medieval church of St Mary Magdalen, built from 1160 to about 1500, is huge, one of the best in England, with a 77m spire. Mostly 15th century, it has a Perpendicular nave and chancel, 15th century east window, a brass which is one of the largest in England, a 1505 oak rood screen, two 1506 Dance of Death paintings, 16th century choirstalls and a 12th century crypt with a treasury including the 1705 church plate set.

The market place is cobbled and the 1777 Palladian town hall ballroom is one of the best assembly rooms in the country for the period. The 14th century White Hart is timber framed and the town has one of the finest Georgian town halls in the country. William Jessop lived in the town and people come today for the bimonthly antiques fairs which are the largest in Europe.

The seven arch stone Trent or Newark Bridge was built in 1775 and widened in 1848. With a 52m span it has pilasters on the piers, cutwaters and decorative lamps. It carries the B6326, the Great North Road. The road passes the cattle market and becomes the A616, running for 1.7km across low embankment and Smeatons' Arches of about 1770, 74 arches in eight groups of 4.6m brick spans, extended on the west side in 1929.

Below the bridge is the *Castle Barge*, a grain barge converted to a two deck floating public house with a great deal of character.

A former railway crossing, 2002 Jubilee Bridge, 2001 King's Marina and aluminium sugar beet factory come before the Grade II Fiddlers Elbow Bridge, built in 1915 for horses. The name comes from the vertical curve at the apex, which is only 150mm thick with a 27m span rising 2.7m.

Soon after this the river becomes edged with high sheet piling under the A46 and Nottingham–Grimsby railway crossings, through a traffic light controlled bend leading to Nether Lock and beyond to the East Coast Main Line bridge. While it is possible for small craft to take out up the weedy bank at the start of all this there is nowhere that it is possible to relaunch until the second railway bridge, launching not being easy, even ignoring railway private notices. The lock keeper is prepared to allow small craft to pass through the lock but even the users of larger craft are faced with having to climb significant ladders to tie up while waiting.

Beyond gravel pits the East Coast Main Line crosses the lattice Newark Dyke Bridge, previous bridges being used in the 1920s for load measurements at high speed because of the straight approaches. A low brick viaduct then takes the line across the main channel. Beyond a sewage works the River Trent is rejoined at Crankley Point. Winthorpe Rack is the navigation channel before and after this confluence.

The A1 crosses at Winthorpe which is marked by the spire of All Saints' church, rebuilt in 1888. Lapwings are seen in the vicinity of Winthorpe Lake in old gravel pits.

North Muskham has a 15th century church with Norman fragments, the Muskham Ferry public house overlooks the river as the name suggests and there is another gravel pit. Holme, site of a temporary Roman camp, faces it across the river, its church having a 15th century porch and a short spire. Both were on the same side of the river until Elizabethan times when a flood moved the channel.

The Oven leads to Cromwell Lock, the last on the river and the tidal limit. There was a Roman bridge here but now there is a lethal design of weir with a long towback and enclosed ends, killing a number of people including ten soldiers in a single incident in 1975. The lock has dredger buckets as flower tubs and is large enough to have produced 9t of fish when it was dewatered in 2003 for repairs. A road, locked overnight, leads to Cromwell with its restored 13th century church and the 17th century rectory which has over 1,000 dolls in the Vina Cooke Museum of Dolls & Bygone Childhood.

Distance
68km from Shardlow to Cromwell

Navigation Authority
Canal & River Trust

OS 1:50,000 Sheets
120 Mansfield & Worksop
121 Lincoln & Newark-on-Trent
129 Nottingham & Loughbrough

Connections
Trent & Mersey Canal – see CoB p189
Erewash Canal – see CoB p82
Grand Union Canal Leicester Line – see CoB p76
Grantham Canal – see CoB p85
Tidal River Trent – see RoB p158

The amazingly slim concrete Fiddlers Elbow Bridge.

13 New River Ancholme

Rennie's straight river across flat countryside

The winding River Ancholme comes alongside the River Rase and runs next to it for 4km from Bishopbridge where it changes its character completely, this being the head of navigation. The flow is augmented by water from the River Trent at Torksey for industrial supply. The name comes from a bridge built for a bishop of Lincoln.

The New River Ancholme flows in a strike valley where the clay has been eroded at the foot of the limestone outcrop of the Wolds. It is a poorly drained watershed, part of the bed of a lake which existed during a late stage in the Ice Age when the mouth of the Humber was blocked by ice. A typical sequence is humus, peat, upper forest bed, brown alluvial clay, blue-grey alluvial clay, lower forest bed and glacial drift.

It was one of the earliest rivers to see significant improvements for navigation, a patent of 1287 permitting work to be done to make it easier for boats to move up from the Humber to Bishopbridge. Most of the work in producing the almost straight New River Ancholme which exists today was done by John Rennie in the period up to 1820, permitting Humber keels and billyboys to work up to collect agricultural produce from this farming area. An authorized link to the River Witham was never cut.

A small sloping weir below the A631 bridge is the head of navigation, beyond which stands an old wharf building, four storeys high, square with a small, pyramidal, slate cap roof, built in dark red brick and now showing its age.

The navigation sets off with a great sweeping bend, a very gentle turn but about as sharp as will be met on this river. Reeds line the edge of the water which is not particularly clean but is satisfactory for swans, coots, moorhens and mallards which frequent the upper end while the occasional flocks of rooks flap their irregular way across the sky.

From time to time a willow is passed on the high banks which carry the full length towpath, forming a public footpath, and block out some of the prevailing westerly wind in this exposed area, together with most of the view.

The flatness of the countryside is emphasized by the fact that there are only two locks, the first at Harlam Hill. A former guillotine gate has been replaced by mitre gates opened with metal poles. A bypass channel leaves under a footbridge on the right before the lock, over a weir which is effectively a grade 1 rapid, but this joins the River Rase down to Atterby Weir. This is about 2m high with two steep steps and a sloping toe so a portage is not avoided. Electric cables passing high overhead at intervals are marked by pairs of conspicuous yellow plastic warning notices on each side, mostly broken in half, it seems.

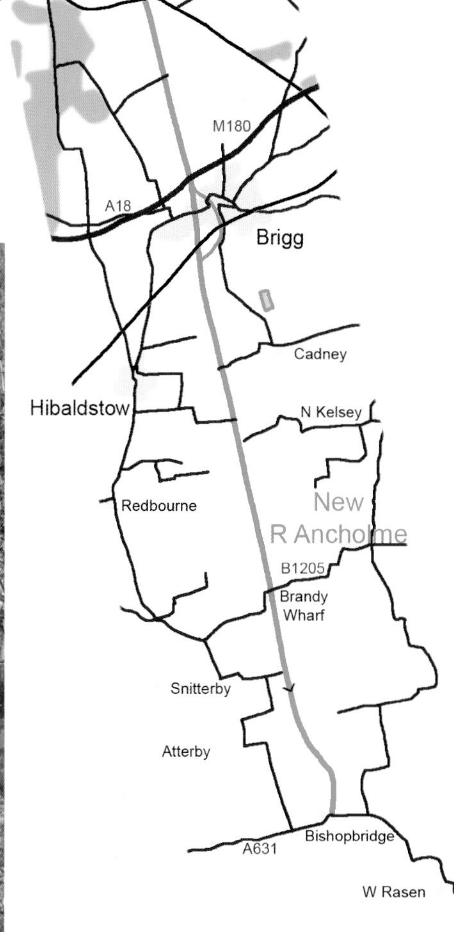

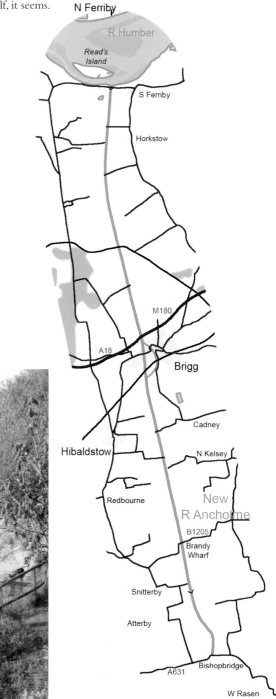

The weir and old wharf building at the head of the navigation at Bishopbridge.

Harlam Hill Lock, now more user-friendly with mitred gates.

Former wharf building and Cider Centre at Brandy Wharf.

The weir at Harlam Hill.

While slender arched bridges across the river, such as Rennie's iron bridge at Snitterby Carr, are not infrequent and show a variety of designs they usually carry only farm tracks as roads tend to cross the carrs to the river and then stop. The one at Brandy Wharf is an exception, carrying the B1025 and being accompanied by the Old Mill which has been renovated from the wharf building, a public telephone box and the confusingly-named Brandy Wharf Cider Centre. Generally, villages are situated well back from the river.

The Lincolnshire/North East Lincolnshire border crosses and then recrosses a couple more times following the Old River Ancholme before disappearing up North Kelsey Beck. Also on the right is the line of the former Caistor Canal, its use forbidden by the Environment Agency, a route which paralleled the earlier Roman road from Caistor to **Hibaldstow**. A substantial Roman building site has been found at Sturton. Other early activity not seen from the water is the former RAF Hibaldstow airfield at Redbourne, where parachuting has replaced the Defiant night fighters of 255 Squadron, and a windmill at Hibaldstow.

As the Old River Ancholme crosses after Hibaldstow Bridge it leaves to the left under a footbridge balanced on two largely undermined abutments below more than half of which it is possible to see daylight.

Pumphouses line the river to remove water from the low-lying carrs. Mostly these are old structures in the dark red brick of the area but a large modern one by Cadney Bridge features an interestingly-shaped wooden top.

Sand Hills, just beyond on the left bank, is conspicuous for its surrounding trees on a largely-treeless route. It seems to be home for an assortment of ducks and geese. Powerlines are also very visible and the first of three sets cross soon after.

Sluice gates mark the end of Kettleby Beck.

The most significant remaining section of the Old River Ancholme is the loop which goes off to the right to visit **Brigg** and, presumably, the site of the original bridge implied by the name. The town is remembered in Delius' *Brigg Fair*, first performed in 1908, his English rhapsody based on a Lincolnshire folk song and dedicated to Percy Grainger, who introduced him to the song. The annual horse fair continues in August.

The New River Ancholme cuts off the loop, creating Island Carr. Passing under the Grimsby–Worksop railway and near the silos of a conspicuous factory and a hidden windmill, it is crossed by the A18, by which are moorings, another old wharf building and the carpark of the Glanford Leisure Centre.

Old and new channels meet and are crossed by the M180 bridge below which the local youth can make a deafening row on scrambling bikes on one bank while rows of anglers' green umbrellas silently line the other. The

The grand chain Horkstow Bridge.

Old River Ancholme takes another loop to the right but Weir Dyke now runs immediately on the right side of the navigation to the Humber.

The Old River Ancholme makes a final cross back on a long straight reach of some 7km, only broken otherwise by the Doncaster–Grimsby railway and a second set of powerlines. All the while the Lincolnshire Wolds are closing in on the right but remain hidden from the river. A cormorant might warn of the approach to the estuary.

Bushes on each side of the navigation line the approaches to Horkstow Bridge, a grand chain suspension bridge which leads nowhere, Rennie's only suspension bridge.

More powerlines cross and then high overhead passes a conveyor belt which serves the large cement works at Ferriby Sluice from a quarry at South Ferriby. In the vicinity of the conveyor are numerous moorings including those of the Humber Yawl Club. Their history involves the direct development of the Humber Yawl from the 19th century sailing canoes as a step towards the yachts of today. The Humber Keel & Sloop Preservation Society have the keel *Comrade* and the sloop *Amy Houston* moored here.

The second and final lock is fitted with tide gates which can be used over the top half of the tidal cycle. The catchment above this point is 73km^2 and this end can be quite rough after periods of flooding.

Although the navigation finishes by the Hope & Anchor public house with parking close by, it is worth taking a look at a couple more local features of interest. Between the chimneys of the cement works and a matching chimney at **North Ferriby** on the far side of the River Humber lies Read's Island. This is a wildfowl refuge used for grazing sheep and was said to have been formed over the wreck of a French cargo boat early in the 19th century.

Turning northeast gives a fine view of the Humber Bridge, built as the world's longest single span suspension bridge.

Looking inland from Ferriby Sluice.

Distance
31km from Bishopbridge to the River Humber

Navigation Authority
Environment Agency

Navigation Society
East Anglian Waterways Association
www.eawa.co.uk

OS 1:50,000 Sheets
(106 Market Weighton)
112 Scunthorpe & Gainsborough

14 Hobhole Drain

Straight across the fens

The Hobhole Drain is one of the Witham Navigable Drains, flowing south across the Lincolnshire fens to the Haven reach of the River Witham and cut at the start of the 19th century. The Witham Navigable Drains were new cuts or improved existing channels for drainage and some carriage of agricultural produce in an area with excellent agricultural land but a flat landscape. From late September to early April the levels are lowered to permit winter rainfall to be handled. It is predominantly straight throughout and over most of its length it has a minor road on at least one side, often both.

It starts at Toynton Fen Side, just 200m short of the East Fen Catchwater Drain. Throughout, the surrounding land is flat, agricultural and below sea level, the drain having banks 2–3m high so that the water level is at least 3m below sea level. At first the surface is totally overgrown with vegetation between two rows of bushes but after 500m it suddenly clears and the water is deep and free of vegetation over its width for the rest of its course. It is relatively muddy but has freshwater mussels.

There is regular noise from jet fighters curving across the sky on training flights. The airfield and aviation museum at East Kirkby are not part of this, the only local noises being the skylarks. Grass on the banks is interlaced with stinging nettles which provide food for red admiral caterpillars while yellow irises add a dash of colour along the waterside.

The Hobhole Drain is almost dry at Toynton Fen Side.

The drain runs as a straight fenland river on its way south.

One of the first farms to be passed is the interestingly-named Boston Corporation Farm.

At intervals the banks have holes through to let side channels enter. These vary from culverts large enough to take a small boat to small brick culverts which are egg shaped in section to maximize the rate of flow at the bottom, scouring out silt and preventing settlement in inverts.

A larger side channel is the Bell Water Drain which leads off to the Steeping River. It is immediately followed by a slipway. Bridge abutments show where there has been a further crossing. Numbered angling contest pegs begin and run for the greater part of 100 positions.

An interesting cupola tops buildings at Midville. Windmills at Fen Side and Stickney remain hidden but the tower of the church at Stickney lies directly along the line of a crossing drain.

Little grebes join the wildlife on the water.

The one compulsory portage comes at Lade Bank Bridge where a pumping station blocks the drain, having been built in 1867 because of problems caused by shrinkage of the peat in East Fen. It is best portaged on the left despite the difficult re-entry and the fact that there is a ramp down on the right side, a route which involves a longer detour past the ornate square brick chimney. Another drain heads off to Lade Bank and there is a disused lock and sluice, Lade Bank Old Lock.

Teasels appear on the banks and pheasants squawk noisily as they sail low over the drain.

The Skegness–Sleaford railway cuts as straight a line across the fens as do the roads and the drain. Because of the oblique angle and the low height at which it crosses, the brick arch resulting is an impressive structure, long, wide and very flat, like the roof of a tunnel under a large building.

A windmill at Leake Commonside and two at **Sibsey** (including the Sibsey Trader Mill) all remain hidden. Indeed, the line of trees on the left bank hide everything except the dog roses, which add a touch of pink every so often, and the red buoy which marks the end of a pipeline.

Powerlines cross and then follow the drain unobtrusively as far as Boston. There are swans on the water. Herons fish quietly and oilseed rape and elder bushes add colour.

The major tributary is the Cowbridge Drain, the two waterways sweeping together with curves which would do justice to a railway engineer. The road itself departs at Haltoft End, leaving the drain to move alone across the country.

A line of foam floating out from the right bank draws attention to a sewage works but even from the top of the bank it is not possible to see the windmills at Butterwick and Freiston Shore or the Rochford Tower on the outskirts of **Boston**.

Despite the lack of a road alongside, the section past Fishtoft is popular with boaters. The banks are also used by anglers and there are a line of white pegs, each with a long line of steps hacked down the bank to it in the earth.

Nunn's Bridge, with a 22m clear span, was the first in situ prestressed concrete bridge built in Britain, com-

Lade Bank Pumping Station with the old lock in the centre.

Distance
22km from Toynton Fen Side to the Haven

Navigation Authority
Witham Fourth District Internal Drainage Board

Navigation Society
East Anglian Waterways Association
www.eawa.co.uk

OS 1:50,000 Sheets
122 Skegness & Horncastle
131 Boston & Spalding

pleted in 1948. It was designed by L G Mouchel & Partners and constructed by G E Buchner with the Witham Fourth District Internal Drainage Board's own labour.

The drain divides just before the Haven, each arm finishing at the Hobhole Navigation Pumping Station which lifts the water to the Haven. Onward passage needs to take into consideration the tides as low tide offers a stream at the foot of two steep banks of glistening mud. This is just 3km from the Wash and the Sea Bank gives protection against flooding. To the east lies the North Sea Camp, an attractively named prison.

The nearest public road ends in a parking and picnic area near to a monument marking the point at which the villagers of Scrooby, later known as the Pilgrim Fathers, made their first attempt to emigrate to America. Breaking the skyline is Boston, particularly the tower of St Botolph's church, better known as the Boston Stump.

Dog roses and yellow irises near Fishtoft.

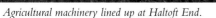

Agricultural machinery lined up at Haltoft End.

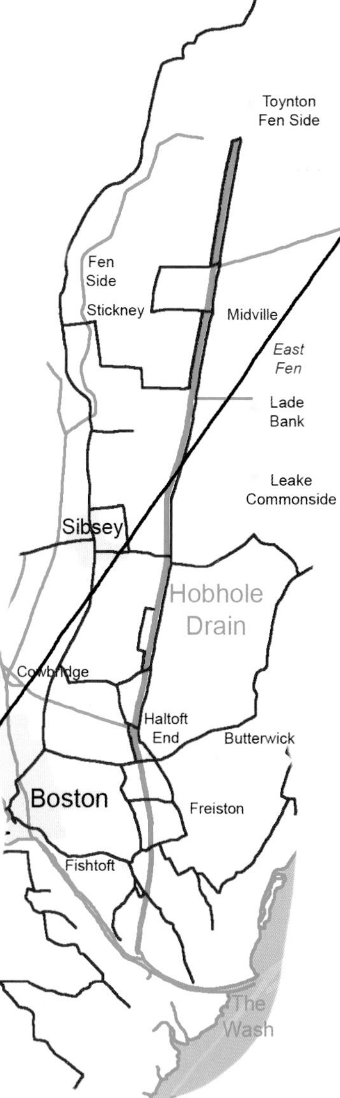

15 East Fen Catchwater Drain

Draining the last great fen in England

East Fen Catchwater Drain starts near the Steeping River at Halton Fenside. It passes 200m from the head of the Hobhole Drain near Toynton Fen Side and has widened somewhat by the bridge near Woolham Farm. This drain was opened in 1643 and developed as part of an early 19th century scheme to drain the last great fen in England, designed by John Rennie for Sir Joseph Banks of Revesby. The banks are high, restricting views of the Wolds to the north.

The fields of grain attract pheasants. One of the most frequent sounds down the drain is the flapping of wood pigeons as they beat their way out of the waterside hawthorn bushes. This is a relatively quiet drain, except for the passing jets in the upper reaches, mostly not being followed by roads.

Between Keal Cotes and East Kirby with its windmill is the 1940s bomber airfield which now houses the Lincolnshire Aviation Heritage Centre with Avro Lancaster bomber, original control tower, blast and air raid shelters, link trainer display, photographs and refreshments.

The banks have cow parsley cutting off in a sharp horizontal line with green lower down, frequently stinging nettles. Dog roses and teasels add colour but the water is opaque and there is frequently a scum of weed, thinly disguised by a carpet of white hawthorn petals in the spring.

A boat may be moored at Stickford in a setting of horse chestnut trees, a pleasant spot to be on a summer's day.

Bell Water Drain leaves from the other side of the road

The drain near Keal Cotes.

Looking across the fen farmland to Stickney with its windmill.

An old brick bridge, now lacking parapets, near Stickney.

Confluence of the West and East Fen Catchwater Drains.

Distance
10km from Woolham Farm to Stone Bridge Drain

Navigation Authority
Witham Fourth District Internal Drainage Board

Navigation Society
East Anglian Waterways Association
www.eawa.co.uk

OS 1:50,000 Sheets
122 Skegness & Horncastle

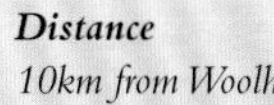

to cross to the Steeping River. A picnic area follows on the line of a former railway.

Windmills in Fen Side and Stickney can be seen from the banks of the drain. Flailing arms might be more conspicuous close at hand as a mole swims across the drain, powerful front paws digging hard and snout held high.

A road bridge, after the sewage works at Stickney, is a concrete structure but only the minimum of the previous bridge has been removed. The supporting steel columns pass through holes hacked into the brick abutments, an arrangement which suggests economy played a greater role than aesthetics in the design of the latest structure.

An abandoned raft shows that it is not just moorhens and mallards which use the drain.

The drain is crossed by the A16. Other roads in the fens are mostly straight but the A16 wanders about, indicating that it predates the drainage of the fens.

At Northlands, East Fen Catchwater Drain joins with West Fen Catchwater Drain to form the wider Stone Bridge Drain. Exit is possible to a minor road on the right where a laminated wooden arch footbridge crosses the drain.

Moorhen's nest near Bar Bridge Farm.

16 West Fen Catchwater Drain

Searching for windmills

St Botolph's Town! Far over leagues of land
And leagues of sea looks forth its noble tower,
And far around the chiming bells are heard;
So may that sacred name forever stand
A landmark, and a symbol of the power,
That lies concentred in a single word.
Henry Wadsworth Longfellow

Cow parsley coats the bank as it leaves Revesby Bridge.

East Kirkby from Kirkby Fenside.

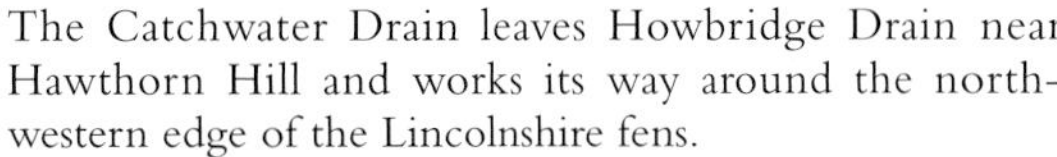

The Catchwater Drain leaves Howbridge Drain near Hawthorn Hill and works its way around the north-western edge of the Lincolnshire fens.

By Revesby Bridge it is a respectable width and has become the West Fen Catchwater Drain. It almost connects with the Medlam Drain at this point but remains separated by a road. These are Witham Navigable drains. From October to March the water levels are lowered to be able to handle floodwater more easily.

The drain was opened in 1634 and developed as part of an early 19th century scheme to drain the last great fen area in England, designed by John Rennie for Sir Joseph Banks of Revesby.

A rope hangs loosely across the drain at Revesby Bridge, as if to dissuade passage further upstream. Across the fields near Revesby is the site of the abbey earthworks.

The banks are high and lined with cow parsley, the white upper halves of the banks stopping in a clearly defined line to leave just green vegetation on the lower halves of the banks. Bushes or young trees usually line one or other side of the drain, mostly hawthorns and elms. There are swans and reeds are present in places.

A 600mm vertical drop weir is a surprising obstruction when the land is only 2m above sea level and the drain is already well below that level.

Fen Farm is served by a rather ugly bridge consisting of a culvert arch with concrete above into which stones have been pushed. There are shallows briefly, the only ones, the rest of the drain being in good condition and the water clear beneath a floating scum of algae and weed which gathers at times. Large fish float on the surface at intervals, a legacy from anglers.

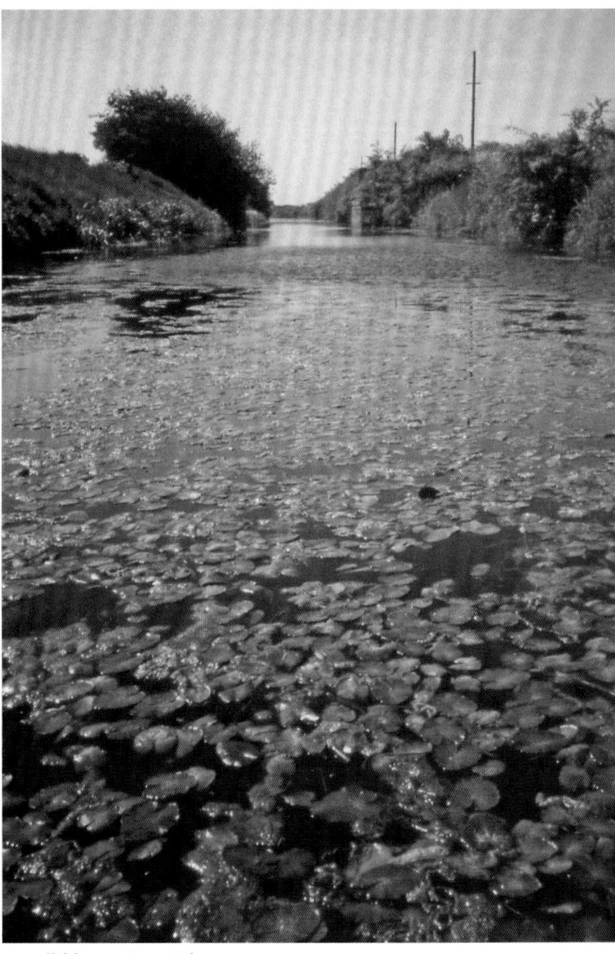

Small lilies at Fen Side.

The magnificent Sibsey Trader Mill.

The windmill at East Kirkby can be seen from the bridge at Kirkby Fenside. Between East Kirkby and the drain is the 1940s bomber airfield which now houses the Lincolnshire Aviation Heritage Centre.

Flying displays on the drain relate to mallards feigning injury to draw boaters away from their ducklings. Voles hide in the waterside grass or scrabble into the water.

Hagnaby Lock now lacks gates. Rabbits scamper around and horses look over fences. This is, perhaps, the best section of the drain with lawns running down to the water, some interesting old farm buildings and a pleasantly rural smell of manure.

The drain widens and the banks become less steep, giving more open views of skylark and kestrel although the cuckoo is heard but not seen. The occasional giant puffball might be found floating amongst the reeds at the edge.

Windmills at Fen Side and Stickney remain fairly well hidden.

At Stickney a low footbridge acts as the limit of navigation for larger craft and a boat is moored to a landing stage next to it, making the point.

Dog rose and teasel join the variety of plant life along the banks. A minor road pulls alongside and there is now a road on one or both sides for the rest of the journey.

West Fen Catchwater Drain is joined by East Fen Catchwater Drain at Northlands to form the wide Stone Bridge Drain which was opened in 1801. Herons and great crested grebes seem quite content with the geometrical exactness of the drain at Sibsey Fen Side as it runs wide and straight between two high banks.

There are two windmills at **Sibsey**, the one nearer the drain being the magnificent Sibsey Trader Mill, built in 1877 by Sandersons of Louth on the site of a previous mill. One of the last erected in Lincolnshire, it is one of the few in England with six sails, worked until 1953 and now restored. The tapered brick tower is tarred on the outside and whitewashed within with a painted white wooden cap.

Swallows swoop at Cowbridge where there is what seems to be an unneccesarily complex junction. Stone Bridge Drain crosses an aqueduct. Short Drain approaches on the right and is piped under the aqueduct to continue on the left as Cowbridge Drain. A sluice lock on the right admits traffic from West Fen Drain which has been joined immediately above the lock by Frith Bank Drain. As it does so, Junction Drain leaves on the left to join Cowbridge Drain, crossed by a low wire which is used for pulling a small boat across for access to a house. To add further interest, a golf course has been sited around the junction and balls come whistling over the water. The local youth gather and swim in the drain to collect the results of slices.

The route ahead now becomes the Maud Foster Drain, opened in 1568 and named after a wealthy Elizabethan landowner. It was enlarged in the early 19th century as part of the fen drainage scheme and is one of the few sections of the Witham Navigable Drains still carrying large boats.

The footbridge from the B1183 and Cowbridge House Inn is one of two remaining from those built by Rennie in 1811. It shows skillful working of cast iron, the ribs being pierced and curved in both profile and plan to give an elegant waisted appearance. The handrails are of wrought iron with gritstone pillars and brick abutments. The cambered footway has a 19m clear span and a 1.1m rise.

The Skegness–Boston railway fits in a river crossing in a 300m length which includes three level crossings of roads.

The approach to **Boston** is grand, a gentle sweep with trees planted at regular intervals along the bank. The drain is then channelled beneath Rennie's other remaining footbridge and between high brick walls, near the far end of which is the magnificent Maud Foster windmill. Built in 1819 and the tallest working mill in England, it has seven storeys of white brick and five sails, restored in 1988.

The red brick Georgian town of Boston was the Old English St Botolph's or Botwulf's town or stone, where the saint founded a monastery in 654. The town grew rapidly in Norman times and received its charter in 1204. Apparently the winds are the result of the struggle between St Botolph and the Devil, who has not yet got his breath back. St Botolph's church, the

Golfers cross the aqueduct at Cowbridge.

Perpendicular Boston Stump, is 86m long with an 83m tower built in stages from about 1425 to around 1510, the tallest in Britain, with an octagonal lantern acting as a beacon from where it is possible to see Lincoln Cathedral and Hunstanton. It is the largest parish church in England, the nave is mostly 14th century with fine carvings, a painted roof and a beautiful medieval oak door and it has 7 doors, 12 pillars in the nave, 24 steps to the library, 52 windows, 60 steps to the chancel and 365 steps to the Stump. It is one of the grandest parish churches in England and was funded by wool.

Boston was the home of Puritanism. The Guildhall Museum has cells which held the Pilgrim Fathers in 1607 after they attempted to leave England for religious freedom in the Netherlands. The second attempt in 1630 was more successful and resulted in the setting up of Boston, Massachusetts. The town has markets on Wednesdays and Saturdays and a fair in May.

There is a college on the right bank of the final reach. Houses face onto the drain.

The drain comes to an abrupt end at heavy sluice doors adjacent to the Fogarty furnishings factory. Beyond the sluices is the Haven, the tidal River Witham with steep banks of silt. Pylons carry power cables high over the river. Container and conventional cranes serve the docks to the right, large buoys stand on the 730m of quayside and silos store produce. Boston was the second most important port in England after London at the end of the 13th century and the fishmarket was famous but the port declined in the 15th century because of floods and silting, reviving a little in the 18th century with riverworks. Trade today is in fertilizers, fruit, potatoes, shellfish, steel and timber.

Maud Foster mill by the drain in Boston.

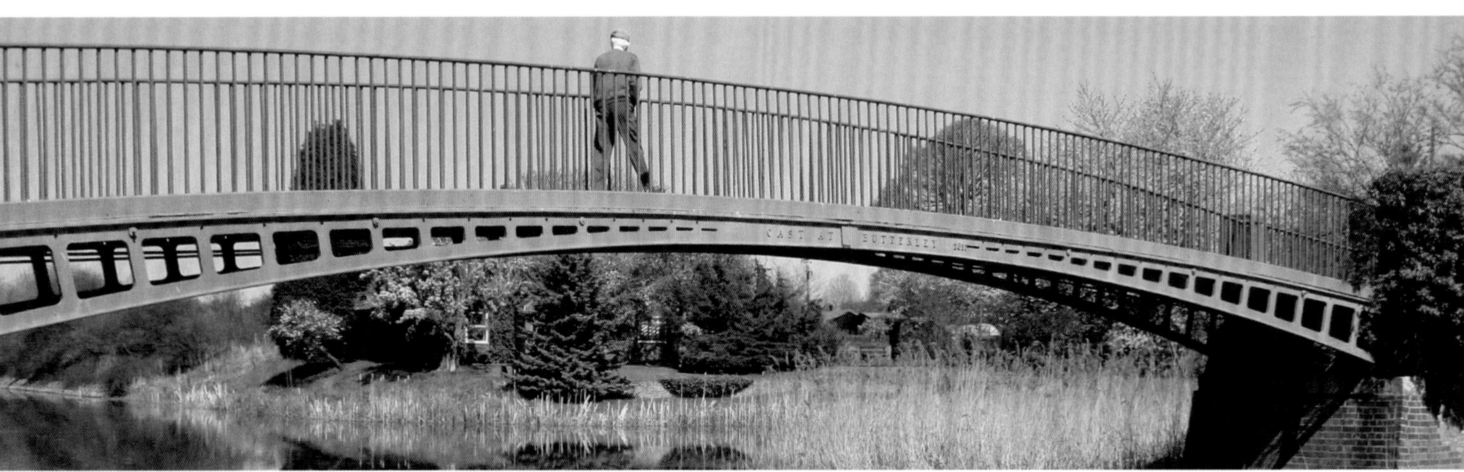

One of Rennie's footbridges crosses Maud Foster Drain.

Distance
21km from Revesby Bridge to Boston

Navigation Authority
Witham Fourth District Internal Drainage Board

Navigation Society
East Anglian Waterways Association
www.eawa.co.uk

OS 1:50,000 Sheets
122 Skegness & Horncastle
131 Boston & Spalding

Maud Foster Drain approaches Boston in a broad sweep.

17 Medlam Drain

A wildlife diary in the mud

Medlam Drain is one of the Witham Navigable Drains. It flows southwards across Lincolnshire to join West Fen Drain. The area is flat, rich, agricultural land reclaimed from the sea. The land is mostly about 2m above sea level so that the drain itself is below sea level. To view the surrounding fields it is necessary to stop and climb up one of the banks but the drain is well sheltered from the prevailing wind. There is the occasional minor road crossing but it runs about 1km to the east of the B1183 and so is quiet with the wildlife undisturbed.

It starts at Revesby Bridge, literally the opposite side of the road from West Fen Catchwater Drain which is to run parallel about 2km to the east. Surprisingly, there is not even a pipe connecting the two drains. Across the fields towards Revesby lie the Abbey Earthworks, some distance from Revesby Abbey.

Eyes have to be kept open if wildlife is to be spotted. Mallards nest amongst the long vegetation just above water level.

Initially the drain is narrow. Pipes run right through the embankments to drains beyond, daylight visible through them in most cases, even the odd egg shaped brick drain, shaped to benefit from maximum velocity in the invert in an attempt to prevent silting.

After Lapwater Farm there is a small wood, opposite which the bank of the drain has suffered a slip. Rabbits

Medlam Drain near its head at Revesby Bridge.

A mallard's nest at the head of Medland Drain.

The drain heads away from Revesby Bridge.

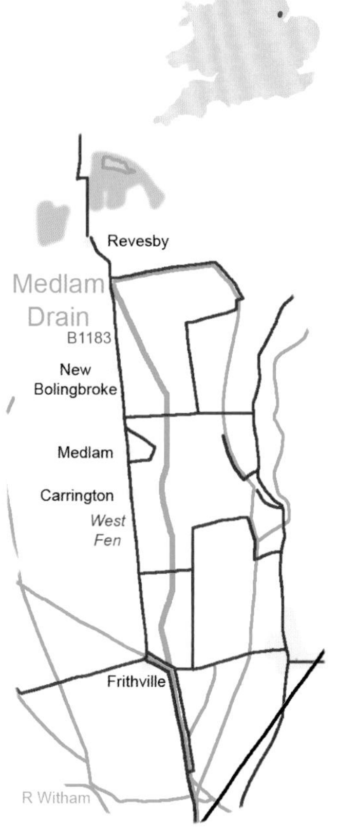

New Bolingbroke including its armless windmill. All pictures show the drawn-down winter water level.

scamper about on the bank. Perhaps their excavations contributed to the problem.

An armless windmill stands at New Bolingbroke. The drain running in from the village is used to get powered boats there and the Medlam Drain is wider from the point where the side drain joins.

Before the drain reaches Medlam Bridge it arrives at what, from a distance, look like large ornamental gateposts on both sides of the drain. In fact, they are no more than the abutments of a bridge which formerly carried a railway line.

In the winter the water level is drawn down. This leaves a muddy verge on each side. The mud preserves a catalogue of bird and animal activity in the form of footprints. There are also many freshwater mussel shells, showing that the water is cleaner than its opaque colour and patches of floating algae suggest. However, it is not clean enough to attract more than the odd immature swan. Moorhens pick their way along the muddy shores and skylarks twitter overhead in the spring. Pheasants whirr across the drain, followed by distant shooting.

Vegetation is mostly in the form of stunted hawthorn bushes. To call them a hedge would be to overstate the case. Clumps of daffodils appear in the spring, to be upstaged by fields of rape.

One of the larger side drains leads down from Carrington Grange.

Mink are attracted by the wildlife diet although some fish are noticeably diseased. The reach after Hackerley Bridge includes anglers' steps cut into the bank.

At Frithville the B1183 passes over as Medlam Drain joins West Fen Drain.

Distance
11km from Revesby Bridge to West Fen Drain

Navigation Authority
Witham Fourth District Internal Drainage Board

Navigation Society
East Anglian Waterways Association
www.eawa.co.uk

OS 1:50,000 Sheet
122 Skegness & Horncastle

The Medlam Drain near Carrington.

18 West Fen Drain

Howbridge Drain starts adjacent to the River Witham at Chapel Hill. It was opened in 1801.

The nearest road approach is at Hurn Bridge, a remote spot with kestrels, pheasants and grouse flying around. A disadvantage of the remoteness has been described bitterly on a corrugated iron panel next to the road in front of the adjacent barn, 'No need to break in, nothing left'.

Tattersall Castle is visible to the north and somewhat closer is **Coningsby** Airfield.

The vegetation along the banks is cow parsley, oilseed rape and water plantains. A single oak tree interrupts the sweep of barley and other arable crops although hawthorn and sycamore are to appear down the banks.

The Catchwater Drain leaves unnoticed on the left.

Buildings at Bettinson's Bridge are in mellow red brick with deeply profiled orange tiles, typical of the area. Castle Dike leaves at Bettinson's Bridge and, beside it, to the southeast stands a windmill.

Tufted ducks frequent the drain at Hough Bridge itself. Roads follow the drain for the rest of its route, Just up the road is New York while the next bridge, a set of concrete arches, comes at Bunker's Hill and is overlooked by the Old Union public house. Chestnut, ash and alder trees flank the drain by the bridge and periwinkle adds a dash of colour as it trails down the wall.

Looking east from Hurn Bridge.

Flattened arches on a farm near the Newham Drain mimic those over the Howbridge Drain.

Approaching the Newham Drain, a farm on the right bank is built with a series of flattened brick arch doorways, an attractive building which complements the brick arches used for some of the drain crossings. Cows express casual interest from the fields and skylarks twitter somewhere above.

Newham Drain crosses and Howbridge Drain becomes West Fen Drain.

Near Westville Farm a drain enters from the Medlam direction, having passed two other Westville Farms in a 3km length, a recipe for confusion.

Frithville, the busiest place on the drain, arrives with a war memorial near the water and a chapel close by. The line turns to the south, the direction in which Medlam Drain is flowing as it enters. The drain is now rather wider and great crested grebes treat it as open water.

Lush's Drain enters near Bank Farm and numbered angling pegs then follow to Cowbridge.

Swallows swoop at Cowbridge where there is a complex junction which gives two routes to the Cowbridge Drain. The first is by taking Short Drain on the left. A boom across the drain protects a set of sluices. These need to be portaged on the right. Almost immediately the drain is piped under an aqueduct carrying Stone Bridge Drain, to appear on the far side as Cowbridge Drain. The whole complex has become the site of a golf course. There is a convenient footbridge

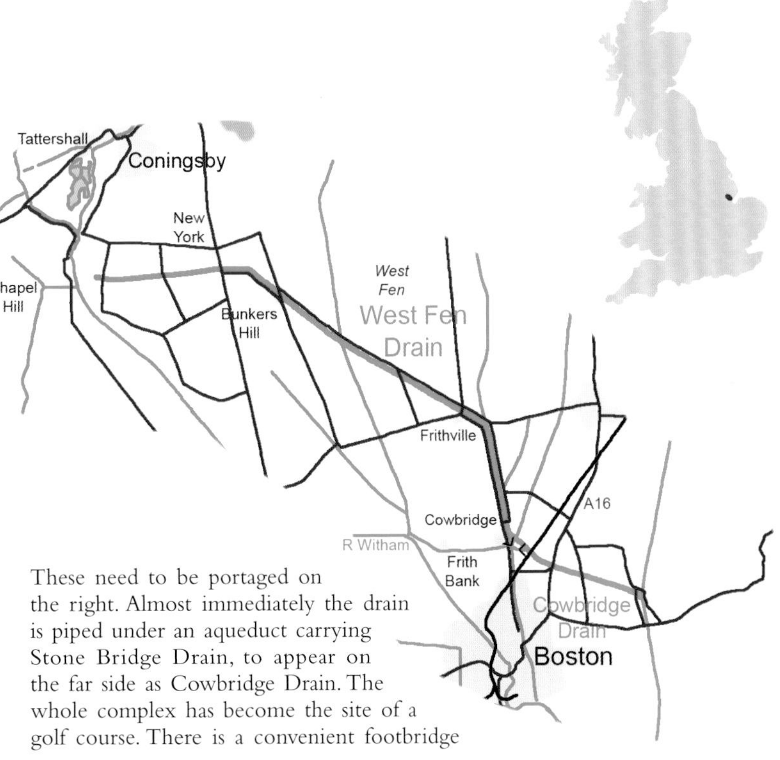

Daffodils at Frithville with the drain drawn down to winter level.

East Fen Lock on the Junction Drain has been incorporated into a golf course as an unusual obstacle.

across Stone Bridge Drain for golfers but there is the risk of low flying golf balls, the warning notice containing information about the potential direction of attack, more for golfers than for the uninitiated.

The other route is to continue, picking up Frith Bank Drain from the right, to Cowbridge Lock with its sluice gates adjacent to a pillbox. The line then crosses Stone Bridge Drain as it becomes Maud Foster Drain above one of Rennie's footbridges and enters Junction Drain.

A low wire crosses Junction Drain and is used for pulling a boat across for access to a house. East Fen Lock, connecting Junction Drain to Cowbridge Drain, has been filled in and provides an interesting tee with golfers having to drive diagonally over the lock, virtually down the line of the portage. The last few metres from the lock to Cowbridge Drain have been abandoned as a swampy area so there is little to choose between the two routes.

Cowbridge Drain is crossed by the Skegness–Boston railway and then by the A16 which wanders in an unfenlike fashion.

Elder bushes flank the drain as it cuts across to the north of **Boston**. At Baker's Bridge there are slots in the brickwork to take stop planks just before the Cowbridge Drain joins the Hobhole Drain on a sweeping curve.

Exit is most easily undertaken by turning up the Hobhole Drain and getting out at the first bridge.

Distance
19km from Chapel Hill to the Hobhole Drain

Navigation Authority
Witham Fourth District Internal Drainage Board

Navigation Society
East Anglian Waterways Association
www.eawa.co.uk

OS 1:50,000 Sheets
122 Skegness & Horncastle
131 Boston & Spalding

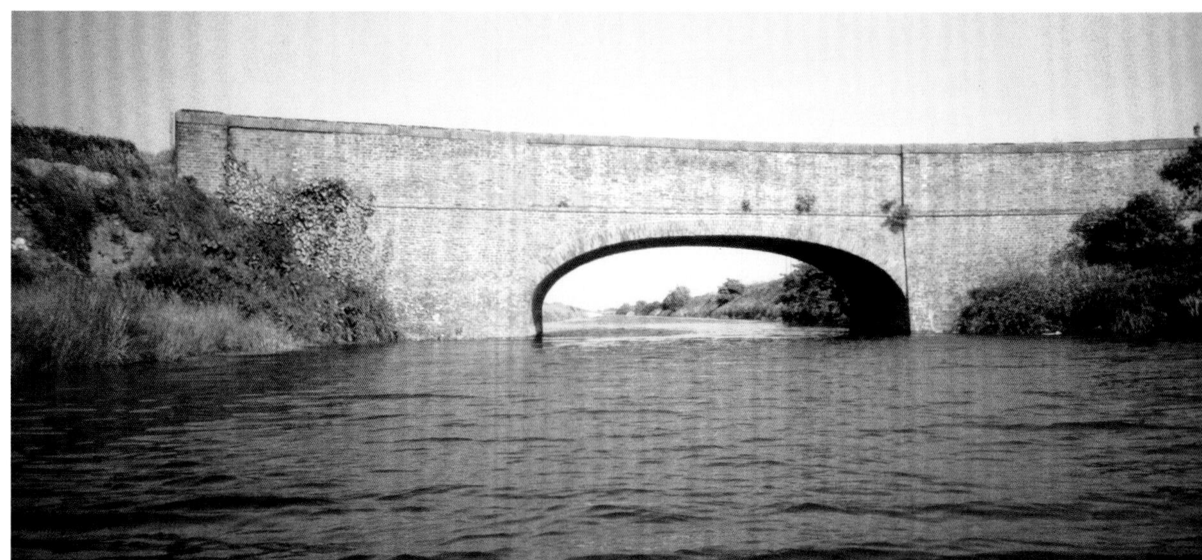

Another flattened arch, this time longer, over Cowbridge Drain.

19 Newham Drain

Flowing up towards the sea

Newham Drain is one of the Witham Navigable Drains, built for land drainage and the carriage of agricultural produce and coal. It starts near Mareham le Fen and flows southwards across Lincolnshire to Anton's Gowt where there is a connection with the River Witham. The area is of rich agricultural land reclaimed from the sea. The land is mostly 2–3 metres above sea level so that the drain itself is below sea level. To view the surrounding fields it is necessary to stop and climb up one of the banks but the drain is well sheltered from the prevailing wind except for the final section, for which there is often a following wind.

Most of the time the route is away from roads and what roads there are take the form of minor country lanes.

A possible starting point is at Moorhouses, nearly in line with the main runway at Coningsby Airfield, 4km away. In the winter the water is drawn down, revealing a muddy shoreline with a few freshwater mussels and quite a collection of flints. The water is murky with patches of floating algae but the occasional immature swan finds the conditions satisfactory while herons and moorhens are at home here. Skylarks sing high overhead in the spring, when coltsfoot and daffodils might be seen along the banks.

Goats are tethered on one bank, mink slip surreptitiously away and pheasants make known their annoyance at being disturbed, not wise with guns being fired in the distance.

A large culvert bridge precedes the crossing of the point where Howbridge Drain becomes West Fen Drain. Most trees in the fens seem to surround houses, like the large ash trees here.

Teasels flower by the bank towards Newham Farm where rabbits chase about and a variety of birds leave their footprints in the mud at the side of the drain. Cattle fences project into the navigation on both sides at one point, suggesting that powered craft are not common here.

Mill's Bridge with four tyres but no vehicle.

The B1184 crosses by Canister Hall, another building surrounded by trees and with hawthorn bushes dotted along the banks.

There is a jetty near Peacock's Farm although it does not appear to see much use. From here the Boston Stump can be seen away across the fields to the southeast.

Castle Dike joins from the right. Newham Drain approaches the River Witham at Anton's Gowt where a lock connects the two. Surprisingly, as the Witham is less than 4km from its tidal limit, boats lock down to the Newham Drain, giving a striking picture of the lower water levels in the Witham Navigable Drains.

The route now becomes the Frith Bank Drain, opened in 1216 and officially a navigation from 1802. Unlike the more recent drains, it bends frequently and is more obviously riverlike in character despite the continuing high banks. These banks support spreads of periwinkle

Crossing the Hough Bridge Drain/West Fen Drain junction.

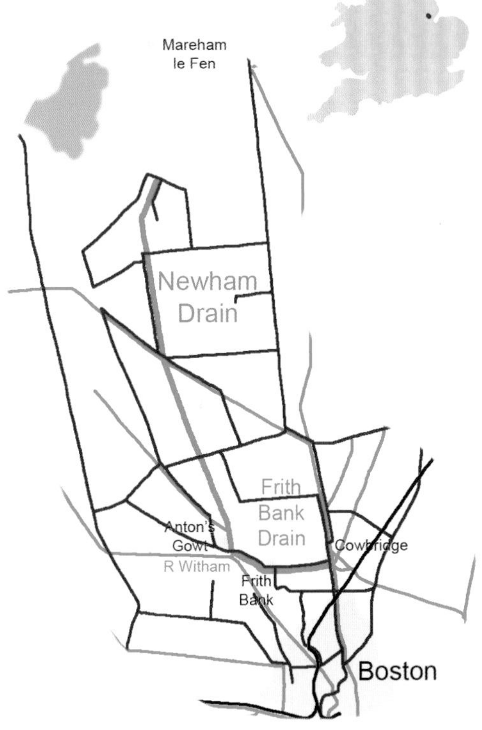

Rich agricultural land which occupies the Lincolnshire fens. All pictures show drawn down winter levels.

in the spring, their blue flowers and beds of dark green leaves offsetting the yellow daffodils which also line the banks. A further flash of blue might come from a kingfisher streaking away.

At winter levels the mud reveals rows of stumps of stakes which have been part of a bank stabilization scheme in an earlier age.

Beyond the B1183 at Cowbridge the Frith Bank Drain returns to West Fen Drain where it meets Stone Bridge Drain, Maud Foster Drain and Cowbridge Drain. Exit is most easily made opposite onto the golf course and back over the lock to where there is roadside parking near the Cowbridge House Inn.

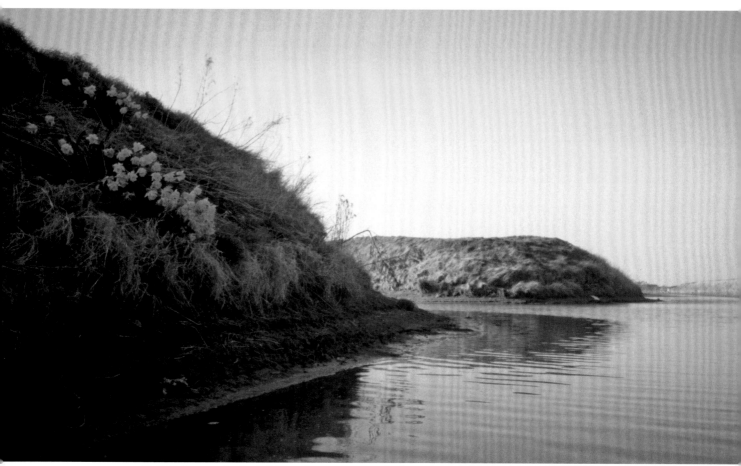

Daffodils bloom at the Castle Dike confluence at its winter level.

Distance
20km from Moorhouses to Cowbridge

Navigation Authority
Witham Fourth District Internal Drainage Board

Navigation Society
East Anglian Waterways Association
www.eawa.co.uk

OS 1:50,000 Sheets
122 Skegness & Horncastle
131 Boston & Spalding

Anton's Gowt Lock leads up to the River Witham high above as it approaches the Wash.

20 River Witham

A concentration of religious houses

By this to Lincoln come, upon whose lofty scite,
Whilst wistly Wytham looks with wonderful delight
Enamoured of the state and beauty of the place,
That her of all the rest especially doth grace,
Leaving her former course, in which she first set forth,
Which seemed to have been directly to the north,
She runs her silver front into the muddy fen,
Which lies into the east, in her deep journey, when
Clear Ban, a pretty brook, from Lindsey coming down,
Delicious Wytham leads to holy Botulph's town,
Where proudly she puts in amongst the great resort,
That their appearance make in Neptune's watery court.
Michael Drayton

Rising near Wymondham, the River Witham flows north then southeast across Lincolnshire to the Wash through low lying fens. With the Fossdyke Navigation it is the oldest inland waterway still in use, having been carrying boats since Roman times. Often it has straight reaches with high banks and slow flow although the levels can fluctuate significantly. As it is a cul-de-sac for those not planning to go out into the Wash it is surprising how many pleasure craft there are using it. In due course it will form part of the Fens Waterways Link but those wanting to stay off the open sea can use it to reach only the Witham Navigable Drains and the South Forty Foot Drain before returning.

In 1810 a local election was fought on a proposal to join the Witham to the Welland at Stamford and then to the Oakham Canal in order to link the fen rivers to the main canal network. At one time the river was controlled by 17 different authorities, hardly assisting strategic planning.

In glacial times the much larger River Trent had drained Lake Humber to Lake Fenland through the Witham Gap, the only cut in the limestone Lincoln Cliff between Grantham and the Humber. This is naturally a poorly drained area, all being alluvial land within the former Lake Fenland.

The inland equivalent of St Michael's Mount was an obvious attraction, becoming the Celtic Lindum, the hill fort by the pool, and then the Roman Lindum Colonia. The Romans built a 17ha walled fort, later adding 23ha of the lower town, the remains of which can be seen in **Lincoln**'s Temple Gardens. The fortress was for the 9th then the 2nd Legion, in 78 becoming a retirement town for legionnaires. The Romans excavated Brayford Pool as a port and, in 120, connected it westward to the River Trent by digging the Fossdyke Navigation.

The city became rich on wool, making cloth including Lincoln green, but failed to progress. Defoe reported

Lincoln's Glory Hole.

that it was in a state of venerable antiquity, dirty, decayed and decaying further with only 13 churches remaining of the 53 there had been at the Conquest, when it was the fourth largest English town in the second most populated county.

The Norman Lincoln Castle on its 5.7ha site dates from 1068 with a Norman gateway, walls with three towers, a large bailey, a mound for the Lucy Tower named after the 12th century Countess Lucy and the 14th century Observation Tower restored in 1825 for astronomy on a smaller mound. The Roundheads captured it from the Royalists in 1644 and it was where the Separatists were tried after their capture in Boston. It has a Victorian prison and a prison chapel designed so that convicts could not see each other. In 1215 one of the four existing copies of Magna Carta was sent here. It was from here that Queen Eleanor's body was taken to Charing Cross.

The Lawn was Britain's first purpose-built lunatic asylum. The Jew's House has outstanding 12th century Norman domestic architecture. The 15th century black and white Cardinal's Hat was named after Wolsey, who had been Bishop of Lincoln. St Benedict's, St Mary le Wigford's and St Peter at Gowt's all have Anglo-Saxon towers.

The cathedral is one of the world's finest medieval buildings and the best sited cathedral, Britain's third largest. The bishop's seat was moved here from the southern edge of the diocese at Dorchester on the Thames after the Conquest for Remigius, England's first Norman bishop. Built in the 11th century by the Normans, only the core of the west front survived an earthquake in 1185. It was rebuilt in the 13th century by St Hugh with three towers and was said to have been the world's tallest building for 250 years. The 165m main spire fell in a storm in 1547 and the ones on the western towers were removed in 1807. Construction is in honey coloured Barnack limestone with an 83m tower containing the 5.5t Great Tom bell. The 1674 library by Wren was for Dean Honywood's books from Leiden, mostly about America. There is notable medieval 13/14th century and Victorian glass with the Seamen's Chapel windows dedicated to the Pilgrim Fathers, John Smith, who named new England and helped establish Virginia, and explorer Matthew Flinders. There is England's earliest and largest eight light window. Romanesque works, a stone screen of about 1330, oak misericords of about 1370 which are among the best anywhere, plate including an Anglo-Saxon bowl from the Bailgate, the best Early English Gothic in the Angel Choir, England's finest collection of 13th century heads and rare cloister bosses from about 1290 can all be found here. The Russell Chantry has 1959 Duncan Grant murals, there are 1984 candleholders to the Gilbertines and a 300mm high imp was causing so much havoc around the cathedral that he was turned to stone on a pillar by an angel. A shrine to Little St Hugh was established after bones found in the cathedral in 1791 were said to have been those of an 8 year old ritually slaughtered by a Jew in 1290 for which 19 Jews were hanged following a confession obtained by torture, a story used in *The Canterbury Tales*. There is a statue of Tennyson, a visitor, with his wolfhound.

An unusual design of footbridge over the river.

Light but inelegant Victorian engineering.

The 12th century medieval Bishop's Palace was one of England's most important buildings, the administrative centre for the country's largest diocese, built by St Hugh. The East Hall with its barrel vaulted undercroft is the earliest example in the country of a domestic roofed hall. Bishop William Alnwick modernized it in the 1430s, adding the Alnwick entrance tower. It was visited by Henry VIII and Catherine Howard, where she was caught being indiscrete with Thomas Culpepper, later used in the trial against her, and was also visited by James I. It was sacked by the Royalists in 1648 and restored in the 1880s with hillside terraces, a heritage garden and one of the most northerly vineyards in Europe.

The Usher Gallery is Lincolnshire's leading art gallery with the Usher collection of enamels and porcelain, Peter de Wint watercolours, Lincolnshire portraits, an Alfred Lord Tennyson memorabilia collection and Nelson items and letters. Other art appears in the Gallery of the School of Applied Art & Design of De Montfort University and the Collection, which has art and archaeology. The City & County Museum in Lincoln Drill Hall has armour and a prehistoric boat from the Witham, the Museum of Lincolnshire Life covers agriculture, industry, social history and a First World War tank and there is the Incredibly Fantastic Old Toy Show.

St Swithin's church is Victorian, there is the oldest Franciscan church in England, dating from 1250, and Greyfriars is a 13th century friary. The Newport Arch, the northern gate across Ermine St, is the only Roman arch still used by traffic. The 15th century Stonebow Tudor gateway has the Guildhall above with an open timber roof, 15/16th century carved bosses, Richard II and Henry VII swords, maces, the best regal insignia outside London, the 1157 charter and a model of the Little Willie tank, the world's first, built in Lincoln. The Council are summoned by the 1371 Mote Bell, the oldest of its kind in Britain. Lincoln also has the restored Ellis Mill with its four sails. Lincoln Arboretum is one of the UK's finest Victorian parks.

Lincoln Mystery Plays are performed every four years. The city has been used for filming *The Life & Crimes of William Pardoner*, *The Da Vinci Code*, *Oliver Twist* and *Young Victoria*.

The Odeon and the Royal William IV public house are conspicuous from Brayford Pool which is used by many swans and mallards. This is where the Witham turns sharply from a northerly to an easterly direction, departing under the A57.

Ahead is the Glory Hole, the 1160 High Bridge on the line connecting Ermine Street, the Fosse Way and the Roman road to Burgh le Marsh. It is the oldest bridge in Britain carrying buildings, the half-timbered structures added about 1450. What can only be seen from the water, however, are the Norman foundations for what is the second oldest masonry bridge in Britain, its 6.7m span with subsequent extensions being more like the structure of a cathedral cloister roof than a traditional bridge. The Grade I bridge has been restricted to pedestrians since 1971. Navigation under it can be difficult if the water level is high or the wind is funnelling through.

The river is fed between concrete walls through the Waterside area with stylized angels reaching over the water. The A15 passes between the Witch & Wardrobe and the Grade II Doughty's Oil Mill of 1863. An unusual footbridge crosses the river, supported from semi circular arches and with steep steps at the ends, visually attractive from the water.

Stamp End Lock is announced by its guillotine gate. The Lincoln–Grimsby railway crosses and then there is an iron road bridge which is so obviously functional with no attempt to tidy up the design that it is almost attractive.

The water is clear with reedmace along the banks but algae grows quickly in the summer to nuisance levels so it is surprising that rowers should choose to site their boathouse here. Sincil Dyke or the South Delph now runs along the south side to Bardney Lock and further drainage channels run outside these so there are four parallel waterways to be crossed by anyone travelling north–south.

The river has produced a ceremonial Iron Age shield, 1.2m long in bronze with a stylized boar.

A railway line branched onto the river bank at **Washingborough** and followed it all the way to Boston but has since gone the way of many other lines and is now a surfaced cycleway and the Viking Way.

Washingborough has stone cottages and is where the Romans began their Car Dyke cut to Peterborough, following the edge of higher ground. The dormitory village of Cherry Willingham stands back from the river on higher ground, as does Fiskerton which was a fishing port despite now being nearly 50km inland. The church has two Norman arches and the village has turned up Bronze Age axes as well as two Iron Age jars found beneath a prehistoric causeway. The area was frequented by Peter de Wint and by pheasants, harriers, herons and moorhens.

Kilometre posts record progress and a footbridge at Five Mile House Farm is a significant landmark. After running 11km east from Brayford Pool almost in a straight line the river suddenly turns southeast. Flags grow along the banks, great crested grebes are on the water, the cuckoo may be heard in the spring, owl boxes are mounted on the bank and angling platforms are by the water.

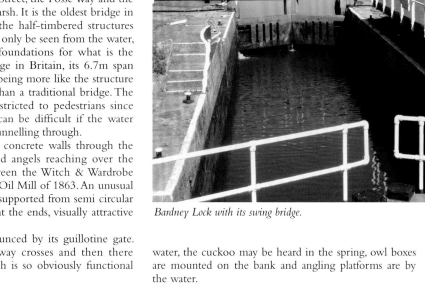

Bardney Lock with its swing bridge.

The Old River Witham leaves through sluices, to be followed by the arrival of Branston Delph to the Sincil Dyke. A wooden carving of a woman looks over the stinging nettles as moorings begin past Branston Island. There is plenty of activity at **Bardney** Lock where a large swing bridge sits beside the centre of the chamber. The Old River Witham rejoins below the lock, having picked up Barlings Eau, and the cycle track changes bank on the former railway bridge as Sincil Dyke finally joins and water lilies grow in the river.

Across the fen are the remains of King Æthelred's 7th century Bardney Abbey. By the 12th century it was one of nine religious houses in 18km, the greatest concentration of monastic communities in Britain. Out of envy the monks of Bardney refused to bury St Oswald so the body was left outside the locked gates overnight. A pillar of light shone to the sky from the body so the monks took the hint and buried him the next day, agreeing never to close their doors again. The question 'Do you come from Bardney?' has the same meaning as 'Were you born in a field with the gate wide open?'

The B1190 crosses over to Bardney where the 15th century

Carving beside the river and the cycleway.

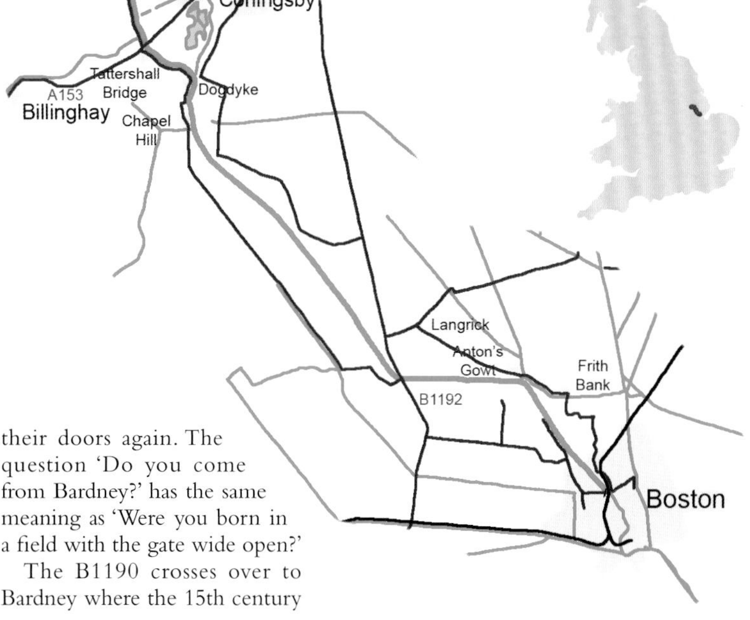

Approaching Bardney Lock under the railway-turned-cycleway.

Bardney sugar beet factory has a gantry across the river.

church of St Lawrence has a medieval brick chancel built by the monks of an 1139 Cistercian monastery.

The village was attacked by navvies working on river improvements so the Riot Act had to be read and the cavalry called out to take them away. The most conspicuous part of the village is a large redundant sugar beet factory with a gantry across the river to more buildings beside an area of pits. The river is lined with cow parsley, hawthorn bushes and willows and is used by coots and blackheaded gulls.

Nocton Delph joins before Southrey, where a slipway with rails runs down to the water. The church of St John the Divine was built in 1898 by villagers, a bellcoted timber chapel, now plastic coated, coloured white on the outside and sky blue inside. The White Horse Inn faces from the other bank. Another statue rises above the vegetation by the cycle track, a rippling silver pillar.

The Metheringham Drain and Catchwater Drain join from opposite sides above where a house has acquired a disused signal box, forming a suntrap overlooking the river.

Kirkstead Bridge takes the B1191 across by the Kings Arms at Martin Dales and the Timberland Delph joins beyond. Abbey Earthworks also include some masonry from another of the monastic sites near the river. **Woodhall Spa** Airfield, 2km from the river, is no longer used but was the base from which the Dambusters flew. Tales of the Riverbank & Timberland Pumping Station Visitor Centre is sited next to the Engine Drain on the west bank, featuring fen drainage.

No longer joining is the Horncastle Canal which followed the River Bain but then cut across from Tattershall and its castle to join the Witham above the **Billinghay** Skirth junction. The old Tattershall Bridge stands downstream of its replacement carrying the A153.

A leisure park has been established in old pits. Dogdyke Pumping Station had a wind pump in 1796, replaced in 1855 by a steam beam pumping engine with a 3.7m beam and 4.3m flywheel driving a 7.3m scoop wheel which drained 6.1km^2. It has been restored and is the only land drainage engine still steamed. It was replaced in 1940 by a Ruston & Hornsby diesel which is retained in reserve in case the modern electric pumps fail. The chimney was removed as it was a landmark for enemy aircraft seeking **Coningsby** Airfield, of which the main runway is 1km away. As well as intensive training with jets doing frequent circuits it houses the Battle of Britain Memorial Flight with the only flying Lancaster in Europe, a Dakota, two Hurricanes, five Spitfires and Chipmunks.

The River Bain joins at Dogdyke with the Packet Inn's pontoons beyond the confluence. Howbridge Drain, one of the Witham Navigable Drains, starts beyond the rushes and embankment on the east side of the river. On the other side of Chapel Hill the Kyme Eau joins with moorings along its final reach.

The course is now clearly artificial. Damselflies, greylag geese, great crested grebes and tufted ducks might be seen and alder trees, dog roses and oilseed rape grow along banks which are remote from people. The line is almost straight for 8km to Langrick Bridge, taking the B1192 across, where the river turns east for a further straight run of over 3km to Anton's Gowt. The lock here on the north side is the only access point to the Witham Navigable Drains at the point where the Newham Drain becomes the Frith Bank Drain at a lower level than the river.

The river then turns southeast again for a further straight run of over 4km to Boston. A viewing platform has been built on the bank and benefits from being able to see far down the river.

Boston is approached past Boston Marina, moorings and a sailing club. Grand Sluice with its lock forms the tidal limit, a cramped location with the A1137 passing

Another sculpture near Stixwould.

A disused signal box near Stixwould makes an ideal sun trap.

Landing at Coningsby over Tattershall Bridge.

The Packet Inn beyond the River Bain confluence.

A cruiser that has seen happier days.

over and the Skegness–Sleaford railway crossing that. The first sluice, built in 1142, decayed and the river became tidal again. The 1500 replacement lasted a century although a failing bridge struggled on to 1807. Meanwhile, new sluices were built in 1766 with three 5.2m spans and a lock which has had steel lifting gates since 1982, this being the oldest tidal outfall sluice largely in its original state. The lock is only open for four hours around high water as the tidal river drains to leave steep mud banks.

Very conspicuous below the sluice is St Botolph's church, the Perpendicular Boston Stump.

Less conspicuous is Fydell House, a small pre-1720 town house with a fine 18th century staircase, owned by the Fydell family who were merchants and local politicians.

A barrage is under consideration for the Haven so that water through the town will be non tidal, making it less restrictive for boats using the Fens Waterways Link when the South Forty Foot Drain obstruction is bypassed.

Anton's Gowt lock leads to the Witham Navigable Drains.

Distance
51km from Brayford Pool to the Haven

Navigation Authority
Canal & River Trust

Navigation Society
East Anglian Waterways Association
www.eawa.co.uk

OS 1:50,000 Sheets
121 Lincoln & Newark-on-Trent
122 Skegness & Horncastle
131 Boston & Spalding

Connection
Fossdyke Navigation *– see CoB p311*

Grand Sluice on the left leads past the Boston Stump.

21 Kyme Eau

A river with an identity crisis

Ornate bridge carrying a road towards Haverholme Priory.

Old sluice gear wheels at Haverholme Lock.

This is a river with an identity crisis. It rises on Willoughby Heath as the River Slea and flows eastwards across Lincolnshire to the River Witham, changing its name to the Kyme Eau after Ferry Farm. The reach from Ferry Farm was used by the Romans as part of the line of their Car Dyke, here the Clay Dyke. From 1792 it was canalized from Carre Street Wharf in Sleaford, being known as the Sleaford Canal or Sleaford Navigation.

The navigation was abandoned in 1878 although half of it was still used until the 1940s, locks now replaced with fixed sluices. The Sleaford Navigation Trust has evolved from the society formed in 1977 and is undertaking restoration, the navigation having the benefit of a towpath throughout although some of it is very overgrown and the route is not clear at Ferry Farm.

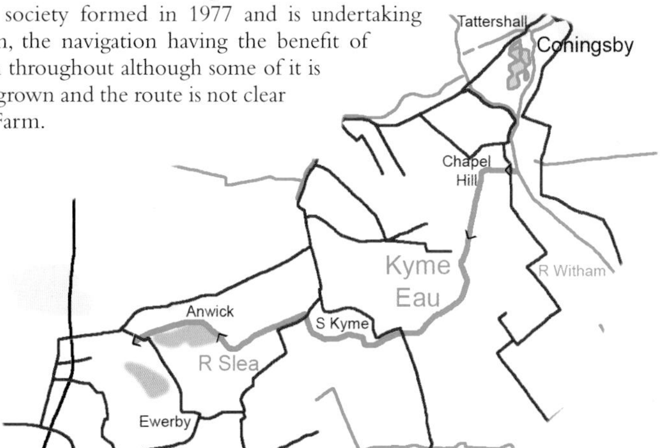

Tattershall
Coningsby
Chapel Hill
Kyme Eau
R Witham
Anwick
S Kyme
R Slea
Ewerby

Haverholme Priory looks down towards the river.

Cobbler's Lock stops larger craft.

A major problem is that this is one of the driest rivers in the country.

Haverholme Lock will be the acting head of navigation when restoration of Cobbler's Lock is completed. Its winding gear is worthy of closer inspection, the iron gearwheels having wooden teeth, some of which are still

Hawthorn and cow parsley blossom below Cobbler's Lock.

Clay Dyke, the Roman canal section.

The castellated tower at South Kyme alone in its grounds.

in place. Paths, a picnic site and a footbridge serve the lock area.

For the first few hundred metres the river will be too dry to use except after rainy spells, when there may be just enough water for a small boat to pick a route through the weeds to the road bridge, which has a parking area.

The bridge is a small but magnificent stone structure with a ball on each corner and a coat of arms in low relief. Doubtless, this stone bridge was built in such fine style as it was the approach to Haverholme Priory, standing back from the right bank, although the coat of arms can only be seen from the water.

A stream on the left brings in more water after the bridge, possibly making the difference to whether it is possible to run the sand and gravel rapids which come at first. A pipe bridge arches over and the river then widens out and becomes deeper for the rest of its distance. The water is clear because of its lack of use by powered craft. There are plenty of reeds along the banks. For a while the right bank is wooded, mostly young elder bushes. Birdlife ranges from the wren to the heron, moorhens and coots also being seen regularly. The left bank is too high to see the nearby village of Anwick and this situation remains unchanged as the river moves into fenland.

Cobbler's Lock has been restored except for its gates, which will be added when bank restoration work has been undertaken upstream. The Old River Slea comes in on the right side below, this natural river course apparently having been abandoned below Sleaford in favour of the navigation route. A new landing stage has been constructed below the lock.

On the far side of Ewerby Waithe Common is the farmhouse at Ferry Farm corner where both banks of the river are a sea of daffodils in the spring.

The sudden change of direction here indicates the short length known as the Clay Dyke. This Roman canal ran from Waterbeach to Lincoln where the Fossdyke took over and it is inconceivable that it was just a drainage channel. It must have been used for transport here and, if so, there is every likelihood that the Romans also used many other rivers for transport.

Carved wooden kingfisher with its catch on the riverbank at South Kyme.

The navigation's triumphal arch at South Kyme.

Craft moored at South Kyme.

Traditional architecture at the first Terry Booth Farm.

Bottom Lock choked with weed.

An owl box at Chapel Hill faces what looks like a wired-off slipway.

The river now becomes the Kyme Eau, taking its name from South Kyme, an attractive village which enhances the river. A large church has neither tower nor spire although a lone castellated tower stands close by, its gaunt three storey window silhouettes looking out over the river.

In the village, mown lawns lead down to the river and there are assorted craft including cruisers and narrowboats. The village ends with a large wooden carving on the bank by Simon Todd of a kingfisher holding a fish. A decorative arch celebrates the navigation's bicentenary in 1994, oddly located where it is easily missed from the road and hard to see from the river because of the B1395 bridge crossing.

Leaving the village, the river turns around more towards the north, now with high embankments in much more open farmland although some farm buildings are dilapidated, particularly at the first of the two Terry Booth Farms.

Bottom Lock has been restored with a guillotine gate at its upstream end. The approach channel is choked with weed, contrasting with the care the Sleaford Navigation Trust have put into a flower bed and plaque on the lock island. Canada geese and kingfishers may be seen in the vicinity and the great crested grebe is also present on the river.

Between the abutments of a former bridge at Bridge Farm are two stakes in the river, marked by a road cone firmly attached to the top of each.

As the river turns onto its final eastwards reach there is an owl box on the left bank facing what looks like a slipway smartly surfaced with chippings but closed off with barbed wire so it must just be for cattle to drink. The river here is 4km from Tattersall Castle by the Horncastle Canal and about 2km from **Coningsby** Airfield.

At Chapel Hill there are automatic flood control gates, usually open. These lead to moorings as far as the River Witham.

Roadside parking is possible by the final bridge over the river.

Craft moored at Chapel Hill.

Distance
15km from Haverholm Lock to the River Witham

Navigation Societies
Sleaford Navigation Trust www.sleafordnavigation.co.uk, East Anglian Waterways Association www.eawa.co.uk

OS 1:50,000 Sheets
121 Lincoln & Newark-on-Trent
122 Skegness & Horncastle
130 Grantham

22 South Forty Foot Drain

Draining the marshes the Romans avoided

The head of the drain at Guthram Gowt needs work.

A trig point just 5m above sea level near Forty Foot Farm.

Barn owl nesting boxes near the head of the drain.

Rich farmland stretches away from the first Forty Foot Farm.

When the Romans built their Car Dyke they followed the toe of the high land where it met the marshes. Later, the South Forty Foot Drain was dug some 4km to the east to drain those marshes, which it does with the assistance of a network of ditches covering the resulting silt fens, at one time an Ice Age lake. Water is brought in from the Car Dyke, from near Bourne and from the direction of Guthram Gowt where there is not quite a connection with the River Glen. Two of the largest channels meet at the remote Forty Foot Farm.

A pair of barn owl nesting boxes on long poles overlook the junction where powerlines cross. Pairs of owl boxes follow at intervals, this being an ideal area for them, away from roads.

From here the course is northwards and then eastwards across Lincolnshire on a totally rural line. Until closed in 1967 it served as the Black Sluice Drainage & Navigation. Now there is little human activity except for farms at intervals and the occasional bridge across but that will change again when the drain forms part of the Fens Waterways Link. Villages stand back on higher ground. Along each side are levées to contain floodwater, preventing views to the sides from the water but providing shelter from the prevailing wind in this exposed area. The banks grow profuse cow parsley, poppies, daisies, oilseed rape, dog roses, elder and ash, teasels, plantains, greater reedmace and sedges with arrowhead in the dark clear water. Skylarks, swallows, pheasants, cormorants, moorhens, mallards and swans frequent the drain and minnows surface in the water.

After a kilometre a pumping station bars the way, the only portage needed. A trig point on top of the levée is 4m above sea level, meaning that water level here is about sea level.

The reaches are straight but slight corners at intervals, particularly at the southern end, prevent views along the drain from becoming extensive. Climb to the top of the bank, however, and rich flat farmland stretches to the horizon. On the other hand, rounding a corner can bring an unexpected meeting with a hare which simply takes a few hops along the bank to sit in the vegetation and watch the boater quietly pass.

A solitary swan swims between dog roses at Aslackby Fen.

Beyond the B1397 bridge the drain turns near another Forty Foot Farm and another trig point, this time 5m above sea level.

Horses seem surprisingly common, grazing amongst the dog rose bushes along the banks. Ducks might be expected at Mallard Hurn but, in fact, grebes patrol instead.

In a landscape which is totally dedicated to agricultural produce and its movement, the balustraded Donington High Bridge carrying the A52 seems unduly ornate. Next to it is the Sloop Inn Restaurant, an equally unexpected source of refreshment.

After the Spalding–Sleaford railway crosses, a moored dinghy reminds of the drain's history as a navigation. At Eau End Farm, Cliff Beck arrives unseen via a pumping station on the left bank at the head of a reach which is crossed by three sets of powerlines passing through a windfarm.

Yellow iris and trefoil brighten the banks but gun cartridges provide a less attractive brightening of the water. Angling platforms are cut out of the bank as the Sleaford–Boston railway comes alongside, to follow the bank all the way to Boston.

Swineshead Bridge, carrying the A17, is the busiest on the drain. On the south side a plough stands in front of a cottage. On the other bank, next to the Barge Restaurant the A1121 leaves to follow the railway along the bank to Boston. The trains are conspicuous while the road traffic is hidden but clearly heard.

Coots and shelducks frequent the widening drain as it is joined from the north by the Skerth Drain. Opposite is Hammond Beck, which is pumped in from behind less steep banks which are grazed, making the numbered angling pegs that much more conspicuous. These contrast with the red hot pokers on the north bank, bursting through the vegetation between the Clay Dike and Hubbert's Bridge, which carries the B1192.

The vegetation covered levée successfully hides **Boston** Aerodrome on Wyberton Fen. The A52 crosses back at Chain Bridge, these days on a rather more mundane structure. Old Hammond Beck is pumped in on the right as the housing of Boston begins and a prominent aerial draws attention to the doors which control the entry of the North Forty Foot Drain.

Water tower and moat alike remain hidden behind the trees in Skirbeck Quarter. Beyond the bridge which carried the former Boston–Spalding railway is a store on the left and, ahead, the large pumping station at the current tidal limit. Black Sluice Lock has been installed for the Fens Waterways Link.

This is the port area of the River Witham which has exceedingly muddy high banks. Any plans to proceed on the river should take this into consideration, arrival being timed to catch high tide.

The Black Sluice Lock connection to the Haven at Boston.

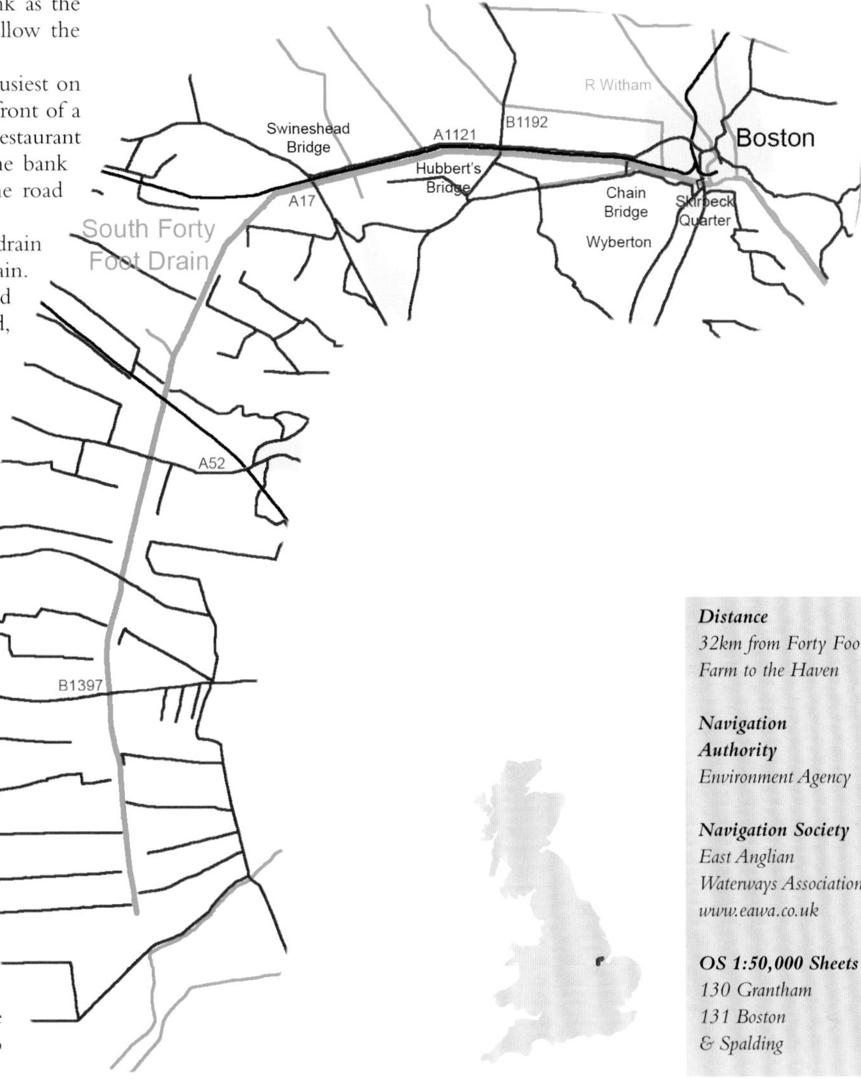

Distance
32km from Forty Foot Farm to the Haven

Navigation Authority
Environment Agency

Navigation Society
East Anglian Waterways Association
www.eawa.co.uk

OS 1:50,000 Sheets
130 Grantham
131 Boston & Spalding

23 River Glen

A minor river destined to become more important

Working the rich agricultural land by the Glen near Twenty.

Teasels along the bank near Tongue End.

Owl boxes by the old railway crossing near Guthram Gowt.

The East Glen and West Glen join at Wilsthorpe to form the River Glen which flows northeast across Lincolnshire. Being little used, the water is fairly clear. This is all alluvial land within what was the glacial Lake Fenland and forms rich agricultural land, much used for growing bulbs. It is a flat area and the river runs shallow to Pinchbeck, frequently straight where it has been modified and with other associated channels, especially the parallel Counter Drain at the head of the navigation at Tongue End.

The navigation begins officially at the confluence with the Bourne Eau although this cut is isolated by a sluice and pumping station. Upstream of the official head of navigation there are Environment Agency notices which warn boats of underwater obstructions on one side of the channel.

The banks are high with clumps of teasels in places, reeds along the edges and willow trees as something of a rarity. Where it is possible to see over, the landscape is of flat fields of crops such as broad beans to the horizon, broken up only by groups of wind turbines, a clump north of Deeping St Nicholas. The rural idyll is also shattered at times by low flying jets.

The squawks of pheasants are heard, larks sing and swans, mallards, moorhens, coots and magpies go about their businesses. A pair of owl boxes stand on the bank beyond piers which used to carry a railway bridge, now removed although its partner across the Counter Drain remains in place.

At Guthram Gowt a former connection to the South Forty Foot Drain is to be reinstated with a lock, after which the drain and the river downstream will form a section of the Fens Waterways Link, the connecting lock already having been installed at the Boston end.

This was a Roman salt working area, a reminder of the former presence of the sea. A nature reserve is sited on the edge of Pinchbeck South Fen.

The A151, which has followed since Guthram Gowt, crosses New Bridge at Pinchbeck West, where there are 48 hour moorings. Following a fire, the New Bridge Inn

Daffodils extend to the River Glen at Pinchbeck West.

Daffodils in profusion on the bank at Pinchbeck West.

Pinchbeck West's windmill.

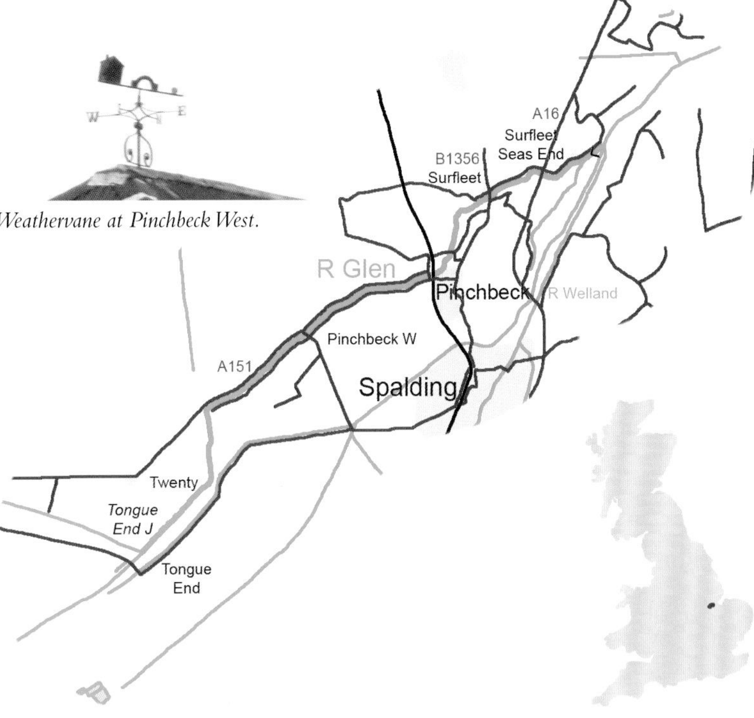

Weathervane at Pinchbeck West.

House, cedar tree and dovecote at Pinchbeck.

Windmill and farm livestock with a difference at Pinchbeck.

Pinchbeck's water tower acts as a landmark by the railway.

may be converted to flats. In the spring the banks are increasingly covered with displays of daffodils. An aerial stands on one site of the river. On the other is a windmill of 1812, armless but with a smart white pixie cap.

Some rather larger houses are seen around Money Bridge, where a moat suggests a significant house was sited.

Spalding Tropical Forest & Rose Gardens Cottage Water Garden Centre occupies 2,000m^2 of glasshouses with oriental gardens, rainforest and desert although a field of alpacas on the riverbank are more interested in boaters. There is another windmill, this time just a tower sited further back from the river.

Pinchbeck's conspicuous landmark is a large white water tower beside the Peterborough–Lincoln railway crossing. Crossgate Bridge leads to Spalding Bulb Museum & Horticultural Exhibition, which has been displaying the industry since 1880.

The river wanders across more fen with shelducks and blackheaded gulls, even the odd hawthorn hedge, until Surfleet, a village which was 3km from the sea in historical times and is where Scott talks in *The Heart of Midlothian* of the possibility of Jeanie Deans being held captive on a lugger for several weeks as it was on the Wash in those days. Here its character changes. It begins with the Mermaid Inn, which had maltings but now has a thatched bar by the river, circular thatched shades over the tables for customers, a mooring pontoon and a plaque on a brick arch promoting the Fens Waterways Link. The adjacent bridge carrying the B1356 has girders which project low over the river from its soffit.

Weeping willows more reminiscent of a Thames back-water lead to the church, an ostentatiously large building, one of several of excessive size resulting from the rivalry between Spalding and Crowland. The tower with its spire leans 1.8m off the vertical, apparently after bowing to a righteous knight. Well, it is not unknown for the elderly to have difficulty straightening up again. Its problems cannot be helped by the weight of a dozen bells. The surrounding trees house a rookery.

On the north bank the owners are proud of the river, lawns and smart gardens sweeping down to the water. The opposite bank has daffodils, later in the spring replaced by reedmace, and the kingfisher is another resident. A slipway allows launching before the Riverside Hotel with more thatched tables by the water. Facilities for boat users on the non tidal part of this river are generally in good condition.

The A16 crosses on the line of what was 42km of almost straight railway from Peterborough to Boston, now abandoned north of Spalding.

Surfleet Seas End is the superior end of the river, including Mediterranean villa arches and a security cam-

A moorhen's nest amongst the reeds at Surfleet.

An arch leads to the Mermaid Inn's thatched bar. Behind, Surfleet's church tower leans.

era covering a landing stage, small boats being moored with increasing regularity. The village is outside the Sea Bank, an ancient earthwork to provide protection against the elements, starting here and running up the west side of the Wash. A large drain joins from the far side of a golf course.

Tidal doors of 1824 prevent passage except at the top end of the tide. The buildings end with the popular Ship, a watering hole overlooking the Reservoir, a hole which often has more mud than water but has tall timber landing points.

The confluence with the River Welland comes just downstream of its confluence with Vernatt's Drain, a difficult environment for the inland navigator connecting up sections of the Fens Waterways Link. No doubt work will be undertaken to remove the tidal bottleneck in due course or, at least, make the wait for the tide a little less messy for boaters.

Weeping willows line the river at Surfleet.

Moorings on the tidal Reservoir at Surfleet Seas End.

Distance
19km from Tongue End to the River Welland

Navigation Authority
Environment Agency

Navigation Society
East Anglian Waterways Association
www.eawa.co.uk

OS 1:50,000 Sheets
130 Grantham
131 Boston & Spalding

24 South Drove Drain

A riot of daffodils

Bales and wind turbines are landmarks in this flat farmland.

Horseshoe Bridge, an early example of reinforced concrete.

A stream arising from gravel workings near Peakirk flows northeast across Lincolnshire to join the River Welland, in time reaching the dimensions needed for a former broad canal. It runs in straight reaches across the fens, the bed of an Ice Age lake. Despite the fact that it flows away from the foot of Kesteven's limestone hills and the local scenery is totally flat, the hills are low enough to hide behind the few hedges, trees and buildings that do appear on this open landscape.

A possible starting point is the Cross Drain between Rectory Farm and Barron's Farm on Deeping Common near **Deeping St James**. A rust coloured ditch runs along the edge of the field from the minor road to meet up with flows over weirs on the Cross Drain from the direction of the two farms to form a channel of canal width although no longer of canal depth. At this point the land is 2m above sea level and the banks are about 2m high, giving shelter from the wind when nothing else does. The water is opaque with floating scum but the surroundings are entirely of crops growing on flat, rich farmland so any pollution is likely to be agricultural in origin.

The many birds include herons, larks, pheasants, tufted ducks, swans, coots, moorhens, mallards, great crested grebes and black headed gulls. Greater reedmace and, more often, bulrushes edge the drain.

To the southeast of Hop Pole the Peterborough–Sleaford railway crosses for the first time on a stretch of line which runs dead straight for 21km. Some 4km to the southeast is **Crowland**.

Near Law's Farm a plank footbridge crosses at water

The South Drove Drain (left) with the North Drove Drain approaching from the distance.

level. If the level is adequate, it may be possible to float over the left end but excessive water will bring the rope handrail into conflict.

Fresh water mussel shells on the bank show that the water is cleaner than its colour suggests.

The South Drove Drain turns north as it approaches the River Welland where Cowbit Wash forms a winter flood area between the River Welland and the New River at Cowbit, the latter with a windmill and a zoo. From here the drain is accompanied by a minor road along the bank as far as Pode Hole.

The A1175 crosses before powerlines, an older trunk road following at Luck's Bridge.

The railway, still on its straight course, comes back over at the edge of Spalding Common. Also appearing in spring are the first of the daffodils along the banks while fields of them can be seen near the drain and glasshouses grow them nearer Spalding. Other yellow spring flowers include coltsfoot and crowfoot.

The following crossing, Horseshoe Bridge, is notable as an early reinforced concrete example, dating from 1910 and perhaps trying to mimic the panelling of older materials.

Pode Hole is a major junction of channels. North Drove Drain flows in from the left and the combined drain is taken in through screens to be pumped on its way. The portage is on the right, left over the A151 and Fenland Cycle Trail bridge and back onto the water in front of the Fisherman's Arms. The pumping station complex is owned by the Welland & Deepings Drainage Board, whose byelaws from the 1870s are displayed on a large board on the front of one of the buildings, just too far away to be read from the road and with another notice prohibiting unauthorized access for those wanting to read them. The buildings include a pumping station museum with steam engines first installed in 1826 although the museum is only open on rare occasions.

Also being pumped in from the left is the Counter Drain. These drains all combine to form Vernatt's Drain, cut by Sir Philibert Vernatti in the 1630s. A pumping station on the left bank of the new wider drain carries the date 1952. The banks are populated by a surprising number of horses although the tranquillity is shattered by jets thundering across the sky to the north.

Steadily, the number of daffodil fields increase. **Spalding** is surrounded by 40km^2 of bulbfields and is the centre of the British flower and bulb industry, using

Pumping stations obstruct the drain at Pode Hole.

1870s byelaws are displayed on the drainage board's buildings.

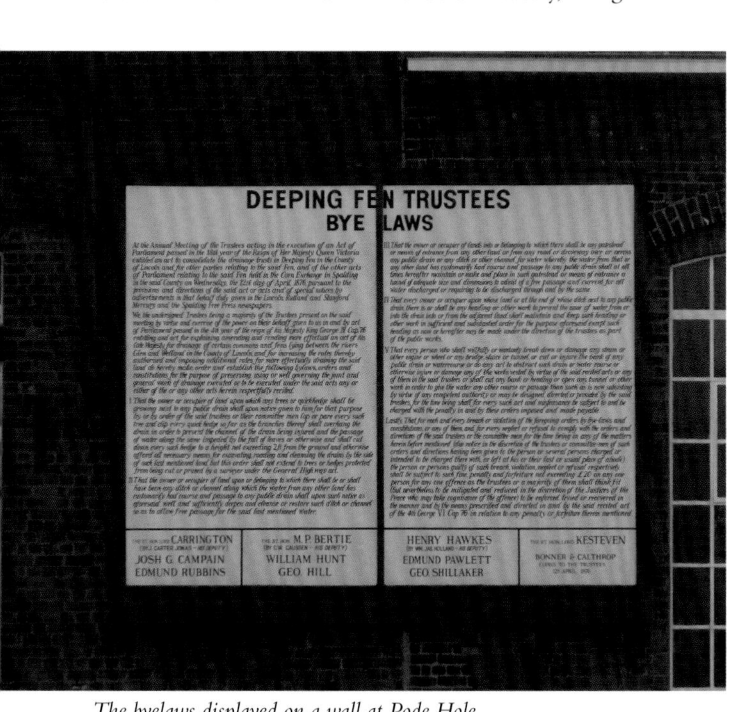

The byelaws displayed on a wall at Pode Hole.

Daffodils growing wild on the bank near the A16.

Owl boxes overlooking fields of cultivated daffodils.

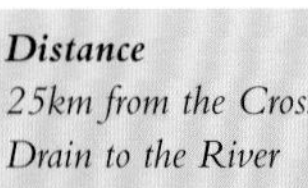

some of the most fertile farmland in the country. A spring trip shows the flowers at their best. A Georgian town, Spalding is the capital of South Holland and has a strong Dutch influence and a long history. The name comes from the Old English spald, a ditch or watercourse, and ingas, the people of an Anglo Saxon tribe, or from the Saxon spalda, a county division. The market has been running for at least 900 years. A feud between Ivo, the standard bearer of William the Conqueror, and St Guthlac's abbey in Crowland continued for centuries right through to the Civil War.

Eventually the railway breaks away from its straight course and turns across the drain as it heads for Lincoln. However, after the B1356, Sharpe's Bridge used to carry the railway for a further 20km on that straight line.

In the distance is the almost detached tower of St Paul's church, unusual for a fenland church in that it is a massive red Victorian structure, built by Sir Gilbert Scott for a wealthy patroness. **Pinchbeck** was a Roman settlement.

The area now grows mostly daffodils and these appear in profusion on the banks of the drain, sometimes swathes of a single variety, sometimes mixes of many kinds, the drain's display of bankside flowers being at their best around Platt's Bridge and where the A16 crosses onto the track of the former railway which it is to follow to Boston.

To the left of the drain on the Blue Gowt is the Pinchbeck Engine & Land Drainage Museum with an 1833 steam beam engine retired in 1952, the year the new pumphouse was built at Pode Hole. The beam engine has a scoop wheel and this was the last beam engine and scoop wheel working in the fens. The museum covers the history of fen drainage.

This was a salt producing area and the enginehouse is built by the 72km long Anglo Saxon Sea Bank although the sea itself is 15km away these days.

Across Pinchbeck Marsh the drain runs parallel to the River Welland, which has been tidal since Spalding, attracting oystercatchers. A high outer bank to the drain allows the fields between the two to act as a wash in the winter and is a suitable site for owl nesting boxes.

Fields of daffodils give way to a golf course at Surfleet Seas End.

Tidal doors lead to the confluence with the River Welland and the River Glen which has picked up the Blue Gowt just outside Surfleet Seas End. Any continuation beyond this point needs to take into consideration the high banks of silt once the tide has dropped. There is limited parking by the confluence, if not too many people are walking dogs at the time, or a proper carpark 200m away in the village.

The Welland joins from the right and the Glen from the left at Surfleet Seas End.

Distance
25km from the Cross Drain to the River Welland

Navigation Society
East Anglian Waterways Association
www.eawa.co.uk

OS 1:50,000 Sheets
(130 Grantham)
131 Boston & Spalding
142 Peterborough

25 River Welland

Britain's bulb capital

Fair Ellayne she walk'd by Welland river,
Across the lily lee:
O, gentle Sir Robert, ye are not kind
To stay so long at sea.
William Morris

Remains of the once-great Crowland Abbey.

From its source near Sibertoft the River Welland flows northeast to the Wash. It is a navigation officially from the Folly River Outfall where it is joined by the Roman Car Dyke which is to be restored as part of the Fens Waterways Link to continue downstream and connect with the River Glen.

The Romans were thought to have used the Welland below Stamford and there was a canal downstream from that town in the 17th century. Just upstream of the confluence there is another junction where the river is rejoined by the 8km Maxey Cut bypassing Market Deeping.

Intersecting the area is the **Peterborough**–Lincoln railway which runs almost straight for 21km to Spalding, a mere half of its original straight line to Boston. In former gravel pits in the midst of this network are the 8ha of Peakirk Waterfowl Gardens with gardens and woodland hosting 700 captive waterfowl, 150 species including ducks, swans, geese, cranes and a breeding colony of Chilean flamingoes.

The channel was improved after the 1947 floods and was straightened and widened after flooding in 1953 so that it is now very wide yet water levels can still change quickly and weed can be a problem as the summer progresses. It is surrounded by alluvial farmland within the former glacial Lake Fenland. Despite the width and banks which are lower than on some rivers in the region there are no striking views. The land is flat to the horizon with crops and wide skies but not even villages most of the way.

Gravel pits on the west side of the river have become the **Deeping** Lakes nature reserve. The river with its weeds might have herons, mallards, greylag geese, coots, oystercatchers and blackheaded gulls.

Peterborough is soon left behind on the east bank so the river flows entirely in Lincolnshire after a wooded decoy is passed, from which direction shooting might be heard.

Most of the drainage is artificial, including the New River which runs parallel on the east side. Occasionally there is a siphon spillway leading off the Welland. Whether the benefits over a simple weir justify the added complexity might be questioned but being plastered with safety stickers does little to reduce the added danger.

An ugly water tower like a silo marks where the B1166 crosses a bridge, low like most on this river, towards **Crowland**, over a kilometre away. The town was founded in 699 by Benedictine monk St Guthlac. Its conspicuous feature is Crowland Abbey, built by Æthelbald in 716 as thanks for regaining his throne without bloodshed. It formed a refuge for Hereward the Wake, as featured in Charles Kingsley's book named after him, but was badly damaged after the Dissolution and again in 1643 by Cromwell. The north aisle remains in use and it has one of the oldest rings of bells in the country, one bell dating from the 15th century.

A notable feature of the town is the Trinity Bridge, built in the 10th century in timber and rebuilt in 1370 in limestone. It is Y shaped, its three steep 3m half spans meeting at 120° to support each other, built by abbey masons perhaps as a parable in stone for the Trinity. It crossed the confluence of the Cattewater, now

The Folly River Outfall. The Maxey Cut joins on the right just out of the picture.

Crowland's triangular bridge once spanned the Welland.

culverted, with the Welland, no longer even visible in the distance. The size of the diminutive arches is a striking lesson on how small the natural rivers were and, with their low gradients, why the fens were so marshy before drainage was undertaken. Until the new channels were cut a habitual problem was fen ague, possibly malaria. This was another Roman salt producing area.

The levées now have very gentle slopes with rock edges to leave the riverside cleaner although reedmace, bulrushes or sedges edge sections. The prevailing wind, used by a windfarm north of Deeping St Nicholas, follows the river so significant waves form in some reaches, matched by waves running along the lines of polyethylene sheet covering swathes of land to force early crops. There are occasional mussel shells. Equally spaced angling platforms stretch away into the distance along the low bank. A few Jacob's sheep might be seen and birds include lapwings, tufted ducks, great crested grebes and moorhens.

Using tulip heads to prepare procession floats for Spalding Flower Festival.

Cowbit stands back from the river but, after powerlines and the A1175 cross, housing begins to appear for the first time. Backed by a rookery, Associated British Bulbs have a large building near one bank of the river facing fields of daffodils grown on the other side. More than half of Britain's bulbs are grown around Spalding, the centre of the British bulb industry with 40km^2 planted. From 1890 to the 1930s the flowers were grown for sale but from then the flower heads were taken off to improve the bulbs. The waste heads have been used since 1959 to decorate floats in the colourful Spalding Flower Festival parade, usually the first Saturday in May, accompanied by such activities as maypole dancing. Although daffodils are still grown in the fields, these days the tulips are grown only for the parade, 8,000,000 of them, mostly in glasshouses. Spalding Pumpkin Festival is in October, this being Europe's largest pumpkin producing area, and potatoes and sugar beet are produced in quantity. The area has high employment and low crime rates.

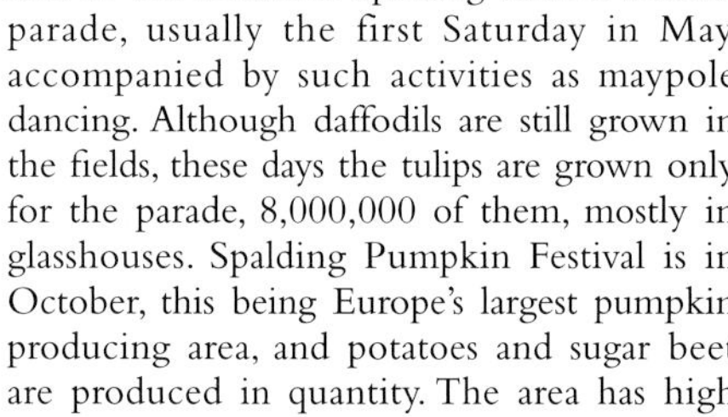

Spalding's fleet of water taxis moored up.

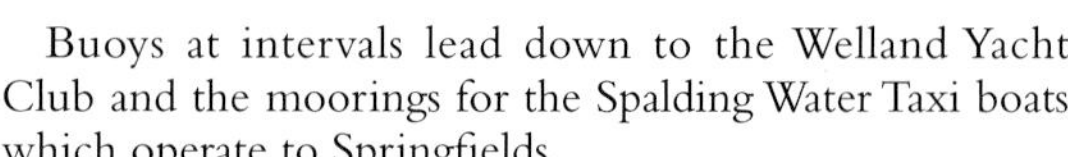

Buoys at intervals lead down to the Welland Yacht Club and the moorings for the Spalding Water Taxi boats which operate to Springfields.

Spalding begins rather austerely with high sheetpiled sides and a sluice where the New River finally joins at Fen End, back from which is the Gordon Boswell Romany Museum with its horse caravans. Just beyond where a railway formerly crossed, the Coronation Channel leaves, built in 1953 to provide a water bypass and prevent flooding in this town which was on the Wash coast in 1086.

Few towns make as good use of their rivers as Spalding does, tree lined avenues down each side, mown grass banks to the water and flowers on the banks. Watering holes overlooking it include the Lincoln Arms, the thatched Olde White Horse, the Lincolnshire Poacher, the Vine and, until a serious fire, the Anchor, now perhaps to be converted to flats. The South Holland Centre caters for the arts. Many of the 18/19th century Georgian buildings show the Dutch influence of the 17th century drainage engineers.

The priory, covering 12ha, was founded in 1052 by Lady Godiva's brother. It was joined by the great castle of Ivo Tailbois, the Lord of Spalding and nephew and standard bearer of William the Conqueror. Rivalry with Crowland grew to involve Hereward the Wake, his uncle, William II, the courts, Bishop Odo, monks, Angers, Anjou, spells, attacks and ambushes on people and animals and a string of dirty tricks allegedly perpetrated by Tailbois. Following the Dissolution, the Prior's Oven cakeshop is all that remains of the priory and castle. The bitter dispute with Crowland continued with the Civil War, however, Spalding backing the Parliamentarians and Crowland the Royalists, Cromwell attacking Crowland in person with a large army from three directions and being faced by Spalding prisoners used as human shields.

The large medieval church of Sts Mary & Nicolas dates from 1284 with extra aisles added to make it almost square, its slim spire rising above its notable 15th century timber roof carried on angel supports and its 1766 brass chandelier. Ayscoughfee Hall Museum & Gardens are based in a 1430s medieval wool merchant's house with great hall, vaulted cellar, ice house, Lutyens war memorial and 2ha garden with 17th century Dutch yew tree walks. It features the fens, drainage, fen skating, agriculture, Spalding and Matthew Flinders.

Spalding Gentlemen's Society Museum promotes the country's second oldest antiquarian society, dating from 1710 and having included Sir Isaac Newton and Alexander Pope as members. It was still new at the time of the 1715 fire which claimed 84 of the town's houses in four hours. Another old society is the Spalding Shipwreck Society, the last around the British coast, paying out a Christmas bonus to the widows of members.

Another unusual church for the fens is the large red brick St Paul's Victorian church by Sir Gilbert Scott, its tower and spire almost separate from the rest of the church.

There are several bridges across, including Spalding Bridge near the Georgian market place. The last carries the A151 near Londis, from where the locality becomes progressively more an industrial estate towards a large Norbert Dentressangle cold store. The tidal limit is at Fulney Lock, built in 1953 as part of the flood prevention scheme with the Coronation Channel, which joins just below. The lock can only be used at the top of the tide.

Set up beyond the channel in 1966 is Springfields, 10ha with one of Britain's best garden shows, herb, knot, sunken, wildflower and woodland gardens, a maze, tulips, hyacinths, daffodils, palm houses, a bulb museum, a carp lake, the Fenscape discovery centre, blown stainless steel statues and an outlet centre. This is the starting point for the Spalding Flower Festival parade at the beginning of May which has been running for 40 years.

Few towns make such good use of their waterfronts as Spalding.

Distance
22km from Peakirk to Spalding

Navigation Authority
Environment Agency

Navigation Society
East Anglian Waterways Association
www.eawa.co.uk

OS 1:50,000 Sheets
131 Boston & Spalding
142 Peterborough

26 River Nene

A rural river producing the capital's leaders

Into a nothingness of scorn and noise,
Into a living sea of waking dreams.
Where there is neither sense of life nor joys
But the huge shipwreck of my esteem
John Clare

The line of the Northampton Arm from Gayton Junction.

The Rothersthorpe Flight looks peaceful enough.

The M1 arch encloses a lock.

Rising north of West Haddon, the River Nene flows northeast to the Wash. It was made navigable to Peterborough in 1761 but the Grand Union Canal Northampton Arm was added in 1815, attracting much traffic from the river to the Grand Union Canal, the route by which most craft approach the Nene.

The original plan of the canal builders was a direct line from Leicester to Northampton but this proved too difficult so the connection was made instead to what is now the main line of the Grand Union Canal. A plateway was built from the main line to Northampton in 1805. A decade later it was replaced by the Northampton Arm of the Grand Union Canal, built for a narrow beam even though the main line and the Nene are wide beam. The former railway has been used for a wide towpath and then for the line of the A43.

The arm leaves the main line at Gayton Junction with its old toll house and passes Gayton Marina. Canada geese, mallards and herons use the water, rabbits are present in number and foxes benefit from these.

The line passes midway between the brick and stone villages of Milton Malsor and Rothersthorpe, the former with the Greyhound pub in 17th century cottages with a playground, the latter with a church containing a Tudor pulpit.

Tiled walls are a feature of the lock cottage by the top lock of the listed Rothersthorpe lock flight. The arm drops 32.9m through 17 locks, the first 13 of which come in 1.5km, bywash flowing in open channels. Four wooden drawbridges cross the flight but appear not to have been used in recent years.

What was once a peaceful route now has the noise of traffic on the A43, to which is increasingly added roar from the M1. The motorway crosses on a large braced concrete arch, before which is a forlorn wire sculpture in a copse adjoining the towpath. It is not simply the M1 here but with Junction 15A and Rothersthorpe Services so vehicular activity is intense.

Approached from the junction but not from local lanes is the Swan Valley development with warehouses near the canal. In 1995 British Waterways lost an important legal case relating to the control of their neighbours and the construction of bridges over and pipelines under the canal.

Osier beds, yellow irises, cow parsley, reedmace, reeds and lilies appear in turn, an environment for azure damselflies and hawker dragonflies. There are big fish in the clear water but the surroundings are changing with a new housing estate being added on the east side by the canal around Wootton or Banbury Road Lock, the narrow

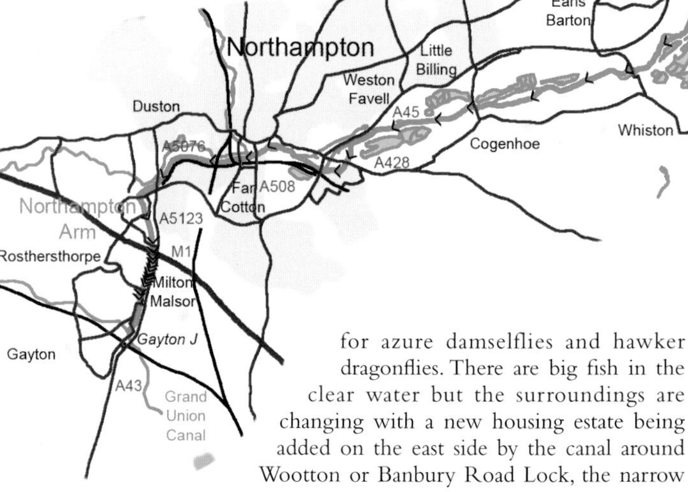

but busy humped bridge over the canal being controlled by traffic lights.

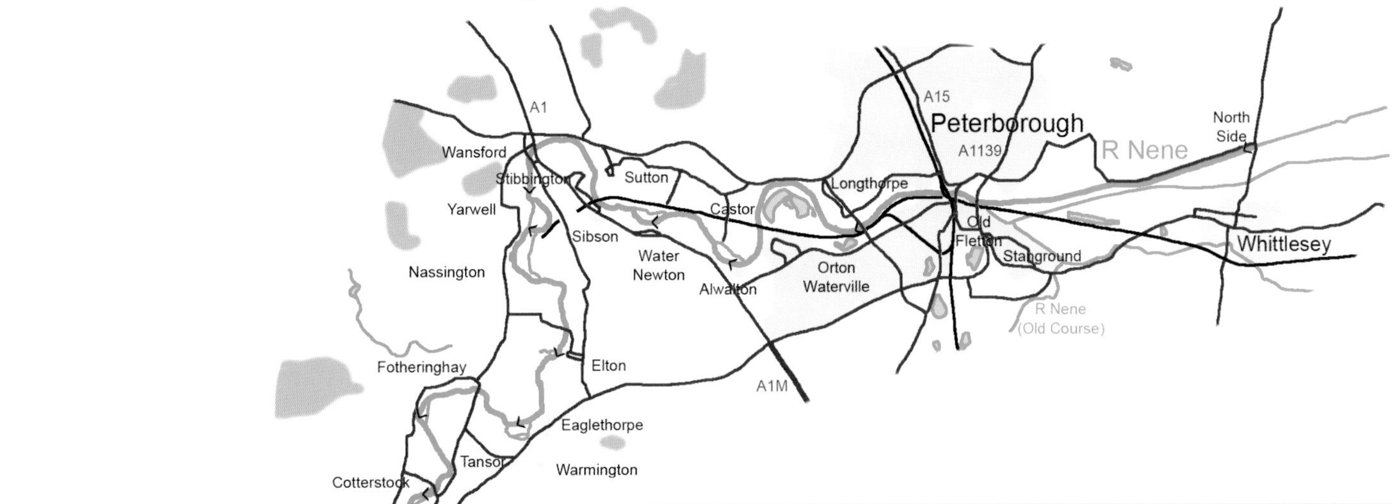

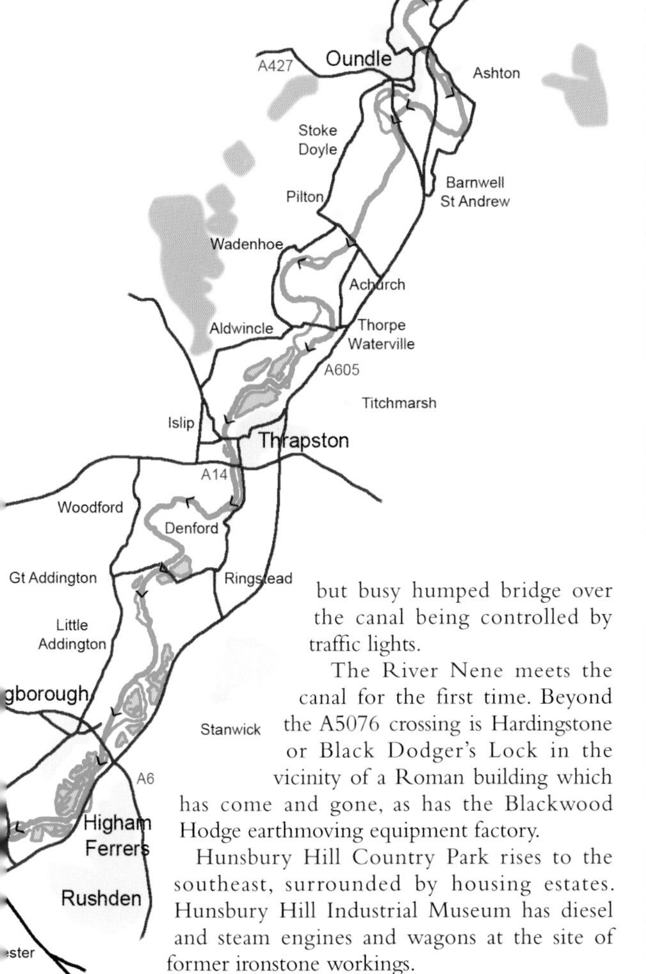

The River Nene meets the canal for the first time. Beyond the A5076 crossing is Hardingstone or Black Dodger's Lock in the vicinity of a Roman building which has come and gone, as has the Blackwood Hodge earthmoving equipment factory.

Hunsbury Hill Country Park rises to the southeast, surrounded by housing estates. Hunsbury Hill Industrial Museum has diesel and steam engines and wagons at the site of former ironstone workings.

Across the valley is the **Northampton** Town Football Club stadium, Northampton Saints Rugby Football Club and, spectacularly, the 127m Grade II National Lift Tower or Northampton Lighthouse of 1982, a freestanding column with three shafts – the UK's only tower for testing lifts.

Duston Mill is older but there was a Roman settlement with a mill and a road from Whilton Lodge, there having been a community here from at least the Iron Age.

Northampton Lock has the Milton Keynes–Northampton railway crossing with lesser lines alongside and to follow across. The final lock, Cotton End, follows the A5123 crossing before the canal joins the River Nene.

The river is almost entirely rural and even Northampton, Wellingborough and Peterborough are passed quickly. The navigation begins at Cotton End opposite the distinctive Carlsberg Tetley brewery of 1973. Purple

The National Lift Tower at Northampton.

The Carlsberg Tetley brewery in Northampton.

loosestrife cloaks the banks while the water itself has algae, becoming an increasing nuisance, especially alongside the A45 although the water clears downstream.

Beside the stone arches of the South Bridge carrying the A508 is the Latimer & Crick warehouse adapted for residential use in an area which has seen further widespread residential development and a new footbridge built across the river. Buddleia adds colour to the banks.

Northampton takes its name from the Old English hamtun, village in the main part of an estate. It was the third largest town in England in 1189, when its charter

was issued, and it had a busy port, the town developing on boot and shoe manufacturing. Northampton Museum & Art Gallery has the world's largest collection of footwear including Roman sandals, Queen Victoria's wedding slippers, Fonteyn and Nijinsky's ballet shoes and boots worn by elephants for crossing the Alps, along with the town's wider history. Leather bottles and a coracle are shown in the Museum of Leathercraft, sited in the 1812 Blue Coat School. The factory system was opposed by shoe manufacturers who had been independent, taking Mondays off unpaid as Saint Mondays in protest.

The Church of the Holy Sepulchre was built in 1100 by Simon de Seulis, the 1st Earl of Northampton, in thanks for his safe return from the Crusades. Based on

Northampton's redeveloped waterfront.

The first of the guillotine locks at Weston Favell.

an original in Jerusalem, it is the largest and best of the four remaining round churches in the UK although it has some battle damage from the Wars of the Roses. In 1170 St Peter's replaced a Saxon church. Semi-circular with angled buttresses, it has one of the finest English Norman interiors and the stone coffin lid of St Ragener, who cured a crippled girl who was praying here.

The medieval market square from 1235 is the largest enclosed market square in England. The town became less enclosed in 1264, however, when Henry III broke down the walls. There was a significant fire in 1516 but not as bad as the one of 1675 which burned down three quarters of the town. Charles II gave a donation for rebuilding All Saints church in 1680, a Grade I building despite being only half its previous size but retaining its 13th century crypt and with fine plaster ceilings, described as the stateliest church of its time outside London. Charles also gave 1,000t of oak for rebuilding the town so May 29th has become Oak Apple Day when an oak wreath is placed on a statue of Charles II.

The Welsh House of 1595 was built for Welsh cattle drovers. Defoe called it the 'handsomest and best built town in this part of England'. To follow was the 1864 Victorian Gothic Guildhall. Charles Rennie Mackintosh carried out his last major commission at 78 Derngate, from the 19th century, which he remodelled in 1916 for W J Bassett-Lowke, the producer of model railways and ships.

To the south of the river is Delapre Park with the 17th century Delapre Abbey, a former Cluniac monastery, one of only two in England, now housing the county

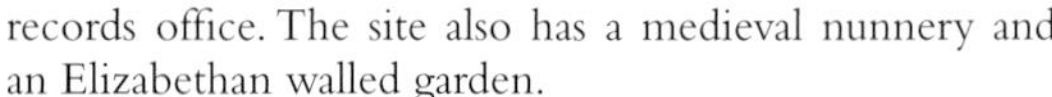

records office. The site also has a medieval nunnery and an Elizabethan walled garden.

The Battle of Northampton took place in 1460 during the Wars of the Roses, when Henry VI was taken prisoner. The town was attacked again in 1643 by Prince Rupert during the Civil War.

There is no towpath but the Nene Way footpath follows the river. The first lock, Northampton, is sited in Becket's Park, where Becket escaped through the town wall gate from the 1164 Council of Clarendon. St Thomas à Becket's Well is a further reminder. A power station and an Avon factory have gone but Northampton Sea Cadets hold their position. Lapwings, golden plovers and migrating birds might be seen around Midsummer Meadow, which runs beside the river, leading to a nature reserve. Rosebay willowherb grows along the banks.

The valley is extensively braided and has numerous gravel pits. The navigation channel is always marked with a small white sign, occasionally hidden by reeds but normally informative, such as below the A45 where the navigation turns off the main channel. Rowers continue on the wide reach to their base, by which is the Nene Whitewater Centre, an artificial canoe slalom course.

The navigation channel passes a Roman pottery site and various sunken cruisers to reach Rush Mills Lock. The A428 and Britannia public house are followed by Abington Lock with its fir trees and dog roses. Weston Favell Lock is the first with a guillotine lower gate, a feature of many of the locks on this river. These were installed in the 1930s for flood control. The Nene floods quickly with heavy rain and Northampton suffered serious flooding in 1998. At such times the locks are reversed, the mitre gates being tied open and the guillotine gates partially lifted. The upper mitre gates have just an open framework above the water so that they weir over into the chamber when closed. The guillotine gate is opened with a low-geared disc wheel, requiring up to 156 turns to lift a gate fully. Below Abington and above Weston Favell Locks are sluices which close automatically across the navigation in times of flood. Water arriving between the two via the wider non-navigation channel is then diverted into old gravel pits and let back into the river below Weston Favell Lock at a controlled rate. These automatic sluices inevitably close the navigation.

Below Weston Favell Lock are huts belonging to Northampton Boat Club and then some superior chalets. A large field of ragwort is edged by arrowhead, where

Kayak anglers at Earls Barton.

A delicate lattice arch farm access bridge near Earls Barton.

The echelon method of getting three cruisers into a Nene lock.

great crested grebes, moorhens and cormorants fish. Horses graze.

Overlooking Clifford Hill Lock is Clifford Hill, one of the largest mottes in the country but with no evidence of a castle, to the extent that there was a bowling green on top in the 17th century.

Below Billing Lock is the restored 18th century Billing Mill with a channel which leads to Billing Aquadrome, a 95ha park in former gravel pits with boating, windsurfing, swimming, a funfair and a miniature railway. Princess Yachts are built here. Billing Lakes are stocked with carp and there are anglers here, on the campsite above the lock and, indeed, in significant numbers all down the river. Billing Wharf is on the river below the lock.

At Cogenhoe, the Anglo-Saxon Cogga's hill, are stone houses and the 12th century St Peter's church. Cogenhoe Lock, bypasses a mill. The odour of effluent becomes more noticeable although whether this is from the water or carried on a westerly breeze from a large sewage works by the aquadrome is not clear. Watercress is no more attractive for it although there is an increasingly healthy growth of duckweed. Teasels also become more frequent.

Whiston and White Mills Locks are to the south of Earls Barton, another shoe manufacturing centre, while the increasingly clear river bends too and fro to Earls Barton Lock, near which was the site of a Roman building.

The views open up past Great Doddington towards Wellingborough, gentle slopes of grain sweeping to meadows. Great Doddington stands above Doddington and Wollaston Locks, its manor house having become a vicarage in days when the church was more affluent. Summer Leys Nature Reserve has hides from which to spot tree sparrows and is one of the best places in the Midlands to see wetland wildlife. Domestic and greylag geese congregate in the banks. Thomas à Becket is thought to have hidden in Hardwater Mill when fleeing from Northampton.

On the edge of the 80ha of woodland forming Irchester Country Park with its woodpeckers and sparrowhawks is Irchester Narrow Gauge Railway Museum, having had an ore railway for its ironstone workings. Little Irchester has Iron Age remains and a Roman town site guarded a ford. Churches to be seen include the 14th century All Hallows' and St Katharine's which has a Catherine wheel weathervane. To the west of Upper Wellingborough Lock is Wellingborough prison.

After the A45 and A509 crossings is the 1866 Victorian

Mill buildings in Wellingborough, located for water transport.

Wellingborough has a surfeit of swans.

The old A6 bridge at Irthlingborough.

Owls have a choice of waterside housing options.

Canada geese below St Mary the Virgin's church at Woodford.

Whitworth's mill. **Wellingborough**, the Old English Wendel's burg or fort, is a Victorian brick town with footwear and clothing industries but it barely meets the river. Weetabix is a better known name from its business enterprises.

The Waendel Walk takes place in May. Water play in the fountains next to the river take place whenever it is warm and swans are fed in a great flock in front of a line of copper beeches and horse chestnut trees.

Between two former railway crossings the River Ise joins and Lower Wellingborough Lock is surrounded by security fencing although there is a small gap at the bottom end for those needing to escape to the adjacent field of horses or the portage platforms. Himalayan balsam is seen increasingly.

The 107m long twin Wellingborough viaducts of 1857 have 14 arches carrying the Leicester–St Pancras railway but one has an easier gradient than the other for freight.

Ditchford Bridge has had a bridge since 1292 but it also acquired a station and was so popular for recreation that it was referred to as Ditchford on Sea. The station has gone and the recreation today takes place on Skew Bridge Ski Lake or as quieter groups setting off in hired canoes from beside Ditchford Lock. Broadholme sewage works and the smells from a recycling plant in an old mill make it less of a holiday venue than in the past.

The river is diverted into artificial cut to accommodate the A45 past **Higham Ferrers**, named after the Saxon hecham – settlement on a hill – and Count de Fereris, who received the manor in the 12th century. The town with its stone houses has a 13th century market cross and was the birthplace of Henry Chichele, Archbishop of Canterbury from 1414 to 1443. It also has associations with H E Bates.

King's footbridge is the longest and highest on the canal system, the EA's response to repeated complaints of damage after collisions with the previous low bridge.

North of Higham Ferrers Lock is **Irthlingborough**, yirtlingaburg having been a ploughman's fortified place. Its various delights include the Nene Park, **Rushden** & Diamonds Football Club, the smell of a tannery and a windfarm near Burton Latimer. A college was founded by John Pyel, a local who became Lord Mayor of London in 1473. St Peter's is a 14th century collegiate church, the porch of which has doors at the four cardinal points and is 12m from the detached 19th century belltower, built to replace a 13th century tower which had developed a lean.

A railway bridge has been dismantled so the next crossing is the 1936 viaduct carrying the A6, a rather utilitarian concrete structure. Beyond is Irthlingborough Bridge, a 14th century Ancient Monument with nine 4m stone spans, its crossed keys of St Peter identifying it with Peterborough Abbey. Nearby was the Dr Martens factory, makers of the uniform footwear for skinheads.

Beyond Irthlingborough Lock are Stanwick Lakes with their great crested newts and terns opposite the Rock UK Activities centre which has children climbing by and canoeing on the river. To the north of the lakes is the site of Mallows Cotton village, abandoned because of the Black Death. Little Addington held Second World War prisoners.

An estate of beehives and then assorted owl boxes precede Upper Ringstead Lock near Great Addington. The former railway down the valley crosses for the first of three times in just over 2km by rail, somewhat further by river, before Lower Ringstead Lock. Boats are hired from the marina at Willy Watt Mill, the name a corruption of willow islands. The site was in use in 1086, since when it has ground grain, bones for fertilizer and for cloth and paper. The ghost of Lydia Atley haunted the area for two decades after going to meet her lover in 1850 until her skeleton was eventually found in a ditch.

The 15ha Ringstead Grange Trout Fishery for trout and salmon was set up in 1980. The 55ha Kinewell Lake Local Nature Reserve has insects, migrating birds and excavations which revealed a 10m diameter Iron Age hut site and the location of a Roman building with a tessellated floor. There is also Blackthorn Lake Marina. Ringstead means circular place and its buildings include St Mary's church with a 13th century tower.

Woodford Riverside Marina is tucked away below the Three Hills tumuli, a Neolithic or Bronze Age burial ground. It is a water tower which is particularly conspicuous as successive reaches point towards it.

The Saxon village of Woodford is dominated by the church of St Mary the Virgin, which looks down over river margins dotted with forget-me-nots and an area where there are signs of old housing towards the river. John Styles lost the church in 1550 because of his Catholic beliefs and fled with the chalice to Belgium, where he died. His replacement, Andrew Powlet, recovered the chalice and a heart. Powlet's ghost was seen by a panel in the rectory in 1862, removal of which revealed the chalice and a letter leading to a heart in a church pillar, where it is now displayed. It may have been that of Roger de Kirketon, the lord of the manor who died in Norfolk in 1280, or of another lord of the manor, Sir Walter Trailly, who died on Crusade a decade later. A 1964 photograph of the altar showed the ghost of a knight kneeling at it.

Woodford House was often visited by the Duke of Wellington and owner General Charles Arbuthnot began mining on his land for iron ore. Woodford Shrubbery or Stone Pit Common was used by limestone miners for illegal drinking sessions. Poplar trees now lead the way to Woodford Lock.

Denford, valley ford, is a village of stone and brick houses and with ridge and furrow remains. The 13th century Grade I Holy Trinity church has ashes and hawthorns among the trees in the nature reserve in the churchyard and there was a windmill on a mound. The river has pollarded willows and Aylesbury ducks with Denford Lock.

The A14 crosses at **Thrapston**, as does a high disused railway viaduct in blue brick. Not least of the crossings is the 13th century medieval bridge of nine arches, five of which had to be rebuilt after a flood in 1795. The market charter was given in 1205 by King John and St James' church is also 13th century with the stars and stripes coat of arms of the Washington family which was later to be used for the American flag. There was an old castle sited in the village and it was also the home of Second World War air writer John Smith.

Islip, meaning slippery place, has the Perpendicular church of St Nicholas and a secret passage from Islip House to the Woolpack Inn. This reach of the river, fringed by weeping willows, is particularly attractive, a credit to the architects of the new housing on the Thrapston side who have left open grass down to the water rather than squeezing in as many houses as possible.

From Islip Lock, accompanied by a mill which is now residential, the locks tend to be more widely spaced and there are more water meadows and less gravel pits although not immediately. Thrapston Lagoon is one of the country's biggest and is used by the Middle Nene Sailing Club. Water birds are attracted. The Gartree Roman road from Leicester to Godmanchester crossed here with a fork going off along the valley to Water Newton, parts of a causeway and bridge remaining. Another subtle change hereabouts is the pronunciation from Nen to Neen.

Titchmarsh Nature Reserve is in 80ha of old gravel workings where Lord Lilford had a duck decoy in 1885 and there are a large heronry and sand martins.

The Environment Agency installed solar panels to operate Titchmarsh Lock but they were stolen so conventional methods continue. Adjacent are a marina, the headquarters of the Middle Nene Cruising Club and the Grade II Titchmarsh Mill, now residential.

Thorpe Waterville has a large medieval thatched barn which was part of a castle and a moat which remains from the Waterville family house. A road leads over the Nene and over the 14th century Brancey Bridge, crossing a tributary, Harper's Brook, to Aldwincle. The name of the stone village means bend in the river. It has a scarecrow festival and two medieval churches. St Peter's has 14th century glass but All Saints' is disused although Dryden was born in its thatched rectory in 1631. There are tench in the river.

Wadenhoe means Wada's spur of land and, with its thatched stone cottages, is probably Saxon although it has a Neolithic mortuary and two Bronze Age barrows. Dominating the approach is the Norman St Michael & All Angels' church with its saddleback-roofed belltower, musical bells and unusual head corbels. There is a memorial to a couple killed by bandits in Salerno in 1824 while on honeymoon but the bloodstains on the floor are not the usual record of some grisly murder but of a lady falling down the steps while arriving late for Harvest Festival. The waterside near the King's Head is particularly attractive but this is not just a picturesque sleepy backwater, having been the first village in the country to have telegraph when local landowner George Ward Hunt became Disraeli's Chancellor of the Exchequer and needed good communication. Wadenhoe Lock bypasses a watermill and the village has a circular dovecote of 1650 and a manor house.

Denford's Holy Trinity church stands back from Denford Lock.

The disused railway viaduct at Thrapston.

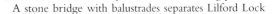

Thrapston's medieval bridge.

Achurch has existed since the Iron Age and takes its name from the Saxon aas kirk, waterside church. St John the Baptist's church was rebuilt by Sir Asceline de Waterville after his safe return from the Crusades, complete with spire, but the folly in the churchyard is Lilford church, rebuilt here is 1788. The houses were rebuilt as an estate in 1830. Achurch Meadow has redshanks, snipe and over a hundred flowering plant species. The Linches were part of Rockingham Forest, also called Bareshanks after Black Watch deserters were caught here in 1743. Notable sons of the village were William Peake, born in 1603, to become Lord Mayor of London, and Alfred Leete in 1882, known for his First World War 'Your Country Needs You' recruiting poster.

A stone bridge with balustrades separates Lilford Lock

Longhorn cattle graze below Wadenhoe church.

St John the Baptist's church, Achurch.

Lilford Park silhouetted above the river in the morning sun.

from Saxon Lilford which was cleared in 1755 for the 97ha Lilford Park. A 1635 Ketton stone Jacobean hall is a vital part of the estate which includes a water tower and children's farm animals. Lord Lilford introduced the little owl to Britain, built aviaries and wrote *The Birds of Northamptonshire*. In 1889 an ox roast was held on the frozen river.

There are moats on both sides of the river, the one at Pilton with a manor house and the Grade II St Mary & All Saints' church. Another moat was dug at Stoke Doyle, a village with an unofficial road sign provided by one of the villagers, twinning it with Barcelona. The river is increasingly used by young rowers and the kite has spread this far.

A restaurant and bar occupy the magnificent 17th century Oundle Mill on a site which was already in use in 875. Alongside is Upper Barnwell Lock and the 15ha Barnwell Country Park is close with lakes, ponds, meadows, hides, the UK's largest colony of noctule bats, newts, angling, bowls and a children's activity area. A minor road bridge is lined underneath on both sides with swallows' nests and is followed by Oundle Cruising Club, Oundle Marina in old gravel workings and the Fairline factory. Coots are other water users.

Below Lower Barnwell Lock the A605 makes two crossings of a long river loop. Between them is Ashton Lock. Ashton is a village of thatched stone cottages, recreated in 1900 by Charles Rothschild. A lead baptism trough is associated with a Roman settlement, the school dates from 1705, the Victorian power station has a bygones museum, the thatched Chequered Skipper recalls that this was the last venue in England for this butterfly before it became extinct, there are Oundle School's Stahl Theatre and Ashton Mill and, since 1965, the village has hosted the world conker championships every October. Polo ponies were trained here by Cream's Ginger Baker and Clark Gable was stationed locally with the USAF.

Oundle Bridge, carrying the A427, was built in 1571 after floods destroyed its predecessor. **Oundle** is the oldest English town built in stone, dating from the Iron Age although most of the current buildings are 17th or 18th century, grey stone with Collyweston slate roofs. The Anglo-Saxon Undels were united or landless people. There was formerly a monastery to St Wilfred, a museum covering the town's Roman and Saxon history. Oundle School, one of the country's largest independent schools, was founded in the 14th century and promoted in 1556 after the Dissolution by grocer William Laxton, who became a Lord Mayor of London. Canal enthusiast Sir Peter Scott was a former pupil.

There has been a market since Saxon times. The 13th century St Peter's church in Early English, Decorated and Perpendicular styles has a 66m spire and a pre-Conquest coffin lid from a 7th century church. The Talbot Hotel was rebuilt in 1626 with a staircase and stone from Fotheringhay Castle. Latham's Hospital consists of almshouses from 1611 and the former White Horse Inn was only thirty years newer. Bramston House is 18th century. Oundle Museum covers local history from Roman times and Southwick Hall has Victorian and Edwardian costumes. Oundle International Festival offers classical and organ music, jazz, theatre and film while the Drummingwell was said to have drummed before important events. Beyond the bridge is the 120m Oundle Wharf cut.

A mill bypasses Cotterstock Lock. Cotterstock had a Roman pottery kiln, the Elizabethan Cotterstock Hall manor with fine gardens where Dryden wrote many of his fables and the 12th century St Andrew's church with ancient deer drawings on an earlier site.

Tansor has St Mary's church with choirstalls from Fotheringhay church. Perio Mill stands beyond Perio Lock with Bluebell Lakes to the east side.

Fotheringhay probably takes its name from fodring eg, foddering island. Approach is dominated by the 1441 Perpendicular former collegiate church of St Mary & All Saints, partly destroyed at the Dissolution but still big with a large lantern tower topped by a gilt coated fettered falcon weathervane, the logo of the House of York who funded the church, and with a pulpit donated by Edward IV. The village of thatched cottages and forge are insignificant by comparison, even with a bright orange windsock flying near the 18th century stone bridge.

Little more than a 12th century motte remains of Fotheringhay Castle, which was built to guard the river crossing. Richard III was born here in 1452 and Mary, Queen of Scots was held here and executed in the former Great Hall in 1587. Scots thistles grow on the mound where she planted them and a ghostly mist is said to form on the river on February 8th, the anniversary of her execution.

The countryside gradually becomes flatter and again a former railway crossing is missing.

For no obvious reason, many of the canoe portage platforms on the river are enclosed by fences with spring loaded gates, requiring an extra person to hold the gate open. Warmington Lock, crossed by cyclists on the Nene Way as well as those portaging, has two sprung gates

Oundle Mill and Upper Barnwell Lock.

just over arms' length apart, requiring two gate holders or methods of propping them open, enough to foil the most intelligent of Houdini cattle tendencies. There is no platform at the upstream end but the steps to the low section of platform at the downstream end are completely enclosed by fence with no gate at all. Many of the other locks on the river have steps which are either padlocked or so convoluted that it is difficult to use them while carrying a boat.

Eaglethorpe was founded by the Danes but depopulated in the 16th century by the expansion of Elton Park. Alders were used for matches and the mill is now occupied by Fired Earth. A dovecote for 800 birds, built from mortar on a wood frame, is an Ancient Monument and there is also a Beaker burial site.

The right bank changes from Northamptonshire to Cambridgeshire before Elton Hall, a house here since the Conquest. The 15th century gatehouse and crypt survived the Cromwell demolition and the hall was rebuilt in 1666 by Sir Thomas Proby, whose family had lived here throughout so there is a mixture of medieval, Gothic and classical styling. There are Gainsborough and Reynolds paintings, Henry VIII's prayerbook and knot, parterre and sunken gardens in which Repton was involved. Elton Park has a Gothic orangery and Ratty Island, named because Kenneth Graham spent many summers here. A Roman road explains the sites of five Roman buildings. Elton means prince's farm while Stocks Green is more modern, the stocks still present. All Saints' church has a William Morris window and Saxon graves. The village has thatched cottages. Elton Lock is below the Willow Brook confluence, accompanied by a three storey mill of 1840 on a site which was in use in 1086.

Sibson Aerodrome stands back from the right bank

Cattle watch the activity at Lower Barnwell Lock.

but parachutes and even a biplane might be seen to show that it is in use while an egret may glide over the river. Again the dismantled railway no longer crosses.

Nassington was the headland dwellers' farm although the Romans built here for ironstone extraction. The 13th century Grade I prebendal manor is the oldest inhabited building in Northamptonshire with a 15th century dovecote, a tithe barn museum, Europe's largest recreated 14th century medieval gardens and fishponds, rare breed pigs, sheep, hens, geese and ducks and prehistoric barrows. The Grade I All Saints' church has a Saxon nave, Saxon cross, cemetery with 65 Saxon graves and 14th century wall paintings.

The 16th century Oundle Bridge.

St Andrew's church by the river at Cotterstock.

A different railway no longer crosses, after which there are a caravan site and moorings, accompanied by a piece of driftwood sculpted into a monster of the deep. Yarwell produced limestone, clay and gravel.

Where the two missing railway lines previously joined beyond Yarwell Lock is the head of the Nene Valley Railway, about to dive into a tunnel. The river loops back to Yarwell where St Mary Magdalene church is partly 13th century. The village was also a producer of newsprint until an explosion in 1855, Stibbington House having papermills in the grounds by Wansford Lock during the 18th and 19th centuries.

The remains of the Old Sulehay Forest stand on the hillside to the west before the bank changes from Northamptonshire to Peterborough after a 3ha nature reserve and before St Mary the Virgin's church with its Saxon windows.

Sheep may safely graze: St Mary & All Saints, Fotheringhay.

The ancient dozen-arched stone bridge carried the Great North Road until 1930 although it has only a single carriageway. It was in use by 1221, when it needed repair. The seven arches at the northern end were built in the 16th century, the next three in 1674 with spans to 7.8m after floods, a 15m span of 1795 replaced a pair lost to a flood and the final arch dates from the 17th century, a total of over 180m with large cutwaters. These days the road is the A6118.

A further flooding incident involved one Barnabee, sleeping out to avoid the plague and choosing a haystack while rather the worse for drink. A flood carried the haystack away with its passenger until colliding with the bridge, waking up the boater. He called up to ask where he was. 'Wansford,' came the reply.

'Wansford where?'

'Wansford in England.' That is the name which now appears on the village sign. Adjacent is the Haycock Hotel of 1670 although some of it is from the 13th century. It has a magnificent walled garden, the wall having kept out subsequent haystacks and flood barriers across the gateways keep out the worst of the floodwater carrying them.

The northbound carriageway of the A1, which follows, crosses a single 33m span of 1930, the largest mass concrete arch on British roads. An aerial stands near the Wansford pumping station intakes for Rutland Water. Also nearby is the 2km^2 Sacrewell Farm & Country Centre with 1755 buildings, a three storey working watermill, Romano-British villas, prehistoric circles and a hedge maze. Neolithic implements have been found.

On the south bank is Stibbington Marina. There have been Roman pottery finds at the 1625 Stibbington Hall, from where there used to be a ford across to Sutton.

The Nene Valley Railway, built in 1838, closed in 1972 and since reopened as a steam line, crosses at Wansford station. Locomotives and rolling stock from nine countries are in use and engine coal has been delivered by narrowboat, being lifted from the river by steam crane. The line has been used for filming *Hannay*, *London's Burning*, *Christobel*, *Octopussy*, *Goldeneye* and *Peter's Friends*. More importantly, it was the line on which the Rev W Audrey based the Thomas the Tank Engine stories.

Water Newton's St Remigius' church was named after the Roman Bishop of Rheims. The 17th century Water Newton House has a perfect setting or would have were it not for the roar of traffic on the A1. Below Water Newton Lock is the three storey mill of 1791 with its mansard roof, striking when seen from downstream. The Roman Ermine Street crossed a fortified ford to reach the Roman town of Durobrivae. Of 2ha and walled with another 1km^2 of suburbs, it was comparable with London at the time. There was a large Romano-British pottery with an intensive industrial site at Normangate Field.

On the north side is Castor with one of the largest Roman buildings in England at the present churchyard of St Kyneburgha's church, built in the 7th century using some of the Roman stone. Rebuilt in 1124, it is one of the best Norman churches in the country with a richly carved Norman tower, an angel roof and three wall paintings of the martyrdom of St Catherine. In 1975 a hoard of 27 pieces of 3rd or 4th century Christian plate, the Water Newton Treasure, was found in the village, the earliest church plate from the Roman empire. Pottery Castorware itself was exported throughout the empire. The name is from castra – camp – abbreviated from Kyniburgacastra, an early nunnery set up by Kyniburga and Kyneswitha, the daughters of Paeda – the first Christian king of Mercia. One day they were attacked by three men and dropped the loaves they were carrying. It was claimed that these formed a thorn hedge which the men hacked through to emerge bleeding, only to fall into a bottomless pit which opened in front of them.

Back Dike flows parallel with the main channel past Alwalton Lock and Peterborough Cruising Club. In the 18th century Alwalton was the head of navigation on the river.

Little remains of Fotheringhay Castle.

St Andrew's church has a 12th century doorway, a 13th century transept tower and the grave of Henry Royce, born in the village. The village was also home in the 1860s to another motor man, Frank Perkins, founder of Perkins Engines.

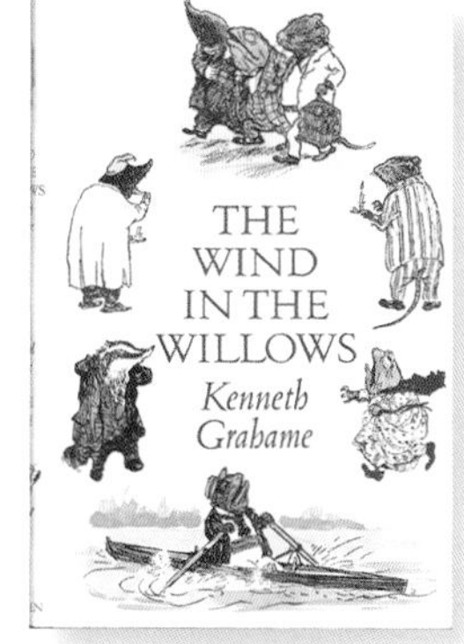

Lynch Lodge was the two storey Jacobean porch to Dryden's house at Chesterton manor, moved here in 1807 as the lodge to Milton Park at the other end of a former 5km drive. Alwalton marble, actually limestone, was produced from a quarry by the Romans. Leofwine gave the manor house to Peterborough Abbey in the 11th century. Many visitors to the village come to the East of England Showground with Britain's second largest agricultural show. As the river enters **Peterborough** completely, Peterborough Business Park fills the gap to Orton Wistow, where the Nene Valley Railway crosses back.

Driftwood art at Yarwell.

The haycock-stopping Wansford Bridge.

The A1 crosses Britain's largest mass concrete road arch.

The 2km^2 Ferry Meadows Country Park stretches for 10km and includes 49ha of linked Gunwade, Lynch and Overton gravel pits from the 1970s, meadows, woods, boating, windsurfing, angling, golf and a miniature railway.

Robin Hood and Little John are stones on the opposite bank. The three arched Milton Ferry Bridge of 1716 in ashlar limestone, with triangular cutwaters and fluted keystones, has two rooms in the north abutment, complete with doors and bullseye windows. Carrying what was never a public road, Defoe was charged half a crown to cross with a carriage in 1724, an exorbitant sum, perhaps making it the highest toll in the country. It now gives access to the 10km^2 Nene Park.

Up from the river is an aerial and, beyond, the Longthorpe Tower of about 1300 added to an existing fortified manor of similar age. With walls 2m thick, it has the best 14th century domestic wall paintings in northern Europe, England's most complete set of the period with *Bible* and East Anglian countryside scenes, although they were only revealed from under their coating of limewash and distemper by the disturbance of a Second World War bomb. St Botolph's church has a leper window.

"Yes, Sir," Percy shivered miserably

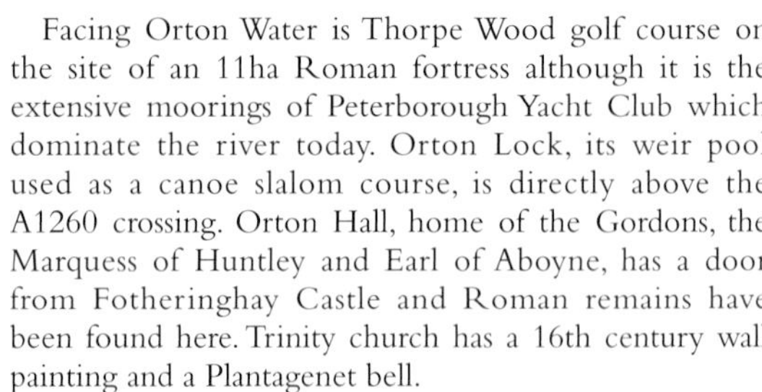

Facing Orton Water is Thorpe Wood golf course on the site of an 11ha Roman fortress although it is the extensive moorings of Peterborough Yacht Club which dominate the river today. Orton Lock, its weir pool used as a canoe slalom course, is directly above the A1260 crossing. Orton Hall, home of the Gordons, the Marquess of Huntley and Earl of Aboyne, has a door from Fotheringhay Castle and Roman remains have been found here. Trinity church has a 16th century wall painting and a Plantagenet bell.

Clear patches in the bank vegetation, marked with numbered angling pegs, front a sculpture park and the regatta course near a cross, holy well and Thorpe Hall, a Sue Ryder home.

Woodston's former staunch was the tidal limit until Dog-in-a-Doublet sluice was built. St Augustine's church tower is partly Anglo-Saxon. The trees lining the river manage to hide most of the city except for the row of bridges in the centre. The first is the Railworld footbridge, the centre itself featuring steam, modern and hover trains and model railways by the terminus of the Nene Valley Railway. It is followed by the Peterborough–Norwich line and then two bridges for the East Coast Main Line. The first is a large Whipple Murphy truss, giving two extra lines of capacity to the two original lines carried on three 20m spans with 2.6m rise, lattice spandrels and fluted columns – the last remaining cast iron bridge on a British high speed route. The 1934 Peterborough Bridge with its stone arches is on the site of Godfrey of Croyland's 1308 bridge and carries one of the A15s under Peterborough's confusing road numbering system. The Charter's Bar and Grain Barge are floating restaurants moored above and below it.

Atheleda agreed to marry Paeda if he converted to Christianity, which he did, founding St Peter's as a Benedictine monastery church in 655. It was destroyed by the Danes in 870 and rebuilt in 972 by St Æthelwold. Even though protected by 150 knights, the Norman prelate Turold and his church's treasure were captured by Hereward the Wake in 1070 but a vision of St Peter resulted in Hereward's taking them back. It was burned down accidentally in 1116 and

The Nene Valley Railway crosses the river.

An idyllic setting at Water Newton (except for the traffic roar).

rebuilt in Barnack limestone with a high wooden roof in 1118–1238. The serious damage by Cromwell's men in 1643, including smashing most of the glass, was not accidental. Peterborough Cathedral is one of the finest Norman buildings in the country, including the earliest painted nave ceiling in England from about 1220, the best example of Romanesque art in Europe. The 13th century Early English triple arched west front is totally unique. There are the remains of the 14th century Chapel of St Thomas of Canterbury, fan vaulting of 1496–1508, a Norman apse, a mosaic sanctuary floor, a font of Alwalton marble, a partly Norman Great Gate and 19th century stained glass by William Morris. It has the grave of Catherine of Aragon, which may have been why it survived the Dissolution and was upgraded to a cathedral, together with the standard of Henry VIII given by Elizabeth II, the grave of Mary, Queen of Scots before she was moved to Westminster Abbey and the tomb of gravedigger Robert Scarlett who buried them both and dug other graves for more than twice the total population of Peterborough.

A medieval vineyard was established in about 1140, the church of John the Baptist dates from 1407 and the Guildhall or Butter Cross from 1671. The 16th century Customs House, scheduled as an Ancient Monument, had a navigation light and is now used by the Sea Scouts. In 1968 Peterborough was designated as a new town and expanded greatly in the 1970s and 1980s. The 1982 Queensgate shopping centre was voted the best in Europe the year after it was opened.

Peterborough Museum & Art Gallery covers local history from 4000 BC, geology, archaeology, natural and social history and has the world's largest collection of prisoner of war work including Napoleonic carved ships and bones.

On the south side of the river former engine sheds have been restored for an arts centre. New Fletton is a name synonymous with bricks. The A1139 crosses, accompanied by Asda, an athletics track, a greyhound stadium and Peterborough United Football Club. A gently stepped embankment lined with weeping willows has a slipway.

Peterborough is 6m above sea level at the edge of what was the glacial Lake Fenland. From here the Old Course of the River Nene, the Stanground Branch, heads southeast under the Peterborough–Norwich railway to the King's Dike while the current course of the River Nene is eastward across obvious fen in a nearly straight artificial cut.

The speed limit is removed for 1.6km from Fitzwilliam Bridge to allow water skiing. Flowing parallel is Morton's Leam, used as the main navigation channel in earlier days.

Water Newton Mill with its mansard roof.

Nene Valley Railway diesel with blood and custard rolling stock.

Milton Ferry Bridge which Defoe crossed at a price.

Assorted bridges in Peterborough.

The line of Cnut's Dyke is crossed and this section of the Nene will form part of the Fens Waterways Link as far as the Roman Car Dyke. *Songs of Praise* came from the 1993 Inland Waterways Festival here, glossing over the vandalism of a specially installed mooring ring by a swan before the concrete had set, requiring replacement.

As the south bank changes from Peterborough to Cambridgeshire the landscape is one of powerlines, wind turbines and brickwork chimneys in addition to the clay pits excavated across the area for the brickworks. The 2.4km^2 Nene Washes nature reserve has marsh and wet meadows, home to blacktailed godwits, redshanks, winter ducks and breeding waders.

The Fen Causeway Roman road crossed near the Flag Fen sewage works. The Flag Fen lake settlement, occupied from Neolithic to Roman times, has been excavated extensively and produced the biggest collection of Bronze Age material in Europe, including England's oldest wheel. The 12ha archaeological park, now partly flooded to prevent drying out, has replica Iron and Bronze Age roundhouses, a museum of finds and rare breeds.

A recent footbridge curves across the river towards **Whittlesey**. In 2006 a submerged car, missing since 1999, was recovered with body parts inside.

Dog-in-a-Doublet Lock at North Side includes a fish pass of 1998. The Dog-in-a-Doublet name came from a leather jerkin made by the publican's wife for the decoy man's terrier after it lost all its fur to skin disease. The river is tidal from here and only useable at certain stages of the tide.

Distance
101km from Gayton Junction to North Side

Navigation Authority
Environment Agency

Navigation Society
Association of Nene River Clubs
www.anrc.org.uk

OS 1:50,000 Sheets
141 Kettering & Corby
142 Peterborough
152 Northampton & Milton Keynes
153 Bedford & Huntingdon

Connections
Grand Union Canal – see CoB p54
Tidal River Nene – see RoB p163

Pylons, wind turbines and brickwork chimneys near Whittlesey.

Dog-in-a-Doublet Lock at North Side, the tidal limit.

27 Whittlesey Dike

The direct route to the fens

From **Peterborough** the River Nene is taken in a series of long straight cuts through Wisbech to the Wash at Guy's Head. This was not always so, the old course of the River Nene twisting across the fens to become a tributary of the River Great Ouse. Various channels provide other route options, the most important of which is that provided by King's Dike and Whittlesey Dike, now the main navigation channel of the Middle Level Navigations from the River Nene eastwards across Cambridgeshire to the River Great Ouse. Thus, it is well maintained. Weed ropes are placed across the river from June onwards.

The River Nene old course leaves the current cut to the west of the A1139 which crosses at the southern end of Peterborough and is crossed immediately by the Peterborough–Ely railway.

Morton's Leam leaves via a sluice at Stanground. Cut in 1478–90 by Bishop John Morton of Ely, it is 12m wide and 1.2m deep, the first large straight cut in the fens to improve the gradient, bypassing part of the old course of the River Nene.

Horsey Sluice on the River Nene old course, where King's Dike leaves, has been converted from a lock to a set of sluice gates so that non-portable craft have no option but to take the new cut. Immediately west of the junction has been used as a swans' nest site.

There is just room for a vehicle between the gas compound and King's Dike. Horsey Hill, site of a Civil War fort, is 300m to the south on the other side of the busy A605 which follows the river for 2km.

The water is opaque because of its use by powered craft. Indeed, some are moored behind houses which occasionally back onto the dike. The banks are low, allowing extensive views. Prominent is McCain's factory for turning the local potatoes from this agricultural area into oven-ready chips.

Willows and teasels dot the banks and skylarks twitter overhead. In due course the A605 crosses and moves away while the dike is hemmed in by a wall of large straw bales.

The dominant feature at King's Dike is the London Brick Company's works with several tall chimneys, wind turbines and deep clay pits between them and the dike, an excavator with a massive triangular frame on the front extracting the clay. A northerly wind brings the pungent sulphurous smell of brick kilns. In 2010 six Bronze Age wooden dugout boats from 1300 BC were excavated from the bed of a former course of the River Nene at Must Farm, in excellent condition with decorative wood carving well preserved, Britain's oldest boats. With them were large quantities of clothing, spears, swords, fish weirs and eel traps.

Beyond the Peterborough–Ely railway, which now crosses over, is a stand of poplar trees, conspicuous in the flat landscape. They surround a former scrapyard, keeping it well hidden and providing a hunting ground for kestrels. With cars piled up behind the screen a notice on the gates reads 'Car park. Patrons only.' This might be read as 'Trespassers will be dismantled.'

Whittlesey is the only place of any size on the dike, having developed on the agriculture and brickmaking which sustain it today. Its windmill is not seen from the dike but the spire of St Mary's church, the finest spire in Cambridgeshire, is clearly visible. There is a 17th century Butter Cross and some notable Georgian housing. As well as a walled garden with Elizabethan herb beds, the museum covers agriculture, hand tools, archaeology, brickmaking, a brickmaker's living room, costumes, local photographs and an exhibition relating to Sir Harry Smith, the 19th century soldier who was the town's most famous son. The Hero of Aliwal public house stands on

The large brickworks beside the cut at King's Dyke.

At Briggate Bend the dike turns sharp right.

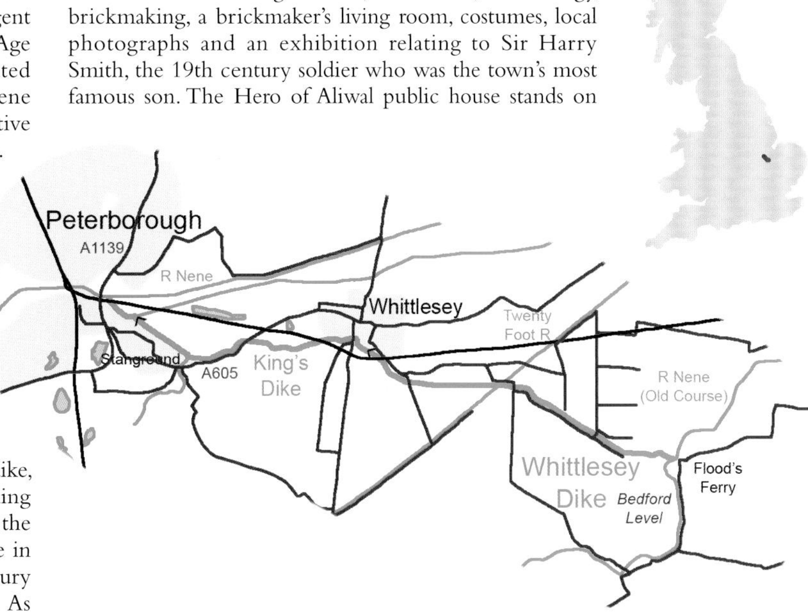

Whittlesey Lock, the only lock on the Whittlesey Dike, has slotted gate tops to let water weir over.

the bank of the dike but another with a notable name is the Letter B, one of an original quartet from A to D.

The dike narrows down with high concrete walls on both sides of the approach to Briggate Bend, the tightest corner for powered craft on the entire inland waterways system.

King's Dike now becomes Whittlesey Dike, tree lined at first, freshwater mussel shells on the bank suggesting the water quality is not too bad.

Whittlesey Lock or Ashline Sluice is the only lock on the dike. Normally, the lower gates are left open with the upper ones acting as a cascade weir. There is a cricket pitch alongside as the water runs into a 2–4m deep cutting. The railway crosses back again and then there is an interesting jumble of sewage works and industrial units together with pleasant waterside housing, one house with its own large swimming pool and slide next to an industrial unit. By Lattersey the dike is out into open fenland with the fields above sea level. Roads are left behind and the dike runs in long straight reaches through the agricultural land of Wype Doles. Kite birdscarers fly above the fields. At intervals there are pillboxes along the bank. Goldfinches might be seen but the most conspicuous feature is a clump of trees at the end of the long straight down to the intersection at Angle Corner and a windfarm to the south. Here, Bevill's Leam emerges from the right. To the left is the Twenty Foot River. Angle Corner Bridge is sufficiently strategic for a swans' nest site.

A large radio ham aerial precedes Bank Farm, near which two unmarked steel joists project into the river just below water level on the inside of a bend. A great crested grebe might perhaps be seen doing some underwater inspection. A long straight follows until bank restoration with flints on the left side and another pillbox on the right lead into the final bend at Flood's Ferry with another windfarm beyond. As Whittlesey Dike joins the old course of the River Nene again a minor road pulls alongside and parking is no problem in the middle of a sea of crops which cover the Bedford Level.

Distance
18km from Stanground to Flood's Ferry

Navigation Authority
Middle Level Commissioners

Navigation Society
East Anglian Waterways Association
www.eawa.co.uk

OS 1:50,000 Sheets
142 Peterborough

The confluence with the old course of the River Nene at Flood's Ferry.

28 Twenty Foot River

A short cut across the fens

Bevill's Leam, the Twenty Foot River and Popham's Eau lead eastwards across Cambridgeshire but are largely unused by powered craft. Most of the land is at sea level so the water level is somewhat lower, all within the area of the Ice Age Lake Fenland. Now part of the Middle Level Navigation, it was mainly cut in 1651 for fenland drainage but also for the transport of agricultural produce, the most common road traffic in the area these days seeming to be tractors and articulated box lorries of agricultural produce. Bevill's Leam originally ran to Guyhirn but the northern part was upgraded as the Twenty Foot River. The flat farmland is very fertile and the Twenty Foot River is through peat, the line running almost straight for the first 17km but wavering just enough to restrict sightlines to a kilometre or two.

The nearest point of vehicle access to Mere Mouth on the Old Course of the River Nene is Tebbitt's Bridge unless the gate is unlocked, when it is possible to drive as far as the pumping station which brings in a side dike just above the sluices which completely block Bevill's Leam.

Bevill's Leam leaves the old course of the River Nene at Mere Mouth, the name referring to Whittlesey Mere, now completely drained. Both the upstream section, the New or North Western Cut, and the downstream section curve into the start of Bevill's Leam so that the River Nene doubles back on itself at this point.

The sluice near Tebbitt's Bridge on Bevill's Leam.

The drainage pumping station by Glass Moor.

Mere Mouth with the River Nene coming from the New Cut on the right and going round a sharp corner to the left.

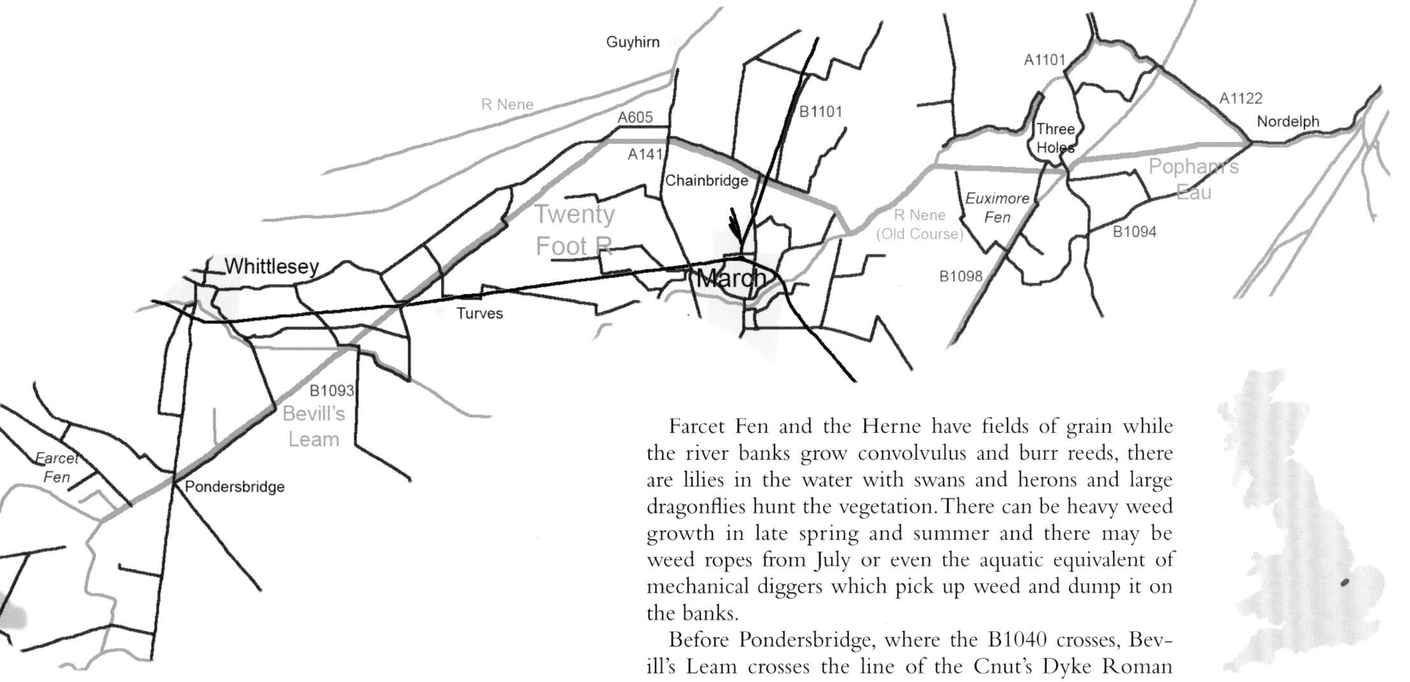

Farcet Fen and the Herne have fields of grain while the river banks grow convolvulus and burr reeds, there are lilies in the water with swans and herons and large dragonflies hunt the vegetation. There can be heavy weed growth in late spring and summer and there may be weed ropes from July or even the aquatic equivalent of mechanical diggers which pick up weed and dump it on the banks.

Before Pondersbridge, where the B1040 crosses, Bevill's Leam crosses the line of the Cnut's Dyke Roman

A warning of submerged piling shows boats are expected.

The fenland agricultural landscape at Warwick Farm.

canal, part of the Car Dyke, a 14m wide canal to drain the fens and take grain from East Anglia to the northern garrisons.

Large angling numbers are to appear along the banks and continue for a good few kilometres, together with large dead fish in the water. Timing is critical for whether this will be a quiet trip or one with lots of company.

Water from a drain is pumped in by a pumping station with a tall chimney on the edge of Glass Moor, which has a windfarm. Moorhens and pheasants join the birdlife as Underwood's Grounds give way to Flag Fen, not to be confused with the better-known one nearer Peterborough.

At Angle Corner the **Whittlesey** Dike is left opposite Bevill's Leam and the B1093 passes over. The channel is the Twenty Foot River as this was the width when it was cut by Vermuyden in 1651 although it is very much wider today. As it crosses Wype Doles there is a carpet of duckweed, hiding an underlay of Canadian pondweed which appears more often as the route progresses.

The Peterborough–Ely railway crosses the river and the Turves near Beggars' Bridge Farm. Great crested grebes dive under the water and cormorants perch on electricity pylons across Kingsland. Angling platforms are spaced at intervals and the bank is otherwise lined with reeds.

The drive to Infield's Farm is along the Fen Causeway Roman road, the line of which crosses the river here. There is a solitary owl box with a view over fields of potatoes and grain.

Finally, at Goosetree Farm the river makes a significant turn to the east although it is possible to portage to a channel which continues the original line alongside the A605 to Guyhirn Corner where another portage onto Morton's Leam leads to the tidal River Nene. Coots and mallards stick with the main river.

Hobbs Lots Bridge takes the A141 over while the next bridge is a footbridge on what was the line of the railway from Spalding to March at the northern end of Whitemoor marshalling yards and now leads towards Whitemoor prison. On the north side of the river the signals are still set but it is a few years since a train last came this way. A little further along are the remains of an extensive brick and concrete waterside structure which might have been anything from fortifications to a wharf.

At Chainbridge, which is now a much more mundane structure, the river is crossed by a former line of the Great Ouse, the B1101 and the Wisbech–**March** freight railway line.

Watching a cormorant downing a large and uncooperative eel on the river can be entertaining.

A further bend after a small sewage works leads to a reach which joins the old course of the River Nene at Twenty Foot End. Dunham's Wood on Reed Fen offers 3ha of fen flora and fauna, sculptures and a 790m light railway. Swans nest along the banks and peacock butterflies explore the vegetation where it remains undisturbed. On the north bank is a large windfarm.

Popham's Eau of 1605 takes off from Low Corner as a straight and broad channel to the north of Euximoor Fen and is frequented by increasing numbers of kingfishers.

Beyond the B1098 bridge it passes from Cambridgeshire to Norfolk where it crosses the line of the Old Croft River, once a major drainage route but now a minor ditch.

Popham's Eau joins the Sixteen Foot Drain and passes under the A1101, the road numbering being confusing in this area. This is the start of Three Holes, as indicated by the attractive carved village sign which features an older and more interesting bridge than the present one.

As the Sixteen Foot Drain heads northeast to become the Middle Level Main Drain, Popham's Eau starts again but as a very different channel from all that has gone before. It is much narrower, especially at first, and reed fringed, starting with an S bend which it easy to miss as it appears so insignificant.

Popham's Eau or Old Popham's Eau, Bertie Popham being its engineer, had more significance as a wartime defence line and a number of pillboxes guard the remainder of its line as it divides North District from South District, on which fields of onions grow and over which kestrels hunt. There are occasional stands of hawthorn. Beyond the powerlines the trees become horse chestnuts and the water becomes progressively more stagnant.

Just before the confluence with Well Creek there is a

Former railway line near March with the signals still in place.

The narrower second part of Popham's Eau.

vertical concrete wall, the water being some 2m higher on the downstream side. Approach needs to be with care to allow trapped swans to escape. The portage is difficult because the river is edged with steep concrete slabs which may be slippery and partially overgrown with stinging nettles. There is a walkway over the dam, closed off with a security fence. The best line of attack would appear to be to the right while passing the fence. However, there has been a wasps' nest in here and the residents do not like being disturbed. Anything louder than wasps are likely to be low flying jets marginally above head height. An alternative might be to use the footpath before the start of the houses in Nordelph and portage out to the B1094.

Nordelph also has a carved village sign beside Well Creek and the A1122. Opposite the Chequers is a carpark and a landing stage with a warning to anglers that boats are the priority users.

The final reach approaching the dam at Nordelph.

Nordelph dam looking back downstream as the river level steps up.

Distance
36km from Mere Mouth to Nordelph

Navigation Authority
Middle Level Commissioners

Navigation Society
East Anglian Waterways Association
www.eawa.co.uk

OS 1:50,000 Sheets
142 Peterborough
143 Ely & Wisbech

29 River Nene (Old Course)

Climbing up to sea level

The River Nene rises at Badby in Northamptonshire and flows to the Wash through the Nene Outfall Cut in Cambridgeshire. Below **Peterborough** it runs through the cut of 1728 and was tidal from Peterborough until Dog-in-a-Doublet Locks were built in 1937. In earlier days it found various routes across the peat fens and the old course can still be followed. Much of it forms part of the Middle Level Navigation as it flows eastwards across an Ice Age fenland lake site, these days very fertile flat farmland. There is heavy weed growth in late spring and summer with weed ropes in place from July.

The East Coast Main Line crosses Yaxley Lode, now deep enough for larger craft.

Pumping station lifting Yaxley Fen water up to Black Ham.

The old course, parts of which are known as the Farcet River and Pig Water, can be followed with difficulty by portable craft.

The head of navigation for larger craft is the East Coast Main Line from Waverley to Kings Cross, crossing Yaxley Lode below **Yaxley.**

A pumping station brings in a feeder from Yaxley Fen and Yaxley Lode becomes Black Ham. Whittlesey Mere was drained in 1851 and now consists of flat farmland, over which the noise of shooting can be heard. To the south of it is the Holme Fen National Nature Reserve with its birch wood, unusually large for the fens. An iron column from the Crystal Palace in London was set in the fen and shows how the surface of the peat has shrunk by 4m because of oxidation of the organic soil since Whittlesey Mere was drained and is still shrinking at 30mm per year. Whittlesey Mere was about 1.5m deep and varied between 6km^2 in summer and 12km^2 in winter, the largest freshwater lake in England until two centuries ago, a place of regattas and skating competitions. One of the vast number of fish left when the mere was drained in 1851 was a 24kg pike, 1.4m long, which is thought to have been England's biggest ever pike, reputed to be one which had grabbed a swan by the neck and pulled it under. Other finds were a prehistoric oak canoe, a killer whale skeleton and a silver chandelier from Ramsey Abbey.

A drain across Osier Fen from Pig Water joins and Black Ham becomes the New or North Western Cut. At Frog Hall it passes under a bridge with concrete blocks piled on top to keep out unwanted visitors. A display of lilac around the abutments improves the scent. Certainly, great crested grebes seem to like the area.

The lowering of the ground has caused many problems, as demonstrated at Mere Mouth where Bevill's Leam leaves, draining all the water through a new pumping station at Tebbitt's Bridge. This large structure is clearly visible and results in the flow beyond this point on the River Nene having been reversed.

A rather older and smaller pumping engine house stands on the bank near Engine Farm at the end of Holme Lode. The river zigzags its way past Old Decoy Farm. Reed buntings scramble about in the reeds at the edge of the river while large and small water lilies appear on the surface, together with algae.

Exhibition Bridge, carrying the B660, is the lowest bridge on the system at 1.6m, enough to keep some craft from using waters northwest of this point.

Looking across Whittlesey Mere to Holme Fen.

The leaning windmill, Ugg Mere.

Pumping station near Engine Farm.

Meeting the New Dyke at Nightingale's Corner.

The river turns through more than a right angle at Nightingale's Corner where New Dyke enters between the abutments of the dismantled Holme–Somersham railway bridge. Also disused on the edge of Ugg Mere is the stump of a windmill with a distinct lean.

At Ramsey St Mary's the B1040 crosses and runs alongside the river for nearly 2km, the only place where the river has significant traffic along its banks although this does not disturb sunbathing fish. The junction must be poorly marked if the number of vehicles nearly missing the turn even in daylight is any indication. The road straight on leads to Ramsey Heights, all of 4m above most of the land in the area, which is at sea level.

By the corner, Ramsey St Mary's church was opened in 1859 to allow for the increase in population after Whittlesey, Trundle and Ugg Meres were drained. It was built in Early Decorated/Gothic style on long oak piles driven through the peat to hard clay. Louvres allow the bells to be heard over New Fen. It had a wooden spire but this was removed in 1920 when it became unsafe, the battlements being taken down in 1974. Features inside include 61 carved heads, mostly of kings and queens.

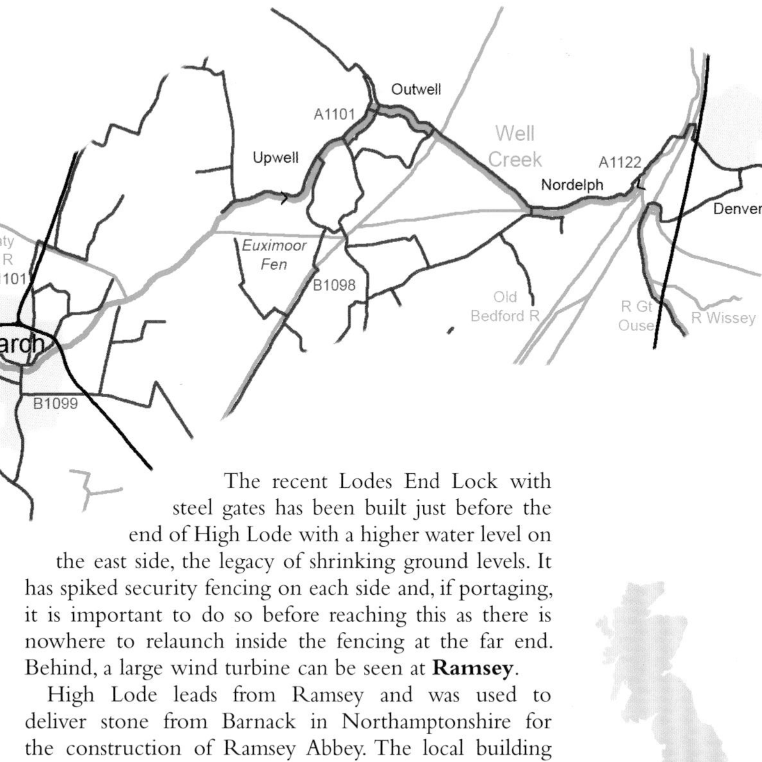

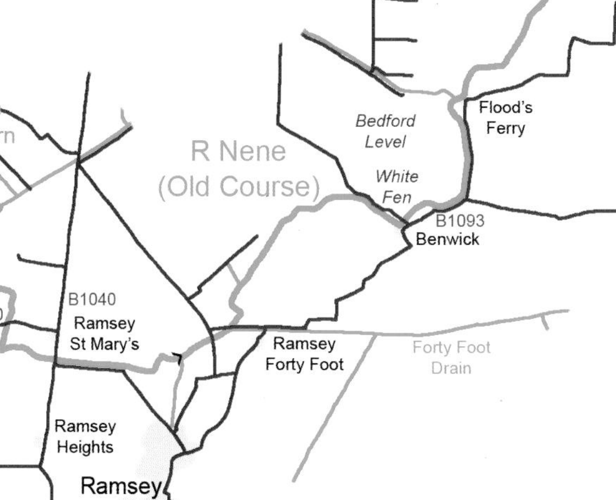

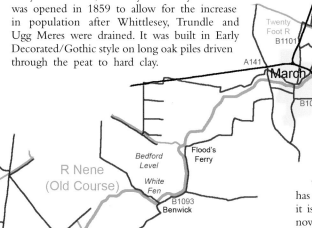

The recent Lodes End Lock with steel gates has been built just before the end of High Lode with a higher water level on the east side, the legacy of shrinking ground levels. It has spiked security fencing on each side and, if portaging, it is important to do so before reaching this as there is nowhere to relaunch inside the fencing at the far end. Behind, a large wind turbine can be seen at **Ramsey**.

High Lode leads from Ramsey and was used to deliver stone from Barnack in Northamptonshire for the construction of Ramsey Abbey. The local building material is noted at Brick Kilns Farm, approached from Saunders Bridge. Beyond the golf course, Bodsey Bridge, again surrounded by lilac, leads to Bodsey House. Near here, the Roman Cnut's Dyke joined from the northwest.

Pillboxes appear on the banks in several locations,

Ramsey St Mary's church.

Lodes End Lock with a wind turbine on the horizon.

Approaching Benwick, a village which appreciates the river.

including at Wells' Bridge where the Forty Foot or Vermuden's Drain enters past Ramsey Forty Foot. The route from east to north is to be a part of the Fens Waterways Link.

The river winds past a camper van sales centre and then heads across farmland with a windfarm behind until meeting up with the B1093 outside Benwick, the first village to treat the river as an asset. There are moorings and kayaks, an old wooden footbridge across the river and new riverside houses. A high aerial fails to hide behind a high immaculately-trimmed hedge in a village which seems to care about its appearance. A cormorant flies over and periwinkle straggles down the embankment next to a drainage pumping station.

Benwick sits among fields of potatoes and strawberries although it is not those which are seen but banks of cow parsley, stinging and white dead nettles and greater reedmace. Likewise, pheasants and cuckoos are heard in the distance but coots, mallards and herons are seen on or beside the river. Swans may nest near a pumping station, one of those draining adjacent sections of the Bedford Level into the river. A pillbox at Copalder Corner is one of several on this section of the river. A more surprising structure is the bridge at White Fen Farm which has a decorative pillar on each of the four corners at the ends of the parapets.

Whittlesey Dike enters at Flood's Ferry, bringing what is a trunk route for powered craft so that the river now becomes a little more busy but not as busy as it will become once it forms part of the Fens Waterways Link from Cambridge to Lincoln. This will be why the local Rotary Club have chosen to site their 2000 sign locating the meridian at this point rather than at one of the other two points where the line crosses the river north of

White Fen Farm access bridge.

Copalder Corner. It will also be seen by walkers on the Hereward Way footpath which now follows the river to Upwell.

Larks and kestrels hover above the banks, cormorants look strangely surreal perched on powerlines and greylag geese cross the river fast and low on final approach. Mussel shells on the bank suggest the water is reasonably clean and assorted waterlilies appear in the water at intervals.

Fox Narrowboats' marina is passed as the A141 crosses over and the river enters **March**. Unusually, the town environment is more attractive and interesting than the farmland one. March began as a wooded island community at least 1,400 years ago and remains wooded today, even if many of the trees are now such species as weeping willow. Earlier, the Romans had a pottery kiln here and it has been suggested that they diverted the river through the gravel ridge here. In Tudor times it was a port and it later became a railway town with the largest marshalling yard in Europe.

Flood's Ferry with Whittlesey Dike entering on the left.

Instead of the high banks, gardens now come to the water's edge with small jetties. One house has a dovecot, aviaries of singing birds, a waterwheel and a windmill or lighthouse. On the south side of the river by the B1099 is Little London with the Acre public house and a folk museum with domestic and agricultural artefacts including a 19th century forge and a fen cottage. The original town was well to the south of the merche or boundary, the river. Notable is the church of St Wendreda which has a 15th century double hammerbeam roof carved with 118 oak angels in flight on the bosses, the best of its kind and the largest wooden church ceiling in England. It was visited by Lord Peter Wimsey in Dorothy L Sayers' *The Nine Tailors*, the title being a reference to the bells, which were brought to March by river. Upwell church is included and many other places in the area are not named but barely disguised.

The Gothic architecture of some of the buildings declines to the New Kashmir Tandoori & Balti House, from where the scents decline to masses of pink and white hawthorn blossom in spring and an undertone of river water. Swallows swoop over the river for insects and great crested grebes search under the surface for their food.

Beyond the Peterborough–Ely railway the landscape returns to embanked farmland. The river is crossed by the line of the Fen Causeway Roman road before Twenty Foot End where the Twenty Foot River joins from the

Marking the meridian.

Gothic architecture by the river in March.

March riparian pride.

Moorings in March.

Houses crowd the river in Upwell. In the spring the banks are a mass of daffodils.

The old church in Upwell.

Trees crowd the river in Upwell.

left. A large windfarm stands on the northwest bank. A little later at Low Corner Popham's Eau leaves to the right. Both channels are artificial and straight. Swans nest along the banks and peacock butterflies explore the vegetation while it remains undisturbed. Beyond Low Corner Farm there is to be a road along at least one bank for the rest of the route.

Marmont Priory Sluice lock, cheerfully decorated with tubs of pansies, raises the water level up to sea level in what is now Well Creek. Large craft going beyond this point will find no further changes of level between here and tidal water.

What used to be an important tributary, the Old Croft River, has largely disappeared but its line is preserved as the Norfolk boundary and B1098 which arrives from the right. Also on the right is a tree climbing dog. Admittedly, the willow tree in question slopes at quite an angle beside the river but an Old English sheepdog is able to bound a long way up it to guard his territory.

Surrounded by orchards, Welle Manor Hall is a 13th century ecclesiastical fortified manor, home of the Norfolk Punch. It is believed to be sited where Hereward the Wake, the last Saxon king, elected to lead his resistance against the Norman invaders in 1070.

After the Globe Inn the water takes on rather a bright green colour, not unlike pea soup. The scenery becomes reminiscent of Friesland which may be a legacy from the Dutch drainage engineers of the past. Daffodils line the banks in spring and watercress grows at the edge of the river. The buildings of Upwell incorporate an element of Dutch styling although one ornately decorated building announces itself as offices without giving any further details.

The A1101 (not to be confused with the B1101) crosses with the Norfolk Cycle Way in front of the Five Bells Inn next to the church and a typical ornate carved Norfolk village sign.

The river becomes very narrow, overhung on one side by a line of horse chestnut trees while a windmill lurks on the other bank. The layout of the river in Outwell is as unreal as it appears on the map. The river doubles back on itself when faced by an embankment topped by picnic tables. Until the late 13th century the line of the River Nene was to Wisbech, accompanied by water from the Great Ouse, Cam, Lark, Little Ouse and Wissey, but a catastrophic storm changed everything. The Wisbech Canal used the line but its only supply of water was from the Nene on spring tides and it was abandoned in 1926, these days only the roads and the county boundary going that way. Earlier it had been the Wellstream, in which King John may have mislaid his jewels. Upwell and Outwell were the important Saxon port of Wella.

Modern boat traffic is now accompanied by the A1122 all the way. A high brick retaining wall in front of the Red Lion makes it a bit gloomy as first but it soon opens out. Another legacy of the Dutch is ice skating. Use of the creek while ice is forming results in an uneven surface for skaters and does not improve the popularity rating.

The village ends after the Crown Lodge Hotel but the river continues to have as many sunken boats as dead fish where it would be better that it had neither.

Mullicourt Aqueduct is the only aqueduct in the fens and is surrounded by road bridges on three sides. One of these had its headroom lowered when an overweight lorry crossed, pushing down its foundations. Underneath is the Middle Level Main Drain, closed to boats because water is pumped into it and it can have interesting water conditions.

The main straight of Well Creek is crossed by powerlines but has the adjacent road hidden by an embankment topped by teasels and inhabited by lizards, the embankment including the Podyke Wall which was built to keep the salt marshes separate from the fresh.

The derelict end of Popham's Eau rejoins at Nordelph,

Mullicourt Aqueduct, the only one in the fens, carries Well Creek over the Middle Level Main Drain.

Nordelph's squat windmill.

again with a decorative village sign near the Chequers. A very squat former windmill comes at the end of a village which has pillboxes giving protection along this section of waterway.

The junction at Salters Lode and Denver Sluice is as complicated as they come, five channels arriving and two leaving. Well Creek is the most westerly of these and there is parking between it and the Old Bedford River.

Salters Lode Sluice lock is manned and has double direction gates but these are only opened to give access to the tidal River Great Ouse when the waters are level. As this only happens once a day for most of the year it has to be one of the less onerous waterway posts. High water is an hour after King's Lynn. A new connection for larger craft to the Cut-off Channel means that more craft will now wish to proceed beyond the sluice at Salters Lode.

Waiting at Salters Lode.

Distance
35km from Yaxley to the River Great Ouse

Navigation Authority
Middle Level Commissioners

Navigation Society
East Anglian Waterways Association
www.eawa.co.uk

OS 1:50,000 Sheets
142 Peterborough
143 Ely & Wisbech

Connection
River Great Ouse
– see RoB p169

30 Forty Foot Drain

Vermuyden's own drain

Boats no longer welcome at Welches Dam.

The name of the Forty Foot Drain has no particular significance as far as its dimensions are concerned. Indeed, it is clear that the first section to Horseway is somewhat narrower than the rest of the route. However, the alternative name of Vermuden's Drain is significant. Cornelius Vermuyden was the Dutch engineer who began reclaiming the fens for the Duke of Bedford in the 17th century and this channel of 1651 across the Bedford Level recalls the origins of the Middle Level Navigation as it cuts across Cambridgeshire. Under the control of the Environment Agency, it is reputed to be the leakiest navigation in the UK. It was in good condition in the 1990s but the first lock now has its gates padlocked and there is sheet piling across the entrance. Only in wet conditions could a small portable boat struggle through the reeds.

There is a convenient RSPB carpark with toilets at Welches Dam, together with a noticeboard giving the latest sightings on the bird reserves and more information in the RSPB visitor centre.

The Forty Foot Drain leaves the Counter Wash Drain about 200m from the Old Bedford River at Welches Dam or Black Sluice, one of the two locks on the river. The lock is the shortest in the UK at 14.3m and was restored in 1991 by the IWA but has been closed off by the EA, officially to prevent leakage. This has prevented boaters exercising the legal right of navigation on the Forty Foot Drain even by short craft.

The lock includes some interesting detailing on the walkway which, instead of being split symmetrically as would usually be the case, opens with the majority of the walkway and railing attached to one gate and only a short piece fixed to the other.

From the walkway it is possible to look 4km down the first straight to Horseway Sluice, a narrow deep cut through agricultural land at sea level, edged with bulrushes.

There are a couple of pillboxes along this reach. Perhaps it was a wartime economy that the bricks used in their construction were weaker than the mortar holding them together, the mortar now standing proud of the weathered dark brickwork.

It is a quiet and remote reach. Some birdlife spills over from the bird reserve and ranges from the high flying skylark, unseen but loudly heard, to the ungainly heron staggering into flight.

Horseway Sluice was reopened in 1985, an unusual lock with open structure gates continuing up above the water to allow excess water to weir through. It is worth

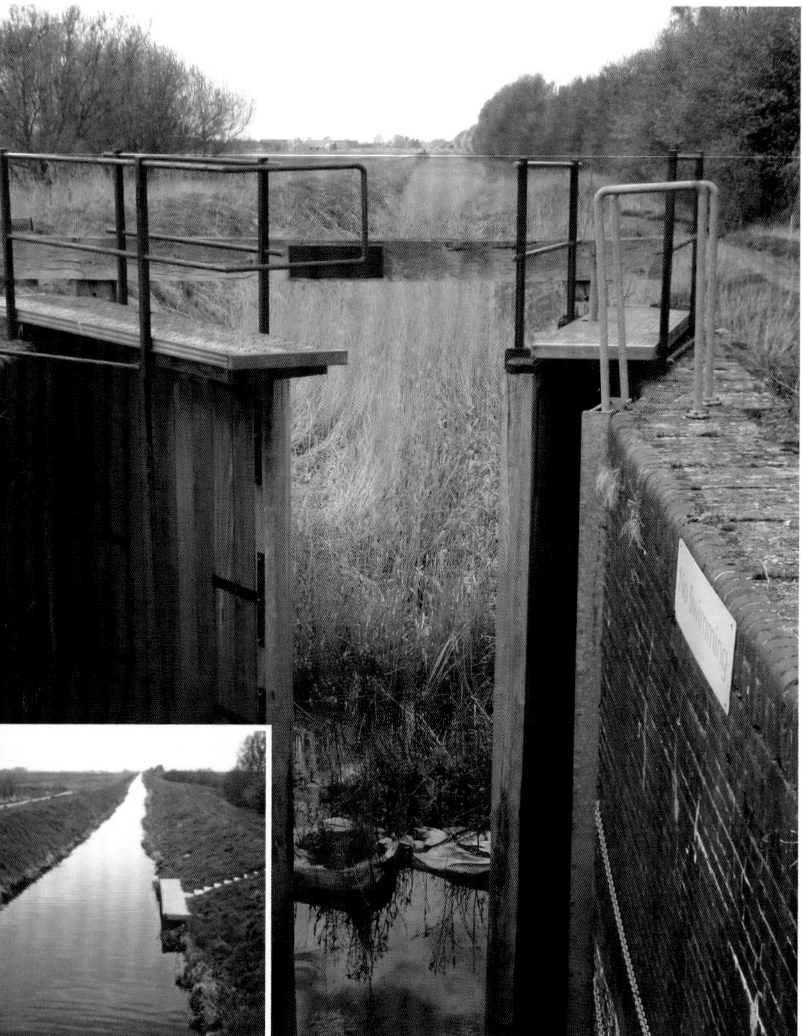

The drain in 1992.

The remote Forty Foot Drain from Welches Dam.

Weathered brick pillbox in Langwood Fen.

Reeds reach to the skeleton Horseway Sluice.

looking at the surrounding countryside, especially outside the growing season when the rich black soil can be seen with the furrows running away unbroken into the distance.

Just beyond the lock there stands a large aerial. The reeds continue on the left of the river but hawthorn bushes take over on the right, giving an extra splash of colour in the spring and autumn.

A little before Hollyhouse Farm the river reaches its most attractive as it enters a wooded section. Certainly, the swans think so.

What appears to be an eyesore of waste straw debris and polyethylene sheeting strewn down the bank is, in fact, carefully placed over water extraction pipes, a situation already passed previously before Horseway Sluice. Although they would not be audible to a powered boat user, the pumps can be heard working quietly by others.

From the B1098 bridge the river opens out to its full width for the rest of its course and is a well maintained drainage channel. Sixteen Foot Corner is at the head of the Sixteen Foot Drain which, with its continuation, the Middle Level Main Drain, runs nearly straight for over 30km to discharge into the River Great Ouse. Both ends of the Forty Foot Drain seem to flow towards Sixteen Foot Corner but this can be academic if the prevailing headwind is blowing as the remainder of the river is wide and exposed.

The corner also brings the first angling peg, number 206.

A pumping station is all that is seen of Chatteris Dock, leading from Nightlayer's Fen. **Chatteris** itself remains hidden to the south, just as Doddington with its windmill lies unseen to the north. Bypassing the two is the A141 which crosses at Curf along the line of a former railway. A weed rope also reaches across in the summer.

The corner crossed by Leonard Child Bridge is the sharpest on the river although there can be few rivers where a 20° bend would be considered something about which to get excited. In addition, it brings a minor unclassified road alongside for the rest of the route, a route which carries a surprisingly heavy traffic load, much of the traffic in the fens being accounted for by large box lorries carrying agricultural produce. The lulls between the rumbles of passing lorries are filled with the twittering notes of skylarks high above the river while the heron stands silent at the water's edge.

The one conspicuous tributary from the south is Fenton Lode or the Twenty Foot Drain which emerges almost opposite Swingbrow.

Puddock Bridge brings a recent drain headwall on the south side and bank repairs on the north side, not to mention another weed rope. By this point the angling pegs are into the 500s, only to begin again at 1 and increase westwards into three figures once more before the end of the river. To the south is a windfarm.

Ramsey Hollow pumping station brings in the hidden Ash Drain, the largest of the remaining feeders.

Geese announce loudly that Ramsey Forty Foot has been reached, not to be confused with the **Ramsey** which lies some 3km to the southwest. The river narrows at this point and there are an arched bridge, unusual for

Near the junction with the Sixteen Foot Drain at Horseway.

the area, a pillbox in front of the George Inn, gardens backing down to the river and a general improvement in the appearance of the river.

By now, though, the old course of the River Nene is in sight at Wells' Bridge, a point overlooked by another pillbox, a motor caravan display area and another windfarm to the north. Freshwater mussel shells on the bank suggest the water is still only muddy.

Distance
17km from the Counter Wash Drain to old course of the River Nene

Navigation Authority
Middle Level Commissioners/ Environment Agency

Navigation Society
East Anglian Waterways Association www.eawa.co.uk

OS 1:50,000 Sheets
142 Peterborough
143 Ely & Wisbech

The arched bridge at Ramsey Forty Foot is unusual on this fenland drain.

31 Sixteen Foot Drain

Britain's lowest hill fort and Sir Peter's crash site

The Sixteen Foot Drain or Sixteen Foot River takes its name from the width when cut by Vermuyden in 1651 although it is now much wider. In the 18th century it was known as Thurlow's Drain.

It runs almost straight the whole way, followed on the right bank by the B1098. In the summer there is significant weed growth with weed ropes being set from July. The water is relatively clear because it receives only limited use, not least because of the headroom at the bridges.

Stonea Camp, Britain's lowest hill fort.

The Forty Foot Drain is left almost at a right angle at Sixteen-Foot Corner near Horseway, the B1098 cutting the corner a little more than in the past, the abandoned section of road being blocked off but still used as a rubbish dump.

Cow parsley and escaped oilseed rape coat the banks, occasionally joined by poppies, with rushes, reedmace and lilies of various sizes at water level. Birdlife includes skylarks, kestrels, pheasants, mallards, coots, greylag geese, great crested grebes and nesting swans while specimens of fish death lie in the reeds.

To the right lies Honey Hill. Something of a misnomer, it was named after Huna, St Æthelthryth's chaplain, and is 5m above sea level at its highest, what passes as a hill in these parts.

The Wesleyan chapel at Stonea.

Aerial activity includes not only microlites but also parachute drops from a white twin-engined plane to a landing strip at Mount Pleasant on Benson's Fen. Wind turbines are visible to the west of Chatteris.

The drain cranks to the right before Honey Bridge, interesting because Thomas Badeslade's map of 1723 shows it stepping to the left at Stony Fenn, presumably Stonea, but being straight here. The first of a couple of platforms is met, accompanied by no mooring notices.

In the vicinity of Wimblington Common the peat fen becomes silt fen, indicative of the Ice Age lake shore. Orange tip butterflies roam the banks of the cut. The B1093 crosses Boot's Braidge.

Canada geese are outnumbered by farmyard geese at Ancaster Farm, where rooks command a rare stand of horse chestnut trees.

To the left is Stonea Camp which has the distinction of being the lowest Bronze Age hill fort in Britain, actually about sea level. It may have been used in resisting the Romans but a Roman settlement was later established. In the 20th century the site was ploughed up but archaeologists have since been back with earthmoving equipment and reinstated it as far as possible.

The B1098 follows the drain almost its whole length.

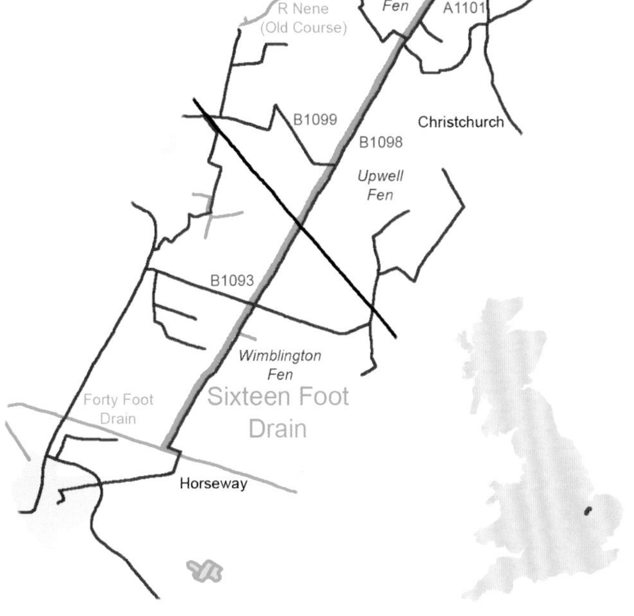

Across the drain a Wesleyan chapel of 1904 has become a private house but retains some interesting architectural detailing.

The Ely–March railway runs dead straight across the fens, crossing the drain at Stonea. The road has a level crossing as well as a bypass taken under a low bridge, avoiding delays for car users.

A pumping station draining Upwell Fen on the right has become a private house beyond Bedlam Bridge carrying the B1099. Chapel of Ease Farm suggests the chapel here was for those who could not reach the main chapel in the area.

Birdlife varies from reed buntings to blackbacked gulls. A rookery occupies a small wood near Christchurch Farm, where the Hereward Way footpath crosses on the line of the Fen Causeway Roman road. This passes through Christchurch where Dorothy L Sayers spent some of her youth and heads towards a large windfarm.

Weeping willows and poplars grow around Iron Bridge, now a low concrete structure like the rest of the bridges, leading to Euximoor Fen, where skittish horses watch from the adjacent field.

At Cotton's Corner the B1098 crosses and finally leaves the drain free of roads for its final kilometre. The bridge is concrete again but on the far side are the brick abutments of a former humpbacked bridge, Frog's Bridge where Sayers would have us believe Lord Peter Wimsey crashed his car one snowy New Year's Eve at the start of *The Nine Tailors*.

The quieter reach may be the haunt of the otter. Halfway down it are hawthorn bushes on each side. Beyond the one on the right is an inlet on the line of the Old Croft River, a major river before the draining of the fens. Now it is little more than a ditch although it is still the county boundary between Cambridgeshire and Norfolk. On the left bank it has entirely disappeared, a featureless ploughed field stretching right across it.

The Sixteen Foot Drain ends at Three Holes, a reference to a former arched brick bridge, the A1101 now passing over a modern structure. Popham's Eau joins from the left, a straight cut from the Old Course of the River Nene. After another 500m it leaves on the right side to run as an equally straight but narrow cut to Nordelph where it joins Well Creek which is at a higher level beyond a non-navigable barrage at its east end. The route ahead to the River Great Ouse continues as the Middle Level Main Drain. However, after 4km it passes under Well Creek at the Mullicourt Aqueduct. No boats are permitted as the pumping station can start with a sudden surge. Non-portable craft can exit to the rest of the waterway network along the western arm of Popham's Eau.

Last vestiges of the Old Croft River.

The arched bridge on Three Holes' village sign.

Distance
15km from the Forty Foot Drain to Popham's Eau

Navigation Authority
Middle Level Commissioners

Navigation Society
East Anglian Waterways Association
www.eawa.co.uk

OS 1:50,000 Sheet
(142 Peterborough)
143 Ely & Wisbech

Popham's Eau comes from the right to join the Sixteen Foot Drain. In summer there is a carpet of green duckweed.

32 Old Bedford River

Britain's most important inland waterfowl site

Despite never being more than 1km from the New Bedford River, with which it runs parallel, the Old Bedford River differs markedly in character, being narrower, much more heavily vegetated and non-tidal.

The cut was made in 1637 for the Duke of Bedford by Cornelius Vermuyden as the main method of draining the fens following ineffectual tinkering for Charles I. It was a bold idea, cutting off over 60 meandering kilometres of the River Great Ouse in an almost straight line. The fens were turned into some of the richest agricultural land in Britain but the drainage experts were hated by the local inhabitants who had earned their livelihoods by fishing and wildfowling. The works collapsed, however, and the good quality agricultural land was lost, along with the sponsors' money. Peat shrinkage of 5m and embanking of channels since the time of construction have left the river above the surrounding fenland.

The Old Bedford River as it leaves Earith.

The Old and New Bedford Rivers each have the outer bank higher than the inner so that the whole of the area between them, the 23km^2 of Hundred Foot Washes, can absorb floodwater or storm surges from the Wash and is regularly drowned out in the winter. The work has done much to prevent subsequent flooding.

The work continues and the Middle Level Barrier at the A1123 at Earith, where the Old Bedford River leaves the tidal River Great Ouse through non-navigable sluices, has been accompanied by a bank improvement scheme which raised the whole of the outer bank as far as Mepal in 1994. Digging is an ongoing process. The Bulwark earthwork on the Hundred Foot Washes may be Roman but the bastions are Cromwellian. There are sand and gravel workings on the other side.

A small memorial beside the river recalls a crash 2km north of Earith involving a Hurricane and a Stirling in 1942 in which nine crew were killed.

At first the river is shallow but after two steps the concrete lined section is left and the river becomes deeper. Although there are occasional collections of debris at first, which make things difficult, these are soon left and the channel becomes easier than its plantlife suggests. Duckweed, arrowhead and carpets of yellow water lilies provide cover for fishes and elvers and confound the relatively small numbers of swans which inhabit only the first half of the river, reducing their aggressiveness. Along the banks are purple loosestrife, thistles and docks. It is an environment which attracts dragonflies.

There is little break up the straight river at first, only a contractor's Bailey bridge, a farm access bridge and the Gullet where the left bank forms a loop back from the river but a set of concrete piers complete the line across the gap although whatever they once carried is no longer there.

There is debris under the bridge at Sutton Gault, avoided by keeping left of centre, no such problem occurring under the A412 viaduct at Mepal, the road first built in 1643 and named the Ireton Way after Cromwell's deputy governor in Ely.

At Welches Dam, named after Vermuyden's engineer Edmund Welche, who built it, the river on this line becomes the River Delph, the

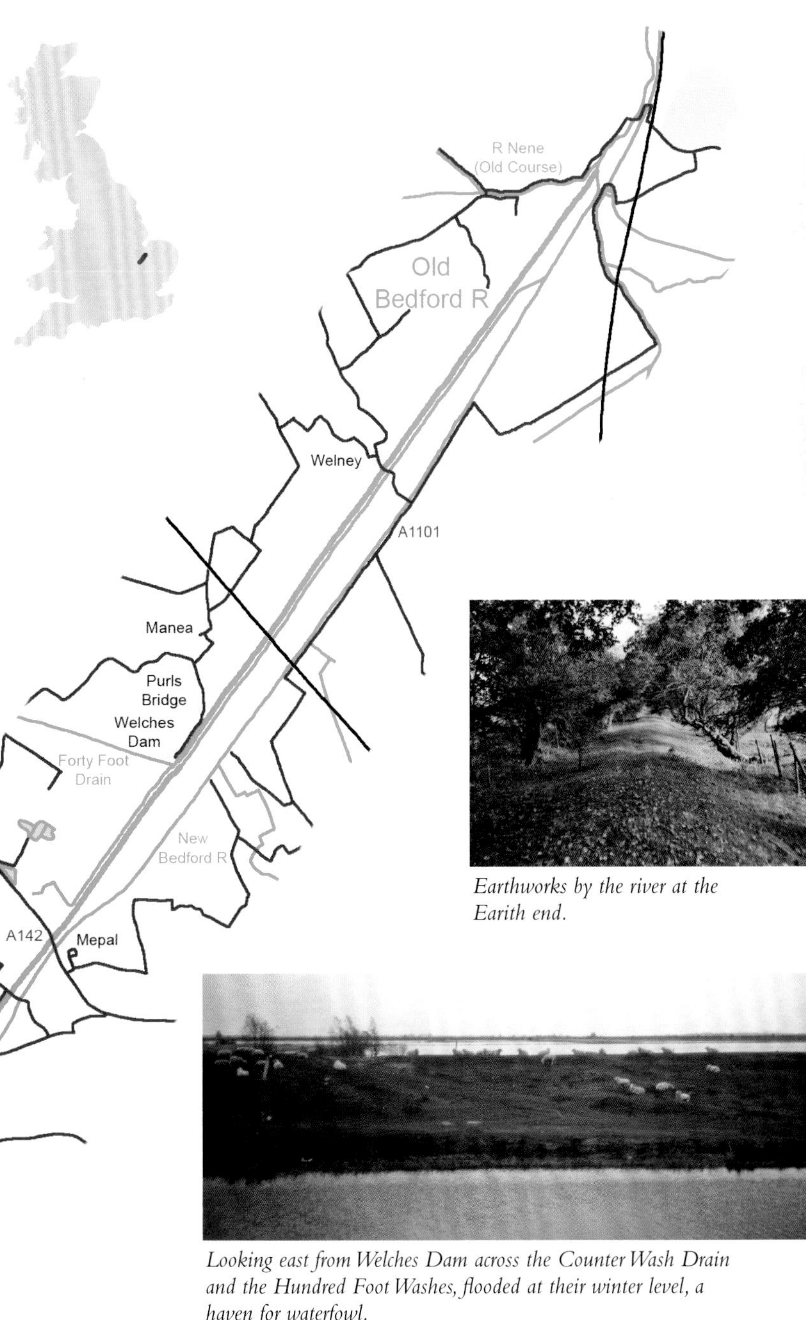

Earthworks by the river at the Earith end.

Looking east from Welches Dam across the Counter Wash Drain and the Hundred Foot Washes, flooded at their winter level, a haven for waterfowl.

The Counter Wash Drain at Welches Dam. The Forty Foot Drain joins by the van.

The pumping station at Welches Dam.

Old Bedford River being lifted up by a pumping station to a parallel line on the outside. At the higher level it is joined by the Counter Wash Drain which has been running parallel (as a flood channel for filling washlands at times of flood) just beyond the top of the Forty Foot or Vermuden's Drain.

In his *Small Boat Down the Years* Roger Pilkington tells of the night in February 1937 when, as a Cambridge student, he joined other volunteers in sandbagging the bank of the Old Bedford River, which was lower than that of the New Bedford River, in an effort to contain flooding. The whole operation was being controlled via the BBC Home Service; at least, that was the theory. The pumping station operator at Welches Dam was not having someone on the wireless telling him how to run his station and when the instruction came for him to throttle back to half speed he responded by increasing to full power.

There is a low bridge just before the pumping station. While it is easier to get out at the foot of the pumping station the draw off area is unguarded. Getting back in on the upper channel is best down a flight of overgrown steps in front of the RSPB centre.

The washes themselves are the largest area of regularly flooded grazing marshland in Britain and one of the world's finest wetlands. They form a textbook example of conservation farming with cattle grazing selected areas but not others, no spraying or fertilizing, progressive cropping of osier beds and willow holts to give a range of habitats and a permanent grassland in summer accompanied by a rich flora with an enormous range of insects, animals and birds.

Present are 44% of British aquatic plant species. Vegetation ranges from the common reed sweet grass, reed canary grass and tufted hair grass through meadow rue, yellowcress, bittersweet and large bracket fungi to such rarities as sulphur water dropwort, slender spike rush, mousetail, whorled water milfoil, tasteless water pepper and fringed water lily. Animal life includes foxes, rabbits, stoats, weasels, voles, harvest mice, otters and mink.

It is the birdlife, however, which makes the washes of international value and Britain's most important inland site for waterfowl. Of prime importance are the 3,000 Bewick's swans which overwinter here from November to March, a prime European site for them, and the blacktailed godwit for which this is the main British nesting site. Also present in the winter are great crested grebe, whooper swan, white fronted goose, water rail, kingfisher, fieldfare, redwing and over 40,000 widgeon. Ruff joust in the spring and in the summer there are garganey, shelduck, lapwing, redshank, reed warbler, goldfinch, redpoll and several hundred pairs of yellow wagtails. Little grebe, heron, mallard, teal, gadwall, pintail, shoveler, tufted duck, pochard, goosander, red breasted merganser, snipe, little owl, short eared owl and numerous rarer species may be seen at any time, a tribute to the farming methods employed and the influence of the Wildfowl & Wetlands Trust, RSPB and Cambridge & Isle of Ely Naturalists' Trust who own over half of the washes.

The visitor centre at Welches Dam has hand-painted displays and exhibits of traditional fenland activities. In the nearby carpark are toilets and, in the nearest corner, some information boards. On one side of one is suggested which birds are likely to be present at the time while on the back are lists of what bird watchers think they have seen and when, a list which is not always believed in its entirety by the warden. A line of some ten hides, dark wood cabins, run along the top of the Old Bedford Barrier Bank between the two parallel rivers, the Old Bedford River having moved to the outside of the high embankment which acts as the northwest bank of the Hundred Foot Washes, these hides now facing inwards. Ornithologists are instructed to approach the hides at the foot of the outside edge of the embankment and not to break the skyline which would disturb the birds being watched. The same should also apply to boaters who should only portage by the pumping station and who should, as far as possible, try to avoid using the river when there is peak interest for the ornithologists. July and August are suitably quiet months, especially on weekdays, while February and March are particularly busy times for the birdwatchers.

At Purls Bridge the Ship Inn may be reached by a ladder thoughtfully placed down the sloping bank. The boarding up the front of an extension on the left is flush with the old part of the building at the bottom but not

The Ship Inn with the 2003 extension at a different angle from the nearer old part. Inside, the list is even more conspicuous.

so at the top, an indication of settlement. Strange angles inside may not be the effect of alcohol.

On the other side of the river the sheep have slots cut in the peat for them to reach the water. These do not always work too well and it is not unusual to find sheep stuck in the silt at the edge of the river, especially when the water level is low. There is no bridge at Purls Bridge.

The Ouse Washes Reserve is the largest wet lowlands grassland habitat in Europe and is flooded in winter with many geese and swans, including the largest UK concentrations of Bewick and Whooper swans, around a series of lakes running parallel with the river.

Moorhens, swallows, martins and blackheaded gulls join the birdlife, reedmace makes an appearance on the banks and empty freshwater mussel shells are left at intervals along the edge of the river.

A girder bridge which carries the railway line between Ely and Peterborough is a most conspicuous feature because of the long distance over which it can be seen although bombers and other aircraft usually make their presence more obviously noticed as they fly over.

After the railway bridge and beyond excavations with draglines visible from the river, the depth becomes less past the Manea Fifties and there is the smell of hydrogen sulphide being given off by vegetation. Both river and railway are straight and level so that the curvature of the Earth can be seen on either.

Colony Farm recalls the 1838 Cambridgeshire Community No 1 or Manea Colony with 60ha being farmed by self-supporting colonists who wore uniforms. The scheme met problems and failed in 1851.

Passing from Cambridgeshire to Norfolk, the river reaches Welney, the A1101 and a sluice usually left in the raised position, allowing craft to pass, the river downstream being rather wider than before.

Something else which used to cross near here was the Old Croft River which drained the Lark and Cam via Wisbech to the Wash. Now it feeds only a few ditches into the Middle Leading Drain, a shadow of its former self.

Welney was a centre for speed skating in the 19th century with such prominent names as Fish and Turkey Smart and Gutta Percha See resident, racing against the Dutch both here and in the Netherlands. Turkey placed a decade of winnings 'in the bank', buried at the edge of the river. The tradition has not completely died as there are still several men using road speed skates in Manea.

The Welney Wetland Centre, run by the Wildfowl & Wetlands Trust, is claimed to be the best viewpoint for the Hundred Foot Washes and has few equals in Europe. It is approached on foot from the southeast side of the Washes. Viewing is generally done from the public hides or the heated observatory for members. The 4km^2 site is flooded in winter. In summer there are a wide variety of wild flowers and it is important for breeding waders and ducks. Gulls and cormorants are seen more often now.

Powerlines cross and then the River Delph, which has followed the northwest side of the Hundred Foot Washes, switches across to the New Bedford River. A little further on, the Old Bedford River crosses the line of the Roman road from Brampton to Water Newton.

Sets of numbers along the edge of the river show that it is used for angling contests.

The sluice at Salters Lode is protected by a single set of doors on each side in diamond formation. These can only be opened briefly to let craft through when the tidal River Great Ouse downstream is at the same level as the Old Bedford River. Almost alongside is Well Creek, the old line of the River Nene. Launching downstream of the sluice is difficult because of the silty banks once the tide has dropped. Those wishing to stop at this point will find a limited amount of parking space beside the sluice although the exit up a rough concrete slope is not easy in itself.

The tidal sluice at Salters Lode, seen from the tidal side.

Distance
33km from Earith to Salters Lode

Navigation Authority
Environment Agency

Navigation Society
East Anglian Waterways Association
www.eawa.co.uk

OS 1:50,000 Sheets
(142 Peterborough)
143 Ely & Wisbech

Connections
River Great Ouse *– see RoB p167, p169*

33 River Great Ouse

Religious thinkers good and bad

Here Ouse, slow-winding through a level plain
Of spacious meads with cattle sprinkled o'er,
Conducts the eye along his sinuous course
William Cowper

New housing replaces the burnt-down mill at Kempston.

Also known as the Bedford Ouse to distinguish it from the others, the River Great Ouse takes its name from the Sanskrit for water. It rises at Greatworth and flows northeastwards to the Wash, having formerly flowed to Wisbech. It was made navigable below Bedford in the 17th century but had to be restored from impassable states in both the 19th and 20th centuries. There were plans in 1811 and 1892 to make a cut from Newport Pagnell, in place again as the Bedford–Milton Keynes Link proposal. There have also been suggestions of deepening the river from the Grand Union Canal crossing upstream at Wolverton.

The head of navigation for large craft is a closed-in weir to the west of **Kempston** Mill. A channel bypasses this but it is overgrown with weeds.

The river generally has little flow in the summer and is followed by the prevailing wind. In spate conditions the locks are reversed by tying open the mitre gates. There is no towpath although footpaths are usually not too far away. Excavation of Roman and Anglo-Saxon sites shows past interest in the river.

Parking at Kempston Mill is hard to find but of good quality when it is discovered. The mill burnt down in 1969 and has been replaced with modern housing influenced by the mill architecture. The water is clear and there are lifebelts beside the river at intervals. Dragonflies and damselflies use the river, which has arrowhead in it and it is edged by loosestrife, sedges, alders and oaks. No effort is made to clear trees which fall across the navigation, which can prevent use by larger craft.

Bedford makes several attempts to reach the river, initially held back by parkland which keeps the housing at a distance. The town is entered past Charles Wells' Eagle Brewery, this being Britain's largest independent family brewery company and the fifth largest overall after taking on Young's.

Canoe slalom gates hang near the railway, a railway depot having been located between the St Pancras–Leicester and Midland–Bletchley lines with a Cambridge–Oxford link proposed.

County Bridge carries the A5141 over before the Star Club with its rowing boathouse and there is some impressive brick building by Queen's Reach.

Bedford was Beda's settlement at Batts ford, a pre-8th century Saxon settlement, fortified in 915 but pillaged by the Danes in 1010. As the county town of Bedfordshire, it has the second oldest charter in England, issued by Henry II in 1166. Town Bridge, carrying the A6, was a ford site. Bedford Castle mound has the remains of a Saxon castle, destroyed in a siege in 1224 by Henry III, the stone used to build the first bridge although the current one, with five Portland stone arches, was built in 1813. A stampede in the town's narrow streets in 1439 killed 18 people.

Bedford Museum, in the former Higgins Castle Brewery, has a farmhouse and cottage interiors, lace making, archaeology, rocks, fossils and natural history. The Cecil Higgins Art Gallery & Museum with 19th century arts is in an 1846 Victorian brewer's mansion.

St Mary's and St John's churches are 14th century and St Paul's is from the 14/15th centuries. St Peter's is Saxon and Norman.

There is a 2.7m bronze statue of Bunyan and the John Bunyan Museum is in the Bunyan Meeting Free Church where he was a minister from 1672 to 1688. He was jailed from 1660 to 1672 and started writing *The Pilgrim's Progress* while in jail again for six months in 1678 for refusing to conform to the established church. The museum has bronze doors and some of the best 20th/21st century stained glass.

A statue also records another prisoner, John Howard, who founded the League for Penal Reform. In 1962 James Hanratty was hanged here for the A6 murder, the last person in Britain to be executed.

Sir William Harpur, born early in the 16th century, became Lord Mayor of London and founded four Harpur schools. The former local lace industry was claimed to have been started by Catherine of Aragon and another branch of the arts was to be enhanced by American band leader Glenn Miller, stationed here during the Second World War.

Bedford's Star Rowing Club boathouse.

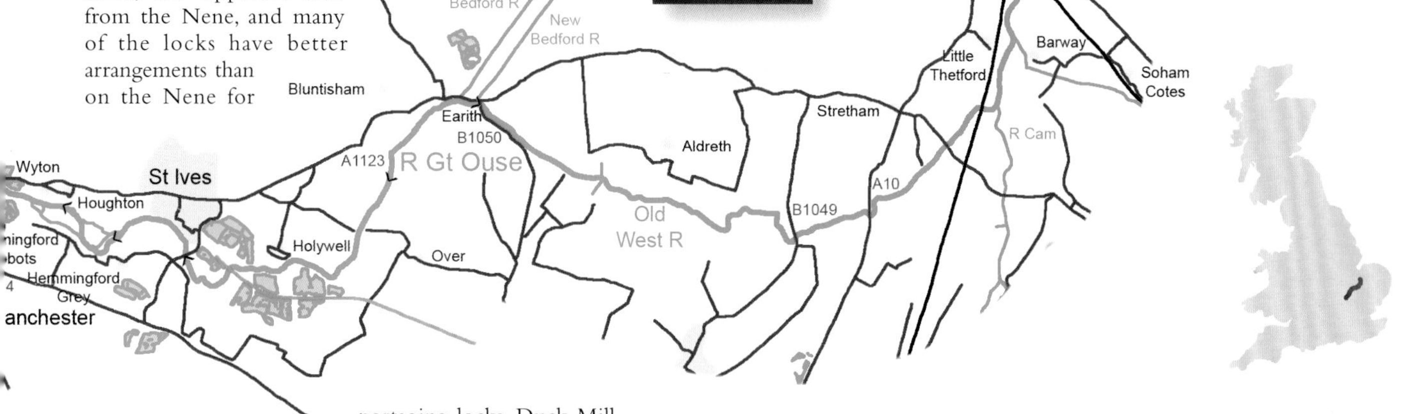

Bedford is the headquarters of the Panacea Society, which has a box belonging to Joanna Southcott, who died in 1814 after claiming that war, disease, crime and banditry would increase until the box was opened in the presence of two dozen bishops, who have declined to cooperate so far. X rays show it includes a pistol. Another of her boxes, opened in 1927 without bishops, contained a nightcap and a lottery ticket.

The Riverside Bar and Bedford Rowing Club face the Swan Hotel. Swans in profusion gather by Embankment Gardens. With Victorian landscaping, this is one of England's best urban river settings and includes a steel bowstring suspension bridge of 1888 and a new bridge of even more striking design over the New Cut. There is a rowing regatta in May and Britain's second largest free outdoor event takes place in even years.

Duck Mill or Town Lock leads off to one side. Guillotine gates are at the top end on this river, the opposite end from the Nene, and many of the locks have better arrangements than on the Nene for portaging locks. Duck Mill weirpool is used on Boxing Day by the local Viking Kayak Club for a rolling competition to address the previous day's excesses. A bandstand is prominent as the river follows the Embankment Gardens.

Beyond the A5140 crossing the former Bedford–Sandy railway has become a footpath and cycleway. The Augustinian Newnham Priory of about 1166 had its stones taken for Bedford Castle by King John. They were returned after the castle's capture but were taken again after the Dissolution for a house in Willington.

Priory Country Park of 1.2km^2 has a 32ha lake with sailing and rowing, winter migrants, great grey shrikes, little egrets, breeding mallards and grass and woodland. Britain's first artificial canoe slalom course, doubling as a flood relief channel, was installed here in 1982. Although subsequent courses have become more advanced, this one is still used for the annual national inter club championships. Priory Marina has moorings and the Sea Cadets have a base. Angling platforms are established amongst the Himalayan balsam, burr reed, hawthorns and sycamores.

Cardington Cross has Smeatons' bridge of 1778, five 1.8m brick arches for the Whitbread brewing family. Beyond are the two Short's airship hangars, 248m x 55m x 53m, one brought from Pulham. After many premonitions, the R101, containing 160,000m^3 of hydrogen, crashed in flames near Beauvais on its maiden voyage to India in 1930, killing 48 of the 54 aboard. In a seance before the official inquiry, the pilot gave the reasons in his own voice and using technical

Impressive brickwork by Queens Reach in Bedford.

Bedford Rowing Club's boathouse.

jargon not familiar to the medium. The huge hangars have since been used for scientific projects.

Cardington Lock takes the river north and clear of a sewage works. Castle or Castle Mills Lock is near a motte while Castle Mill Airfield is defunct. The A421 crosses, missing Howbury Hall, and a set of powerlines follow the valley, crossing the river five times before the A1 is met. The earthworks for Risinghoe Castle are also missed narrowly.

Terns, herons, kingfishers and moorhens use the river and Gadsey Brook joins before Danish Camp, a Norwegian log cabin at the heart of an outdoor activities centre. Willington stands back from the river with its 16th century stone dovecote for 1,400 birds, stables and the Perpendicular St Lawrence's church. Beyond Willington Lock the right bank becomes Central Bedfordshire until returning to Bedford at Wyboston. Old Mills Lock site is no longer used.

Barford Bridge is one of the gems of the river. It had eight stone arches after 1429 but was extended in stages until there were 17 arches, refurbished in the 18th century using brick and with cutwaters on the upstream side. Behind the Anchor Inn is All Saints' church, also partly 15th century. Great Barford Lock has an anchor concreted to the base of a crane as a feature and a weir which is deeper in the centre for gauging. Swallows, longhorn cattle, chub, watercress and water lilies are found variously around the river.

Beyond Roxton Lock the River Ivel joins, formerly a river navigation from Bigglewade with a canal link from Shefford but the planned connection with the River Lee was never made.

The Dane Gannock built a castle in 921 but it was attacked by Edward the Elder, Gannock and his sons being killed. St Peter's church is 14/15th century and the half-timbered Gannock House is also 15th century but Tingey's House is from 1534. Although in Elizabethan style, Tempsford Hall was not built until 1898 and is the Keir construction group's headquarters.

Roxton has the 14th century St Mary Magdalene's church with a 15th century tower and there is also a thatched Congregational church with Gothic windows and a wooden veranda.

The A1 crosses on two bridges. The first, Tempsford

Bedford's Embankment Gardens reach as the navigation leaves.

Cows graze by Great Barford's ancient bridge.

Bridge, was rebuilt in 1820 from Yorkshire gritstone and sandstone with three round arches plus additional flood arches. It takes the northbound carriageway but is difficult for this standard of road as it is set at right angles to the river. The other bridge of 1961 is on an easier line. Between them are Kelpie Marine and moorings. There are the remains of Tempsford Staunch which flooded the area when closed for ferry traffic for the Great North Road before the bridges were built and was a contender for Bunyan's Slough of Despond.

Market gardening is a feature of Wyboston and there is a nature reserve, Wyboston Leisure Park and a golf course around Wyboston Lakes with the noise of water skiing and jet boats. In 1297 four people were drowned from the ferry and the ferryman himself was drowned in the 14th century. There are increasing numbers of lakes down the valley left after sand and gravel extraction. Reedmace is seen increasingly.

St Dennis' 12th century church is disused. Little Barford power station is a 680MW gas turbine plant. Four sets of powerlines cross the river. Poet Laureate Nicholas Rowe was born in Little Barford in 1674.

With the A428 the river passes from Bedford into Cambridgeshire. A campsite, lifebelt, skateboard park and swings give notice of arrival in a built up area.

The trapezoidal Eaton Socon Lock is close to River Mill Marina and the 19th century mill. The Normans had a vineyard in Eaton Socon and Dickens mentioned the 13th century White Horse mail staging post in *Nicholas Nickleby*. The 1826 Cage jail has two brick cells, a wooden bed and chains. St Mary's church was funded by the Saxons, the current building erected in 1930 with a notable rood screen after an extensive fire. Castle Hill or Hillings had an 11/12th century Norman castle.

The 12th century Norman church in **Eynesbury** was rebuilt mostly in Early English style with 14th century oak benches, an ornately carved 17th century pulpit and a tower which was rebuilt after collapsing in 1685. The 21 year old Eynesbury Giant, James Toller, who was 2.48m tall, was buried under the font in 1818 to deter body snatchers. A giant who stood on the Coneygear Field Roman fort site and threw spears at Eaton Socon earthworks may have been an incorrect folk memory of a Roman ballista.

St Neots is the largest market town in Cambridgeshire, the name from a Cornish saint buried in the former Saxon priory of 974, the bones possibly stolen from Bodmin. It was partly ruined by the Danes in 1010 with a Benedictine priory rebuilt about 1081, to be destroyed at the Dissolution. The market charter came from Henry I in 1130, the market square being one of the country's largest and oldest and having a column provided by brewer John Day in 1822 to dispense clean water. A Georgian coaching town, it has over 200 listed buildings including a 15th century shop. One of the best buildings in the town is the 17th century Brook House.

Interesting housing at the Hen Brook confluence leads along the waterfront to Bridge House, the Drunken Duck, weeping willows and the B1428 bridge. The first bridge in 1180 had 73 wooden spans, to be replaced about 1600 by a stone bridge and by the modern one in 1965. Being a strategic crossing, it was the site of the 1648 Civil War Battle of St Neots. The town had a heronry, has a folk festival in May and was home to the Miles quads, the first in Britain to survive.

St Neots Museum is in the Victorian former police station with a 1907 Edwardian cell and magistrates' court. St Mary the Virgin's church was called the Cathedral of Huntingdonshire, as it then was, in 15th century Perpendicular style with a 40m Somerset style tower, carved oak altar of about 1600, Victorian stained glass, an 1855 Holditch organ, animal roof carvings and a painted roof at the eastern end. An 18th century oast house is the basis for an arts centre. The Priory Centre is by the

Great Barford's Anchor Inn and All Saints' church.

A drawbridge fronts new housing approaching St Neots.

Eaton Socon Lock, the first of several of trapezoidal design.

The Hen Brook confluence in St Neots.

The East Coast Main Line at Offord Darcy.

Brampton Mill has a working water wheel.

river near St Neots Rowing Club and a slipway while Priory Hill Park has an open air swimming pool. Lammas Meadow was used for cricket from 1845, golf to 1890 and ice hockey and speed skating when it was flooded and frozen.

24
THE CIVIL WAR 1642-51
fought between the forces of KING
& PARLIAMENT: Pikeman

Ouse Valley River Club have moorings outside the town towards Crosshall Marine's base. After the River Kym confluence the navigation route leads left off the main river to St Neots or Papermill Lock where the mill which introduced paper in continuous rolls has been replaced by housing. For portable craft, relaunching on the downstream side of the B1041 is difficult because of the high side.

This is the start of Little Paxton, now much larger than Great Paxton, but it needed much rebuilding after many houses were destroyed by fire in 1945. Paxton Hall was built about 1738 for the son of the Bishop of Lincoln. St James' stone church has a 12th century chancel and a 15th century tower. Around the eastern side of the village is the Paxton Pits nature reserve, 75ha of lakes, meadow, grassland, scrub, woodland and hides with winter wildfowl, nightingales and the second largest breeding colony of cormorants in England. There is now a windfarm.

The East Coast Main Line has been running down the valley and now comes right alongside the river. A pre-war race was run between a boat, a train, a car and a plane, presumably with some handicapping.

At Great Paxton the 11th century Saxon minster has its chancel 3m higher than the nave.

Offord D'Arcy had willow beds and a 17th century manor house which was rebuilt with a false third storey, no doubt to impress. Both Offords were lace centres, Offord Cluny being granted to the French Cluny Abbey. All Saints' church dates from the 13th century.

Offord Lock leads past mills to Buckden Marina, surrounded by chalets and lodges.

The former Kettering–Huntingdon railway used to cross before the river turns away from Brampton, from which it is kept by gravel pits. The village has a Bronze Age burial site. Henry I, Henry II, Henry III and King John each stayed at a house here but then it was lost to floods in 1348. The 14th century church has notable carved oak stalls. Pepys' parents had a house here and, although he rarely visited it, he buried some money in the garden in case the Dutch invaded, found in 1842.

Brampton Lock is another of trapezium shape, below Hinchingbrooke Country Park, 69ha of woodland, meadows and wetland with kestrels and foxes, an Iron Age farm reconstruction and classical concerts in the Hinchingbrooke Performing Arts Centre. Hinchingbrooke House has building work from 12th century Norman to the 20th century, using Ramsey Abbey stone, including the gatehouse which may have been imported from Ramey Abbey. The 13th century Benedictine nunnery site was given by Henry VIII to Cromwell's ancestors at the Dissolution and it was visited by Elizabeth I and James I. In 1603 five year old Oliver visited and was claimed to have given young Charles Stuart a bloody nose but they probably never met, confusion arising between Stuart and Oliver's mother's maiden name of Steward. The house was sold to the Earl of Sandwich in 1627, responsible for bringing Charles II back to England, but it was the 4th Earl, John Montague, who gave the name to the world in the 18th century by calling for beef between slices of bread to save time while gambling. The house is now Hinchingbrooke School 6th form centre.

The East Coast Main Line passes over the river on a pair of red bridges, one of which is significantly lower than the other. Port Holme island is claimed to be the largest meadow in Europe at $1km^2$ although Oxford's Port Meadow might contest this. It has rare wild flowers including snake's head fritillary, marsh dandelion, great

The waterfront at Huntingdon's historic bridge.

burnett and brown sedge so it has been declared a SSSI. In the past it was used for horse racing and the first local plane flight took place here in 1910.

Godmanchester Lock is trapezium shaped. The town has Bronze and Iron Age remains. It had 10ha of the Roman town of Durovigutum with a fort, barrows, mausolea, 2nd century baths, a villa and other substantial buildings. The name is from the Anglo-Saxon Godmund's Caester and it was one of England's first boroughs, with a 1212 charter from King John. Offspring of freemen born and continuing to live in the town have free use of the extensive common lands granted by King John. The 13th century church of St Mary the Virgin has carved choirstalls from Ramsey Abbey, possibly on a Roman site. In the 14th century the residents murdered the vicar. Those who refused to contribute to the 1623 rebuild of the tower were imprisoned. Queen Elizabeth's Grammar School dates from 1559 although many of the town houses are 17/18th century, often timber framed. Island Hall is an 18th century mansion with Georgian panelled rooms and the gabled Gothic-style town hall dates from 1844.

Thomas Weems was forced to marry his girlfriend in 1818 when told that she was pregnant but she was not and he eventually strangled her. He was seen, hanged and his body dissected and used for electricity experiments. Hers was displayed in its coffin on the bar of the White Hart.

The area was unhealthy with typhoid into the 19th century. Cook's Backwater is crossed by the wooden Chinese Bridge, an 18m span 1960 replica of Gallier's 1827 bridge, allowing access to Port Holme. Poplars lead towards Huntingdon Boathouse.

Huntingdon has long been an important crossing point. It is where the Via Devana meets the line of Ermine Street and where the A14 crosses. The B1044 crosses the Old River Bridge of about 1332, replacing one lost to floods in the 13th century. One of the finest medieval bridges still in use, it has six stone arches up to 10m wide. The towns on each side could not agree on a line before starting so they did not meet properly in the middle. A chapel to St Thomas à Becket was sited on the Huntingdon side and a footbridge was added in 1966. Cromwell replaced part of the bridge with a drawbridge to defend the town but the Royalists approached in 1645 from the opposite direction. The Old Bridge Hotel faces across to warehouses converted to residential accommodation.

Although Palaeolithic and Neolithic tools and weapons have been found, the town's Saxon name is from the Old English hunta tun, huntsman's estate. It was in existence by 659, had a fortress from 870 and was a county town from 921 when Edward the Elder recovered it from the Danes. There was an Anglo-Saxon mint from 955. The 1068 Norman castle of William the Conqueror was destroyed in 1174 but Castle Hills with their fire beacon remain an Ancient Monument. A market town, it was also a port until the 13th century when the Abbot of Ramsey built a weir at Hemingford Abbots and a lord built another at Hemingford Grey to block navigation and increase their own tolls.

The town's charter was issued in 1205 by King John and there is much Georgian architecture with 150 listed properties and a Town Park with a maze. It was a coaching centre which became a railway centre but the town is no longer split by the railway to Cambridge.

Oliver Cromwell's grandfather owned the George Hotel, which suffered a bad fire in 1865 although some of the 17th century courtyard and rare wooden gallery remain. The hotel was used for Shakespeare performances and was reputed to have been used by Dick Turpin. Oliver was born in 1599 in a former house on the site of the 1285 Augustinian friary, rebuilt in the 19th century as Cromwell House and now used by the Huntingdon Research Centre. Cromwell and Pepys were both educated at the grammar school, formerly part of the 1160 Hospital of St John the Baptist and now the Cromwell Museum. The Grade II 16th century Falcon Inn was Cromwell's headquarters and Charles I also had a headquarters here but it is presently closed.

There were 16 churches until the Black Death, which claimed half the population. Now there are two. All Saints' church is 14/15th century Early English and Victorian with a fine chancel roof, a good organ chamber, an excellent stained glass window and Cromwell tombs. St Mary's church is Norman, rebuilt in the 13th century with a Perpendicular west tower rebuilt after a 1607 collapse.

The Grade II Cowper House with its fine 18th century front was the home of William Cowper from 1765 to 1767 and now houses newspaper offices. Castle Hill House of 1786 became the Second World War headquarters of the Pathfinder Squadrons. The town has a War Museum and the Huntingdon Trading Post includes a Blacked-Out Britain Museum.

Former Prime Minister John Major represented the constituency for 22 years, for a while with the largest majority in the country.

Great crested grebes and Canada geese are not deterred by increasing algae. Huntingdon merges into Hartford, which has produced Stone, Iron and Bronze Age remains near the pre-Roman ford and Saxon graves. The 12th century All Saints' church stands on the bank. The Hartford Hoard of 1,108 nearly mint English and French coins from 1450 to 1503, found in 1964, is now in the British Museum. There is a 16th century half-timbered manor house, the 18th century Hartford House on the bank and the 1804 Barley Mow with a stone from the former St Benet's church in Huntingdon.

Godmanchester Gravel Pits ceased extraction in 1986 and are now a nature reserve. Mill House and Hartford Marina accompany floating caravans and Daylock Marine Services have a carvery.

Wyton has the 13th century medieval church of St Margaret & All Saints of brown cobbles, now disused despite having Second World War airmen's graves.

Houghton Lock has rollers which have not seen recent use and lead to a channel in similar state. The Grade II five storey weatherboarded mill of the 17–19th centuries is the oldest on the river, now a gallery of local art. It is on a site given to the abbot in 974 by the founder of Ramsey Abbey but abbey tenant farmers were forbidden

All Saints' church by the river in Hartford.

The manor house at Hemingford Grey with its chess pieces.

The thatched village of Hemingford Grey.

St James' church in Hemingford Grey with its truncated spire.

from using any other to grind their grain. There were three wheels, two replaced by sluices for level control and the remaining one electrically powered. Potto Brown was a miller who allowed religion into all aspects of his life, taking his account books to church so that he could discuss his debtors with God.

St Mary's church dates from the 13th century. Charles James Fox married his mistress, Mrs Armitage, in 1795 and managed to keep it quiet for seven years. The village has 17th century houses, the Three Jolly Butchers, a square with a thatched clocktower, a Gothic village pump, the ridge and furrow Houghton Meadow and the Trout Stream. Various braided channels are each called Back Water.

Hemingford Abbots was the site of a Paleolithic/ Mesolithic camp. It was the ford of Hemma's people from the 8th century, the abbots of Ramsey Abbey taking control in the 10th century, and was the setting for Dendy Sadler's *Thursday* and *Friday* paintings of jolly friars catching and eating fish. The Grade I Perpendicular 14th century medieval church has a tall spire, a yellow brick chancel probably from the 19th century, part of the roof painted black and a Roman coffin from the Ridgeway.

The moated manor house from about 1130 is the oldest continually inhabited house in England, in a 1.4ha garden with more than 200 old roses and topiary in the form of coronation and chess pieces. John Gunning's daughter, Elizabeth, married the Duke of Hamilton secretly in Mayfair at midnight in 1752, without banns and using a curtain ring, a scandal which led to the Marriage Act two years later. It was the former home of Lucy Boston, the setting for her Green Knowe books and housing her patchwork collection. The village has a number of brick, timbered and thatched cottages and the 17th century Axe & Compass with its award winning restaurant.

The medieval 1160 church of St James in Hemingford Grey lost part of its spire in 1741 to a hurricane, lightning or the Devil, who had threatened to take it if the Cardinal did not damn all non-Catholics from the pulpit. The Grade II 1697 Hemingford Grey House conference centre has a plane tree only five years younger than the building, predating most of the 18/19th century thatched and timbered brick houses in the village. The name comes from Reginald de Grey, who became lord of the manor.

Holt Island is a 2.8ha nature reserve with former osier beds.

The river front in **St Ives** includes Floods Tavern, St Ives Rowing Club and the 1933 Norris Museum, the museum for Huntingdonshire with a mammoth tusk, a model ichthyosaur, flint tools, Civil War arms, armour, Cromwell items, 16/17th century witch trials, Napoleonic prisoner of war carved ships and ice skating.

There was a ford here at what was the tidal limit before locks were installed. The ford was superseded by a bridge in 1107. The current St Ives Bridge was built in 1415–26 by Ramsey monks, a packhorse bridge in Barnack limestone. There are four Gothic spans of 4.0–9.1m and two rounded arches of 4.9 and 6.4m from 1716 to replace a drawbridge placed by Parliamentarians in 1645. The chapel of St Leger rises straight from the river, one of three remaining bridge chapels in England, had two more storeys added for a while and also served as a toll house, being damaged by the great town fire of 1680.

Formerly called Slepe, the Saxon for muddy, the town was renamed St Ives after the Persian Christian missionary bishop St Ivo, who died here in the 7th century and whose bones had healing properties when found about 1000. It became a place of pilgrimage until they were removed to Ramsey Abbey. All Saints' church is built on the site of Slepe with some 12th century work and a 13th century arch but is mostly 15th century. The

St Ives ancient bridge with its bridge chapel.

slender spire has been rebuilt three times, the last in 1924 after it was hit by a First World War bomber, killing the pilot. There is a 13th century font, an Elizabethan pulpit and a large organ of 1893. The 1860 Free Church has a 47m spire, claimed to have been intentionally taller than that of the parish church. The Roman Catholic church of the Sacred Heart by Pugin was moved from Cambridge and rebuilt. Since 1675 Whitsun *Bibles* have been given to six boys and six girls of good report, under 12 and able to read them, the children needing to roll dice to qualify, the cost funded by the income from Bible Orchard under the terms of the will of Dr Robert Wilde.

The first charter was in 1110 from Henry I and the market is 800 years old. The town received international trade and there were large Easter fairs. Cheaper cloth was sold in St Audrey's Lane, corrupted to tawdry, although the same explanation has been given for St Audrey's Fair at Ely.

The oldest building is the manor house from about 1600 but there are some 170 listed buildings. Quay buildings are 18th century. The Waits has 18/19th century houses facing onto a triangular green with the remains of Middle Ages ploughing strips. The Golden Lion Hotel, a 19th century coaching inn, has the ghost of a lady in green who pulls bedclothes off the bed and opens doors.

Cromwell lived in the town for five years and there is a bronze statue of him from about 1901, given after it had been declined by Huntingdon.

An 1854 steam mill on the south side of the river is now flats. The River Tea Rooms and the Dolphin Hotel face the water downstream of the bridge.

Between the A1096 and St Ives Staunch is Jones Boatyard. Gravel pits are extensive but the river is now moving into the fens, this being the start of the glacial Lake Fenland with dark alluvial soil, some of the country's best agricultural land but sinking at 20mm per year. The Cambridgeshire Guided Busway crosses. Fen Drayton Lakes have hobbies, terns, geese and, to start 2013, a migrant seal.

An ancient ring village from prehistoric times, Holywell takes its name from a spring with healing properties in St John the Baptist's churchyard. The church was in existence by 890 and it has a 16th century tower of stones from Ramsey Abbey. The wisteria-covered Ferry Boat Inn is at what was the site of a monastic ferry used by Hereward the Wake to escape William the Conqueror. Part of the inn is as old as the church and alcohol was sold on the site from 560 so it claims to be the country's oldest. Juliet Tewsley committed suicide in 1050 over unrequited love for a woodcutter by hanging herself on a willow tree on the site so she was buried in unconsecrated ground. A stone marking her grave is in the bar and on the March 17th anniversary she walks along the path to the bar and points to it.

Levées begin here, a characteristic of the fens. The meridian is crossed between the isolated Pike & Eel Hotel and Brownshill Staunch or Over Lock, conspicuous because of a gravel conveyor crossing the river above it. Forget-me-nots grow along the bank.

Brownshill Staunch, the tidal limit, with a gravel conveyor.

It can be tidal from Brownshill Staunch although the range is limited and, even then, only at spring tides. Two barges are moored below the lock as a floating landing stage for boat crews.

In 1947 a serious breach of the south bank flooded many square kilometres of Ouse Fen, the hole being sealed by building a dam around army amphibious vehicles. Formerly there were osier beds. There are marsh marigolds now.

The spire draws attention to St Mary's church at Bluntisham which has an unusual three sided apse from the 14th century. The Queen Anne rectory, now Bluntisham House with a doorway from Slepe Hall in St Ives, is where Dorothy L Sayers was raised.

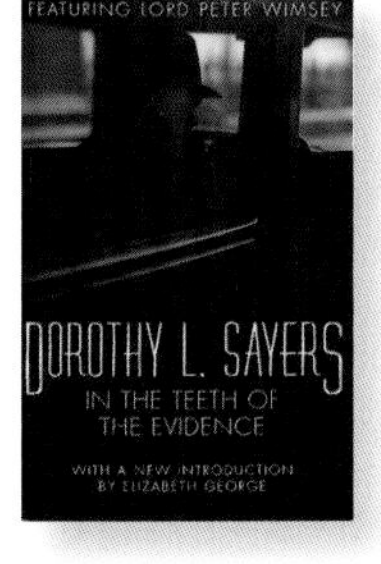

Bandy, the precursor to ice hockey, was invented at Bury Fen, a site used for major ice skating contests.

Also beginning here in 1836 were builders merchants Jewsons, who had limekilns at the entrance to what is now Westview Marina and the Quiet Waters Boat Haven.

Piers from the former St Ives–Ely railway stand on each side of the river and the Roman Car Dyke line is crossed. A Romano-Gallic bronze statue, possibly of Emperor Commodus, was found in 1826 and is now in the British Museum.

Earith, meaning muddy landing place, has a high street with fine early 19th century houses. The Crown, Old Riverview Hotel and Bridge End Stores advertise themselves to boaters.

The Old Bedford River leads off to the left before the river arrives at the Hermitage, a most interesting spot. Although the Great Ouse is tidal upstream, Hermitage Lock has its gates fitted so it is non-tidal downstream. Instead, the tidal flow is taken by the New Bedford River or Hundred Foot. Hire craft are not allowed to use it. Many would not do so anyway as the River Great Ouse or Old West River downstream of the lock is prettier despite being 16km longer and much slower.

The level on the east side is higher than on the west. There is no natural flow in the Old West River until

The Hermitage. The tidal New Bedford River goes under the A1123 while the lock leads to the non-tidal Old West River.

The narrower Old West River near the Hermitage.

Pope's Corner, only what comes in from pumping stations or from the River Cam. The B1050 crosses and runs along the bank at first before turning away. The lock name comes from a 15th century hermit who had to mind the bridge and a causeway. The river is narrow and bank full between reeds so there are sets of markers at each end so that boaters can check their speeds. The line of the Roman Car Dyke follows the river for a while. There are few landmarks. Vegetation includes blackberries and willows which produce three cricket bats from the bottom 2.1m of each tree. Birds include green woodpeckers, barn owls and marsh and hen harriers. Seals can get here despite the locks and there are also bream, carp, roach and tench in the river.

Aldreth Bridge is on the line of the ancient Aldreth Causeway to Ely which was the base for Hereward the Wake, the last Saxon leader to resist the Normans, who killed his brother. He began his defence in 1067. William the Conqueror is said to have built a wooden causeway from Aldreth with the help of a French witch. Hereward attacked near the bridge in 1070 by setting fire to the causeway and many Normans died in the marshes, harassed by Saxon archers. Hereward killed 14 singlehandedly. He was captured in 1071 after being betrayed by the monks who showed the Normans a path through the fens in exchange for an amnesty. The story was used in 1866 by Charles Kingsley in his *Hereward the Wake*.

The B1049 crosses at the former Twenty Pence Ferry, a pre-decimal name, Twenty Pence Marina still in business although the public house of that name has closed. Coots and greylag geese swim around the sedges.

Beyond the A10 crossing the Lazy Otter is next to the old road, the Stretham Ferry Bridge on the Roman road from Cambridge to Ely, but it cannot accept more than a single boat under 11m long on its jetty, which is also too high for small craft to use so they are expected to get out onto the angling platforms on the other side of the river and walk round. There is no way to get in from the adjacent marina except for their customers.

Beyond Stretham Wooden Bridge is Stretham Old Engine, an Ancient Monument. This Victorian steam beam pumping engine, used from 1831 to 1925, has been restored. With a 7.3m beam and 7.3m flywheel, its 11m

Stretham Old Engine is an Ancient Monument.

The fens are vulnerable to winds.

Ely Cathedral rises above the fens.

The Cutter Inn in Ely is a popular wharf area.

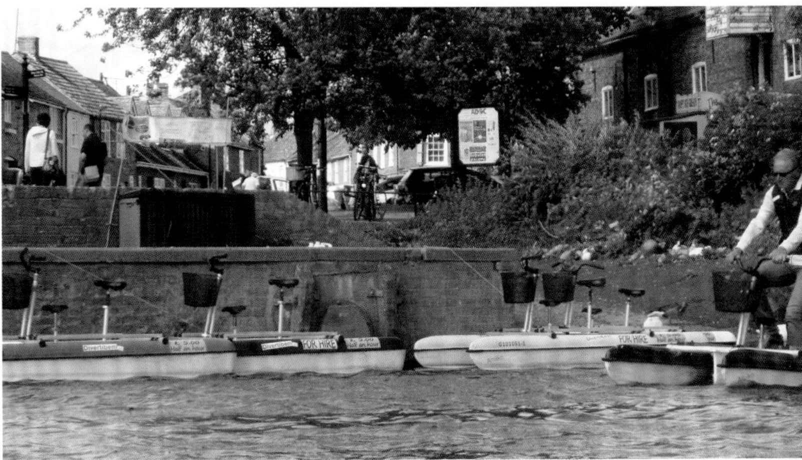

Waterbikes are hired out in Ely.

diameter scoop wheel feeds the river 1.2–3.7m higher at 30m^3 per revolution or 120m^3 per minute. With a 24m chimney, it is the last engine of its kind working in the fens. When the bank collapsed in the 1919 floods it ran continuously for 47 days. There is also a diesel engine which was used from 1925 to 1943.

The A1123 and the Liverpool Street–King's Lynn railway cross before Pope's Corner where the River Cam joins and the channel widens considerably and becomes the Ely Ouse to Littleport.

Little Thetford has St George's 14th century ragstone church and a thatched brick roundhouse. During the Bronze Age there was a river crossing from Barway. Soham Lode joins where 11th century weapons have been recovered from the river so this might have been the way William the Conqueror approached Ely. Jets fly low across the fens and wagtails hop about by the river.

The Stowmarket–Ely railway crosses and the A142 follows over Ely High Bridge beyond the railway station. Ely Station Dock has closed and Tesco has opened here. The Bronze Age causeway was the first land approach to **Ely**. Beyond the Bridge Boatyard the Liverpool Street–King's Lynn railway crosses on the Cutter Railway Bridge before arrival at the Ely waterfront with the Boathouse Restaurant, Riverside Inn, Cutter Inn and Waterside Restaurant.

Ely comes from the Latin elge, Old English el-ge or Saxon elig, eel island. It was said that St Dunstan changed the 10th century monks into eels after finding most married or living with women.

It is for Ely Cathedral that the city is best known, the Ship of the Fens, on top of a small hill and visible from all directions over the flat landscape. A Benedictine monastery for monks and nuns was founded in 673 by St Æthelthryth but burned in 870 by the Danes. The medieval monastic buildings around the cathedral are the largest collection in England, including King's School, founded in 970, one of the oldest English schools. Edward the Confessor studied here as a prince in 1010 and it was granted its charter when he was crowned. William the Conqueror visited the church alone while the monks were eating and left a reward of 1 mark on the altar for betraying Hereward the Wake. They chased him to Witchford, apologized and were fined 700 marks. They melted down the church ornaments to pay the fine but their ingots were underweight so they were charged an additional 300 marks.

The current cathedral building, 76m long with a 22m high ceiling, was built by the Normans from 1080 to 1189 with a 66m West Tower and a hammerbeam roof supported on carved angels. The Octagon Tower was built about 1325 by the monk Alan de Walsingham after the previous tower collapsed in 1322. Rising above the fens, it has magnificent tracery with a lantern weighing over 400t held 30m above the floor with no visible means of support but actually on eight 19m x 760mm x 510mm oak trunks. The lantern has 14m span and 330mm rise and this is one of the greatest structural engineering feats of the Middle Ages, the oaks thought to have been brought by water from Chicksend near Shefford. St Ovin's Cross is Saxon. In the 10th century the monks stole the remains of St Withburga from Dereham to place with his sister, St Æthelthryth, in Ely, but a healing holy well formed in the empty tomb, drawing pilgrims to Dereham, the spring still being there. The Lady Chapel of 1321 was the largest in England with some of the best delicate carving and tracery in Britain although only one statue retains its head. The choirstalls are also 14th century. Bishop Matthew Wren was imprisoned in the Tower for 18 years for supporting Archbishop Laud. The cathedral was closed for 17 years from 1644 after Cromwell drove the congregation out of a choir service which he thought unsuitable. Also thought unsuitable was orange seller Nell Gwynne, who used to sit in the bay window of a shop facing the Bishop's Palace where Charles II stayed. She was moved to where she was not visible to the public as the bishop objected to the king's association with a commoner. The nave has a painted ceiling and there is a memorial to an engine driver and fireman killed when a boiler exploded. A plane tree is said to be England's oldest and largest.

The most northerly Norman vineyard was planted in the city. The motte had a 12th century bailey. St Mary's church dates from the 13th century and Oliver Cromwell's half-timbered house was built in the 14th century as a tithe store, then used as the rectory of Holy Trinity and St Mary's. Cromwell lived here for about a decade after inheriting some local land in 1636 and it became a brewery and inn in the 19th century. It has 17th century furnishings and a haunted bedroom. While here, Cromwell was employed as a church tax collector.

The tiny market city has narrow streets, Georgian architecture and timbered houses. Ely Stained Glass Museum is the only one on the topic, sited in the cathedral with glass from the 13th century onwards. The Ely Museum at the Old Gaol features the fens, archaeology, medieval history, the Cambridgeshire Regiment and crafts. One of the city's prizes is a Russian cannon from Sebastopol.

The slate-roofed maltings of 1868 became the Maltings public house and concert hall in 1971. The Ely Folk Festival takes place in July.

Between the two railway bridges the water in Ely is very active, from the King's School Boat Club to waterbikes being hired near a slipway. Ely Marina is here and the *Viscountess Bury*, built for Edward VII, carries 60 people. Domestic ducks and geese are found with Muscovy ducks.

Until the sugar beet factory closed in the 1970s there were beet barges moored six abreast. Now it is a warehouse and the greatest water activity is in Roswell Pits, used by Ely Sailing Club.

The Great Ouse used to run via Prickwillow and then follow the line of what is now the residual Old Croft River to Wisbech while the Little Ouse flowed to King's Lynn. In 1827 an artificial cut was made to Brandon Creek to link the two Ouses and the water now all heads for the eastern side of the Wash through long straight reaches, used by Cambridge University trial rowing eights.

The Ely–Norwich line crosses Adelaide Railway Bridge where, in 2007, a derailment left aggregate wagons hanging over the side of the bridge. They were lifted clear by a 1,000t crane but not until a 1.2km approach road had been built for it.

Adelaide Road Bridge carries the B1382 from Queen Adelaide, named after a former inn. There is a Herb Garden here, also with wild, woodland and water gardens.

Distinctive pumping station brickwork in Southery Fens.

The River Lark joins halfway down a 5km straight reach.

Littleport is on a fen island. Cnut is said to have been refused refuge by drunken monks but was sheltered by the fisherman Legres, whose wife had been raped by the monks and beaten after he tried to rescue her. Cnut's fleet attacked with many monks killed and the rest forced to build Littleport, Legres installed as the first mayor. Sandhill Bridge by the Swan Restaurant is also called Bulldog Bridge from a large dog seen crossing at dusk. In the Middle Ages a friar attempted to rape a servant girl but a large dog pulled him off and killed him although he stabbed the dog. Even if these stories were untrue it is clear that the Ely monks were getting a bad press generally.

A split goosefeather was a token to enlist the support of fenmen and was used by both sides in the Civil War, including by Charles I at Littleport to pass Roundhead sentries. Cromwell was said to have had permanent disquiet not because of the execution of Charles but because it took place after he had been shown a split goosefeather.

St George's church has a 15th century tower.

The Littleport Riots took place in 1816 when farm workers returning from the Napoleonic Wars faced unemployment and starvation because of the land enclosures. The Riot Act was read and the cavalry called from Bury St Edmunds. One person was killed, several wounded and 80 arrested. They were later tried by the Temporal Court of the Bishopric of Ely, who sentenced 24 to hang. Such was the public outcry that the judges feared for their own lives and the punishments were reduced to five Littleport Martyrs hanged, nine transported and ten imprisoned for a year. The riots led to the Vagrancy Act of 1824 and the Metropolitan Police Act to set up the first modern police force in 1829. A more recent local antagonist has been rugby's Clive Woodward.

A marina is located in a former railway dock before the A10 crosses back over Littleport Bridge to follow the bank as the railway leaves. Mildenhall Drain, one of the larger channels, is pumped in beyond powerlines in a sparsely populated area.

The river moves from Cambridgeshire to Norfolk with the arrival of the Little Ouse River and the Ship Inn at Brandon Creek. There are ghosts of murderers who were noosed and left to hang as the tide dropped and of soldiers who were buried in the bank and left to drown as the tide rose.

Another pumping station brings in Creeks End Mill Drain at Southery Ferry which was to serve Southery, built on an island of Kimmeridge clay. Denver Cruising Club is also based here.

The bed of the Ten Mile River, as it has now become, is lower than the bed of the tidal New Bedford River with which it is converging, another facet of the complex drainage of the fens. The Middle Level Leading Drain is pumped in before Ten Mile Bank, where Hilgay Toll Bridge crosses. The Liverpool Street–King's Lynn railway crosses for a final time before the confluence with the River Wissey. The Environment Agency have been considering an iconic aqueduct to carry boats over the New Bedford River to Salters Lode, avoiding the need for many to go onto tidal water.

The popular Jenyns Arms and moorings are ports of call for many above Denver Sluice and tidal water beyond. The Jenyns Arms has a rather new-looking tariff of rates in old coinage, to cross the river bridge, attached to its wall. Denver Sluice gates were built to operate both ways, to keep out tidal water, to retain enough water for navigation and to discharge water as appropriate. The first sluice was built in 1652 by Vermuyden, bursting in 1713 with extreme floods and high tides. It was rebuilt in 1750 by Labelye and replaced in 1834 by Rennie using three 5.3m gates to which an extra 11m sluice was added in 1923. Double guillotine gates can both be raised together for flushing, a dangerous situation, when red lights are shown as a warning to keep away. The Cut-off Channel, New Bedford River, Old Bedford River and Well Creek all bring water. The Relief Channel was added in 1965 to discharge water as its two ends are at different states of the tide and there is a 3.4m drop along its length. This complex web of routes offers great potential for boaters, much of which has yet to be realized. This area was the setting for Graham Swift's novel *Waterland*.

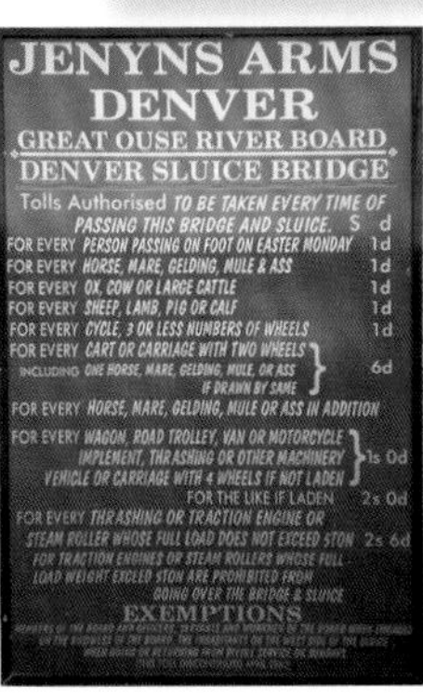

The Jenyns Arms at Denver Sluice.

Distance
99km from Kempston to Denver

Navigation Authority
Environment Agency

Navigation Societies
Great Ouse Boating Association www.goba.org.uk, East Anglian Waterways Association www.eawa.co.uk

OS 1:50,000 Sheets
142 Peterborough
143 Ely & Wisbech
153 Bedford & Huntingdon
154 Cambridge & Newmarket

Connection
River Great Ouse – *see RoB p167*

34 River Cam

The world's best punting location

Ah! surely not in singless of heart
Should I have seen the light of evening fade
Upon the silent Cam, if we had met,
Even at that early time; I needs must hope
William Wordsworth

In the rivalries between Oxford and **Cambridge** the Backs win hands down as the supreme setting for punting. On a sunny summer's day the water, the banks and the carparks are packed as people converge from around the world to this historic centre of learning.

The River Cam rises near Widdington and flows north to the River Great Ouse, followed by the Fens Rivers Way. The glacial Lake Fenland reached nearly to Cambridge and this fenland river flows with little current. The Roman name of Granta was taken from the British Celtic for marshy river. Vermuyden proposed the Cut-off Channel from Grantchester to Denver Sluice in 1638 but it was not dug until the 20th century and then only below Barton Mills on the River Lark. The 1812 London & Cambridge Junction Canal from Bishop's Stortford to Clayhithe was never built or it would have connected the Ouse to the main canal network. Likewise, a vaguer plan to connect to the Stour in 1888 never came to anything.

Cambridge was a 5th century Saxon market town. It was used as a Danish army base and became an 11th century Norman centre. Its life as an academic town dates from the 13th century. Unlike Oxford, it does not have a manufacturing history. The 31 colleges have produced 62 Nobel Prize winners, 13 Prime Ministers, 9 Archbishops of Canterbury, Prince Charles, Professor Stephen Hawking, A A Milne, Samuel Pepys, Thomas Shadwell, Guy Burgess, Donald Maclean, Anthony Blunt and Kim Philby to name a few. Cromwell was MP from 1640 to 1653 and seized the mayorship in 1642. The city has been used for filming *An Unsuitable Job for a Lady*, *Bliss*, *Cold Enough for Snow* and *Silent Witness* and is where Defoe had Moll Flanders stealing linen.

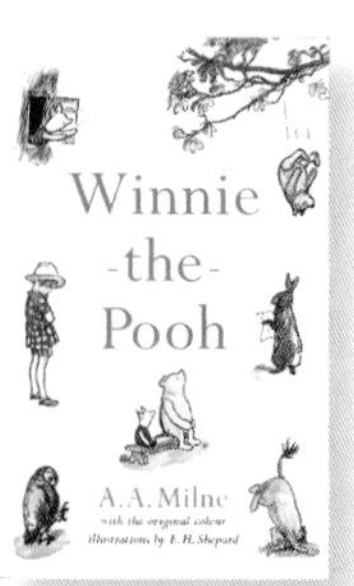

King's Mill punt rollers define the head of navigation for anything not portable although many of the punts and canoes on hire below are taken upstream. A Cambridge speciality is a double width punt complete with chauffeur who gives a guided tour to those who simply wish to sit back.

King's Ditch of 1265 became an open sewer so Hobson's Conduit was constructed in 1610 to bring water via Hobson's Brook to flush it out, by 1631 serving ornate drinking fountains at Emmanuel and Christ's Colleges. Carrier Thomas Hobson became mayor and hired out his horses in strict rotation, known as Hobson's choice.

The Scott Polar Research Institute has a memorial to Scott's 1912 journey to the South Pole.

Downing College was established by Sir George Downing who served Cromwell but switched to Charles II to suit the requirements, becoming rich as his colleagues were executed. His 15 year old grandson married his 13 year old cousin, did a two year Grand Tour and returned to find her a maid of honour to Queen Anne. This was politically unacceptable so they never lived together and he left his estate to found a new college although most of the money was taken up in legal fees fighting his wife.

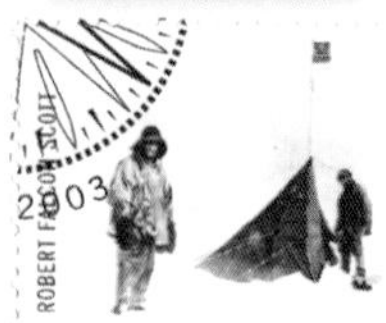

The Fitzwilliam Museum is in an 1848 building with Corinthian portico and shows Egyptian, Greek and Roman antiquities, ceramics and furniture, being one of the best outside the major cities and one of the earliest British public picture galleries. The lions outside are reputed to roar, get down for a drink or go inside when midnight strikes.

Porterhouse College was founded in 1284 by Hugh de Balsham, Bishop of Ely, for 14 fellows but students had already been in Cambridge since fleeing Oxford riots in 1209. Those present included William Brewster and Massachussetts Governor John Winthrop. There is a University Museum of Archaeology & Anthropology and the Sedgwick Museum has fossils and rocks.

Emmanuel College was founded in 1584 by Sir Walter Mildmay, to be Elizabeth I's Chancellor of the Exchequer, with strict rules for producing Protestant preachers, students including John Harvard. The 1666 chapel was by Sir Christopher Wren. Little St Mary's church or the church of St Mary the Less is 14th century.

Sir Christopher Wren's first completed building the previous year had been the chapel of Pembroke College, which had been founded in 1347 by the widowed Countess of Pembroke. The 17 year old Lady Marie St Pol de Valence had married the 50 year old Earl of Pembroke but he had been killed in a jousting tournament the same afternoon. Ridley was to be a Master.

The Museum of Zoology includes fossils and extinct species while the Whipple Museum of the History of Science has scientific instruments in the original Cambridge Free School. Fitzbillies Restaurant is a favourite student cakeshop with a secret recipe for Chelsea buns.

St Catherine's College of 1473 is near Silver Street Bridge. Rhode Island founder Roger Williams was here, as was Erasmus, who imported his own wine rather than drink the local beer. The college was poor but in 1623 it was found that the Master, John Hills, owed it a large sum and the college silver had disappeared.

Queens' College by Queens' Bridge was endowed in 1448 by Margaret of Anjou and Elizabeth Woodville, the latter's husband, Edward IV, having murdered Henry VI, the husband of the former. The 1449 Old Court has unchanged medieval brickwork and a sun and moon dial which allows the time to be told by the shadow of the moon as well as that of the sun. Charles Darwin was here and his son, Horace, became the first chairman of Cambridge Scientific Instruments. It was used for filming *The Student Prince*.

It was claimed that the 12m span Mathematical Bridge had been built across the Cam in 1750 without any fixings and that it had been taken to bits by the Victorians to see how it had been done but they had not been able to reassemble it so bolts had to be used, as they are now. A counterclaim is that it has always had bolts, which would beg the question why anyone should want to take it apart unless it was to replace it as a result of deterioration, the current replica being built in 1904.

The Museum of Classical Archaeology is 19th century but St Botolph's church is mostly 14th century with a notable font cover of 1637.

Corpus Christi College of 1352, founded by the townspeople, is the best surviving early medieval college in Cambridge, with a statue of Master Matthew Parker, later Archbishop of Canterbury, the original nosey parker. Other students have included John Smith, the Father of

Virginia, Christopher Marlowe and John Fletcher. An early 20th century ghost is thought to have been Master Dr Henry Butts who hung himself in his room in 1632 as the result of depression over the number of students dying of the plague. A 17th century ghost was that of a student meeting the Master's daughter but suffocating while hiding in a kitchen cupboard. A 16th century passage ran to the 11th century St Bene't's church, short for St Benedict's, with a Saxon tower, the city's oldest building. Fabian Stedman invented change ringing here and wrote the first campanology book in 1668.

As well as two medieval wall paintings the 16th century Eagle public house has the signatures of Second World War pilots on the ceiling. King's Parade shops were founded in the 16th century but are now mostly 18/19th century.

King's College's Gothic chapel of 1446–1515 is 88 x 12 x 29m high. Started in magnesian limestone, it was completed in Weldon stone with the join visible from the north but has some of the best Perpendicular architecture in England with a notable Perpendicular window, an oak screen given by Henry VIII, excellent woodcarving and fan vaulted ceiling, 16th century stained glass and *The Adoration of the Magi* by Rubens as an altarpiece. There is an exhibition of its construction. The first word of the carol *Once in Royal David's City* starting the *Festival of Nine Lessons & Carols*, broadcast from here on Christmas Eve, is the moment many people take to be the start of Christmas.

King's College itself, using Ramsey Abbey stone, had its first stone laid by Henry VI in 1441 to take scholars from his school at Eton. In the 17th century two bursars left with the funds and another changed his name to avoid paternity problems. Rupert Brooke and E M Forster were students, the latter comparing Cambridge unfavourably with Oxford in *Howards End*. Douglas Potts was another brilliant student but lived in a fantasy world, threatened a shopkeeper with a gun in 1930, was questioned by a tutor and a detective and shot both of them and himself. The college was used for filming *Sylvia*.

King's College bridge was moved upstream in 1824. Henry VI had seized land for the Backs, the townsfolk only agreeing if it was put to good use so it is still used to graze five bullocks. The Backs were developed in the 16th century but no landing was allowed and barge horses had to walk on gravel in the river as the banks belonged to the colleges. It is an area of punts, canoes, rowing boats, skiffs, bicycles, lawns and weeping willows.

The 1440s God's House teachers' college was developed in 1505 by Lady Margaret Beaufort, mother of Henry VIII, with a notable pre Reformation chapel and a 1643 Fellows' Building which was the university's first in Classical style. A mulberry tree is one which Milton planted or under which he wrote *Lycidas*. The Fellows' Garden has the ghost of a clergyman.

Clare College of 1326 was rebuilt in 1338 and in 1638–1715 after fires. Fellow Hugh Latimer was also burnt to death. The college was used for filming *Honey for Tea*. Clare Bridge of 1640 is the city's oldest over the Cam and one of England's oldest in Classical design. The 23m structure has three spans of 6.4m. Mostly in Ketton ashlar limestone, it has structural problems but only carries light loads. Much is made of the number of balls on the parapets, not a round figure as a slice is missing from one facing the river on the left end, a practical joke in masonry.

The 1348 Gonville & Caius College, the first name usually being omitted, used Ramsey Abbey stone. In the 17th century Titus Oates devised the Popish Plot which resulted in the executions of 35 innocent people for allegedly plotting to kill Charles II. His father had not been too savoury, either, charging simple housewives to be baptized in the Cam regardless of the temperature.

Trinity Hall of 1350 has an Elizabethan chained library. Master Stephen Gardiner backed Henry VIII's divorce, making Mary illegitimate, but then supported Mary's legitimacy claim. Fellow Leslie Stephen had taken up holy orders but had to relinquish them after running a race half naked in 1854 because of the heat.

Garret Hostel Bridge has been in existence since 1573. The 1960 version has a 26m span, an early post tensioned concrete design only 530mm deep at the crown, making it easy for punters to negotiate.

Behind Corinthian columns is the 1730 Senate House which governs the university. The 15th century Great St Mary's church has a 17th century tower and chimes from 1793 which were later copied for Big Ben in London.

Trinity College used Ramsey Abbey stone and is the largest Cambridge college. It was founded in 1546 by Henry VIII and has a portrait of him by Holbein and a statue of him holding an orb and a chair leg as a 19th century student joke. Wren's library of 1695 has an elaborate wooden coat of arms by Grinling Gibbons. The Tudor Great Court is the world's largest quad. The clock strikes each hour twice. A race takes place round the quad, 347m to be covered in 43

Cambridge's Mathematical Bridge.

King's College Chapel.

Clare College is a substantial building with river frontage.

Clare Bridge is the city's oldest. The odd ball is on the left.

seconds while the clock strikes noon twice. *Chariots of Fire* was filmed in Trinity Quad although the race itself was filmed elsewhere. Trinity has produced 28 Nobel Prize winners and has an apple tree descended from the one which inspired Isaac Newton. The chapel has memorials to Newton, Francis Bacon, Lord Macauley and Lord Tennyson. The college did not allow dogs so Byron got a bear cub and bathed with it in the fountain. The statue of him is one refused by Westminster Abbey because of his gambling and drunken lifestyle. Young bedmaker Elizabeth Butchill ended up in many of them with their occupants. She killed her ensuing baby and flushed it down the toilet. Her uncle was suspicious and informed the police, following which she was executed publicly in 1780.

Trinity Street has Tudor timber framed and Georgian red brick houses. Trinity College Bridge of 1765 has three arches of 5.5–6.1m in early semi-elliptical Classical style, built of Ketton ashlar stone and Portland stone.

Girton College was Cambridge's first college for women. The ghost of a Roman centurion has been seen here.

St John's College was founded in 1511 by Lady Margaret Beaufort with a Tudor roof to the Hall and a 1516 three storey red brick turreted Gate Tower with a statue of her. William Wordsworth, William Wilberforce and Lord Palmerston were here, Cromwell used it as a prison and there is a ghost of the Master Dr Wood who died in 1839 but appears as in his poor student days. St John's Old Bridge or St John's Kitchen Bridge of 1712 by Wren has three stone arches, the lowest on the river through the Backs, with 1879 and 1947 floodmarks. The 1671 level is marked on the New Bridge of 1831, known as the Bridge of Sighs because of its resemblance to its namesake in Venice, its 12m span allowing students across but preventing access once the gates are locked. St John's Cripps Building is said to be the best 20th century building in Cambridge.

Kettle's Yard has 20th century paintings and sculpture. A 16th century timbered farmhouse and 17th century White Horse Inn closed in 1934 form the basis of the Cambridge & County Folk Museum with an eel catcher's trap and gleve and fen overshoes for men and horses.

Magdalen Bridge, the Roman Via Devana on a chalk spur of the Gog Magog Hills, was the Great Bridge which gave the city its name. It has had timber bridges from Saxon times and a cast iron bridge of 13m span since 1823, a steel portal frame having been hidden inside its envelope after it sagged. A motte guarded this strategic crossing. After William the Conqueror's Cambridge Castle became disused the stones were taken for reuse elsewhere in the 15th century.

Magdalen College of 1542 had been the 1400s Buckingham College for Benedictine monks. Its benefactors were the 2nd Duke of Buckingham, his son and the Duke of Norfolk, all being executed for treason between 1483 and 1521. Later benefactors were to be Baron Audley of Walden and Thomas Cromwell, who both helped get rid of two of Henry VIII's wives. Students included Charles Kingsley and Samuel Pepys, whose library of 3,000 books is preserved.

The redundant church of the Holy Sepulchre of about 1130 was by a crusading military monastic order, one of four round churches in England, now a brass-rubbing centre.

Sidney Sussex College was founded in 1596. Oliver Cromwell studied here for a year from 1616 until his father died. His head was buried in the antechamber in 1960.

The Quayside has a former bonded warehouse, a drain with a man's head outlet and bronze lion heads with rings. Canada geese and swans look for handouts around Jesus Green Lock, which has curved balance beams and a swing footbridge across the chamber. Powered craft are not allowed upstream of here between March and September because of the carnage which would result with the punts. There are moorings alongside Jesus Common, including a houseboat, as red and white horse chestnut trees line the river.

Jesus College of 1497 was founded by John Alcock, Bishop of Ely, using the buildings of a 12th century convent. The chapel was restored by Pugin. Cranmer married barmaid Black Joan when he was supposed to be celibate so he resigned his fellowship but he took it up again when she later died in childbirth. When it had been St Radegund's Nunnery there had been a reluctant Sister Benedict who had a relationship with a monk from Barnwell Abbey, to which it was connected by a tunnel. A child carried letters between them until she informed and they were both excommunicated. Abbey House is on the site of an Augustine priory and is haunted by a creature like a large furry penguin, which also haunts Merton College. It also has the ghost of a squire, an armoured man, a black nun, a white head and an ill tempered spirit.

Beyond Victoria Avenue bridge are the college boathouses alongside Midsummer Common, many rowers being active as far as Baits Bite Lock. Absent from here is the Free Press public house in the city, which was registered as a boat club. The common has had a Midsummer Fair since the Middle Ages, opening with the mayor giving pennies to children.

Barnwell was noted for prostitutes serving students. When Robert Browning caught a disease off one in 1876 he responded by slashing the throat of another, 16 year old Emma Rolfe, whose body was taken to the 16th century Fort St George in England public house, not accessible by road. Browning gave himself up and was hanged.

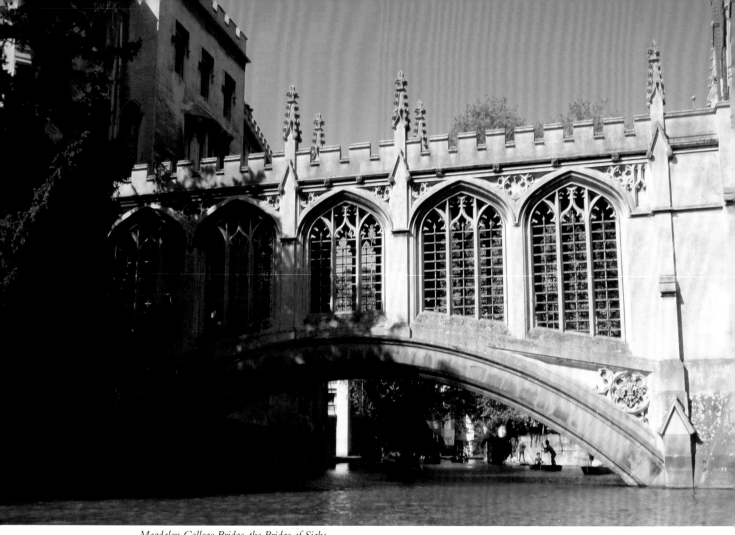

Magdalen College Bridge, the Bridge of Sighs.

Anglia Ruskin University is here to the east of the other colleges.

The A1134 Elizabeth Way crosses the river near the setting for Stourbridge Fair, one of the greatest in Europe, started in King John's time to support the local Leper Hospital of St Mary Magdalene, of which the Norman chapel remains. A tall chimney marks the Museum of Technology, a Victorian beam engine pumping station with steam and gas engines and a printshop in a former gasworks site.

A modern arched bridge with twin cycle and footways snakes across the river to Chesterton where there are the 14th century Chesterton Tower, the Jacobean Chesterton Hall and the 13th century church of St Andrew with 30 carved human pew ends from about 1420.

A heavy girder bridge carries the St Pancras–King's

A cycleway snakes across the Cam as rowers pass beneath.

The Museum of Technology in an old gasworks.

Lynn railway over to leave the city behind. Cow parsley, buttercups, reeds and hawthorn bushes with moorhens and mallards are more typical of Long Reach. Fen Ditton has thatched and 16/17th century houses, a 1635 Hall built around a medieval house and an 18th century Old Vicarage.

St Mary's church is 14th century. A church court fined former sexton and gardener Edward Smith £42/7/6 in 1849 after he made libellous statements about the chastity of the rector's wife and was forced to read a recantation but 3,000 riotous spectators packed the church, derided the rector and his wife as they went home, carried Smith in triumph to the Plough Inn and left a trail of damage at the church and vicarage.

Like the Thames Tideway there is a section which requires craft to cross to the wrong side of the river to make it easier for rowers who are racing. There are bumps rowing races, Lents in February and Mays in June.

The A14 crosses by Biggin Abbey, the 14th century retreat of the Bishops of Ely, before reaching Baits Bite Lock at Milton.

Horningsea was an Iron Age site. The Grade I St Peter's church of the 13th century is on the site of a 9th century Saxon minster. A seat is carved from a fallen willow tree, of which numbers are now appearing along the banks. There are lilies in the water and cormorants join the birdlife. From time to time pillboxes defend the river.

The end of the Car Dyke joined the river upstream of Clayhithe and there was a Roman pottery.

Waterbeach has the earthworks of the Franciscan Norman Waterbeach Abbey for nuns. St John's church is partly 13th century.

From here the river enters a more fenland setting with low banks, making it quite open and windswept, Cam Sailing Club being located to take immediate advantage.

The Cam Conservators cease to be the navigation authority directly above Bottisham Lock, which is run by the Environment Agency and less user friendly than the previous locks.

Levées control the river as teasels grow sporadically and poplars are planted at intervals. Swaffham Bulbeck Lode, which can be weedy, enters through a guillotine lock between Bottisham Fen and Swaffham Prior Fen. Reach Lode enters beyond Tiptree Marina in a similar manner at Upware by the Five Miles Inn, shortened from its title of Five Miles from Anywhere, No Hurry. Despite the distance it has been used by students, as it was in 1850 to declare the Upware Republic. Some twenty years later it was used to proclaim Richard Fielder the King of Upware, His Majesty's Pint being a 27l jug. The Idiots and Beersoakers student clubs both met here. It was rebuilt in 1980 after a fire.

Searchers for a farmer missing for three days in the fog met his ghost, which said where he had died on the first day. Despite wishing to be buried in Wicken he was buried at Soham so he still haunts the area until his wishes are fulfilled.

Approaching Bottisham Lock at Waterbeach.

Woods are less common on the lower fen reaches.

Wicken Fen is Britain's oldest nature reserve, the last undrained fen with reeds, sedge, scrub, 300 plant species, open water, warblers, marsh and hen harriers, breeding snipe, 5,000 insect species and 200 spiders. Water is being pumped into this area to keep it wet, the opposite of the situation throughout the rest of the fens. Currently covering 5km^2, the National Trust would like to extend it in a vast swathe all the way to Cambridge.

The A1123 crosses on a bowstring bridge at Dimmock's Cote, along from a chalk pit which has produced ammonites. There are osier beds and the area grows one of the largest celery crops in Britain. The fenland encourages herons, great crested grebes, coots, oystercatchers, tufted ducks, shelducks, curlews and snipe. Ahead, Ely Cathedral makes its first appearance on the skyline. The Fish & Duck Marina is present at Pope's Corner as the larger Cam joins what is here the much narrower Great Ouse, most of its water no longer passing this way.

A steam launch, one of the quietest boats on the river.

Distance
23km from Cambridge to the River Great Ouse

Navigation Authority
Conservators of the River Cam / Environment Agency

Navigation Societies
Great Ouse Boating Association www.goba.org.uk, East Anglian Waterways Association www.eawa.co.uk

OS 1:50,000 Sheets
143 Ely & Wisbech
154 Cambridge & Newmarket

35 River Lark

A landscape retained by drainage engines

In fitness for the urgent hour,
Unlimited, untiring power,
Precision, promptitude, command,
The infant's will, the giant's hand;
Steam, mighty Steam, ascends the throne,
And reigns lord paramount alone.
Lark Engine House of Burnt Fen

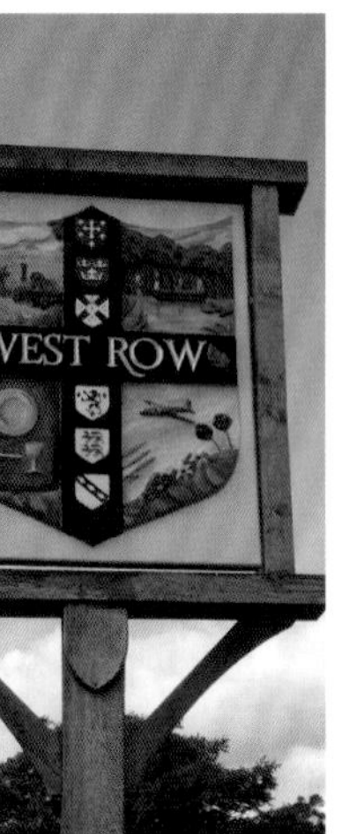

The River Lark emerges from the lake at Plumpton Hall. It was formerly a navigation below Bury St Edmunds but these days large boats can only reach Jude's Ferry at West Row, the top turning point for long craft. King's Staunch below Wamil Hall is a further obstruction to non-portable craft. There are plans to extend the navigation to **Mildenhall**.

At the far end of a plantation of poplar trees the Lee Brook (the downstream extension of the River Kennett) enters, bringing with it the Cambridgeshire border. Suffolk stays with the right bank of the river for another 8km to Lark Grange, though.

A cut at **Isleham** brings the only working lock on the river, prominent notices saying that only anglers may have access to the lock area. The natural course of the river wanders past it with a weir at Waterside. Isleham Marina and a development of chalet houses are located on the island.

With the two channels reunited, the river is broad and runs almost straight for 7km in a cut which may have been made by the Romans across the South Level of the Bedford Level, named after the Duke of Bedford who financed the reclamation of the fens. There are levées on both sides and the northeast bank is edged continuously with corrugated asbestos sheeting. The levées hide the rich peat-black farmland which is at sea level here, significantly below river level. The area is crossed with

The vegetation has a windswept look below Isleham.

Isleham has the River Lark's only working lock.

The former mill near Cock Inn Farm.

Prickwillow Drainage Engine Museum.

A southeasterly wind will aid progress downstream. A prominent marker is a squat octagonal former mill with inward-sloping walls and an octagonal tile cap roof situated on the right bank near Cock Inn Farm, itself graced by a pair of spiral brick chimneys. Mostly, though, the commonest dwellings are the small windbreaks placed at intervals for goats which graze the banks. Otherwise only roofs are seen over the levées.

At Mile End the river suddenly deflects through 90°, bending back even more sharply at Prickwillow in front of the Drainage Engine Museum. This was the line of the River Great Ouse until 1830. The 19th century church has a 17th century marble font which came from Ely Cathedral.

The final 3km to the River Great Ouse are windswept and featureless but for a railway bridge, powerlines and a road bridge at each end.

At one time all the rivers in the area discharged to the sea at Wisbech but a catastrophic storm in the 13th century forced them to flow via King's Lynn.

Distance
16km from West Row to the River Great Ouse

Navigation Authority
Environment Agency

Navigation Societies
Great Ouse Boating Association www.goba.org.uk, East Anglian Waterways Association www.eawa.co.uk

OS 1:50,000 Sheet
143 Ely & Wisbech

drainage ditches and pumping houses at intervals empty them into the river. How much truth there is to the tales of Hereward the Wake is not known but they do set the tone of the fens admirably.

This is very often an open route with most of the interest being provided by the other craft on the river.

The last bridge as the Lark joins the Great Ouse.

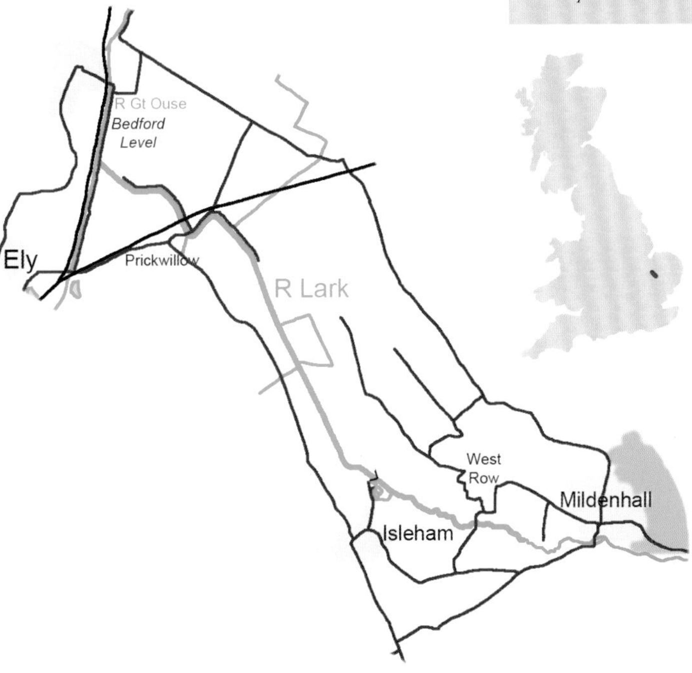

36 Little Ouse River

Flint and fen

Brandon Bridge in brick and flint.

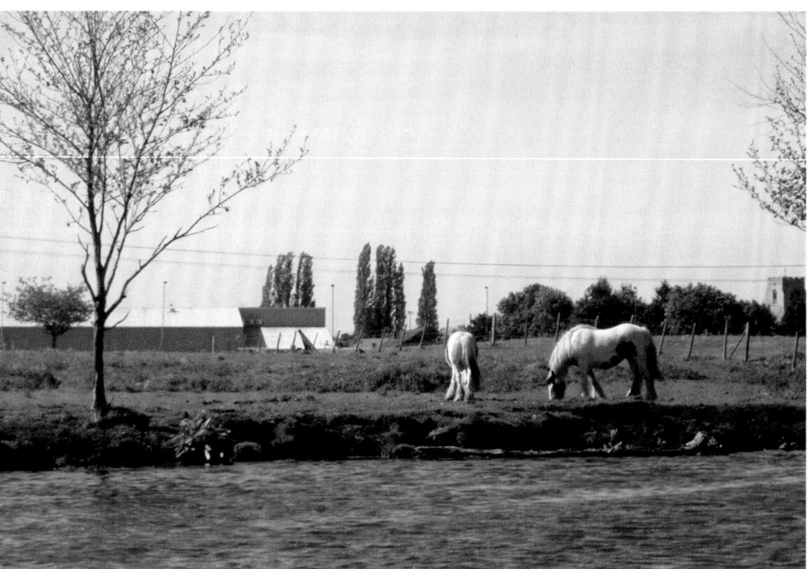
Brandon's church stands away from the centre of the village.

The Little Ouse continues to the left while the sluices on the right lead down to the Cut-off Channel yet the arrow on the right, pointing at these sluices, says 'Navigation Channel'.

The B1113 runs along a sand embankment at Redgrave. Springs under the sand flow eastwards as the River Waveney and westwards as the Little Ouse River, Brandon River, Brandon Creek or Thetford River. These may both have been parts of an overflow channel from the glacial Lake Fenland. They might have been used by the Vikings in the 8th century to drag their boats through this alluvial section and there have been petitions for a through route for craft in water since the time of Charles I, a route still being requested by powered craft users. Fison's had fertilizer traffic below Thetford until the Second World War and there are plans to restore this at least and repair the derelict locks although there is little summer flow.

Brandon, the present head of navigation for powered craft, is on the edge of Breckland, the driest part of the country, with sandy heathland covered by 200km^2 of Thetford Forest, Britain's second largest forest and the biggest lowland pine forest.

Here since Anglo-Saxon times, Brandon has been a centre for the flint industry with over 300 mines in the area. It was the last British location for the gun flint industry although the dust was bad for lungs. The bridge carrying the A1065 gives a grassy approach to the water at its northeast corner and, like many of the houses, is built of brick and small flints.

The Ram Hotel of 1349 is Brandon's oldest building but many buildings are Georgian, including the Brandon House hotel. Brandon Heritage Centre in the old fire station shows flint, fur and forestry since Neolithic times.

The Bridge House Hotel stands by the river as it departs from the village, initially forming the county boundary between Suffolk on the left bank and Norfolk on the right, mostly remote from buildings.

The Environment Agency's only active lock on the river is at Brandon Staunch, built only 12.1m long in 1995 so most powered craft cannot get through although they come up this far, narrowboats needing up to twice this length of lock. The river is edged by alders, willows, hawthorns, reeds and stinging nettles and used by mallards, moorhens, Canada geese, swans and cormorants. To the south of the river are the 17th century Brandon Hall in flint and brick and St Peter's church on a pre-Norman site, some of it 14th century and the rest from 1873 with the unusual churchyard activity of allotments.

A mast stands beside the Norwich–Ely railway bridge, the railway never being more than 900m from the river as far as Botany Bay. At intervals pumps extract water from the river. The site of Sheepwash Staunch is unmarked.

Hockwold cum Wilton is located by the spire of the 14th century church of St James, which has fishponds which were recorded in the *Domesday* survey.

This is the start of the fens, edged by the Cut-off Channel to take surplus water, passing under the river in a siphon, a grade separated interchange with water diverted down through sluices. Floating barriers cross the front of the draw off channel, to which an EA 'Navigation Channel' arrow points. The river navigation channel is actually through the sluices on the left. Wilton Bridge takes the B1112 over.

Bulrushes grow along the banks with lilies in the river and with Egyptian, greylag and domestic geese, herons, great crested grebes and terns. A large stand of woodland on New Fen is out of character. So, on misty nights, is a barge with chanting monks and the corpse of St Withburga which has been reported drifting towards Ely.

The remains of Crosswater Staunch hide among more

Woods have grown up on New Fen.

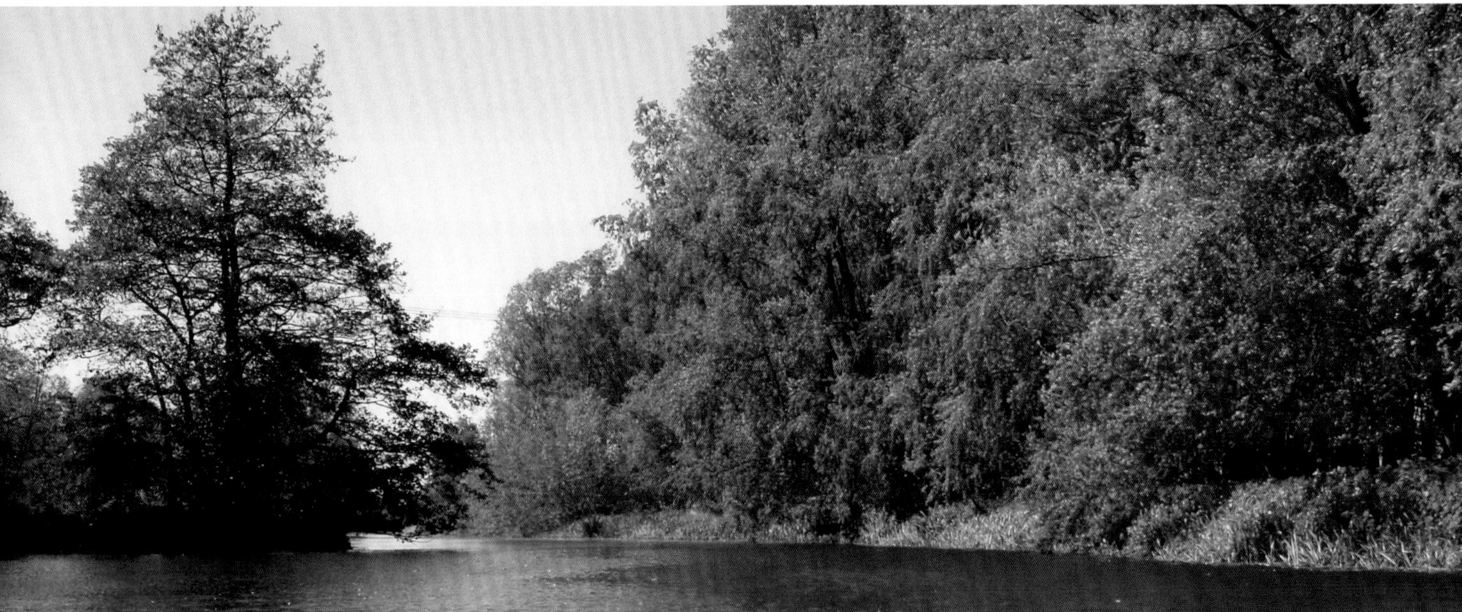

Wooded section near Botany Bay.

trees by the south bank. From here the river is in artificial cut. The old line can be seen by the county boundary until Plantation Farm and then along the line of the A1101 to Littleport. This route shows some of the best rodham in East Anglia, where darker soil marks the lines of the former riverbanks.

At Botany Bay the Little Ouse is joined by Lakenheath New Lode or Stallode and then by **Lakenheath** Lode, Lakenheath Old Lode or Cross Water. Decoy Fen is camouflaged by weeping willows.

A trig point a metre above sea level marks where the south bank becomes Cambridgeshire. It is watched across the river from a pumping station by a straw angler in a green John Deere overall, empty beer glass in one hand and a rod with a catch of sacking in the other.

Cow parsely on the banks adds spring colour with lines of poplar trees on the south bank forming windbreaks. Moorings at Brandon Bank include the antidote to houseboats, built on fast pontoons with a tall chimney and a ship's wheel on the top deck. Saddleback Bridge collects weed as it crosses to Little Ouse where the 1869 former church of St John is built of brick and small flints. To the south is Burnt Fen, where Hereward the Wake was the 11th century arsonist.

Brandon Creek has more moorings and the kingfisher before arrival at the A10. The Ship Inn, site of an old forge, brings customers aboard at the confluence with the River Great Ouse.

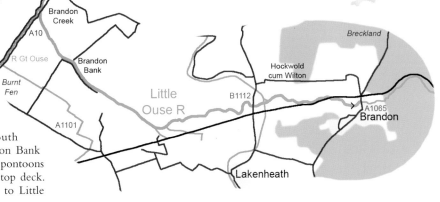

The remains of Crosswater Staunch.

Unlike most houseboats, this one at Brandon Bank has fast catamaran pontoons and a ship's steering wheel.

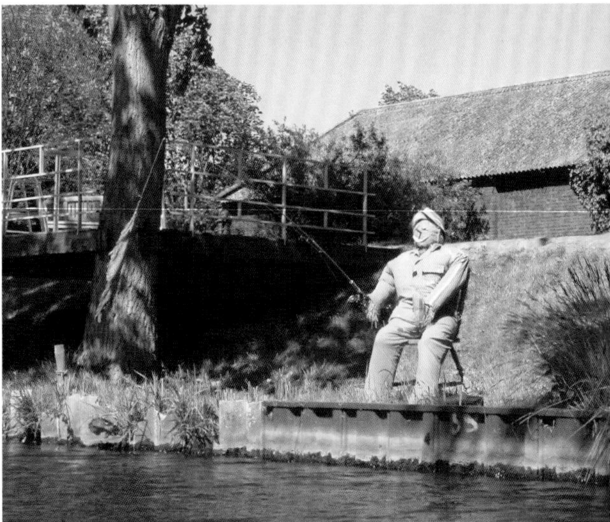

A dummy with beerglass, rod and catch of sacking.

Distance
22km from Brandon to the River Great Ouse

Navigation Authority
Environment Agency

Navigation Society
Great Ouse Boating Association www.goba.org.uk

OS 1:50,000 Sheets
143 Ely & Wisbech
144 Thetford & Diss

The Ship Inn as the Little Ouse joins the Great Ouse.

37 River Wissey

The world's largest sugar beet factory

The River Wissey rises at Shipdham very close to the source of the River Yare but finds its way to the sea in the opposite direction, westwards across Norfolk to join the River Great Ouse. At one time it reached the sea at Wisbech but a catastrophic storm in the late 13th century diverted it to its present route through King's Lynn.

Cruisers can reach Whittington. On a good day the vegetation stalks covering the footpath will have been mown off to ankle height for much of the way down the navigation. Strong headwinds affect this exposed fenland countryside when the prevailing westerly wind blows. There are geese and it is one of the last rivers to have native white clawed crayfish.

After being crossed by the A134 bypass the river brushes the edge of Stoke Ferry.

Ahead, a set of guillotine gates mark a grade-separated river crossing with slip road. The Cut-off Channel which skirts the fens passes underneath and there is a connection down to it to discharge excess water from the Wissey although the EA do not allow the channel's use despite being the riparian owners for almost all of it. A tall aerial at Wretton and a large factory at Methwold are prominent without revealing their functions.

Virtually anything of any size is prominent here although there are more trees and bushes to be seen than in some parts of the fens, willows, birches and hawthorns. Blackberries can be picked from the water in places and coltsfoot and teasels add colour in season. Mallard, coot and moorhen are the birds of the river with kestrels hovering overhead, overshadowed by passing bombers from the various airbases.

Little is seen of the land, which is flat, rich, black farmland, but the noise of tractors may be heard over the raised banks and from time to time there is a solitary pumping station, used to pump into the higher river from the drainage channels crossing the fens. They, too, seem derelict and boarded up but water may be seen boiling up in the side channels which serve these buildings.

Approaching Wissington in the middle of Methwold Severals, the river widens into a series of lakes with islands. The village itself consists almost entirely of an enormous sugar beet factory, the world's largest, with a row of silos and conveyors leading in all directions. This provides central facilities for all British sugar beet factories. The occasional sugar beet floats away down the river to freedom. The footpath leads through the middle of an aggregate yard with large items of plant manoeuvring.

Woods beside the river across Hilgay Fen.

The world's largest sugar beet factory is by the river.

Pumping stations are passed, often apparently derelict.

The largest village on the river is Hilgay where there are moorings on both sides above the bridge and nondescript boats moored downstream. Manorial earthworks on the hillside on the left are followed by the village. The A10 crosses and then the river is into open country again, crossing between Fordham Fen and Great West Fen until reaching the Cambridge–King's Lynn railway bridge, the last feature before Ouse Bridge Farm, which stands on the far side of the River Great Ouse at the confluence.

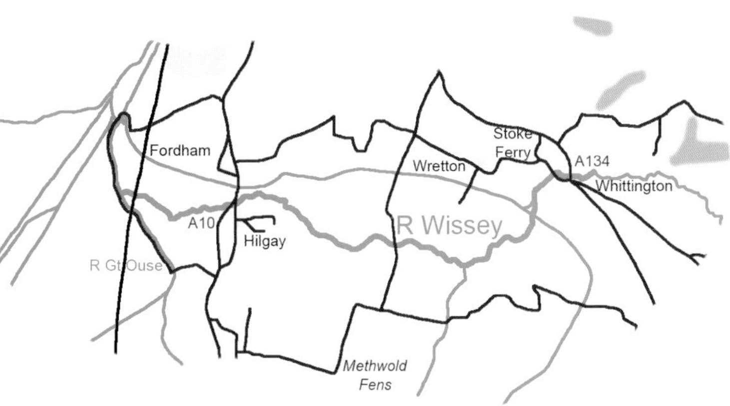

A fen feel to the river below Hilgay.

The railway bridge upstream of the confluence with the Ouse.

Distance
15km from Whittington to River Great Ouse

Navigation Authority
Environment Agency

Navigation Society
Great Ouse Boating Association www.goba.org.uk

OS 1:50,000 Sheet
143 Ely & Wisbech

38 Relief Channel

Protecting boaters and landowners

The Denver Sluice gates across the Relief Channel.

Denver Sluice is one of the largest drainage installations in the country and is the most complex arrangement with two major sets of sluice gates. The River Great Ouse, here also known as the Ten Mile River, arrives after receiving water from the River Wissey and other fenland rivers and is stopped by a set of sluices with a lock. Downstream of the lock is the tidal New Bedford River cut, soon to be joined by the Old Bedford River and Well Creek, the old course of the River Nene. The two Bedford Rivers have higher outer banks to store floodwater between them as a continuous wash but even that was not enough. In the 1947 floods 150km^2 of land was inundated. It is common for boats travelling down the Great Ouse to have to lock up onto tidal water. In times of flood the water upstream of the sluice could only flow away at low tide. The solution was to take the water from upstream of the sluice in a channel parallel to the Great Ouse and have a new confluence above King's Lynn, where the low tide level is 3.4m lower than at Denver. The Relief Channel was completed in 1959. Feeding into it directly below Denver Sluice is the Cut-off Channel, dug a few years later to intercept water from the Lark at Barton Mills, the Little Ouse and the Wissey, originally planned also to pick up the Cam at Grantchester. The idea was not new. Vermuyden had prepared a drawing of the scheme in 1638.

The channel runs northwards across Norfolk, nearly all as gentle lefthand bend, roughly following the eastern shoreline of the Ice Age Lake Fenland. Peat shrinkage has meant that the land has generally dropped about 5m in the area.

It was near here that the Fen Causeway Roman road crossed and the Fen Rivers Way footpath now follows the River Great Ouse, also crossing at the sluice. There are concrete steps down to moorings, this being the cruising limit for many boats. Coots, mallards, swans and cormorants paddle through the duckweed and lilies, dragonflies and red admiral butterflies hunt along the shoreline bushes and reeds and Denver Sailing Club have their base in the middle of it all. In the distance is Denver Mill, a restored Grade II cornmill of 1835. Jets burn over, a regular feature of the fens.

Denver Sluice was built in 1652 by Vermuyden. It burst in 1713 under the load of a surge tide and exceptional floods, not an altogether unpopular event as it was a barrier to navigation and trade. The Swiss Labelye rebuilt it in 1750 and it was reconstructed in its present form by Rennie in 1834. Below it the tidal river is fast with high banks of silt once the tide drops, a difficult place for cruisers.

The proposed Fens Waterways Link will come down the River Great Ouse and up Well Creek. The Environment Agency hope to avoid cruisers having to go onto tidal water by making a cut westwards to the south of the Jenyns Arms and taking an aqueduct over the New Bedford River. This is currently being talked of as an exotic glass aqueduct although a design competition may open it up to other possibilities.

When British Waterways and the Environment Agency were each putting their cases for taking control of all deep water navigations British Waterways said that they would open the

Silos on the edge of Downham Market.

Passing Downham Market on the section adjacent to the railway.

Relief Channel to navigation if they were given control. The EA, who control the channel, responded by building a lock themselves to allow cruisers to bypass the Relief Channel sluice by locking down onto the bottom end of the Cut-off Channel. Canoeists had not needed this but were not allowed to use the Relief Channel until it was opened to large craft. The lock includes portage platforms at convenient height. In the small print on the lock on the side away from the portage trail is a note that cruisers may not use all of the channel. The lock was completed in 2001 and it was estimated that it would draw 2,600 boats a year to the channel.

Below the sluices is a thick raft of floating algae, blown by the wind. Docks, ragwort, teasels and brambles add their colours to the gravelly banks of the broad cut in their seasons.

An aerial marks the arrival of the A1122, the only major road across the channel. In 1720 Defoe reported that there was an ugly wooden bridge over the Ouse but all the drains in the area were navigable. A chapel of ease for pilgrims going to Walsingham has become the Hermitage Hall all faiths religious centre. The EA have provided extensive mooring pontoons, also useful for visiting **Downham Market**, a town which is fronted by silos.

Downham Market is one of the oldest market towns in Norfolk, a pre-Conquest hillside settlement (or as near hillside as it gets in these parts) dating from Saxon times. In 1646 Charles I, disguised as a servant, stayed here on his rather roundabout way from Oxford to Newark to meet up with the Scottish army. It was also where Nelson went to school. Using mellow carr stone and red and yellow brick, it has 17th century Dutch architecture influenced by the immigrant drainage engineers and also has an unusual black and white clocktower. The Noncomformists were strong here. In the church is a 15th century oak chest and a unique 17th century glass chandelier.

The station is by the bank of the channel which follows the Liverpool Street–King's Lynn railway closely for the next 4km. Beyond a sewage works the route returns to being entirely rural. Adjacent fields are grazed by sheep and horses with cows beyond while the flying wildlife ranges from crows, herons, pheasants, plovers and curlews to tortoiseshell butterflies.

Wimbotsham is a marshy area. Beyond Stowbridge there are lines of posts coming out from the left bank to form artificial reefs, difficult to see as they are cut off at water level.

A railway bridge across towards Watlington shows how its line has been closed since the channel was cut.

Wiggenhall St Mary Magdalen, sheltering behind a rare stand of poplars, was famous for its eels and they are still to be found in the channel, home also to moorhens and kingfishers. Beyond the river the church has notable Jacobean panels and 15th century glass.

In Roman times the River Nar joined the River Great Ouse near Wiggenhall St Peter but now it flows north and the confluence is in King's Lynn. A drainage channel pumped into the Relief Channel clears the area of excess floodwater.

By now the banks have become more reedy. There is a small gap which allows landing on the left before Abbey Farm but an adjacent tree has a large number of wasps beneath it in the summer.

On each side of the river are large no entry and turn round signs. For cruisers, the nearest moorings are 3km back upstream at Wiggenhall St Mary Magdalen, where it is possible to leave the boat, walk a kilometre and catch a train the remaining 9km to King's Lynn. Wiggenhall St Mary Magdalen is hardly the most obvious new boating destination. There is no lock to allow passage back to the tidal river at the sluice at the northern end of the channel, even if the EA were to allow use of the channel this close to King's Lynn. The only through route for non portable boats to King's Lynn remains the tidal River Great Ouse. However, as the Relief Channel takes much of the water, the natural river course is now silting badly, making it difficult for larger craft to pass. There is potential to make much better use of this facility.

Turn round sign at Abbey Farm bridge.

Distance
14km from Denver to Wiggenhall St Peter

Navigation Authority
Environment Agency

OS 1:50,000 Sheets
(131 Boston & Spalding)
(132 North West Norfolk)
143 Ely & Wisbech

Connection
River Great Ouse – *see RoB p169*

39 River Ant

Thatching, reed cutting and interesting windmills

Dilham Staithe with the former brickworks dyke beyond.

The River Ant rises at Antingham and flows southeast across Norfolk to join the River Bure rather than taking the much shorter journey to the North Sea by flowing northeast.

In the early 19th century much of it was canalized to form the North Walsham & Dilham Canal. The section above Swafield Bridge was closed in 1927 but the lower section was in use until 1935. The public navigation right below Swafield Bridge has never been rescinded but does not relate to the present owners, an unusual but not totally unique situation. It is not maintained as a deep water navigation. The upper end of the River Ant no longer welcomes larger craft, which are directed to Dilham.

Dilham Staithe has been made welcoming to visitors. Its amenities run to several moorings, a couple of roadside parking spaces and the Broadlands Arts Centre. The name is derived from dill, reflecting its agricultural location. At the head of the staithe is Brickworks Bridge, leading to what is now a private dyke.

A row of small houses back onto the narrow Tyler's Cut. Most have their own mooring spaces and it looks as though their users must choose their craft to suit the spaces available as some fit so precisely.

Various private dykes join Dilham Dyke in a waterland lined with alders, reeds and lilies, the haunt of mallards, swans, herons, kingfishers and Canada and greylag geese.

The armless Moy's drainage mill faces Broad Fen, a marsh, where

Dilham Dyke lined with reeds and trees.

A former mill stands back from Dilham Dyke.

the dyke joins the River Ant at the Smallburgh River Junction. At the time of construction of the canal Broad Fen had the characteristics of a broad and so no further excavation was required. A sign upstream on the river says no entry to 'non motorised craft', perhaps not what is intended.

The river is immediately wider, wide enough for a line of chalets on pontoons moored along the edge. A speed limit of 6km/h is imposed. Houseboats line the bank and Wayford Bridge Inn stands by the A149 crossing. A marina caters for the powered boat hirers. Virtually the last building in the village has the appearance of a disused clubhouse, Doric pillars fronting the river and hinting that there could have been times when blazers and boaters were the dress code.

A Roman road ran west from here to Water Newton although no evidence of it has been found to the east.

The run down to Barton Broad has just one feature to break up the reeds and occasional trees, the magnificent red brick Hunsett Mill of 1698 at Chapel Field, complete with sails and a large fantail. This oasis of splendour sits on the edge of the marshes.

The wide Stalham Dyke feeds Sutton Broad which, despite its name, is now just a navigation channel through reedbeds.

Great crested grebes and blackheaded gulls alike frequent the main channel which is used by large sailing craft as well as the columns of powered boats.

Barton Broad is 1.5km^2 of SSSI and nature reserve, exposed to a crosswind, to the delight of sailors. There are sailing schools operating from moored boats and pontoons and it was on this broad that Nelson learned to sail. The speed limit is eased to 9km/h for the length of the broad.

The Broads are flooded medieval peat diggings. They are shallow and steadily drying out. Bordered by reeds, they have rare wild plants and animals, otters, Britain's largest butterfly, the swallowtail, and such birds as winter wildfowl, garganey, bitterns, bearded tits and marsh harriers. In the face of protests from Natural England, the Broads Authority cleared the water in the broad by using curtains of bubbles to exclude fish, allowing water fleas to develop and remove the cloudiness. The previous depth has also been recovered by excavation. The Broads are noted for their remarkable sunsets and the dry climate, especially early and late in the year.

Several channels lead off Barton Broad to Barton Turf Staithe, to Catfield Wood End Staithe and the Old Lime Kiln Dyke to Neatishead. A trip boat operating here is the *Ra*, Britain's first solar-powered passenger boat.

Back on the river, Irstead has some magnificent thatched and half-timbered cottages. Across a green stands St Michael's church of flint and stone in Decorated style.

Chalets on pontoons at Wayford Bridge.

Near the approach to Crome's Broad is Clackrack Mill, the only surviving hollow post mill with its original scoop wheel. A 19th century structure, it was moved here from Ranworth Marshes to the south in 1981.

After Reedham Marsh with its nature reserve and nature trail, How Hill Staithe is reached with another windpump. Boardman's Mill is an open framed timber trestle windpump with a turbine. The Ant produces reed for thatching. The staithe has a thatched boathouse and stacks of reeds drying out for thatching, transported by small boats. Close by is an imposing mansion with fine water gardens and many miniature canals.

Another fine windmill stands on Turf Fen, an area of reeds cut for thatching. Built in the 1880s, this mill is unusual in having two paddle scoop wheels.

The River Ant was used as one of the first sites to try the Bestmann Green System of bank stabilization. Rolls of coconut fibre 300mm diameter in mesh nets are staked down and planted with reeds to absorb boat washes. They look much better than sheet piling and allow animals to climb out of the water.

A further sail-less windmill stands beside the river at Browns Hill and there is a final small one at Ludham Bridge where the A1062 crosses, the last road access point on the river. From here the river is tidal although any effects are minimal.

Beyond the rookery is Horning Hall with its chapel site. There was also a monk's causeway in the vicinity.

The River Ant joins the River Bure opposite Ward Marsh which is used for reed cutting. The Bure runs southeast in a straight reach from the confluence although the previous route was a large meander round Ward Marsh.

Hunsett Mill and cottage.

The windmill at Turf Fen with How Hill beyond.

Clackrack Mill with Boardman's Mill in the distance.

How Hill Staithe, boathouse and drying reeds.

Cut reedbeds at Turf Fen.

Distance
15km from Dilham to the River Bure

Navigation Authority
Broads Authority

Navigation Society
East Anglian Waterways Association
www.eawa.co.uk

OS 1:50,000 Sheets
(133 North East Norfolk)
134 Norwich & the Broads

Connection
River Bure – see RoB p175

40 River Bure

The first boat hire centre

Youths enjoy the weirpool at Coltishall.

One of the most important of the Broads rivers, the Bure, rises at Melton Constable and flows southeast across Norfolk to Breydon Water. For large craft the head of navigation is the disused **Coltishall** or Horstead Lock although there is a wooden walkway with ramps at the ends for portaging small craft past. The lock is best approached on land from Horstead, there being parking by the disused mill if it is not all taken up by canoeists and swimmers playing in the millpool's white water.

Canoe Man runs guided canoe tours from the village to another base at Wroxham. It can be congested as this is the prettiest part of the Broads. Poplars, sycamores, alders, horse chestnuts, pollarded willows and reeds line the river with its greylag geese, mallards, moorhens and swans.

Heavily pruned trees cover a lawn at Coltishall Manor House at the start of Coltishall Common, Coltishall Staithe and the New Rising Sun. There is free mooring and free parking for those walking or drinking but no parking for anyone wanting to launch or recover even the smallest of boats. This is a haunt of Black Shuck, the demon hound.

Anchor Wood recalls past use by trading vessels. Mussel shells show the river to be relatively clean. Smart gardens indicate arrival at Belaugh and its staithe, as does the mainly Norman church of St Peter. From here the river is almost continuously wooded to the River Ant except for a built up area at Wroxham. There is a neatly thatched boathouse near Juby's Farm as the river makes a 4km loop which progresses it just 600m. The woods are thick enough to hide Belaugh Broad and a windmill opposite the church tower at **Wroxham**.

Wroxham is the Capital of the Broads, an area of medieval peat diggings which have become flooded and, since the arrival of the railway in 1880, have been popular for boating, this being the original boat hire centre. Before the railway crossing is Bridge Broad, made accessible for use since 1979.

The railway used to fork on the north side of the river. The former Great Eastern line has been brought back into use to Aylsham with the 381mm gauge Bure Valley Railway laid in 1990 as the longest narrow gauge line in Norfolk. Rattling along, mostly behind steam engines, are boat trains connecting with Broads cruises.

Wroxham Bridge, carrying the A1151, connects the twin villages of Wroxham and **Hoveton** and is tight

The final hamlet in Coltishall.

Thatched boathouse near Joby's Farm on the Belaugh loop.

for powered craft and on an awkward line. For hirers coming upstream it is the first and most difficult obstacle they will face. For those on land there are numerous facilities, the Golden Fish, the Star of India, Wherryman's Restaurant and Hotel Wroxham amongst others. Hoveton, said to be the prettiest village in the Broads, also attracts many to Roys, claimed to be the world's largest village store. Marina facilities are extensive. Many houses with moorings are built around the numerous inlets on both sides of the river. The traffic from these with the continuous traffic in both directions on the river and the wildlife from great crested grebes to a black swan mean there is always plenty to see on the water. This is home for three of the last eight wherries built on the Broads, two of which are being restored.

Clear of the villages, on the east side is Wroxham Broad, used for sailing, the biggest of the deep freshwater Broads.

The Belaugh loop with and without reeds.

Greylag geese use a rare low bank at Wroxham.

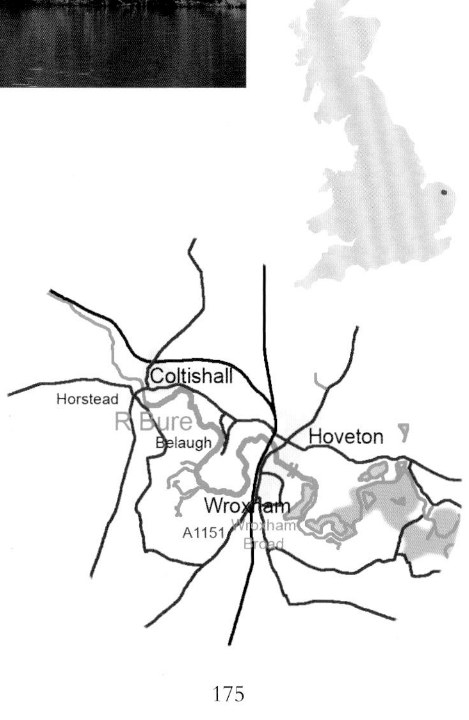

Greylag geese and goslings by the River Bure.

The narrow gauge Bure Valley Line with Blickling Hall *about to take the Easter Eggspress from Wroxham to Aylsham.*

The A1151 bridge in Wroxham is tight for boats.

Distance
11km from Coltishall to Wroxham Broad

Navigation Authority
Broads Authority

Navigation Society
East Anglian Waterways Association
www.eawa.co.uk

OS 1:50,000 Sheets
(133 North East Norfolk)
134 Norwich & the Broads

Connection
Tidal River Bure – see RoB p174

Not so much a house as a small estate.

41 Chelmer & Blackwater Navigation

One of the shallowest canals

Roding (that names eight churches) –
Banks with the paigles dight –
Chelmer whose mill and willows
Keep one red tower in sight –
Arthur Shearly Cripps

The importance of **Chelmsford** even in Roman times was shown by their name for it, Caesaromagus, but it did not become a city until 2012. That importance did not diminish any when John Rennie completed the Chelmer & Blackwater Navigation in 1797, linking the county town of Essex with the estuary of the River Blackwater. Following the collapse of the Chelmer & Blackwater Navigation Company, management was taken over by the Inland Waterways Association in 2005, trading as Essex Waterways Ltd, the first canal trust, but ownership remains with the old company.

Springfield Basin at the head of the canal has new commercial and residential buildings around it but a black shiplapped building remains on the wharf.

Springfield Basin, the head of the canal.

Timberyards which surrounded the end of the canal and which had projecting roofs received delivery of timber by barge until 1972. Until 1960 the barges had been horsedrawn. Their shape was unique with wedge shaped bows. After the horses were retired, the barges were fitted with large diesel powered outboards and one of these barges still remains on the canal for maintenance purposes. The only remaining timber is in Travis Perkins' yard.

The first part of the towpath is missing and it needs to be joined via an alley next to Travis Perkins' yard. It is then overgrown until near the first lock after which it is in good condition throughout. The bridge below the first lock is typical of Rennie's work with an elliptical brick arch.

The former Chelmsford bypass.

The navigation now leads out into the River Chelmer. Just above the junction a four storey mill has been replaced by housing around a dock. A concrete viaduct with four distinctive pinnacles carries the old Chemsford bypass over the river and a viaduct crosses its busy roundabout with the A130. The Chelmer Village retail centre is just up from the river. On the hilltops on each side are massive aerials, one being on the premises of Marconi, one of Chelmsford's most important industries. Britain's first regular broadcasting, a news service, was done from here.

Over much of its line the navigation is completely pastoral. The ruling depth is only 600mm, being one of the shallowest canals in the country, and it twists and turns between low banks, making it an interesting route and allowing views all around. Lock cuts are short and the whole route has been constructed as economically as possible.

The navigation approaches the white weatherboarded Barnes Mill by Barnes Mill Lock and its footbridges. This area has been surrounded by a sprawling housing estate.

On the other side of the river the A1114 holds **Great Baddow** at bay on its hillside, the tower of the fire station rising above the rooflines like a tentpeg through the cloak of houses. Even low hills are clearly seen in a predominantly flat landscape so the hill bearing Little Baddow, **Danbury** and Blake's Wood with its hornbeam and chestnut trees is a distinctive landmark.

A museum at Sandford Mill waterworks has Marconi radio equipment, including the hut used for the world's first scheduled radio broadcast in 1922. Forking left takes the cut to the next lock, overlooked by the large sewage works at Brookend and the first of a couple of pillboxes.

Footpath signs have yellow butterflies as their waymark. Willow trees have been planted on banks on various reaches, some used for making cricket bats. On others there are hawthorn bushes. Lower down the banks there are teasels, stinging nettles and white dead nettles, greater reedmace and other reeds and finally water lilies and marsh marigolds in the river itself.

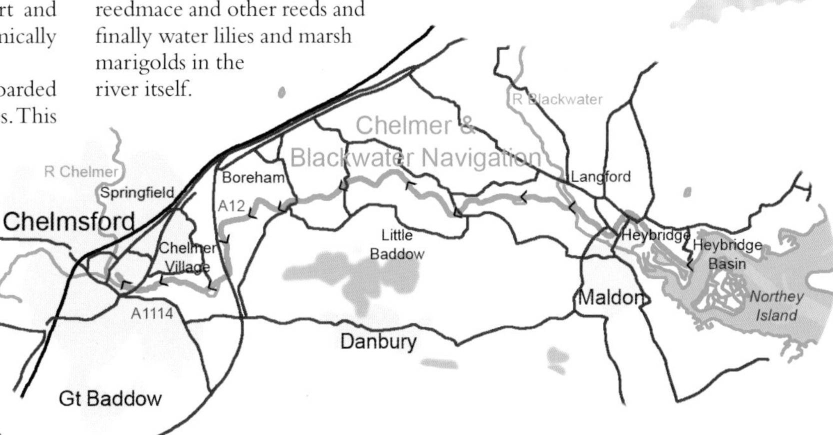

The converted Barnes Mill.

Tree-lined reach below Little Baddow Lock.

Two lines of pylons flank the A12 Chelmsford bypass which curves round alongside the river for a couple of kilometres. The bridge is followed by another modern bridge, this time a steel footbridge with heavily reinforced corners, looking as though it has lost a couple of supporting columns.

A large lake has appeared by the next lock, no doubt the remains of a borrow pit for the adjacent bypass. It is used by swans.

Most locks have concrete launching platforms at their lower ends but Stonham's Lock does not have one, requiring those portaging to launch over the top of asbestos sheet piling.

An avenue of mature poplar trees leads to Little Baddow Lock. Across the fields the slim tower of the church watches over Boreham while Little Baddow church, on the other side, is Norman.

The river passes under another footbridge, similar in

The company office at Paper Mill Lock with the Victoria *moored opposite.*

Summer dawn at All Saints church, Ulting.

The unusual weir at Paper Mill Lock.

Beeleigh flood gates.

shape to the previous one but in wood and with the expected columns present.

Along the river there are frequent warnings of flood danger on the roads, a danger emphasized by the lack of building close to the river. It may have been canalized for centuries but it is still untamed.

A paper mill used rags to make quality paper. Paper Mill Lock is the site of the best of the canal's traditional buildings, one being used as the canal office. There is also a slipway with numerous boats moored, including *Victoria*, the canal's trip boat. The weir is fascinating, too, changing direction halfway down its face with two crooked guide vanes to assist the flow.

The river runs out into completely open country and if any buildings can be seen at all it is only because the banks are so low. At some points the land to the right is below river level. On the other hand the River Ter arrives unnoticed on the weir backwater at the next lock.

All Saints at Ulting is a beautiful little wood spired 13th century church on its own beside the river, surrounded by trees, its setting the epitome of peace in the English countryside in summer although it was an important pilgrimage site in the 14th century. Nearby, however, the landscape has been disrupted by gravel extraction.

Hoe Mill Lock is crossed at its lower end by a concrete bridge in place of the usual brick arch, rather more decorative than most concrete bridges. The landing platforms under the bridge are wide and there are two routes to them, either across the road or by lowering the boat down the hole in the concrete platform joining the lock to the bridge on each side and then climbing down the iron ladder after it. Britain's first sugar factory was built below here in 1833.

Pipe bridges cross the reaches above and below the next lock. The second is a conventional girder affair but the first has a pair of striking pipe arches which spring from blue engineering brick abutments.

Mallards are joined by cormorants, the only indication of the proximity of the sea.

After Beeleigh Lock the River Blackwater and the disused Langford Cut emerge from the left and the river passes over a weir on the right into tidal water. The towpath is carried across the weir on a long trestle walkway and the cut carries on ahead through a flood lock. The brick span across the lock carries the track leading from Langford with its Museum of Power in a steam pumping station to Maldon Golf Club, situated between the navigation and the tidal river channel.

Two railway bridges cross the cut, trackless since the Beeching axe fell. This is one of the few cases of where a

Bentall's four storey factory in Maldon.

canal remained commercial after the railway closed down, possibly because the railway did not follow the canal line directly but took a more roundabout route.

The steepled church and some of the older buildings of **Maldon**, which received its royal charter in 1171, look down from their hillside while a large Tesco store occupies the fields near at hand.

The old channel of the River Blackwater diverges to the right and the canal comes into its only built-up area at Heybridge.

IWA workers at the moorings in Heybridge Basin.

A large four storey brick block was Bentall's agricultural machinery factory, supplied with raw materials by canal. Across the water are modern houses and, behind them, an old school, the decorative styling of which suggests a Dutch influence. A cemetery chapel stands nearby in grounds graced by copper beeches and cedar trees.

The grounds of the jaded Heybridge Hall meet the canal.

Swallows swoop around over the water and arrival at the end of the canal is signalled only by the sudden appearance of lines of high-masted craft of all kinds moored along both banks of the cut. Here, cruisers rub shoulders with fishing smacks, oyster smacks and drifters, a tremendous assortment of craft.

The final lock at Heybridge Basin has balance beams encased in metalwork and an additional flood door which opens onto Collier's Reach of the River Blackwater estuary, an area mostly of mud flats with the tide out, a waterway which was perhaps once the estuary of the Thames. Opposite is Northey Island, a dissected maze of saltings, levées and creeks owned by the National Trust, a Grade I site for overwintering birds and for saltmarsh plants. On land, the final lock is overlooked by a line of traditional timbered Essex houses, the last of which is the Old Ship, with the Jolly Sailor just down below in an area which smells of ships' chandlery and where lines slap in unison against aluminium masts in the breeze.

Buildings at the end of the navigation.

Collier's Reach at low water. Northey Island lies opposite.

Distance
21km from Chelmsford to Blackwater Estuary

Navigation Authority
Essex Waterways

Navigation Societies
Chelmer Canal Trust www.chelmercanaltrust.co.uk, East Anglian Waterways Association www.eawa.co.uk

OS 1:50,000 Sheets
167 Chelmsford
168 Colchester

Connection
River Blackwater – see RoB p207

42 River Stort (Navigation)

Falling short of the Cam and fens

The remains of the canal basin in Bishop's Stortford.

The River Stort was made navigable between 1766 and 1769 by Sir George Duckett for barges to carry agricultural produce and malt. The work only reached Bishop's Stortford. Had it continued a further 50km to the Cam and the fens then its commercial significance would have been much greater. In 1911 it was acquired by the Lee Conservancy, who spent a decade rebuilding the locks, but commercial traffic ceased in the 1940s. With its narrow, winding, wooded course it is today one of the prettiest navigations in the south of England.

The terminus in **Bishop's Stortford** has been realigned. Neighbours include Marks & Spencer, Sainsbury's and Lussmanns by the River. A stream emerges from a dark culvert and assorted ducks and swans waylay the departing boater, demanding food.

An old wharf crane faces onto the main river channel, around which there has been much new building. A large set of maltings have found fresh uses as flats and are approached by the complex Goods Yard Footbridge. One of the occupants is a Chinese restaurant and there are various other eating opportunities behind it.

A coach station has been located alongside the

An old wharf crane remains on the river outside the canal basin.

The old maltings in Bishop's Stortford, now with new roles.

navigation by the Tanner's Arms. Nearby on the other bank is the Old Vicarage where Cecil Rhodes was born in 1853, now the Rhodes Arts Complex & Bishops Stortford Museum, featuring the explorer's life and Zimbabwe and Zambia.

Across the road from a petrol station backing onto the river is the half-timbered Baan Thitiya Thai restaurant in a former public house.

A timberyard and sewage works follow and then the town is left behind. The Cambridge–Liverpool Street railway crosses, has a frequent service including the Stansted Express and is never more than 600m from the navigation over its entire length. The M11, too, follows the valley as far as Harlow but is 1–2km off and isn't noticed, unlike the jets which take off over this reach from **Stansted** airport, the end of the main runway of which is some 4km away.

The Essex border comes in on the left and the river is the county boundary between Essex and Hertfordshire for most of the rest of its length.

South Mill Lock is the first of the 15 wide beam locks. These usually have steep banks around them but most have a wooden ladder down to a launching platform below the lock for ease of relaunching portable craft. The direction of the navigation is not usually indicated because low bridges over the natural course of the river make the route suitably obvious to larger vessels.

The river runs through planted woodland for most of the way to Twyford Lock where the large Georgian Twyford Mill has been divided up into a complex of flats. A 300mm high plate on the wall of the lock shows the working head agreed between the canal owners and the mill owners, similar indications being given further down the navigation. Below the lock is a footbridge consisting of a narrow flat plate laid on top of an I beam and two handrails out in V shape as it crosses the river.

Also crossing the river might be seen a vole with its nose out of the water as it paddles furiously or the rust, white and pale blue of the jay as it flits from one bank to the other.

The large wooded ring of Wallbury Camp flanks the left bank before Spellbrook Lock and a nearby attractive thatched cottage.

The first cut of any length comes at Tednambury Lock where there are sweeping views to the natural channel at Little Hallingbury Mill and its boatyard, a line of narrowboats and cruisers moored on the river rather than the cut.

Great Hyde Hall, set in a wooded park on the hill to the left, was built in 1806 by Sir Jeffrey Wyatville in Tudor style. The view in that direction is enhanced, after the railway crosses back over Kecksy's railway bridge, by the low ground to the left. The 1987 storm hit a row of mature willow trees on the right bank, leaving a line of upturned roots.

Sawbridgeworth Lock has a former clapboarded mill and a row of houses which may be renovations of disused buildings or may be new, most tastefully done and suited to the location, whichever is the case.

The central spindle and base of another canal crane remain on the following bend. The church further back dates from the 14th century and has many monuments, brasses and elegant 18th century gravestones.

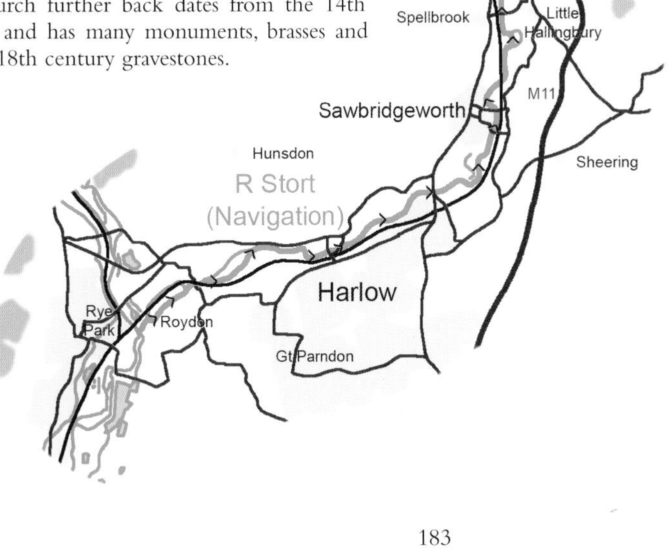

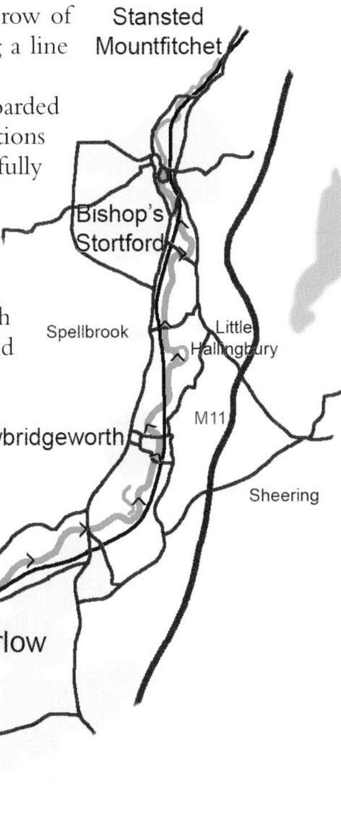

The complex Station Yard Footbridge over the river.

Maltings in the town are similar in style to those in Bishop's Stortford but are much more extensive, sited alongside the navigation in order to benefit from the barge traffic. Again, they are a base for the Riverside Pizza and other fast food options.

A large area of old buildings has been flattened and the houses have been replaced with new houses just above Sheering Lock. The Harcamlow Way long distance footpath crosses at this lock and the lower lock gates are actually sited immediately below the footway and so have to be power operated. The other lock gates on the canal are operated by balance beams but it is only relatively

Twyford Mill has been converted for residential use.

One of the level marker plates, this one at Twyford Lock.

A footbridge based on a single steel beam.

Looking from Tednambury Lock towards Hallingbury Mill.

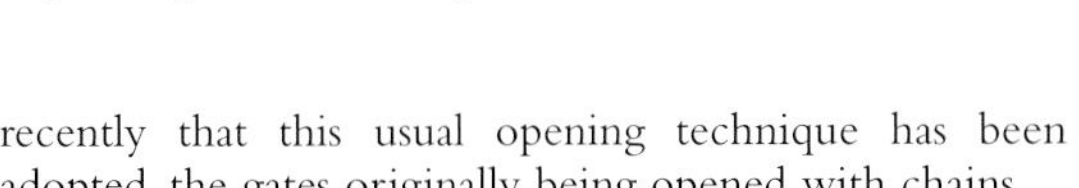

recently that this usual opening technique has been adopted, the gates originally being opened with chains.

Soon after the lock come moorings and boatyard for cruisers.

Adjacent to Feakes Lock is Pishiobury Park. It was remodelled as a castellated mansion in 1782 from a Tudor house by James Wyatt and still contains some Tudor and Jacobean work inside. Landscaping and its lake were by Capability Brown. Rowneybury House, a former school for disabled children, is now known locally as Beckingham Palace after two of its owners.

Harlow is introduced by the Coho Brasserie. Across the road is the Harlow Mill steakhouse where canned music and orders are presented to the passing world over a public address system. Harlow Lock is where the original village of Harlow was sited. Below it a selection of gas holders and chimneys can be seen as the most conspicuous part of an industrial estate on Temple Fields, a Romano-Celtic temple site. Despite the factories through the trees, the navigation remains largely rural with the right bank totally unspoilt.

Followed by both the Harcamlow Way and the Three

Lockside cottages at Sawbridgeworth Lock.

Traditional timber buildings by Sawbridgeworth Lock.

Part of Sawbridgeworth's maltings complex.

New housing with moorings in Sawbridgeworth.

A wrought iron gate opposite the Moorhen at Harlow.

One of the exhibits on the River Stort Sculpture Trail at Latton Lock.

Forests Way, the river moves on down past the Moorhen and Harlow Town station to Burnt Mill Lock.

This is the site of Harlow new town, planned in 1947 by Frederick Gibberd as a London overspill town for 80,000, one of eight and now seen as a breakthrough in town planning with its traffic-free pedestrian area.

A large block, assault course and climbing tower are the property of Harlow Centre for Outdoor Learning with plenty of young people taking part in various activities on the water and high above it.

An attractive church belfry precedes Little Parndon Mill above Parndon Lock, now an arts and crafts centre.

The partly boarded Mead Lodge above Hunsdon Mill Lock in its immaculate garden has to be the most beautiful property on the navigation at the point where the river and navigation make their longest separation of 1.5km. Also leaving at this point is a road which leads up to Hunsdon House at Hunsdonbury, not visible from the river but remembered by the Playford dance of the same name. Prominent across Hunsdon Mead Nature Reserve between the river and navigation is Briggens, another large country house.

Roydon Lock had an 18th century Gothic lock cottage. Unfortunately, this flooded every time the lock was left full and it has been replaced with an uninspiring modern house, noteworthy only for the coat of arms built incongruously into the wall at the far end. On the other hand, an interesting old brick canal building graces the opposite side of the lock.

Modern properties in a new housing development include some interesting houses on pillars with only single rooms and car parking space below elevated first floor accommodation on raised platforms. Set back from them is a 13th century flint church.

As the next mill is approached at Roydon the river weirs off to the right while the navigation departs under a blind bridge on the left rather than taking the main channel which leads straight to the mill.

A Gothic-style lock keeper's cottage survives at Brick Lock. A coat of arms on the front has George Duckett's initials prominently displayed and gives the date as 1830. By now a ridge of low but distinctive hills has risen along the south bank of the navigation and gravel workings have been landscaped into a lake on the opposite side.

Lower Lock was surrounded by a shanty town but this has been cleared and levelled.

One thing that does not change is the giant Rye Meads sewage works, noticed if the wind is from the northwest.

The Stort crosses the River Lea and joins the River Lee Navigation just above Fielde's Weir Lock, with the 720MW Rye House gas fired power station as a backdrop.

Exit is possible at Fielde's Weir Lock via a road which runs up past the power station from Dobb's Weir.

Activities at Harlow Centre for Outdoor Learning.

Little Parndon Mill is now an arts and crafts centre.

A unique footbridge at Parndon Lock.

Mead Lodge above Hunsdon Mill Lock.

Cruising below Hunsdon Mill Lock.

Roydon Mill offers some off-line moorings.

Distance
22km from Bishop's Stortford to the River Lee Navigation

Navigation Authority
Canal & River Trust

OS 1:50,000 Sheets
166 Luton & Hertford
167 Chelmsford

The Gothic-style lock keeper's cottage at Brick Lock.

43 River Lee Navigation

Separating the pagans from the Christians

With that, I saw two Swannes of goodly hewe,
Come softly swimming down along the Lee;
Two fairer Birds I yet did never see
Edmund Spenser

The River Lea, Lee or, formerly, Ley (hence Leyton) has long been used as a navigation. It may even have been used by the Romans as a transport route to St Albans. Improvements began in 1424, using the first Act of Parliament for the improvement of a British river, and in 1430, the first example of an English statutory body borrowing money for public works. Locks were added in the 17th century and the modern navigation reached **Hertford** in the 18th century although it was not until 1930 that 100t barges could travel up to Hertford. A wide beam canal, it has been heavily used below Enfield, mainly for the timber trade. Locks are unusual in having bollard pins recessed into the walls at low levels in addition to the normal bollards on the top. Some of the non-mechanized lock gates do not have balance beams and have to be opened with ropes. The drop from the towpath to the water is often quite high, especially at the downstream end. The navigation has a towpath throughout. In flood times it carries a great deal of land drainage water although it can be weedy at the top end.

The valley could have resulted from north–south folding, the Taplow terrace extending from the

The River Lea at Hertford from the head of the River Lee Navigation.

Modern housing in Hertford is complementary to the old maltings in the town.

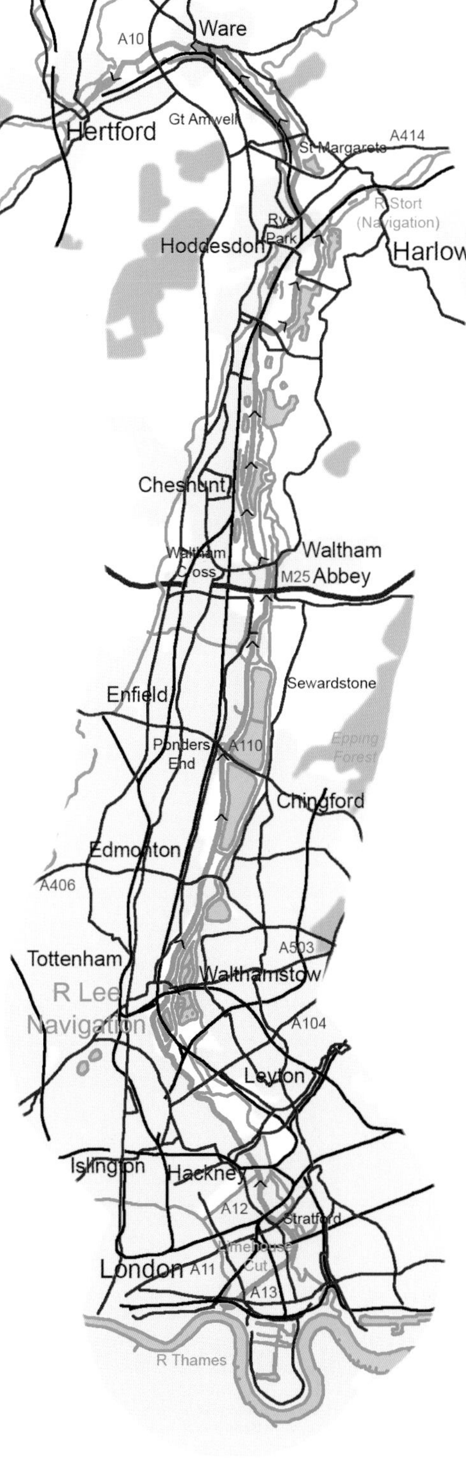

river originally being very marshy, some of the marshland remaining.

The river separated Danelaw from Saxon Wessex, in other words the pagans from the Christians. In the Middle Ages the lower end was recorded as being used by butchers for washing the carcasses of dead animals despite the state of the water.

Throughout most of its length the navigation is followed closely by railway lines.

The navigation leaves the River Lea at Hertford in front of a large old maltings, one of several in the town with McMullen's brewery of 1827, taking most of the water from the river with it. Narrowboats are moored and the navigation and town complement each other. The town was often invaded by the Danes in the 9th century until stopped by Alfred the Great, who pursued them up the river in 896.

The Old Barge is a public house at the head of navigation.

18th century gazebos add interest to the navigation at Ware.

All the buildings hereabouts are well-presented and many are of great historical significance, particularly the castle, built in 1100. King Alfred's son built the first fort in wood and the Normans built the stone walls and mound. It was stormed in 1216 by the French. Edward VI succeeded to the throne while staying here but it was also where Bolingbroke drew up charges against Richard II, leading to his dethronement in 1399. A 12th century curtain wall remains, together with the 15th century gatehouse, which was extensively altered in 1800. The castle was sold by Charles, son of James I, to the Cecils. Important prisoners have included King John of France and David Bruce of Scotland. Elizabeth I granted the town's charter. Hartford in Connecticut was founded by former resident the Revd Samuel Stone.

Other notable buildings include two mediaeval churches, the first national synod being held here in 673 when archbishop Theodore of Tarsus united the Celtic Christians with those in the south and set up the dioceses. The country's oldest house built for the Quakers was completed about 1669. A museum features local history and archaeology as well as geology and natural history. Darwin's partner, Wallace, lived in Wallace House, Captain W E Johns was brought up in Biggles House and the Shire Hall appears in *Pride & Prejudice*.

Modern housing with styling to complement the maltings rooflines follows before Dicker Mill Bridge with its Sea Cadet base. The Scouts also have their own slipway beyond some car repair workshops.

Lock cottages often have small gables and contrasting brick courses. Beyond Hertford Lock the navigation heads out into the water meadows to rejoin the River Lea. The Meads have never been ploughed and have rare plants under a yellow sheen of lady's bedstraw, pollard willows, 11 varieties of dragonfly, lapwings, yellow wagtails, waders, gulls, ducks and swans.

A brick building and penstocks on the right are the head of the New River, constructed parallel to the River Lea in 1609–13 to supply drinking water to London. The A10 sweeps across the floodplain on an 800m-long viaduct and the river flows into **Ware**, dominated by GlaxoSmithKline's pharmaceutical works where the navigation takes a detour past the rosebeds at Ware Lock, operated by the Environment Agency although the rest

Swing bridge across Stanstead Lock at St Margarets.

Residential development of old maltings by Stanstead Lock.

of the river is managed by the Canal & River Trust. To the right can be seen one of the ornate pumping stations on the New River. On the other side is the priory, built from the remains of a Fransiscan friary founded in 1338 by Thomas Wake, the lord of the manor. The Roman Ermine Street crossed near here. A stranger building is Scott's Grotto, a folly of six unlit rooms covered in shells and linked by underground passages.

18th century gazebos over the river are particularly attractive, these being what remain of 27 originally.

Ware, from the Saxon for weir, was the second largest malting centre in the country, the Granary of London, and lightermen from Ware were rewarded with Freedom of the Port of London for continuing to take food into quarantined London during the Great Plague.

A plastic-coated Saracen's Head and modern shops in the centre of Ware contrast with the fine early industrial weatherboarded warehouses, now converted into flats. Notable are the Ware Flour Mills of 1897, now with pretty domestic curtains, and Wickham's Wharf near the Victoria. This medieval community became a coaching town. St Mary the Virgin's church spire is prominent on its battlemented clocktower. The 3m square Great Bed of Ware, which could sleep a dozen people, is now in the Victoria & Albert museum in London. Perhaps a cormorant may be found fishing under the bridge.

Beginning here is the Lee Valley Park, 40km^2 of vital recreational green artery running 37km to Docklands. Begun in 1967, it was the first of its kind in Britain.

The navigation brings long, wide, straight reaches with the occasional lock after the River Lea is left to the east. There are former gravel workings after Hard Mead Lock but the sides of the wide valley are rural. Since 1983 one pit has formed the Amwell Quarry Nature Reserve and ornithologists are frequently seen with cameras on tripods, trying to snap hawfinch, smew and over a hundred other species.

Stanstead Lock at St Margarets is unusual in that it has the top paddles on the gates and has a swing bridge over the lock beside a housing development with a spire above the roofs of former maltings.

St James' church with its 15th century open timber south porch and 16th century brick north chancel chapel at Stanstead Abbotts (Anglo Saxon for stony place of the abbots of Waltham) is redundant and lies to the east of St Margarets.

Powerlines cross backwards and forwards, the River Lea rejoins and the A414 crosses over.

The large Rye Meads sewage works at **Hoddesdon** remains unseen from the river. Adjacent is a spiral brick chimney on the brick gatehouse of the former Rye House of 1443 (owned by ex-Parliamentarian army officer Richard Rumbold), named after an island where the 1683 Newmarket Plot was hatched to ambush Charles II and the future James II by blocking the lane with an

Short longboat in front of the glass-walled Broxbourne Lido.

Herts Young Mariners Base at Cheshunt.

upset cart. The scheme failed when they passed by a week early and many of the conspirators were put to death, Rumbold fleeing to the Netherlands.

Ambushes were carried out by a particularly territorial swan. Not only had he capsized canoeists but he had been known to leap into the cockpit of a cruiser to attack the driver. Deportation to another part of the country failed as he found his way back. He considered his territory to end at the bridge by the station and did not bother to pursue boats any further.

Rye House station began as a request stop, using a red flag, tickets being sold by the public house landlord, who sent his family by train to St Margarets each day to boost sales. The main line of the railway crosses from **Harlow,** bringing Stansted Express trains serving Stansted Airport. From the same direction comes the River Stort (Navigation) and the River Lea now has Essex on the left bank, having been in Hertfordshire so far.

Rye Meads Nature Reserve has kingfishers, ducks, woodpeckers and kestrels. The Showman's Guild ground is a winter site for travelling fairgrounds.

After Fieldes Lock, powerlines converge on Rye House power station.

Hoddesdon is known for its clocktower in the centre of the town and its fair in June. The Fish & Eels stands nearby.

Dobb's Weir Lock cottage is another with small gables and contrasting brickwork.

After Carthagena Lock the river goes right while the

Rafters on the Olympic canoe slalom course.

navigation cuts between the giant indoor Broxbourne Lido with its wave pool plus fleet of hire boats and a short version of a Viking longboat and the Crown. It is overlooked by the flint tower of the church of about 1450, which has a memorial to tarmac inventor John McAdam. Broxbourne is from badger stream.

Near the Broxbourne Rowing Club are glasshouses in profusion around Keysers Estate.

The natural river channel goes left at King's Weir into an area of lakes and braiding.

Cheshunt Lock has been laid out with picnic tables and has many orchids nearby in the early summer.

Lakes on the right at **Cheshunt** are the Herts Young Mariners Base. One youth who went there in his summer holidays was Harry Webb, better known as Cliff Richard. Cheshunt is from a Roman fort in a wood.

Tesco's headquarters are at Cheshunt because Jack Cohen began his business by buying fields and greenhouses in the valley of the Lea.

The river re-enters from the left after Waltham Common Lock.

Waltham Lock was the site of a 1571 pound lock with mitred gates, only a decade after the first pound lock on the Exeter Canal although first improvement of the river took place here in the 12th century.

The Royal Gunpowder Mills in the abbey mills were located between various river channels and were used from 1561 to 1991, served by barge, now open as Gunpowder Park. The willows and alders, now with many siskins and heron nests, were used for making charcoal as an ingredient of gunpowder.

The Lee Valley White Water Centre, based on the Olympic canoe slalom course for 2012, was in doubt because of local contamination levels. However, borehole water is stored in a 1ha artificial lake and treated on site to swimming pool standard for 13.5m^3/s flow falling 5.5m down a 300m course, fed by five pumps. An additional 160m intermediate course falls 1.6m.

It is possible to look up the road to the Norman abbey church at **Waltham Abbey**, Waltham meaning weald homestead. The church was founded in 1030 and nominated a mitred abbey in 1184. (It was rebuilt in the 12th century in a style similar to Durham Cathedral.) A blacksmith in Montacute dreamed of a treasure buried in a local Somerset hill in the 11th century. With the help of other villagers he dug up a stone crucifix. It was placed on a cart but a team of 24 oxen were unable to move it until Cnut selected a hunting lodge at Waltham as its destination, after which there were no problems. A Viking hall recently discovered near Waltham Abbey could be the building. Harold was cured of paralysis by the cross and is reputed to have been buried at the abbey memorial to him after the Battle of Hastings. Waltham Abbey was chosen as a centre for learning and religious instruction by Henry II as an atonement for Becket's murder. The abbey is one of the most outstanding Norman buildings in Essex and became one of the richest and most important abbeys in the country. Richard II took refuge here during the Peasants' Revolt. Cranmer was staying in the town in 1529 when he began to discuss Henry VIII's marriage, leading to the break with Rome, the Reformation and the Dissolution of the monasteries, Waltham being the last in England to be dissolved in 1540, when residents included composer Thomas Tallis. A 14th century chapel is noteworthy, as is the brick west tower of 1556. Only half the original abbey church remains. Tennyson's *Ring Out Wild Bells* was inspired by the campanology and *Hark, the Herald Angels Sing* was given its tune here. The church now dates mostly from the 19th century but has a Norman nave and aisle, a 14th century south chapel, a 1420 lych-gate, a 16th century tower and a fine Burne-Jones east window dating from 1861. There are further interesting archaeological remains in the grounds and the Epping Forest District Museum in a pair of Tudor buildings. The town's charter dates from 1244.

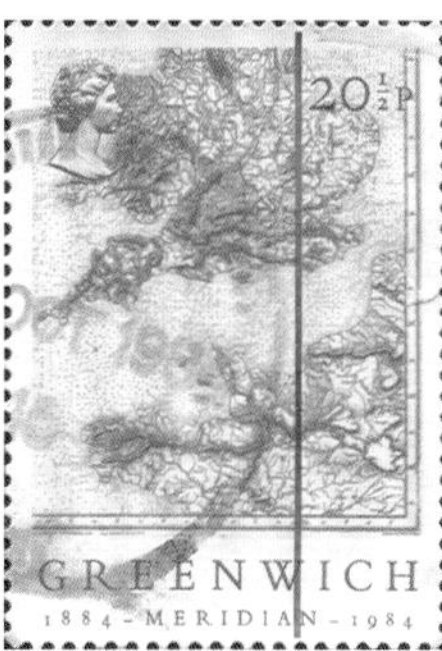

Waltham Cross takes its name from the Eleanor Cross at its centre, one of the dozen places the coffin of Eleanor of Castile rested on its journey to Westminster Abbey, erected by Edward I.

The 201st **Islington** Sea Scouts have their base on the left just before the viaduct carrying the M25 London Orbital Motorway, the world's longest ring road at 200km and the busiest motorway in Europe.

Timber wharf cranes strike wild silhouettes at Upper Clapton.

Trans-shipment depot with overhanging roof.

To the west of the viaduct it runs through one of its two tunnels. During the course of construction the navigation was realigned. At the viaduct the right bank becomes Greater London and the boundary with Essex pulls away over the next 4km.

After Rammey Marsh Lock the navigation meets the river momentarily and a weir operates between the two. Another possessive swan operated from here down past the Greyhound nearly to Enfield Lock.

Enfield Lock has another cottage with small gables and contrasting brick courses. When navigation improvements were completed in 1581 there were riots over loss of trade previously landed and now passing through, with locks being burned, bank damage and violence to lock keepers.

The river has been used as a source of water since the 17th century with major extraction at Chingford, its valley dominated by 13 great reservoirs which run for 6km, also used for ornithology and angling. The Lea reservoirs supply 15% of London's water. The river has been diverted to the left of the valley while the navigation keeps to the right. King George's Reservoir has great crested grebes, yellow wagtails, cormorants, kingfishers, long established heronries and a good selection of winter wildfowl.

In about 1730, the village of Sewardstone had Dick Turpin running the family butcher business. He took to stocking his shop by stealing livestock when finances were difficult, a capital offence. A couple of his cattle were recognized by their unusual markings and he had to take to the road, eventually becoming the most notorious of the highwaymen.

Guns were also the trade of the Royal Small Arms factory next to the navigation from 1816 to 1987, now the Enfield Island Village but with the original clocktower. Their best known product was the Lee-Enfield rifle, named after American designer James Lee rather than the river.

Powerlines cross to the 410MW gas-fired Enfield power station and then run south along the line of the navigation to Edmondton, often along both sides of the navigation.

Mossop's Creek was dug in the 1890s for gravel barges but is now accompanied by a smelter.

Opposite the second reservoir with its King George V Sailing Club and angling was a wharf with a large trans-shipment depot canopy overhanging part of the navigation.

The A110 crosses towards an obelisk of 1825 on Pole Hill, acting as the north marker for Greenwich Observatory and defining the meridian, which the navigation closely follows, having already crossed it on occasions.

Parties of Scouts from nearby Gilwell Park at **Chingford** are frequent users of the towpath.

The 14th century Ponder family gave their name to this end of Enfield. From Ponder's End Lock all locks are mechanized and all but Pickett's Lock are duplicated.

Late glacial deposits were found near here. The landscape is now buildings and reservoirs. William Girling Reservoir has a nature reserve and angling.

Sir Joseph Swan worked here from 1886 on the light bulbs he had invented and Sir James Dewar made his first Thermos flask here.

Pickett's Lock offers the Lee Valley Athletics Centre with squash, yoga, swimming, sauna and solarium while a golf course is fitted in next to the navigation. The BT Tower, Gherkin, Tower 47, Alexandra Palace, the EU's tallest building, the Shard, Canary Wharf and other features of the London skyline progressively become visible.

Shortage of space is such that a recent road has been constructed between the legs of a power pylon.

After **Edmonton** incinerator the A406 North Circular Road crosses. This is followed by various businesses including the Leaside Café. A sludge main across the navigation makes a convenient perch for a heron.

Banbury Reservoir has the Banbury Sailing Centre and angling while Lockwood Reservoir has a nature reserve and angling. Tottenham Marshes have various plants probably imported accidentally from Asia and America with barge freight. Meanwhile, exercise bars are set up at intervals on the towpath for those who need a workout. **Tottenham** has suffered from riots at various times and was the touchstone for the 2011 riots across English cities.

Stonebridge and Tottenham Locks lead to the A503 and North London Lines which cross between Tottenham Hale (the Saxon Totta's home corner) and **Walthamstow** by the Narrow Boat.

The river rejoins the navigation and the railway passes over before the navigation moves to the west of the two parts of Warwick Reservoir with nature reserves and angling and past the Markfield Beam Engine & Museum which houses the beam engine which pumped sewage from 1886 to 1964. The earth mounds are spoil from Victoria Line construction. Copper Mill was built about 1800 to process copper brought from the Pool of London. Modern flats in red brick next to the river at Tottenham are not unpleasant and tennis courts and parkland follow the Lea Rowing Club which precedes a marina. The next clubhouse is the Leaside centre at Upper Clapton, a canoeing facility developed in the 1960s in an old Bostik glue factory and since having produced top competition paddlers.

The railway crosses over again by the Walthamstow Marsh Nature Reserve, some of the last natural marshland in London. A V Roe had a workshop under an arch and flew 300m in his Yellow Peril in 1909, the first powered all-British flight, despite being ordered off local land by a landowner.

The Leaside centre on the former Bostik glue factory site.

Artwork house of wood blocks under the A12 at Hackney.

The approach to Lea Bridge is constricted for larger craft and the many rowing boats because of the tight bends. The popularity of the Lea Bridge area is emphasized by the succession of public houses including the Anchor & Hope (one of the smallest public houses in England and often called the Tolly after its previous owners) and Prince of Wales (renamed in 1997 as the Princess of Wales by the landlord although not by the locals). After the A104, water level at Lea Bridge is controlled by actuated sluices on Pimms Brook to ±25mm to avoid barges grounding or damaging superstructures on the bridge.

The wildlife sanctuaries become more unusual with the Middlesex Filter Beds Nature Reserve having many butterflies.

Tower blocks dominate through Clapton Park although there are playing fields with 73 football pitches on Hackney Marsh, **Hackney** having been named after the Dane Haca or Hacon. This is now London's East End. Down to the A12 the banks are marked out with canoe race training distances.

Behind the Olympic media centre, hockey centre and handball arena in the 2.5km^2 Queen Elizabeth Olympic Park on the left bank are the Eton Manor Paralympic tennis and archery centre, to become a hockey, tennis and football centre, 6,000 seat velodrome with 250m track designed to set records and a fencing hall.

Lesney's Matchbox Toys were made here until manufacture was moved to Macau. The site is now called Matchmakers Wharf. Homerton was Hunburgh's farm, owned by the Knights of St John in the 14th century. The bridge over the navigation has its parapets edged with vertical pieces of slate, only marginally more aesthetic than broken glass.

Near the former Clarnico mints factory the HS1 Channel Tunnel rail link passes under to Stratford station and the North London Line crosses over beyond the 6,500 seat handball arena.

The Hertford Union Canal or Duckett's Cut heads to the right at Old Ford.

Old Ford Locks have large satellite dishes next to the canal. They could also be reached by high tides until 2000 when tides were excluded at Bow Locks to prevent silt from being deposited at low tide. This abandoned industrial area has such birds as cormorants, herons, kingfishers, kestrels and gulls plus butterflies in quantity. The ford is where the Roman road between Colchester and London crossed the Lea.

Four lock cottages were used as a studio for the *Big Breakfast Show* for a decade. The Old River Lee joins on the left past the 2012 Olympic Games main stadium site through Old Ford tide gates. The stadium covers 16ha, seats 80,000 and is surfaced with Scunthorpe turf. Adjacent is the AncelorMittal Orbit, the UK's tallest sculpture at 114m with viewing platforms at 76 and 80m

The Hertford Union Canal heads away towards the Gherkin.

The main Olympic stadium for 2012.

above the ground. The aquatics centre is behind with 1ha of water in three pools. Four skeletons were removed from a prehistoric settlement on the site during its construction. The 2,500 capacity for spectators was increased to 17,500 for the Olympics.

The Northern Outfall Sewer Embankment crosses just below the confluence, part of **London**'s first sewer, built by Bazalgette in the mid-1860s, and carries the Greenway path and cycleway on top. Signs are constructed from sewage pipes.

The final Olympic site is the warm up athletic tracks on the opposite bank from the Bryant & May match factory where the first women's trade union was founded. This followed the 1888 Match Girls Strike over dangerous working conditions relating to the handling of phosphorous.

Successive railway bridges take over a freight line and the Great Eastern line. Suddenly there is road traffic everywhere and road signs alongside giving lane directions for the Blackwall Tunnel.

After the Bow Back River joins on the left, former high tides were indicated by the scrape marks on the underside of the long A11 bridge. The Bow flyover carriageways pass both sides of a 1311 church. This was the position of the original Bow Bridge built by Queen Matilda after Empress Maud nearly drowned in the ford in the 12th century and named after the stone bridge shape. It has probably been nearly as many centuries since Bromley was a bramble wood. A 2011 bridge for cyclists and pedestrians continues underneath the road as a suspended route.

The Channelsea River leaves on the left, sweeping round a corner to Three Mills. The listed Clock Mill with its oast house style malting roofs was built in 1817 with a 1750 clock. It is now offices. The Grade I House Mill was built of timber with a brick facade in 1776 on a pre-*Domesday* site by the Huguenots to prepare malt for the gin trade, all gin having been imported until then. The alcohol produced was so pure it was later used for cordite and so this was the site in 1941 of the first bombing raid on London during the Second World War, demolishing the miller's house, subsequently rebuilt as the British Waterways information centre between the mills. House Mill ran for eight hours of the tidal cycle and was the largest and most powerful tidal mill in Britain, if not the world. The third mill was a windmill. Grinding out the films is a studio which has produced *Bad Girls*, *Footballers'*

The magnificent Three Mills, tidally powered, by the River Lee.

Wives, *Kavanagh QC* and the first *Big Brother* programmes amongst others.

The London, Tilbury & Southend line crosses on a massive lattice girder bridge by seven gasholders now used to hold natural gas on the former Congreve Rocket site. Bow Tidal Lock gives access to Bow Creek for large craft from four hours before high water to two hours after, there having been a proper lock here from 1850. The flotsam on the water has to wait. This is near the line of the former Hackney Brook.

Limehouse Cut was completed in 1770 to give a quick route to the Pool of London. While quieter than the main river, it is susceptible to the prevailing wind as it sets off in a straight canyon beneath the A12 and the Docklands Light Railway. High buildings, one of which carries the Spratt's logo in peeling letters, give little to indicate the origin of the Bow Common name.

By the Bromley Stop Lock the A13 Commercial Road and Docklands Light Railway pass over while hidden beneath is the Limehouse Link. Hawkesmoor's magnificent St Anne's church of 1712–24 stands out in this formerly rough dock area.

Formerly the link to the Thames was direct but this was closed in 1968 and only the 1864 link with the basin used.

Limehouse Basin opened in 1812 as the Regent's Canal Dock although the name Limehouse comes from the 14th century limekilns there. The 4ha basin in London's formerly tough area of Chinatown has been a collecting point for wood and other debris floating down the Regent's Canal as well as for herons, cormorants, tufted ducks, blackheaded gulls and great crested grebes. Now all that has changed with a marina development, public houses, shops, housing and offices. In 1981 the political Limehouse Manifesto was launched here.

Landing is difficult in the Limehouse Basin for small boats because of the high sides. In the absence of anything better, moored Canal & River Trust workboats make useful floating pontoons.

Limehouse Cut goes right at Bow Locks, towards Docklands.

Distance
45km from Hertford to Limehouse Lock

Navigation Authority
Canal & River Trust

OS 1:50,000 Sheets
166 Luton & Hertford
(176 West London)
177 East London

Connections
Regent's Canal – see CoB p96
River Thames –see RoB p229

44 River Thames

England's royal river

How many a brimming river swells its waters deep and clear,
The Windrush and the Cherwell and the Thame to Dorset dear,
The Kennet and the Loddon that have music in their names,
But no grandeur like to that in yours, my own mast-shadowed Thames.
William Cox Bennett

Kemble's claim to the source of the Thames, still little more than a puddle even after months of rain. Behind is the embankment of the Thames & Severn Canal.

Like the Mississippi, the Thames defies the convention that a river's source should be at the head of the longest arm. Thames Head is near Kemble but the River Churn takes a longer line from Seven Springs to their confluence. It has also been suggested, mischievously, using volume as the criterion, that the source should be Swindon sewage works via the River Ray.

This is the royal river, its name from the Sanskrit tamasa, dark water. The upper reaches are also known as the Isis although there is debate about how far this alternative name extends.

The river has followed its general direction for some 58,000,000 years and has taken its present course to the North Sea for 450,000 years. Cnut brought 160 ships up to **Cricklade** in 1016 and barges were still working up to Waterhay in the 19th century. The 1852 Cricklade Bridge is now the official head of navigation as it is too low for any craft to pass under.

However, the head of navigation on this major river is far from accessible and involves climbing over a wall next to the bridge. The river is narrow, fast and twisting as far as Lechlade. The Environment Agency do not clear fallen willow trees from the navigation as far as Lechlade, so that there are more strainers on this section than on all other official English navigations added together. As it is popular with novice canoeists setting out to make their descents over several days, this makes it less safe than it should be. Small gravel rapids are encountered in these upper reaches in drier weather, reeds and hawthorn bushes also intruding into the channel. Capsizes are not unknown.

The river was not made fully navigable until after the finish of the canal age, even though the lower end was part of Brindley's Grand Cross scheme. There had been four flash locks above Lechlade but these were abandoned after completion of the Thames & Severn Canal, which runs parallel as far as Lechlade. Frustration with the state of the Thames led to a series of proposals, linking the Kennet & Avon Canal with the Basingstoke Canal to avoid the Thames below Reading, the Hampton Gay Canal to run from north of Oxford to London and lines from Lechlade or Kempsford to Abingdon or Wallingford and Reading or Sonning to Monkey Island or Isleworth, together with the Wilts & Berks Canal and the North Wiltshire Canal. Indeed, when the Oxford Canal and the Grand Union Canal were linked it was found quicker to send boats from Abingdon to London via Rugby rather than using the Thames, where they might sit for weeks in the shallows, waiting for water. Now the river is strictly regulated and the Environment Agency decide where they hold floodwater.

Cricklade, meaning hill near a passage or river crossing, was claimed to have had a university from 1180 BC although a college established in 650 AD by Penda, King of Mercia, was more likely. This specialized in Greek and was moved to Oxford in the 9th century by King Alfred.

The Romans had a minor settlement where the Ermin Way crossed with a bridge over the Thames and a causeway taking in the Churn. St Augustine was said to have converted the Anglo-Saxons in 597. This was the frontier between Saxon Wessex to the south and the Danes in Mercia to the north, Alfred crossing here to fight the Danes in 878. Fortifications against the Danes were in place a couple of years later and town walls remain.

The 12th century St Sampson's church has some Saxon material and a fine turreted tower of 1552 by the Duke of Northumberland, with massive arcading,

The official head of navigation on the Thames in Cricklade.

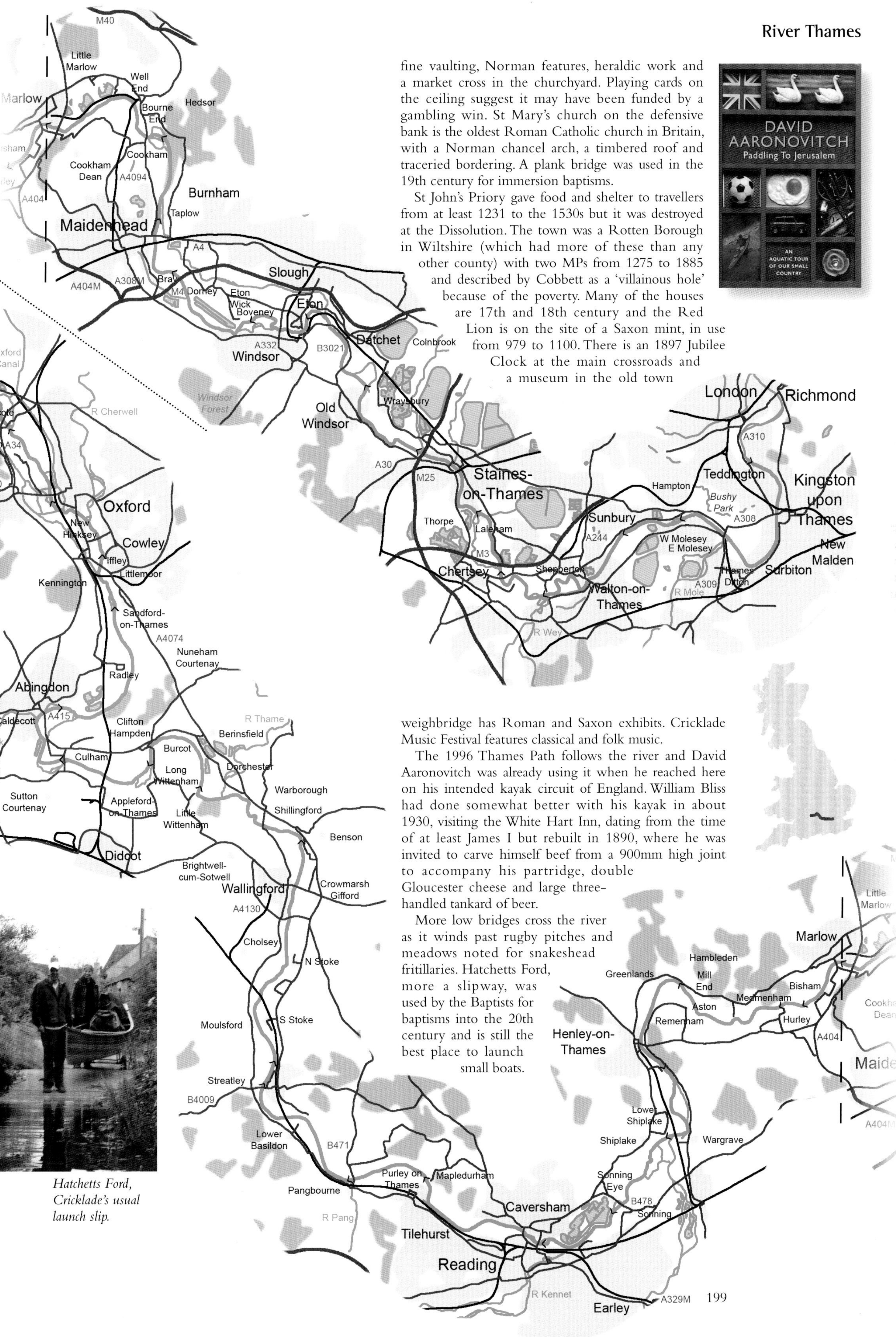

fine vaulting, Norman features, heraldic work and a market cross in the churchyard. Playing cards on the ceiling suggest it may have been funded by a gambling win. St Mary's church on the defensive bank is the oldest Roman Catholic church in Britain, with a Norman chancel arch, a timbered roof and traceried bordering. A plank bridge was used in the 19th century for immersion baptisms.

St John's Priory gave food and shelter to travellers from at least 1231 to the 1530s but it was destroyed at the Dissolution. The town was a Rotten Borough in Wiltshire (which had more of these than any other county) with two MPs from 1275 to 1885 and described by Cobbett as a 'villainous hole' because of the poverty. Many of the houses are 17th and 18th century and the Red Lion is on the site of a Saxon mint, in use from 979 to 1100. There is an 1897 Jubilee Clock at the main crossroads and a museum in the old town weighbridge has Roman and Saxon exhibits. Cricklade Music Festival features classical and folk music.

The 1996 Thames Path follows the river and David Aaronovitch was already using it when he reached here on his intended kayak circuit of England. William Bliss had done somewhat better with his kayak in about 1930, visiting the White Hart Inn, dating from the time of at least James I but rebuilt in 1890, where he was invited to carve himself beef from a 900mm high joint to accompany his partridge, double Gloucester cheese and large three-handled tankard of beer.

More low bridges cross the river as it winds past rugby pitches and meadows noted for snakeshead fritillaries. Hatchetts Ford, more a slipway, was used by the Baptists for baptisms into the 20th century and is still the best place to launch small boats.

Hatchetts Ford, Cricklade's usual launch slip.

St Mary the Virgin's, Castle Eaton.

The line of the North Wilts Canal having been built over in Cricklade, the restorers now propose to bring it in next to the River Key, use the course of the Thames to get under the A419 and then turn north parallel to Ampney Brook to join the Thames & Severn Canal 500m from the Thames.

The A419 bypass of 1975 is the last major road until Oxford, over which distance Lechlade is the only significant settlement. Salmon began to disappear from the river after 1810 with the increasing use of the WCs but there are trout above Lechlade. There are teasels, damselflies, moorhens, magpies, terns, blackheaded and other gulls and buzzards.

There can be a rapid at Eysey footbridge and there are the remains of a chapel, the church having been destroyed in 1953.

The riverside hamlet of Kempsford.

Photographing a mink on a branch.

The River Ray joins before Water Eaton footbridge and Water Eaton House. There are few landmarks as the river winds between fields of crops in unbroken countryside.

As the river moves from Wiltshire to Swindon on the south side and to Gloucestershire on the north side a riverside tree house precedes a heavy girder bridge over the river at Castle Eaton, shallows and the first riparian public house on the river, the 18th century red brick Red Lion, which has pétanque and a picture of an earlier bridge. The 12th century church of St Mary the Virgin, its stone roof recently restored, has an 1861 bell turret by William Butterfield in the centre containing a 13th century sanctus bell and has Norman doorways, a 13th century chancel and a carved wooden Elizabethan pulpit. The manor house was fortified in 1311.

On a normal day the glimpse of a dome might be the only evidence of RAF Fairford with its 3.7km runway, the venue for the Royal International Air Tattoo, the world's largest military air show. This NATO airfield is used by the USAF, was a test site for Concorde, hosted Gulf War B52s and was designated an emergency landing site for the Space Shuttle.

A 40ha battlefield on the south bank at Kempsford is where the Iron Age Hwiccians fought the Wessex Saxons in 800 and there are Saxon earthworks on the north bank, used as the basis of the castle of the Lancasters, demolished about 1700 but with a 12th century tower and stone wall remaining. The Norman church of 1336 has a Decorated chancel, a 1385 Perpendicular tower by John of Gaunt, a memorial to his wife, Blanche, and Lancaster red roses on the ceiling. Nailed to the door is a horseshoe shed at the departure of the 4th Earl of Lancaster after his son had drowned in the Thames. Chaucer visited and wrote *Chaucer's Dream* and *The Book of the Duchess* for the marriage of Blanche and then her death a decade later.

On moonlit nights the Lady of the Mist might be encountered, walking on the water and singing or leaping in with a shriek. She was the wife of Henry, Duke of Lancaster, killed by him after false accusations were made against her during the Barons' Wars.

The George is named after George IV, a friend of Lord Coleraine of Kempsford Manor, who later fled to Paris to escape his creditors. Manor Farmhouse uses the stables but its cellars could be those of the castle. The vicarage is 17th century and there are other 17th century and 18th century houses in the village.

Hannington Bridge of 1841 has three skewed brick arches, frequently with shallows or rapids, Hannington Wick having been the site of a Roman crossing with a Roman villa present.

There is an enclosure site in a field opposite Upper Inglesham, beyond which a channel joins from the River Cole. Mallards and tufted ducks inhabit an environment with lilies and sedges.

St John the Baptist's church was built in the 11th century on a pagan mound at Inglesham, although it is now mostly 12th century. It has the shaft of a Saxon cross in the churchyard but a Saxon Madonna and Child carving has been moved inside for protection. William Morris oversaw the restoration with its 13th century wall paintings on ochre and red checked sloping walls, Norman nave, 13th century chancel with 14th century stone reredos, 1468 font, 15th century screens, Jacobean pew for the squire and pulpit with canopy. The Inglesham Village site is to the east while Inglesham Polo Club meet at Lynt Farm.

Although some powered craft ascend a little further until stopped by fallen trees, most take the head of navigation as being the confluence with the River Coln and the end of the Thames & Severn Canal of 1789. Of particular interest beyond the weeping willows is Inglesham Roundhouse, the first of several along the canal, possibly at the whim of landowner the Earl of Bath to match his folly in Cirencester Park. The building is now in the ownership of a canal enthusiast as canal restoration takes place from the Stroud end. The ground floor has stables, then a 5.1m diameter kitchen and dining room with a bedroom above and then a lead-lined inverted cone to funnel rainwater into a tank.

Shelley rowed here from Old Windsor in 1815 with Mary Godwin, Charles Clairmont and Thomas Love Peacock but they were stopped from continuing along the canal by the £20 toll. It was where Jennifer finally stormed away from Mark in *Boogie up the River*.

A downriver trip is known as a Thames Meander, as described to London in *Hornblower & the Atropos*. Some narrowboats fly high pennants above Oxford to make themselves more visible. Boats moor along the banks but, as this is the effective head of navigation for many on what is probably our most important river, it is surprising that there is no public landing stage and only brief parking nearby.

Swans hang about in a flock by the Riverside pub, expecting to get fed.

Ha'penny Bridge carries the A361. The **Highworth** to Burford turnpike mailcoach road and bridge were proposed, planned and built in a few months in 1792. The stone bridge's semicircular navigation arch was built high enough to clear ships' masts with the arch stones laid radially. Fears that the large arch would collapse have proved unfounded, nothing more serious dropping off than the local youths. The name refers to the toll, from which churchgoers were excluded, other pedestrians being excused after a revolt in 1839 and the toll being removed from vehicles in 1875 although the tollbooth remains at the north end.

Lechlade on Thames, Leach load or the gateway to the Cotswolds, was Ladingford in Compton Mackenzie's *Guy & Pauline*. An old wool and market town, it has been settled since 2500 BC but has mostly 18th and 19th century Cotswold stone houses and the 18th century New Inn in red brick. A medical university was moved to Oxford.

St Lawrence church of 1476 was built of Taynton stone on the site of an earlier rare sanctuary church. It has a stone spire, altered after a 1510 fire, and is buttressed, in Perpendicular style. The pomegranate symbol on the vestry door relates to Catherine of Aragon, who later owned the manor. There are angel roof bosses and 15th century brasses to the Townshend family. One of the chapels is to St Blaise, the patron saint of woolcombers, combs being painted on the reredos. Shelley composed *A Summer Evening Churchyard, Lechlade* here, the churchyard containing the 18th century Church House and a fine gazebo. The Old Vicarage dates from 1805.

The town loaded Gloucester cheese, Cheshire salt and Taynton stone for St Paul's cathedral. There is an annual flag festival.

The south bank becomes Oxfordshire (or Occupied Berkshire to some) as the river reaches a stand of poplars, Himalayan balsam appears on the banks and the first of the pillboxes is met. There were 5,000 pillboxes along the Thames, forming Stopline Red.

The first of the 44 locks, St John's, receives water at 76m above sea level. Red boards are shown at locks when the river is in spate and yellow boards when the flow is rising or falling. The wide beam locks are all manned, the far gate being operated by a pole and hook. It took a flash 70 hours to reach Sonning, 117km downstream. Watching from behind a chain is a statue of Old Father Thames in Portland cement, a copy of a statue of Neptune by Rafaelle Monti in 1851 for the Great Exhibition in Hyde Park. This statue was recovered from the ruins of the Crystal Palace fire in 1936 and taken to Thames Head but moved here for safe keeping in 1974 because of damage by students.

Inglesham Roundhouse at the end of the Thames & Severn.

St John's Bridge of 1886 takes the A417 over a single arch. In 1229 King John contributed 20 marks to the first stone bridge here, kept by seven monks who had no personal possessions and slept in a communal room in their clothes. His wife, Isabella, founded the Priory of St John the Baptist in St John's Priory Park, to be dissolved by Edward IV. The Cotswold stone almshouses of 1472 have become the haunted Trout Inn, where Aunt Sally is played. The River Leach joins from the north and the River Cole from the south.

Ha'penny Bridge in Lechlade.

St Mary the Virgin's church dates from 1200 with a Norman zigzag chancel arch, a 15th century Perpendicular tower, 16th century pulpit panels probably painted by Jan Gossaert and a pair of Burne-Jones windows. The Queen Anne Old Parsonage of 1703 has a walled garden and was left to the National Trust by American author Peter Stuckley but with the stipulation that the tenant must have American literary connections.

The hamlet of Buscot has seen a surprising amount of industrial activity. The Cheese Wharf dispatched 3,000t in 1809. Australian Robert Campbell built the former Berkshire Distillery by the Thames in 1879 to make alcohol from sugar beet and beetroot, moved by narrow gauge railway and exported to France from Brandy Island. He carried out agricultural and irrigation experiments and used a steam pump to supply a reservoir at Buscot House, on the far side of the A417, lined with chestnut trees which look striking in their spring blossom. A canal led to a brick and tile works at Buscot Wharf.

Buscot, Burgweard's cottage, is a model village of 1879. At Buscot Lock, Bliss watched an otter giving her kit a

Old Father Thames, in safe keeping at St John's Lock.

swimming lesson. There are common sandpipers and the 30km^2 Buscot Park also has room for a heronry.

Eaton Weir and the last flash lock on the river were removed in 1936 near where the north bank becomes Oxfordshire.

Kelmscott, Caenhelm's cottage, was the summer residence of Arts & Crafts Movement founder William Morris from 1871 to 1896, and

The historical Radcot Bridge on what is now a backwater.

Stream warning at Shifford Lock.

has now accepted his spelling for the name. The 1570 Elizabethan Lower Farm in Taynton stone became the Grade I Kelmscott Manor, which he shared with his wife, Jane, and her admirer, Dante Gabriel Rossetti, making the trip from Hammersmith in a large punt. He collected riverside plants for colours and patterns and his *News from Nowhere* ends here. Visitors included G B Shaw and W B Yeats, whose sister, Lily, was an apprentice here to Morris' daughter, May, in her embroidery workshop.

St George's church is Norman from about 1190 with a Norman doorway and font, 14th century medieval wall paintings of Cain and Abel and a Burne-Jones window. Morris is buried in the churchyard. The 1902 Memorial Cottages by Philip Webb for Jane have a carving of William over the front door and there is also a 1934 Morris Memorial Hall by supporter Ernest Gimson.

Grafton Lock has a 19th century stone cottage. Grass snakes and Canada geese might be seen in the vicinity. A windfan has been located near where powerlines cross.

The A4095 crosses what is now an island at Radcot, reed or red cottage. The current navigation channel is crossed by Jessop's single span Cradle Bridge of 1878. Overlooking the cut is the 19th century Swan Hotel accompanied by a 14th century stable block and a dovecote which was a chapel. Crossing the original channel is the Grade I Radcot Bridge of about 1225, possibly based on a Saxon bridge of 958. In Taynton stone, it is the oldest bridge on the river and has two pointed ribbed arches with a round 3.7m arch between them. This arch was damaged in the Battle of Radcot Bridge in 1387 during the Peasants' Revolt by Henry Bolingbroke to trap the Earl of Oxford, Richard de Vere, who was on his way south to support Richard II. De Vere lost his horse, sword and armour but swam to safety and escaped in the dark though some of his men were stabbed. This battle led to the Merciless Parliament the following year. The central arch was repaired in 1393 but the keystone settled. A niche may have held a memorial cross. The bridge was taken again in the Civil War by Lord Goring's Royalists on their way to join the king in Oxford. May Morris, daughter of William, campaigned for the bridge to be saved before the First World War.

There is a moat and the Garrison Field earthwork where the Royalists defending Faringdon under Prince Rupert met the Parliamentary cavalry in the 1645 battle. Radcot House is 17th century, the Knights Hospitaller had a preceptory at Friars Court Farm and there is evidence of ridge and furrow farming. Wharves were probably established here in the 12th century and Taynton stone was taken to Oxford colleges, London and Paris.

Sharney Brook joins before the Grade II Rushey Lock, rush island, the earliest paddle and rymer lock on the Thames. Rushes were collected from as far away as Abingdon for chair seating, including for Salisbury Cathedral. When the lock cottage served as a guesthouse the guests included the Astors, Douglas Fairbanks and Errol Flynn. On his tour, Bliss was summoned to the weir to help W G Grace extract a fish hook.

Tadpole Bridge of 1789 has a single stone arch and was tolled until 1875. The 17th century Trout no longer has a Mr Herring as the landlord. This is where Jennifer finally joined Mark in their journey from London to Lechlade in *Boogie up the River*.

Powerlines cross before the 2.5km^2 Chimney Meadow national nature reserve with greylag geese, curlews, snipe and waders. Crossing the river is Tenfoot Bridge of 1869, the name from the width of the former flash lock.

From Chimney the Shifford Cut of 1897 avoids a

Linking the Maybush and Rose Revived at Newbridge.

Paddles and rymers in use at Northmoor.

The ornate Swinford Bridge is still tolled.

meander through Duxford with its ford and weir. The cut ends at Shifford Lock, in 1898 the last to be built on the Thames. Perhaps a stoat might be seen.

The Great Brook, a 19th century irrigation channel, joins at Shifford, where there is erosion around a towpath bridge. Shifford, Saxon for sheep ford, is where Alfred held the first recorded Parliament in a field in 800, the outdoor venue chosen to avoid the risk of surprise attack. A Georgian church was rebuilt in 1863.

Oxfordshire Bit's pollarded willows mark an old meander and Hall Ham was the site of a watermill and wharf. There is an undercut bend below Harrowden Hill, a limestone outlier where UN Weapons inspector Dr David Kelly was claimed to have committed suicide in suspicious circumstances in 2003.

The Grade I 15th century Newbridge, carrying the A415, was originally built about 1250 by French Benedictine monks from St Denis who were based at Deerhurst Priory on the Severn. Crossing the Thames and the Windrush, which joins here, it has six pointed arches of Taynton stone with spans up to 5.8m, some with their ribs cut away. One of the oldest on the Thames, it has cutwaters on the upstream side, extended up as pedestrian refuges. The Royalists defended it in 1644 during the Civil War but Waller crossed by boat and made a successful surprise attack a few days later, breaking the bridge to stop the Oxford Royalists.

The 16th century Maybush at the south end is on the site of a 15th century hermitage used by the bridge-keeper. At the other end is the Rose Revived, where it is claimed that Cromwell's drooping flower perked up after being stood in a flagon of ale. It also has been a hermitage as well as a wharf and a toll house and was considered old in 1462. In the Berkshire days the pubs had different closing times, resulting in a late exodus across the bridge.

Crayfish might be found in the river and hawker dragonflies along the banks as the Thames is diverted through the Oxford clay vale around a Corallian limestone scarp. Hart's Weir Footbridge is named after one of the numerous Hart's Weirs on the Thames, influenced by the ubiquitous Hart family.

Northmoor Lock has the last remaining paddle and rymer weir. In 1766 William Flower, the 2nd Viscount Ashbrook, courted and married Betty Rudge, the daughter of the ferryman, their descendants including the Duchess of Marlborough.

The powerlines cross back between Appleton, with its 16th century thatched cottages, and Eaton. A rusty windfan stands by the river with just a single blade remaining, like a windblown daisy.

Bablock Hythe was Babba's stream landing place, a ford since Roman times. The ferry was established by the monks of Deerhurst Priory in 904 and featured in *News from Nowhere* and in Matthew Arnold's *The Scholar Gypsy*, where this was still considered to be the 'stripling Thames'. Keats planned *Endymion* here. Skinner's Bridge was burnt down in the 1930s by Oxford students. The ferry is now run by the Ferry Inn. There is a static caravan site and a Physic Well is found up the hill to the east.

The Farmoor Reservoirs were constructed in 1976. As well as storing water they are used for sailing, angling and birdwatching. Species include water rails with hobbies, 1,000 swallows and 15,000 house martins in the summer, little stints, turnstones and ruff in the autumn and teal, wigeon, scaup, pochard, goldeneye, longtailed ducks, redheaded smew, goosanders, divers, Slavonian, rednecked and blacknecked grebes and even spotted sandpipers, Caspian terns and longtailed skuas in the winter, when ornithology is at its best.

There is also a hide on the Pinkhill Meadow Reserve, designated in 1990. After the lock at Pinkhill, Pinca's

Wytham Great Wood covers Wytham Hill.

place, powerlines cross to Farmoor and there are bases for Oxford Cruisers and Anglo Welsh.

Beating the bounds of Cumnor in the 18th century involved the ferryman in bringing the vicar 6s 8d in a bowl of water and the vicar then crossing to the Oxfordshire side and holding onto the reeds to claim the whole river.

The Grade II Swinford Bridge, carrying the B4044, is one of the two remaining toll bridges over the Thames. It was built in 1769, probably by Sir William Taylor for the 4th Earl of Abingdon at the request of George III, who had fallen off the ferry. It has nine semicircular arches, the centre three larger with balustrades over them. Tolls are collected from a shelter rather than from the toll house at the north end, raising £200,000 per year. The bridge was sold for £1,100,000 in 2010. It pays no tax, in perpetuity, and no other bridge is permitted within 5km of it.

Swinford meant swine ford while Eynsham was Aegen's place. A priory here was destroyed at the Dissolution. The lower end of Eynsham Lock can be difficult because of the power of the eddy caused by the weirstream. It is followed by the Wharf Stream or

The remains of Godstow Abbey at Wolvercote.

Oxford's Osney Bridge stops larger craft from passing.

Eynsham Canal and then by the Old Canal or Cassington Cut from Cassington Mill and by the River Evenlode.

Opposite these confluences is Wytham Hill, covered by Wytham Great Wood, more than 2.4km^2 owned by Oxford University. The wood has nightingales and deer and is where Sir Charles Elton carried out his early ecology work.

The Thames becomes braided through **Oxford,** with the natural channel buried. The Thames Conservancy Act confirms the right of navigation on all channels leaving the Thames and returning to it but the Environment Agency do not attempt to keep these navigations open. Clearing of trees on the Seacourt Stream has been undertaken by the Thames Traditional Boat Society.

The Duke's Cut leaves from the most northerly point on the Thames, to connect with the Oxford Canal, a link provided by the 4th Duke of Marlborough. By King's Lock, Pixey Mead is cut for hay on an ancient rotation system with lots being drawn in June using 13 Mead Balls in a ceremony which has continued for nearly a millennium. The river bends around Hagley Pool and passes under Thames Bridge, carrying the A34 Western By-Pass. Building bridges and sliding them into place is an established technique but a whole viaduct deck was slid sideways into place just north of here at Wolvercote. The church at Wolvercote has the grave of J R R Tolkien.

The north part of Godstow Bridge is 17th century and crosses the weirstream, the Royalists holding it in 1645 against Parliamentarian artillery. The section over the lock cut dates from 1892. Godstow House, God's place, was founded in 1138, used as a hospice for Godstow Nunnery and rebuilt in the 17th century. Now the Trout Inn, it has a Chinese bridge of about 1880 to a garden which contains peacocks. It was visited by Bill Clinton when daughter Chelsea was an Oxford student and has often been used for filming *Inspector Morse*.

Godstow Abbey was built in 1133 after Lady Edith Launceline saw a beam of light here from Binsey. The nunnery was consecrated in 1139 in the presence of King Stephen. A storm damaged the tower in 1764, the navigation later cut through the graveyard and it was painted by George Price Boyce. It is where the Fair Rosamund, Jane Clifford, the mistress of Henry II, was educated and then buried after her death in 1176. It is not true that she lived in a secret bower in a maze or was poisoned by Queen Eleanor but she may have lived at Woodstock. The ghost of a White Lady was seen and there was the scent of heather from her tomb with the danger of its becoming a shrine so the bishop had her body exhumed and buried outside the walls. The nunnery was largely destroyed at the Dissolution but there are some remains. Wytham has its own abbey.

Locks are all mechanized from Godstow. Some say that the Isis name only applies from here to Iffley Lock. From here to Medley the students used small boats with large sail areas and the reach is also used by St Edward's School rowers. Speed measuring posts are installed here, one minute being the minimum approved time between them.

Port Meadow, Portman's Eyot or burgher's island, is 1.8km^2 of the most studied piece of ground in the country. It was given by Alfred in the 9th century for help in defending against the Danes and has creeping marshwort, round fruited rush and plovers. Freemen of the city of Oxford have grazing rights for cattle, horses and geese and it has been grazed for a millennium. It was a Royalist campsite during the Civil War, was a First World War aerodrome and received Dunkirk evacuees during the Second World War. Annual Sheriff's Races for amateur horses for charity were started at the north end in 1680 and it has been used for ice skating during times of winter flooding.

It has been used for various wagers. In 1774 a blind gelding won a 16km race against a broken winded pony for 100 guineas. A carpenter ran 80km in 10 hours in 1787 and a stone was thrown 165m in 1799 for £40. A racecourse was set up with someone walking 1,690km in 20 days. In 1762 it was used for early games of cricket.

Round Hill is in the centre of the meadow. Black Jack's Hole was popular for suicides and for catching pike.

A well on the west side had cures for eye, stomach pain and infertility problems. It cured Algar, the suitor of the 8th century princess St Frideswide, who lived by it, after he touched her and was blinded. St Margaret's church was founded by St Frideswide and its first recorded vicar was Nicholas Breakspear, who became the only English Pope, Adrian IV.

This reach is where Lewis Carroll, Christ Church maths don Charles Dodgson, told the stories which became *Alice's Adventures in Wonderland* in 1862, during boat trips. The well became Alice's treacle well and her governess, Miss Prickett, the Red Queen, lived at Binsey.

Binsey was Byni's island. The 17th century thatched Perch pub was known as Binsey Cathedral for its flouting of the Sunday closing law. It was visited by Louis MacNeice and Dylan Thomas and frequented by A E Coppard and the ghost of a suicidal sailor. There are trees on a line of poplars that Gerard Manley Hopkins wrote about being felled. Medley Sailing Club is based here and Bossom's boatyard makes wooden punt poles which go to Cambridge because Oxford uses aluminium ones. George Wither wrote about the former Medley Weir and David Aaronovitch, here hitching a ride on a boat, wrote about being pelted at the arched iron Medley Footbridge of 1865.

Castle Mill Stream was the main channel of the Thames until 1227, when monks cut a new channel, to rejoin the Castle Mill Stream below what is now the site of the railway bridge. Unlike Cambridge, Oxford does not make good use of its river, its assets being largely hidden from the water and the river environment mostly indifferent until Folly Bridge.

The Bulstake Stream leaves to the west past the Tumbling Bay, a male-only bathing place which, of course, did not involve bathing costumes. Water quality was used as the excuse for closing down this amenity, used by everyone from dons downwards.

In the opposite direction the Sheepwash Channel emerges under an arched iron footbridge, the route used by boats coming off the Oxford Canal and intending to continue downstream. Their next obstacle is Osney Bridge of 1889, carrying the A420. This cast iron bridge has only 2.3m of headroom, the lowest on the river below Lechlade, and this prevents many craft from travelling further upstream. It is on the site of a monks' stone bridge which had collapsed four years earlier, killing a girl. It was also the site of an uninvited boarding party in *Boogie up the River*.

In 1995 the railway station, which features on the opening page of Max Beerbohm's *Zuleika Dobson*, had the proud boast that improved security had reduced the number of thefts from its carpark over the year from 46 to a mere 16.

Osney was Osa's eyot. In 1222 it was the location of the first English martyrdom of a Jew, the former deacon Robert who had converted to marry a Jew.

Oxford is at a gap in the Corallian limestone ridge. It is usually taken to be the ford where oxen crossed but it may be significant that the Old English for salmon was *ehoc*. Confusingly, the River Ock is downstream at Abingdon.

Over 2,000 years ago, Lud had the realm of southern England measured and discovered that Oxford was at the exact centre. Oxford had a minor Roman settlement. St Frideswide built a monastery in 727 and began the walled town. In 912 Oxford was used by Edward the Elder as a buffer between Wessex and the invading Danes and it was mentioned in the Saxon Chronicle that year.

Oxford colleges. Christ Church is in the right foreground, Magdalen tower to the far right and the Sheldonian dome in the left middle distance. Tha Thames is off the bottom of the picture, flowing left to right.

Æthelstan established a mint in 925. Cnut held a council of Saxons and Danes here. It was the sixth largest town in England in 1066 and it was still the fifth largest in 1781.

The 1071 Norman motte and bailey Oxford Castle accompanies the Saxon stone St George's tower. Queen Matilda, dressed in a white cloak, escaped King Stephen's forces from the castle in 1142 by crossing the frozen Thames to travel to Wallingford. The castle remained a prison until 1996 but now takes paying guests, the first British prison to make the conversion to a hotel and shopping centre. Earlier, the Wesleys had visited prisoners.

The 1258 *Provisions of Oxford* document by Simon de Montfort and the nobles led to Magna Carta and Parliament yet the city was Royalist in the Civil War. Hitler had planned to make it his capital and a 1973 1:10,000 Soviet map of Oxford had metric contours while the Ordnance Survey's maps were still imperial.

There are 900 buildings of architectural or historical interest in the city centre and the best concentration of urban gardens outside Japan. With its 653 listed buildings, the city was Hardy's Christminster, especially in *Jude the Obscure*. Oxford English is the benchmark of English speech yet it is the city of lost causes. It was Arnold's city of dreaming spires yet, appearing to have a pathological hatred of the motor industry which has supplied a significant part of its wealth, it has also been called the city of screaming tyres.

Oxford has the oldest English speaking university and this was in existence by the 11th century. Alfred debated with the monks for several days in 872. When Thomas à Becket was exiled to France in 1167, Henry II ordered students home from France in order to prevent them from associating with him. They gravitated to Oxford. There were town and gown riots for two days in 1355, during which many students were killed.

Oxford University students have included Dr Johnson, Sir Walter Raleigh, Pope Alexander V, Earl Haig, explorer Richard Burton, actor Richard Burton (remembered by the Burton Theatre), Evelyn Waugh, Beau Nash, Beau Brummell, Shelley and a couple of dozen prime ministers. It produced the <, > and ∞ symbols and Boyle's Law. Penicillin was first tried on patients here. Charles and John Wesley of Christ Church met with other students to form the Methodists, both being ordained here but John becoming itinerant after being banned for his 1744 University Sermon. Robert Burton wrote *The Anatomy of Melancholy*.

Richard the Lionheart was born in the former

Beaumont Palace and John was also born in Oxford. The Randolph Hotel is now a local building of note, where Aaronovitch enjoyed the fire drill.

Worcester College was established in 1714 on the site of a Benedictine college, monks' cottages surviving with a lake and a library containing Inigo Jones' design drawings. Green College was a newcomer in 1981 while Somerville College was established in 1894 for women.

The Bate Collection of historical musical instruments includes Handel's harpsichord.

The ghost of Archbishop Laud rolls his decapitated head around the floor of St John's College, founded in 1437, in 2ha of gardens by Capability Brown. Trinity College, founded in 1555, includes part of the 14th century Durham College, a quad by Wren and 1713 Lime Walks. Balliol College, founded in 1263 by John Balliol as a penance after insulting the Bishop of Durham, has 700 year old oak gates, some of the oldest in England, still showing scorch marks from the burning of Latimer and Ridley in the road outside, where there is the Martyrs' Memorial to the pair and Cranmer. The 14th century Master John Wycliffe translated the *New Testament* into English.

Blackwell's, opened in 1879, is one of the world's largest bookshops. Its children's bookshop was a British first and still has the largest stock.

Brasenose College of 1509 is named after the brass knocker on the door although some of it dates back to the 15th century. One of the fellows was Walter Pater, at the centre of the Aesthetic Movement. The Sheldonian Theatre was built for Oxford University chancellor Archbishop Gilbert Sheldon in 1669. It was the first full sized building by Wren, who was a professor of astronomy at the time. It was based on Rome's Theatre of Marcellus, semicircular with columns at the front. The Ashmolean Museum, built in the 1840s, contains Britain's oldest collection, started in 1683 with art and archaeology and including the 9th century Alfred Jewel and Guy Fawkes' lantern. Other attractions include the Oxford Playhouse and the New Theatre. The Bodleian Library, started for Sir Thomas Bodley in 1602, is Europe's oldest with over 7,000,000 books, receiving a copy of every new British book. With it is the Perpendicular Divinity School with Oxford University's oldest building, an unchanged lecture room of 1490. It has a fine vaulted ceiling and a copy of Caxton's first English book.

A college founded in 1386 just has to be called New College. With much Gothic material, its chapel has a jewelled crosier from the Bishop of Winchester and it is the only college restricted to fellows. Outside, New College Lane has modern gargoyles. The domed Classical Radcliffe Camera of 1749 with tall Corinthian columns was built for Sir John Radcliffe, the first circular library in England. From 1238, St Edmund Hall is the last medieval hall, with the original well in the quad. Hertford College's Bridge of Sighs is a copy of the one in Venice. The Clarendon Building, built in 1715 by Hawkesmoor, was occupied by the Oxford University Press but is now the headquarters of Oxford University. All Souls, with a medieval hall, was built in 1438 as a memorial to Henry V and Agincourt. John Wesley taught in Lincoln College of 1427. Exeter was founded in 1314 and Jesus in 1571.

Oxford's oldest building, from 1040, is St Michael at the North Gate, with a Saxon tower and Cranmer's cell doors. It is a church where Shakespeare was a godparent in 1606 and Wesley preached. The University Church of St Mary the Virgin has a 13th century north tower, a 14th century spire and a Baroque south porch of about 1637 with twisted columns. In 1555 it was where Cranmer, Ridley and Latimer were condemned to burn, these days being used for the more peaceful activity of brass rubbing.

William Morris opened a cycle shop in 1902, making his first car in 1913, the Morris Oxford, founding Nuffield College on the profits. The 13th century Carfax Tower has outlived the 14th century St Martin's church, 99 steps leading to the top and a pair of quarter boys to strike the quarter hours. Other attractions include the Covered Market and Modern Art Oxford.

Magdalen College was built in 1458 for William of Waynflete, Bishop of Winchester. The Perpendicular Great Tower of 1492 has ten bells and fine gargoyles, was the first English building to have a clock fixed to the outside and was used by Charles I to view the Siege of Oxford. James II removed the college president in 1687 and imposed his own Roman Catholic candidate. Most of the fellows were expelled for resisting and it was made a Roman Catholic college. The youngest don was 17 year old Henry Phillpotts in 1795.

Celebrations on May Day morning may have begun as pagan fertility rights or as a Requiem Mass for Henry VI. The ritual includes jumping into the Cherwell from the bridge, often with serious injuries as the country's future intellectuals fail to check the depth first. Past students have included Oscar Wilde, Dudley Moore, Compton Mackenzie and John Betjeman with his teddy bear, a concept used in *Brideshead Revisited*.

Merton College, in Decorated and Perpendicular styles, was funded in 1264 by Walter de Merton, Lord High Chancellor of England. Moved from Surrey, it has the world's oldest continuous university library, in use since 1373, with the first quad, 14 original 13th century stained glass windows in the chapel and what is probably Geoffrey Chaucer's astrolabe. Merton Street, cobbled and with 17th and 18th century townhouses, is often used for period films.

Oriel College was founded in 1324, Oxford's first royal foundation, by Edward II, although the building is all more recent. Corpus Christi, founded in 1517, has a complex sundial containing 27 other sundials and had the distinction of being the only college not to give its plate to fund Charles I. Queen's College was founded in 1341 for Philippa, wife of Edward III, although the buildings are now unrivalled Palladian from the 18th century. On Christmas Day a boar's head is served on a silver tray, a throwback to Norse custom.

Shelley was expelled from University College in 1811 for writing a subversive atheist pamphlet but they relented and put up a statue of him after he drowned. The oldest of the 38 colleges, it was founded in 1249, by which time students had already been present for a quarter of a century.

Alice's shop is one of the oldest Oxford buildings, a sweetshop used by Alice Liddell, who lived across the road at Christ Church College where her father was a don. This is the largest college, known as the House, used by Charles I as his Civil War base and from where he escaped the 1645 Roundhead siege of the city. It was started in 1525 by Wolsey on the site of St Frideswide's Priory and has a great hall 35m long with a hammerbeam roof. The dining hall has paintings by leading artists, especially early Italian. The chapel serves as Oxford Cathedral, England's smallest Anglican cathedral, with a noted vaulted choir, the world's only cathedral which is also a college. The 1682 octagonal top by Wren is Tom Tower with the first English spire. Great Tom is the cathedral's loudest bell, weighing 7t, named after St Thomas of Canterbury, the largest to come from Osney Abbey at the Dissolution. It sounds the hours during the day plus 101 at 9:05pm, 9pm local time, to call back 100 students as there were in 1621. Gladstone was one of the students.

The University of Oxford Botanic Garden is the UK's oldest, the world's oldest scientific garden, with 8,000 species including tropical plants and those in alpine rockeries and pools.

Marshall Jones Brooks was the first person to jump 6 feet here in 1876 and 25 year old Roger Bannister used the Iffley Road track in 1954 to be the first person to run a mile in 4 minutes.

Charles II held his last Parliament here. Oxford Literary Festival is held in March and Oxford Open Water Week is in the middle of the summer.

The city has been used for filming *Inspector Morse*, *Brideshead Revisited*, *Harry Potter*, *Iris*, *Shadowlands*, *Wilde*, *A Fish called Wanda*, *The Madness of King George* and *Waiting for God*. C S Lewis and J R R Tolkien were members of the Inklings literary group who met in the Eagle & Child. William Golding was an English literature student, Colin Dexter was given the freedom of the city and Philip Pullman is a local resident. Defoe's Moll Flanders and an extravagant husband blew £93 in a twelve day visit to the city. Evelyn Waugh's *Brideshead Revisited* saw much of its early action in the colleges, Scott's Guy Mannering was a student, as was Tom Brown, and Tibby Schlegel was a student in E M Forster's *Howards End*. It was visited by Frankenstein and was Sypolis in Richard Jefferies' *After London*, when the Thames had become the Lake. Edmond Halley was here.

In 1933 it had the first lollipop lady and, in the 1970s, the first humps to be placed on a public road, the ones in question now being on at least their third design.

Osney Lock was built in 1790 by prisoners from the jail. The Augustinian Osney Abbey was founded in 1129 by Robert d'Oyley and made a cathedral for four years at the Dissolution, eventually being dismantled and the stones used for Civil War defences. A 14th century stone barn remains with part of an arch in a boatyard. A mill was built about 1227 by the monks while more recent activity began in 1874 with the manufacture of Frank Cooper's Oxford marmalade.

Trill Mill Stream has an underground section which was explored by canoe by T E Lawrence. Bulstake Stream rejoins by a monument to a man drowned in 1889 after saving two children.

Osney Railway Bridge of 1850 was rebuilt in 1898 and carries the Oxford to Didcot Parkway line. Masts support the structure of the ice rink, large Virgin hot air balloons sometimes taking off from the adjacent recreation ground, beyond which Castle Mill Stream rejoins. A former railway bridge served a gasworks which closed in 1958 while a pipe bridge of 1886 was opened to pedestrians in 1972. The river is edged by sandbags as it sweeps round to Grandpont.

Navigation is possible either side of the island, on which there was a mill with a pound lock on the south side. A shop was a tollhouse of 1844 although tolls were stopped six years later. A castellated red brick house has balconies and statues of women who worked here when it was a brothel. From 1911 it was the home of historian Robert Gunther who founded the Oxford Museum of History & Science, the exhibits of which include a blackboard used by Einstein in a 1931 lecture, which someone was just prevented from being cleaned in the nick of time.

The Saxon oxen ford was probably near Grandpont and Christ Church Meadow was the site of the first settlement. From 1085 a bridge by Robert d'Oyley was attached to a 42 arch causeway, now buried. The bridge was replaced in 1827 by Ebenezer Perry's Folly Bridge which carries the A4144.

The bridge was named after the 13th century defensive tower at the northern end where the Franciscan friar Roger Bacon lived with his observatory and laboratory and wrote his *Opus Majus* which was used as a basis for science for centuries. He was the first European to give a formula for gunpowder and predicted the car, plane and submarine. The tower was demolished in 1799.

The eastern end of the island is occupied by Salters Steamers, founded in 1858 as college boatbuilders and now running passenger cruise vessels on the river, everything from quiet scenic tours to mobile discos. They built craft for the D-Day landings and made landing craft, minelayers and gunships for wartime. During the Blitz they had two passenger vessels in use as hospital ships between Staines and Oxford. They originally occupied a former grain warehouse on the north bank, now the Head of the River pub, the name relating to rowing boat races on the Thames in Oxford. This is where the Three Men in a Boat turned back downstream.

Grandpont House was built in 1785 over a braid for the town clerk, Sir William Elias Taunton. It was later used by the unpopular magistrate Thomas Randall, who tried to limit pub opening hours.

Unusually, the Cherwell confluence points upstream so that the two rivers are in opposition. A flood on the Cherwell in 1663 resulted in a bore travelling 2km up the Thames. On other occasions the Thames has flooded the Cherwell. A lower cut was made in 1884 to provide a better route for the Cherwell's water.

The Cherwell is the centre of the city's punting activity although this has declined since Edwardian times, when there were over a thousand punts on the river. Oxford punters use the low end, which gives more stability as the centre of gravity is lower but begs the question why there is a platform at the other end, if not to be stood on, as used by Cambridge punters.

University boathouses line the Gut and there were 27 college barges at one time. Frenetic rowing activity takes place, many trying to emulate Matthew Pinsent, who trained here. Torpids take place in February and Eights Week is in May, as described in *Zuleika Dobson*.

New Hinksey takes its name from Hengist's eyot, where the Weirs Mill Stream leaves. The Riverside Centre with its slip is at the centre of more boating activity with the Sea Scouts, Falcon Rowing & Canoeing Club, the Sea Cadets and the Army Cadet Force in an assortment of craft.

Donnington Bridge of 1926 takes the B4495 past the site of what was Salters yard, early users of reinforced concrete with shuttering but burnt down by the Suffragettes. On a cooler note, a student drove an Austin 7 across the river on the ice in the freeze of 1963.

By now the city has been left behind. Iffley, with its thatched limestone cottages, was established in 941 as Gifteleia. The Isis Farmhouse pub came into being in 1842, converted from a farmhouse built at the turn of the century with a scull suspended from the ceiling and a skittle ally in the former morgue. It can only be reached from the towpath or the water, beer being delivered by punt until 1979. Merton College had a toll until the 1950s but coffins were not allowed to pass and had to be rowed across the river. Surrounding wet meadowland has adder's tongue fern, common meadow rue and marsh marigolds with roe and muntjac deer.

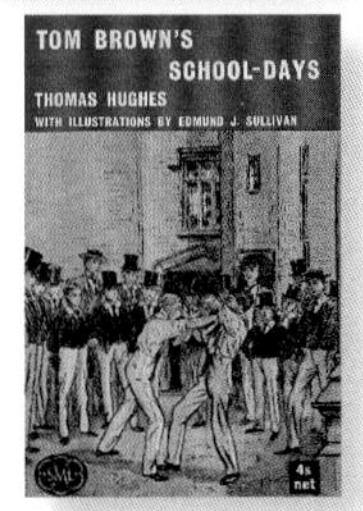

The rowing race course begins at a bronze bull's head with the start signal being given by cannon outside the Isis.

Iffley Lock became the first pound lock on the Thames in 1631 and has been painted by Peter de Wint. The mill here was lost in 1908 to a fire. An ornate stone bridge crosses the channel to the boat rollers, a channel also crossed by a small copy of Cambridge's Mathematical Bridge.

St Mary's is one of the finest Norman churches in the country, built in 1170 with a great west front, 15th century stained glass, a 1995 John Piper window, tower arches, a Norman font and carved stonework suggesting links with Reading Abbey and Santiago de Compostela.

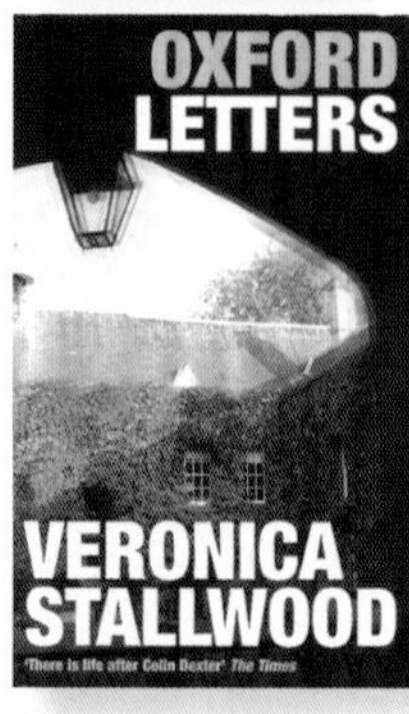

Coffins had to be brought by river rather than carried over the lock in case they created a right of way. The rectory is contemporary with a 1500 wing added.

Isis Bridge takes the A423 over. The Hinksey Stream joins before Kennington Railway Bridge, which used to take a line from Oxford to High Wycombe but now runs only to the BMW works at **Cowley**. A daily train of 50 blue wagons carries 330 lefthand drive Minis on two decks to Sheerness for export. Between Kennington and Littlemoor the Fiddler's Elbow takes the river past Rose Isle.

Sandford-on-Thames was given to the Knights Templars by Thomas de Saunford in 1240. The Norman church, rebuilt in the 19th century, has an annual Alice sermon on a theme from *Alice's Adventures in Wonderland* to recall Charles Dodgson's first sermon, delivered here in 1862. Temple Farmhouse includes parts of the Knights Templars' grainmill of 1294, which produced paper until 1982. Some of the mill is also included in the King's Arms, which occupies an inn site used since the 15th century, incorporating oak ceiling beams made from barge timbers. The 17th century Sandford Lock is 2.68m deep, in 1973 becoming the first with underfloor filling. A weir feeding Sandford Pool is Sandford Lasher. Drownings have included Michael Llewelyn-Davies, the adopted son of J M Barrie, the inspiration for Peter Pan, the boy who never grew up. The monument in the middle of the weir lists five drowning victims.

Six sets of powerlines cross between here and Appleford.

Radley College boathouse has a conspicuous presence at Lower Radley. In *Down River* Geoffrey Boumphrey recalls sculling back here from Nuneham Island after eating 11 boiled eggs. Alice was also rowed down to Nuneham on occasions.

A tumulus is tucked away behind but Nuneham Park rises on the east bank with the Palladian Nuneham House, built in 1756 for the 1st Earl of Harcourt on the site of an earlier house. He used stone from his house at Stanton Harcourt, brought by barge, because the quarry could not produce the stone fast enough, having a large order to fulfill for Blenheim Palace. With twin carriage drives, it was designed by Stiff Leadbetter with landscaping by Capability Brown in the 1770s. Despite the poor Lower Greensand it was described as the best in the world, now with a miniature golf course. Victoria and Albert spent part of their honeymoon here and the house is now leased by Oxford University to the Brahma Kumaris World Spiritual University as a religious retreat centre. The chapel, now closed, was built on the domed All Saints' temple by Athenian Stuart. There is the 1616 Jacobean Carfax Conduit stone fountain, moved from Carfax in 1786, but the 17th century Old Barn Farmhouse was destroyed by troops camping here before D-Day. The medieval village spoiled the view so it was moved to the A4074 in the 1760s. One of the most important planned villages in the country, Nuneham Courtenay was advanced for its time, described as Auburn in Oliver Goldsmith's *The Deserted Village*. The most conspicuous building from the river is the boathouse of 1756. This is an area for the Loddon lily or summer snowflake, like a large snowdrop. Oxford University's Harcourt Arboretum is on the A4074 but Lock Wood is by the river with bats, owls and kestrels.

The Culham Laboratory was built on a former Fleet Air Arm airfield in a loop of the river, the most important piece of equipment being the Joint European Torus, the world's biggest machine for studying hot plasma nuclear fusion as a power source, a project drawing scientists from a range of European countries.

Nuneham Railway Bridge carries the railway back across in an area where gravel pits have been filled with waste ash from Didcot power station, the howls of protest tempered by the fact that they are an excellent environment for orchids. Beyond the bridge, trials bike tracks loop up and down the hillside at Warren Farm. This reach of the river was the site of the **Abingdon** Waterturnpike murder of 1787.

The Back Water or Swift Ditch used to be the main channel of the Thames and contains the remains of a stone lock of 1624, the oldest surviving pound lock in Europe. Kingfisher Canoe Club attempt to clear the fallen trees which block the navigation. On the other side of Andersey Island, which had a church of St Andrew, Abingdon Lock is on the 1052 channel. The Abbey millstream was cut in about 960 although different streams have been used for navigation over different periods.

Abingdon-on-Thames, named after Aebba, is one of the oldest continuously occupied locations in Britain, since the Iron Age around 500 BC. Over the years there have been a number of missed opportunities for the town. The Benedictine St Mary's Abbey of 675 was sacked by the Danes, rebuilt in 955 by St Æthelwold and rebuilt in the 12th century by the Normans to be larger than the current Westminster Abbey. It was the sixth richest in England and occupied 1.2km^2 of land but was destroyed at the Dissolution, leaving only some of the smaller buildings, the 15th century gatehouse, the timbered long gallery with its unusual chimneys, the bakehouse, the granary and the 13th century Checker Hall which was the exchequer or the abbot's wine cellar but is now the Unicorn Theatre. St Edmund of Abingdon became Archbishop of Canterbury in 1233. The 14th century water mill became the Upper Reaches with the millwheel still a feature in the Mill Wheel Restaurant.

In the canal era a link from the Grand Union Canal to the Wilts & Berks Canal would have made Abingdon a more important transport node but the section from Aylesbury to Abingdon was never built.

It is uncertain whether Brunel intended to take the Great Western Railway to Abingdon but is was certain that it would have been rejected by the town in 1837. Instead, Brunel used the village of **Didcot** for his junction. Realizing their mistake, Abingdon had a spur from Radley in 1856 but its lifetime was limited, They also bid for the railway workshops but these were sited in Swindon.

Horse race meetings on Culham Heath were also lost.

Morris Garages, MG, moved their factory to the town in 1929 to produce more sporty models than were coming out of Oxford. Models included the one-off Old Speckled 'Un runabout. The factory closed in 1980 and production moved to China although enthusiasts still make pilgrimages to Abingdon.

Morlands developed in 1711 from abbey brewing, in 1979 producing Old Speckled Hen for MG's jubilee. The brewery was later bought by Greene King, demolished for housing and the production moved to Bury St Edmunds.

Until 1867, when it lost out to Reading, Abingdon was the county town of Berkshire but in 1974 the town and the whole of north Berkshire was designated as part of Oxfordshire. With its Georgian houses and a Monday market since 1086, it received its charter from Philip and Mary in 1556. It has over 300 listed buildings although the post war town centre rebuild is not of the best and is overdue for replacement.

Abingdon Bridge of 1417, also known as the Burford or White Hart Bridge, was built by the Guild of the Holy Cross and rebuilt in 1927 as an eight arch structure with a causeway in an attempt to win back trade from

The Head of the River at Folly Bridge.

Wallingford. It carries the A415 back over past the Nag's Head.

The 12th century church of St Nicholas has the graves of John and Jane Blackwell, who died on the same day in 1625 after a life together. The 13th century St Helen's church is the second widest in England at 33m. With five aisles, it is wider than it is long. Its Lady Chapel of 1391 has the best painted ceiling in England, surviving the Reformation and Cromwell as it was too high to reach. The 46m high spire is prominent from the river, a narrow slipway leading up towards the church. The Long Alley Almshouses of 1446 are also noteworthy.

W Lee, five times the town mayor, died in 1637, leaving 197 offspring. Since a 1700 dispute over the horns from an ox roast there has been a June Morris dancing battle between the Vineyard and Ock Street men for black ox's horns, the winning dancers electing the Mayor of Ock Street.

Abingdon County Hall of 1682 on arches, by Christopher Kempster, is the grandest of its type in England, now demoted to a museum. Since 1760 it has been used at important occasions such as coronations to throw buns from the roof to the crowds. The Michaelmas Fair is the longest street fair in Europe, followed a week after by the Runaway Fair, a second chance for labourers and domestic servants to find better or any employers. The disruption of the build up and breakdown of the modern fairs on two successive weeks suggests that their original concept may have outlived its usefulness.

The Napoleonic Old Gaol of 1811 has been a swimming pool but has now been converted to housing. Unchanged is the Broad Face, its inn courtyard covered in wistaria. This is the upper limit of Swan Upping.

The town saw 690mm of snow in April 1908, 45mm of rain in just over an hour in 1913, a temperature of -19°C in February 1947 and marble-sized hailstones in May 1992. A lecture in December 1981 by the director general of the Met Office, on attempting to modify the weather, had to be postponed twice because of snow and ice.

One of the first recorded strikes was by local apprentices objecting to being served meals of salmon from the Thames every day. Beyond Kingcraft and the Old Anchor Inn, the River Ock joins. Across its mouth is a low cast-iron bridge of 1824, replacing a multi-pointed arched stone bridge. Confusingly, it was built by the Wilts & Berks Canal company although the former canal end, just along the bank, is blocked off by sheet piling, as indicated by an Environment Agency notice. In the winter of 1895 it was possible to skate from here to Swindon along the canal. The junction was painted in about 1860 by George Vicat Cole while Henry Petter's *Abingdon by Moonlight* used a similar location at a similar date.

College boathouses without rowers present.

Approach to the rollers at Iffley Lock.

There was a Second World War gun emplacement near the end of Saxton Road with an anti-tank ditch to Marcham. These days the river's users include great crested grebes, Barnacle geese, racing dinghies, Kingfisher Canoe Club and the boats of Abingdon Rowing Club and Abingdon School, whose boathouse is the largest timber-framed building in the UK. Craft also emerge from Abingdon Marina. The Swift Ditch appears under the stone Culham pack bridge of 1416, now superseded.

Beyond the sewage works is Jubilee Junction of 2006, a token 150m start of a new line for the Wilts & Berks Canal. As piecemeal restoration of the canal goes ahead it is important to get powered craft using it but Thames Water's repeated proposals for a large reservoir to the west

College barge style at Iffley.

of the A34 have placed planning blight on the restoration. The reservoir would straddle the line of the canal but Thames Water would build the emergency drawdown channel to canal dimensions and allow craft to use it. This would include the expensive route crossing the A34. Without this, a more economical route could be found, even with Caldecott housing built over the original line of the canal.

Opposite the junction is the Culham Cut of 1809. Until the start of the 15th century Culham reached west to the river but now stops short. The Victorian church with its 1710 tower replaced a 9th century Saxon chapel. The grey stone manor house from the 15th and 17th centuries was an Abingdon Abbey grange with massive topiary and a 1685 dovecote for 4,000 birds.

Culham Lock was rebuilt early in the 21st century but with a high side below for those portaging small craft. The Environment Agency promised to come back the following winter and make it safe for users but, several years later, this has still not been done. Beyond the Waggon & Horses was Culham College, an 1823 Church of England teacher training college set up by Samuel Wilberforce, the Bishop of Oxford. From 1978 it became the European School, a multilingual school based around a core of pupils who were children of Culham Laboratory scientists, attracting other European families to the area to benefit.

The natural course of the river flows round to Sutton Pools, a particularly attractive reach of the Thames at Sutton Courtenay, overlooked by the house of Asquith, where he signed the document to declare the First World War. The channel leads towards the site of a former mill which made high quality paper for banknotes, recovered from an explosion in 1869 but closed in 1897. A footbridge and fence close off the route to a former lock.

Sutton Courtenay had a Roman villa and a Saxon farm. A 5th century Germanic brooch was found here. The manor was given to Abingdon Abbey in 688 by Ine, King of Wessex. Henry I's daughter, Matilda, the Empress Maud, was born here in 1101 and Henry II gave it to Reginald Courtenay in 1177. The east wing survives with a Norman hall added in 1192 by Robert de Courtenay, including a finely carved Norman doorway. The 13th century abbey was a grange of Abingdon Abbey, extended in 1285. Both the abbey and the manor were owned by *Observer* editor David Astor. The Dalai Lama visited the abbey, which was used by Tibetan refugees, becoming a Christian conference centre in 1980. The 14th century All Saints' church has a two storey 16th century Tudor porch and the conspicuous tomb of Asquith but also the less obvious grave of Eric Blair, George Orwell, who was accepted at Astor's suggestion after other churches had declined this atheist.

Asquith's great-granddaughter Helena Bonham-Carter moved with Tim Burton to a house previously occupied by Princess Margaret's secretary. When asked to review two British restaurants for a magazine, the Fish was one selected by Raymond Blanc. Ferry company LD Lines is operated from here on a site recently vacated by construction company Amey.

A 199m high chimney on the former MoD Central Ordnance Depot is the most conspicuous feature of Didcot A power station, which drew water for its six cooling towers from beside a slipway to the Thames and returned it just downstream, slightly warmer. It was started in 1965 and closed in 2013. Didcot B is much less conspicuous. Some smoke might be seen from steam engines in the Didcot Railway Centre. The area has seen much gravel extraction, the pits then being filled with London refuse and hills rising from the floodplain.

The arched lattice Appleford Railway Bridge of about 1880 takes the Oxford–Didcot Parkway railway across for the last time, replacing a low wooden bridge of 1843. Appleford-on-Thames has been the scene of two railway crashes, the second of which destroyed the signal box, and was one of the last two GWR stations to have pagoda-style shelters for passengers. The bridge inspired the use of the village for the rehearsal for the Arnhem Landings, four participants dying but many lives probably being saved during the real thing and much parachute silk being made available on the black market.

John Faulkner was a winning jockey from 8 to 74 years old and died in 1933 at 104 with 32 children. Arthur Napper won a traction engine race in *Old Timer* in 1952 for a firkin of ale, leading to the traction engine revival. Thousands of Romano-British coins were found on his land. The village also produced the 4th century Appleford Hoard of pewter plate, now in the Ashmolean Museum.

The Appleford Brewery Company is run by Morlands' former treasurer from Brightwell-cum-Sotwell, the village's former pub was used in the filming of *Any Human Heart* and Hawkwind used to rehearse in the village. The church of Sts Peter & Paul is partly 7th century

The boathouse at Nuneham Park.

Saxon and includes a Roman piscina and a Samuel Green organ.

The Clifton Cut of 1822 leads to Clifton Lock, which was not built for another 13 years. The natural course of the river loops past Long Wittenham, leaving past Clifton Weir where dangerous extensive anti-intruder screens have been erected which remove any chance of throwing a rescue line to anyone in the weirpool.

The originally Iron Age village was named after the 5th century Saxon King Witta. One of the first buildings is the Pendon Museum, founded in 1954 with OO gauge railway layouts, perhaps the best in the world. As well as the Madder Valley model there are vast 1930s Dartmoor and Downland models. Supporters model individual buildings for inclusion. Such is the detail that a magnifying glass is mounted at one point in order to see a robin perched on a fork in a garden, miniscule at this scale.

St Birinus preached from the village cross in 634 and rather more noise has been made at the Plough with its moorings, especially during the Wittfest music festival. Thatched cottages and the Vine & Spice stand on the main street. The first landlord of the former Machine Man pub of 1864 had the first steam thresher in the area and also made the bricks used for the bridge.

St Mary's church, built in 1120 by lord of the manor Walter Gifford, the 3rd Earl of Buckingham, is on a 6th century barrow used for pagan burials and Saxon weapons have been found. The church has a 12th century Norman lead font, perhaps the only one of its kind in England with its original base after the villagers encased it in wood to prevent it from being melted down for Civil War bullets. The smallest effigy in England may be that of Gilbert de Clare, the Earl of Gloucester, who died on crusade in 1295 and whose heart may be buried here although his body is in Tewkesbury Abbey. The vicar was a meteorological enthusiast, recording 898mm of rainfall in 1880.

The thatched cruck Barley Mow of 1350 is where some of *Three Men in a Boat* was written. It was burnt down in 1975 but has been restored.

The riverbed here is sandstone and is where the Lord Mayor's barge grounded in 1826, returning from Oxford. This gives good foundations for the red brick Clifton Hampden Bridge of 1867 with its six Tudor arches. Sir Gilbert Scott used the local bricks for the design he had sketched on his shirt cuff. It has pedestrian recesses over the cutwaters and a tollhouse at the east end although the toll was removed in 1946.

Clifton Hampden was named after John Hampden and has 17th century thatched cottages. St Michael & All Angels' church of 1180 on its cliff has Norman origins but was renovated in Victorian times by Sir Gilbert Scott for Henry Hucks Gibbs after he inherited most of the village in 1842. It has a small spire and a Norman stone carving of a boarhunt. It also has the grave of Sergeant William Dykes, who began the Battle of Waterloo when he fired a shot accidentally, later being court marshalled by Wellington. Gibbs, the 1st Lord Aldenham and governor of the Bank of England, had his own gun problems when he accidentally shot off his right hand. He had the parsonage built for an uncle and a son converted it to a manor house. Clifton Manor has the heads of Marlborough and Prince Eugene on columns in the garden. Courtiers House has the ghost of the beautiful Sarah Fletcher who hung herself in the face of neglect by her husband. The Plough Inn is noted for its curries and the village was used by former Abingdon School pupils Radiohead to make recordings.

St Helen's church in Abingdon.

The mouth of the River Ock, despite what it says.

Abingdon School boathouse with its massive timber roof.

Because of the sandstone bed, Burcot, Brydingscot or Bryda's cottage, was the head of navigation until 1636. A Bronze and Iron Age settlement on a loop of the river, it also had Roman occupation. The Cheshire Home is on the site of John Masefield's house, destroyed in a fire.

Berinsfield, begun in 1956 on a former airfield, has a church built with volunteer labour. It adjoins gravel pits which are used for sailing and attract winter birds but destroyed the Dorchester cursus in their excavation. Speed measuring posts are installed here.

With the Thames and the Thame, the Dyke Hills form an Iron Age double defensive earthworks. Day's Lock, named after 17th century residents, is the main gauging point for the Thames. A former lock keeper became so irritated with people breaking bits off his hedge to drop in the river that he cut a box of them and offered them for use at 5p each for the RNLI. This developed into the annual World Poohsticks Championships, run from the footbridge, with the Poohlympics every four years, children having as much chance as adults of winning.

Little Wittenham has the 14th century St Peter's church with a 15th century tower, 17th century memorial to MP Sir William Dunch and a figure of his wife, Mary, Cromwell's aunt, who lived in the manor next to the church. The manor has been developed with building styles from many periods, including a ballroom floor which retracts to reveal a swimming pool.

The 90m high Sinodun Hills, from the Celtic seno dunum or old fort, have also been referred to as Mother Dunch's Buttocks or the Berkshire Bubs. They are topped by the Wittenham Clumps, beeches which are the oldest recorded woodland in Britain. They form the Cuckoo Pen. If the cuckoo can be trapped within them then summer will last for ever, presumably not good news for the springtime bluebells. The Poetry Tree is a beech carved in 1845 by Joseph Tubb. Behind Round Hill is Castle Hill, site of an Iron Age hill fort used by the Ancient Britons, Romans and Danes. The Money Pit is said to contain an iron treasure chest which was found by a villager but a raven said it was not for him so he buried it again. It was not among the items uncovered in a *Time Team* dig.

The 1km^2 Little Wittenham nature reserve of 1982 contains grassland, the Earth Trust Centre, the Timescape Exhibition and Little Wittenham Wood, one of Europe's most important wildlife sites, including oxeye daisies, bats, kingfishers and kites. Oxfordshire County Council pay for public access with an annual red rose. Artist Paul Nash has used it on occasions, including for his *Landscape of the Vernal Equinox*.

Some say that the Thame and Isis join here to form what the Romans called the Tamesis, the Thames. Near the mouth of the Thame, on the Roman road from Towcester to Silchester, which crossed each of these rivers near here, was Dorchester, the British Dorcicon, the Roman Dorcina Castra, then Romano-British, then Anglo-Saxon settlement. It had a fort and pottery kiln.

Old Timer *in action in Appleford.*

Part of the Appleford Hoard in the Ashmolean Museum.

It also had the court of King Cynegils of Wessex, who was baptised in the Thame in 635 by St Birinus in the presence of King Oswald of Northumbria, marrying Oswald's daughter, uniting them against the pagan King Penda of Mercia and making England Christian. Birinus built a Saxon church that year, serving as a cathedral until 1092, the site now being used for the 61m Dorchester Abbey of Sts Peter & Paul, mostly from 1140 to the 14th century, predominantly Decorated. The west tower is from 1602. The abbey is noted for its 14th century Tree of Jesse window, statues merging into the stone tracery, Norman lead font of about 1170 and 13th century alabaster crusader drawing his sword, an effigy of Sir John Holcombe which is one of the best funery sculptures in England, believed to have influenced Henry Moore. The Lady Chapel has a 1354 effigy of John de Stonor, Edward III's Lord Chief Justice of England, and 14th century medieval wall paintings. St Birinus' chapel has glass from about 1225. From about 680 the Mercian bishopric of the diocese of Lincoln reached the Thames and was administered from its southern extremity. Wessex control was moved eventually to Winchester by Alfred and Mercia to Lincoln by William the Conqueror. The Cloister Gardens are on the original monastery site while the Abbey tea room is in the abbey guest house and the Dorcester Abbey Museum is in the only 14th century part of the Augustinian monastery to survive the 16th century destruction.

It was a coaching town with ten inns, the octagonal toll house by the Thame bridge being used until 1873. The 15th century George with its galleried courtyard was the abbey brewhouse while the 16th century Fleur de Lys Inn was a smithy and bakery with a capped wall alongside. The White Hart Hotel is also 16th century. Halliday's is one of the largest antique showrooms in England. The Roman Catholic church of St Birinus was by William Wilkinson Wardell in 1849. The town was used for filming *Howards End*.

Warborough has a church with a good Early English chancel, a Georgian vicarage and a manor house of 1696.

Shillingford has 18th century houses and a particularly well placed house at the start of the village. W B Yeats started *Meditations in Time of Civil War* while living at a Wheeler's End house. The village was the birthplace of Vivian Stanshall of the Bonzo Dog Doo-Dah Band, the plummy inebriated narrator on Mike Oldfield's *Tubular Bells* remix. The village name is from Sciella's ford. The 1827 Shillingford Bridge, founded in the 14th century and overlooked by the 18th century Shillingford Bridge Hotel, has three stone arches but has not always proved popular. One night the tollkeeper's wrist was caught in a knot and tied to a lamp post. Recently, half of the bridge has been converted to a footway with traffic lights installed to control single line traffic, resulting in lines of waiting traffic but pedestrians rarely seen. A push button light, to be used to stop one line of traffic when a pedestrian wished to cross, would have been a much cheaper option with less delay and less exhaust fumes. Beyond the bridge is Rush Court with its moat.

Benson, from Bensington or Baenesa's farm, is where the Romans crossed the ford near what is now the lock. Offa had a palace and won the 777 battle between Mercia and Wessex but his losses began Mercia's decline. Benson Airfield hosted the Queen's Flight until 1995 and has an interesting variety of aircraft using it, mostly helicopters. It was the photo reconnaissance headquarters during the Second World War and has a weather station which often records the lowest temperature in England. In 1935 rain was recorded for about 10 minutes falling from a clear sunny sky. Pioneering meteorologist William Henry Dines is buried at the 13th and 14th century Norman church of St Helen's, which has a Georgian tower with a 1794 clock from Whitehall's Horse Guards, the '9' wrongly transcribed as 'XI'.

Charles I sold the Saxon manor in 1628 and Monarch Court House was the Red Lion where he held a Civil War Privy Council meeting. Benson was a 19th century coaching village with the Georgian former Castle Inn, the Regency former White Hart and the Crown.

Those arriving by water find an estate of static caravans and alder trees around the Waterfront Café. Benson is at the start of the river's longest reach between locks. Benson Lock is unusual in having a cast iron base and walls at the bottom with steel gates.

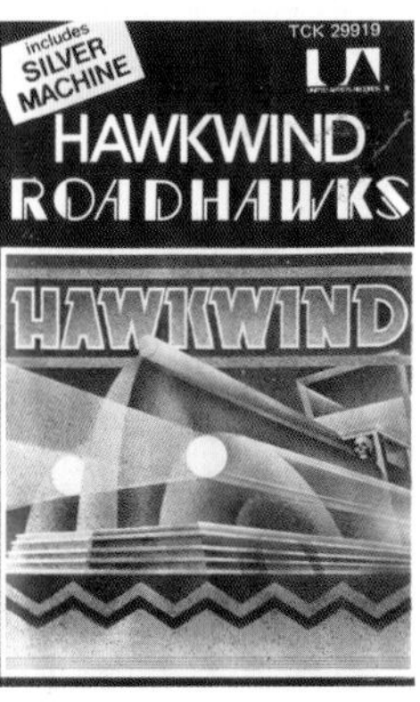

Crowmarsh Battle Farm at Preston Crowmarsh adjoins Howbery Park, where Jethro Tull invented the seed drill in 1701. The red brick Victorian house was built for MP William Blackstone but it bankrupted him and was to be damaged badly by a falling chestnut tree in a January 1934 gale. The park had North American servicemen and then central European refugees during the Second World War. It was developed by the hydraulics research station, HR Wallingford, the 1970s Maplin Building holding a large model of the Thames estuary, used for numerous planning experiments. There are a number of scientific small business offices and the Environment Agency have Red Kite House, offices with lots of environmentally friendly features but a price tag which has been a closely guarded secret, alleged to have been about twice what a normal office would have cost. The Centre for Ecology & Hydrology is here and the former north of Berkshire is administered from the Oxfordshire side of the river.

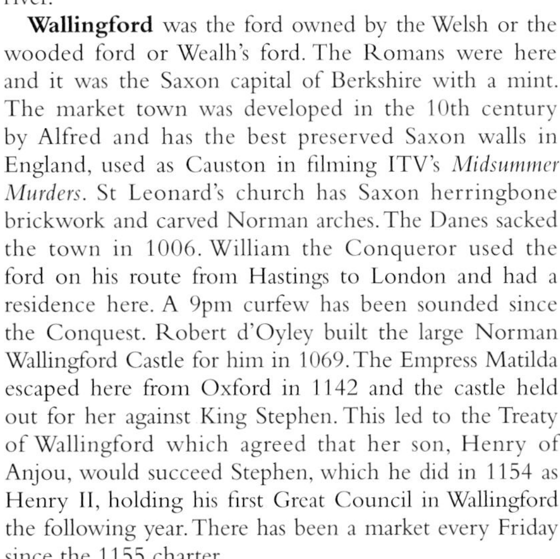

Wallingford was the ford owned by the Welsh or the wooded ford or Wealh's ford. The Romans were here and it was the Saxon capital of Berkshire with a mint. The market town was developed in the 10th century by Alfred and has the best preserved Saxon walls in England, used as Causton in filming ITV's *Midsummer Murders*. St Leonard's church has Saxon herringbone brickwork and carved Norman arches. The Danes sacked the town in 1006. William the Conqueror used the ford on his route from Hastings to London and had a residence here. A 9pm curfew has been sounded since the Conquest. Robert d'Oyley built the large Norman Wallingford Castle for him in 1069. The Empress Matilda escaped here from Oxford in 1142 and the castle held out for her against King Stephen. This led to the Treaty of Wallingford which agreed that her son, Henry of Anjou, would succeed Stephen, which he did in 1154 as Henry II, holding his first Great Council in Wallingford the following year. There has been a market every Friday since the 1155 charter.

The town suffered from the Black Death. Princess Joan, the wife of the Black Prince, died here in 1385 but it was where Catherine de Valois met Owain Tudor, leading to the Tudor dynasty. St Mary le More's church has a 15th century tower and Dick Turpin stayed in the 15th century Tudor George Hotel where the Tear Drop Room has a pattern of tears and soot made by the landlord's daughter after her Royalist sergeant fiancé was stabbed. The 500 year old Flint House contains Wallingford Museum, including coverage of the castle.

Clifton Hampden bridge and church on its ridge.

Day's Lock with Dorchester beyond.

Wittenham Clumps on the Sinodun Hills.

Attractive property at Shillingford.

The 14th century Grade II Queen's Head has an aisled hall and a ghost and was where Cromwell hid in the chimney recess before the battle for Wallingford Castle. This was England's last Royalist place to hold out against Cromwell, lasting 16 weeks until Charles I surrendered in 1646, but was destroyed, the stone being used for other buildings including the tower of St Mary le More's church. The castle is now a nature reserve.

The Lamb Arcade used to be a coaching inn, used by William of Orange on his way to the throne. The Jacobean town hall of 1670 is now an art gallery, containing the charter, Gainsborough portraits and a memorial to local MP Airey Neave, who had been tipped as a future prime minister but was assassinated at Westminster by an INLA car bomb.

Some of the 274m Wallingford Bridge remains from the 1250 structure by Richard, Duke of Cornwall, but most is from 1751. There are 17 arches and a causeway to the east, five of the arches over the river. Three of the arches suffered after Cromwell installed a drawbridge. The central arch was lost to a flood in 1809 and that year the bridge was widened so that arches are rounded upstream but pointed downstream. Next to it is the Boat House pub.

Many houses are Georgian 18th century buildings. The redundant 1777 church of St Peter, with its open stone tower, was restored by Sir Robert Taylor, the first Oxford University professor of English law, who compiled the first understandable study of English Common Law and is buried inside.

Like Abingdon, Wallingford rejected the railway and is now on a branch from Cholsey, run by enthusiasts. Artist George Dunlop Leslie lived in the town and Sheila Hancock learned to swim in the river as an evacuee although there is now an open air pool by the bridge.

In May 1950 a tornado formed, travelling away to the North Sea at Blakeney. The town was cut off in January 1994 by trees felled by a storm.

On the east side of the river, Crowmarsh Gifford is named after Walter Giffard, the standard bearer of William the Conqueror. It has a small Norman church, 17th and 18th century houses and, near the Grade II Bell Inn, a shop with a penny farthing mounted on the wall. There used to be an airstrip. Newnham Warren has the redundant St Mary's church.

Wallingford has the longest straight reach above Henley so there are Wallingford Rowing Club and Oxford University Boat Club boathouses here and the Oxford University boat race crew use it for training.

The Queen Anne Winterbrook House was owned by Agatha Christie and was the model for Miss Marple's Danemead. Wallingford became Market Basing. Some of the Miss Marple stories were written here, including *Three Blind Mice*, based around Mongewell Park, staged in London as *The Mousetrap* since 1952, the world's longest running play.

To the east of the 1993 Winterbrook Br, crossed by the A4130, is the Centre for Agricultural Bioscience International which issues farming advice to Third World countries. Grim's Ditch runs up from the river for nearly 6km to Nuffield.

The Georgian Mongewell Park was rebuilt in 1890 in William and Mary style, its icehouse stocked from the Thames. It acted as a First World War hospital. An American millionaire and atheist had the path sunk so that he did not have to see congregations attending the tiny redundant church of St John the Baptist, which has a Norman doorway and arches and the grave of Shute Barrington, the Bishop of Durham. Bomber Command used the park during the Second World War to study Dambusters raid pictures. From 1948 to 1997 it had Carmel College, Europe's only Jewish boarding school, producing such pupils as Roland Joffe and Arcadia Group owner Philip Green.

At North Stoke the 13th century Grade II St Mary the Virgin's church has medieval wall paintings from 1300, a Jacobean pulpit, brick pinnacles on a 1725 tower, a unique sundial and the grave of Dame Clara Butt. Michael Caine lived in the 17th century Rectory Farmhouse and the Springs Hotel had a guitar shaped pool installed by owner Ian Gillan of Deep Purple. A former mill was fed by local springs and features a window in the kitchen floor.

The Victorian Fair Mile mental hospital at Cholsey has been redeveloped for housing.

The listed Moulsford Railway Bridge has two pairs of elliptical brick spans at an acute skew, carrying the Great Western Region main line. The 27m spans rise 6.9m, this and the corresponding Gatehampton Bridge being the first of their kind.

Moulsford, from the Old English mul's ford, mule's ford, begins with Moulsford Prep School, established in 1961. Gilbert Scott's 1846 church is on a 13th century chapel site, tucked away by the river like Sheridan Marine. The 17th century manor house was owned by Kevin Maxwell and used for filming *Midsummer Murders*.

The Beetle & Wedge was the Potwell Inn in *The History of Mr Polly*, which H G Wells wrote while staying

Brunel's skewed Moulsford Bridge.

here. G B Shaw was also a regular visitor. The Egyptian House, by John Outram, was built in 2000.

The former ferry has been replaced by a footbridge to take the Ridgeway Path. South Stoke is a village of 16th and 18th century timbered and thatched houses with the 16th century Perch & Pike in brick and flint. Ridgeway Brewing is a modern venture. The 13th century Early English St Andrew's church was restored in the 1850s but retains an ancient 13th century lancet window, a 14th century font and a 1659 monument to Griffith Higgs, the chaplain to the Queen of Bohemia. There is a granary on staddle stones and a medieval dovecote for 2,000 birds.

The west bank now becomes West Berkshire.

The Olde Leatherne Bottel adjoins the Goring Thames Sailing Club at Cleeve Spring, which has been noted for its curative powers for eyes, ulcers and corns. After the longest reach, Cleeve Lock begins the shortest reach on the Thames. Cleeve Mill is 17th century. An island is owned by Pete Townshend of the Who. Cleeve has a cliff and the BBC recorded nightingales here in the 1930s.

Goring, named after Gora, had a ferry from Henry I's time, run by Goring Priory before the Dissolution. Sixty people were drowned in 1674 when the ferry overturned and there were more deaths in 1810. The last ferryman and innkeeper of the Swan at Streatley was Moses Saunders, who changed to boatbuilding, his company becoming part of Saunders-Roe Navigation, noted for its hovercraft. This is where the Ridgeway joined the Icknield Way but Goring Lock deepened the water across the ford, which was used until 1797. The 270m Streatley & Goring Bridge carries the B4009, built in 1837 and replaced in 1923 in reinforced concrete to look like timber. It is no surprise that the Oxfordshire end of the bridge has a lower speed limit than the Berkshire end, with the inevitable Oxfordshire speed humps beyond the railway.

Streatley was mentioned in the 637 Saxon charter. The Swan at Streatley was owned briefly by Danny La Rue while Geri Halliwell is a more recent village resident and George Michael is local, too. The village has Georgian houses along the street which was the Ridgeway, Europe's oldest road, and then the Roman Ickleton Street. King Ine granted land here for a monastery. The Morrell brewers owned much of Streatley until the Second World War, living in the 1765 Streatley House while their staff occupied other houses and there was a gabled 19th century malt house.

A monk and a nun were buried in unconsecrated ground in the garden of the Bull in 1440 after being killed for having a relationship. Unsurprisingly, the pub is haunted. St Mary's church had a tower added in the 15th century and was rebuilt in 1864.

The Goring Gap is probably Ice Age, cut where the pre chalk meets the chalk and the London Basin. The Chilterns, with their beeches, meet the Berkshire or North Wessex Downs, powerlines buried underground to keep the views pristine. The river has Edwardian boathouses. There was an Augustinian nunnery with the Norman St Thomas of Canterbury church, probably built in about 1100 by Robert d'Oyley. It has a Norman turret beside the tower, a 1290 bell still in use and a 1912 rood screen of oak from the Trafalgar ship HMS *Thunderer*. There are early brasses including those for the Whistler family and for Henry Aldington in 1374 in Norman French but in English for his wife 25 years later, suggesting a change of language in use.

A mill was present in 1086 but an 1805 painting here by Turner was left unfinished. Pete Townshend used his studio to record *Quadrophenia* and other albums. The John Barleycorn offers a husband sitting service.

Grim's Ditch now continues on the west bank. The Grotto is a house on the site of a shell chamber and rock pool of 1720 for Viscountess Fane of Basildon Park, who was drowned in the well and haunts it. Her summerhouse was extended in the 19th century by MP Arthur Smith and became the headquarters of the Institute of Leisure & Amenity Management. Groundbreaking narrowboater Chris Coburn lives locally.

Gatehampton Railway Bridge has two pairs of skewed brick arches with 20m spans and 5.8m rise with a 2.9m gap between them, the second of Brunel's sets of bridges of this kind. For water troughs, a supply of water is needed, tracks have to be level and they have to be an appropriate distance from other water supplies. They all came together here and this was the site of the first GWR water troughs.

There were a Roman villa and grain drier here and the earliest British relics of post-glacial man with Stone Age items. Lord Alfred Douglas and Oscar Wilde rented Ferry Cottage near the Whistler's Gatehampton Manor in 1893, Wilde beginning *An Ideal Husband* here with local place names for the characters. The house was later extended as the home of Bomber Harris.

Lower Basildon has a 13th century church with a 1734 tower and the 1740 grave of Jethro Tull, who was born here in 1674. There is a monument to Sir Francis Sykes and a sculpture of teenagers Harold and Ernest Deverell who drowned while swimming in the Thames.

The Georgian Palladian Basildon Park was built in 1783 in Bath stone by John Carr of York for Sir Francis Sykes of the East India Company. From 1838 it was owned by James Morrison, the world's largest draper, but it was derelict by the Second World War and it was used for wartime training of British and US soldiers. The publishing Iliffes restored it in the 1950s with a large octagon room, Anglo-Indian room, shell room and fine plasterwork, pictures and furniture, set in 1.6km^2 of park and woodland. It was used as Netherfield Park in the filming of *Pride & Prejudice* and for *Dorian Gray* and *The Duchess*. The name was used in 1911 for Basildon Bond writing paper.

Hartslock nature reserve with hanging woodlands and good yews rises up with monkey orchids and chalk plants and butterflies.

The Child Beale Wildlife Trust also has 1.6km^2, intended to prevent building on this reach. There are rare birds and animals, statues, fountains, a model boat display and a miniature railway. The tithe barn has been converted to Beale Park Maritime Centre with a rolling exhibition of craft from Eyemouth International Sailing Craft Association, the collection formerly held by Exeter Maritime Museum. The Beale Park Boat Show takes place in June around a former gravel pit. Coombe Park is on the east side of the river.

A row of Edwardian houses by the river at Pangbourne are known as the Seven Deadly Sins as they were claimed to have been for the mistresses of store owner D H Evans of Shooters Hill House. Beyond Pangbourne College boathouse is the Swan at one end of the weir, built for Civil War soldiers, where *Three Men in a Boat* finished. It was formerly on a county boundary so there were different closing times at opposite ends of the bar. The Boathouse is where Jimmy Page lived and Led Zepplin was formed.

Pangbourne was Paega's people's stream. Ceolred, Bishop of Leicester, gave the Pangbourne estate to King Beorhtwulf in 844 in return for the freedoms of Abingdon and other monasteries, the charter following in the 9th century. The village features in the Sherlock Holmes story *The Adventure of the Hanging Tyrant*. Kenneth Grahame, the secretary of the Bank of England, lived in Church Cottage, where the garden shed was the circular village lockup. E H Shepard came for ideas for illustrating *The Wind in the Willows*.

There are 16th and 17th century houses and the Cross Keys is 16th century. St James the Less' flint church has many hatchments, a 1718 tower and the rest rebuilt in 1858, its Gabriel window used on a Christmas postage stamp. The River Pang joins, as does a drainage pipe from the Atomic Weapons Establishment at Aldermaston.

Whitchurch Lock, tucked away on private land, was originally turf sided. Whitchurch-on-Thames comes from white church. The Norman mill had been built by 1086 and St Mary the Virgin's church was built in flint on a Saxon site but is now mostly Victorian although a Saxon head carving maybe a gargoyle. Whitchurch Bridge, built in 1792 with the present Victorian construction in 1902, carries the B471. The white iron structure is the second of the two on the river still charging tolls for vehicles although pedestrians have been free since decimalization.

The village was the birthplace of architect Sir John Soane. The 18th century lock keeper's house became the Greyhound pub in 1830, the adjacent building being the local lockup.

The south side of the river has the Adventure Dolphin centre with much youth water activity. It was more serious when troops trained for the D-Day landings by building Bailey and pontoon bridges across the Thames. Toilet blocks and a sewage works stand back across the recreation meadows.

Bozedown Alpacas is the leading stud farm in Europe with over 800 of these animals. Boze Down Vineyard faces Westbury Farm Vineyard which has produced wine from some 6.5ha around an Elizabethan farmhouse since 1970.

Hardwick House is on an estate given by William the Conqueror to Robert d'Oyley. In Restoration red brick, with some 14th century work, it has complex plaster ceilings. Richard Lybbe was visited by Elizabeth I and Charles I was allowed to come here to play bowls while a prisoner at Caversham Park. It was damaged and looted by the Roundheads in 1643, the hidden money never being found. Shephard used some of it when drawing Toad Hall and Toad had some of the aspects of owner Sir Charles Rose. Powerlines are taken under this reach.

Mapledurham Lock was the first on the Thames to be mechanized in 1956. Mapledurham was the village by the maple tree. The watermill, recorded in *Domesday*, is partly 15th century. With wooden machinery, 2.1m head and a 3.7m diameter undershot wheel, it is the only working mill on the Thames and grinds wholemeal flour. It featured on the cover of Black Sabbath's debut album. An incongruous large Archimedes screw has been built alongside with an illuminated panel to record the power being generated.

Mapledurham House was 15th century, rebuilt in 1588 Elizabethan brick with an E plan in honour of frequent visitor Elizabeth I. It was a Catholic stronghold for the Blount family, as shown by oyster shells round one window, priest holes and escape passages. There are fine 16th century ceilings and oak staircases with 16–18th century paintings. It was fortified for Charles I but damaged in the Civil War. It was a model for illustrations of Toad Hall, was Soames Forsyte's country house in *The Forsyte Saga*, was Studley Constable in *The Eagle has Landed* and has been used for filming *Vanity Fair*, *The Wind in the Willows*, *Class Act* and *Inspector Morse*. Alexander Pope undertook the landscaping, being visited by Martha and Teresa Blount, who inspired some of his poetry. Almshouses are Jacobean from 1613. St Margaret's church of about 1200 has Norman origins, restored in the 1860s with a tower cap and a screened off Catholic chapel from the 14th century with a rare oak-timbered arcaded ceiling. The unconsecrated family chapel of 1797 is in Strawberry Hill Gothic style. The 1830 vicarage was by the vicar, Lord Augustus Fitz-Clarence, the illegitimate son of William IV.

Major Storey opposed the use of the banks at Purley on Thames in the 19th century. He threw the meal and crockery of a group of women picnickers in the river, for which they thanked him, having been loaned by his wife. A cormorant was resident on the island for many years.

Hartslock Wood rises above the river.

Some of the activity on the water at the Beale Park Boat Show.

Some of the Seven Deadly Sins at Pangbourne.

Much of Purley Park, designed in 1800 by James Wyatt, is now a housing estate. St Mary the Virgin's church is on a Norman site and has a 17th century tower. Purley Marina is located between the church and the railway.

The south bank changes from West Berkshire to Reading at the Roebuck Ferry. The railway, above a blue brick retaining wall, holds **Tilehurst** at bay as the river divides round Poplar Island, Appletree Eyot and, beyond Reading Marine Services and the Fisheries, St Mary's Island. The north bank also becomes Reading, the Warren and Caversham Heights being the more expensive end of the town. Caversham was Caphere's village, now with Victorian villas and boathouses and residents who might not be the people best able to appreciate their prime view of all that remains of the 1971 Reading Festival, Reading Rock Festival, the UK's longest established, on the other side of the Thames Side Promenade. Located on the south bank around Coombe Bank, the festival uses 13km of fencing and consumes over 1,100m^3 of lager during the weekend. Beyond, a flyover is being built to ease Reading's rail bottleneck.

The river can be busy with kayaks and rowing boats here. Large numbers of swans and Canada geese hang about in front of Reading Rowing Club, where people feed them.

A small Norman font of Purbeck marble, found in

The brewer's father, Fred Maggs or Mr Chubb, was lock keeper at Whitchurch.

a garden, may have been from a shrine. It is now in St Peter's church with its Norman doorway. A 20th century rector swam in the Thames every summer day for 20 years. An interesting gazebo of 1663 stands in **Caversham** Court. The shrine of Our Lady of Caversham was a place of pilgrimage in the Middle Ages. St Anne's well cured eyes and an angel with one wing brought part of the rope Judas used to hang himself, the head of the spear which pierced Christ and the knives which killed King Edward the Martyr and Henry VI.

Caversham Bridge was first built in 1219 with a chapel to St Anne on the central island. There were Civil War skirmishes here in 1643 during the siege of Reading. The current bridge, built in 1926 in reinforced concrete, was the world's longest Mouchel-Hennebique system structure with 38 and 32m spans. The Holy Ghost chapel at the south end became the White Hart Inn, now the Crowne Plaza. Stone from the chapel was used in 1959 for Our Lady & St Anne's church. Piper's Island is followed by Fry's or De Montfort Island where a duel in 1163 between Robert de Montfort and Henry, Earl of Essex, was watched by a large crowd including Henry II. Essex was run through but recovered and stayed in the abbey. The entertainments today include the Island Bar & Restaurant, Thames Valley Cruising Club and Caversham Boat Services.

Reading Bridge of 1923, carrying the B3345, is also a Mouchel-Hennebique reinforced concrete structure. Its main span was the longest in the country at 55m. The road passes between major offices of Thames Water and the Environment Agency, whose craft licensing office will not sell a licence over the counter. Aaronovitch interrupted a boat break in here.

Reading was an Iron Age settlement named after Reada, becoming Roman then Saxon then a red brick Victorian town, Hardy's Aldbrickham, which developed on biscuits, beer and bulbs. Huntley & Palmers, a Quaker company started in 1822, was the world's biggest biscuit company, saving biscuit breakages by using water transport, the site used by them until 1970 and now used for the Prudential offices. Simonds were brewing from 1785 and Suttons ran the world's first mail order seed company from 1806. Austin Reed was formed here with the first shop in 1900 and Reading is now claimed to be one of the top ten retail destinations in the UK.

Henry I had to stand aside for the wagons of Thomas of Reading and other cloth merchants but decided they would be useful allies and established the yard for them, the length of his arm, presumably half his span. Someone who did not move aside was Sir Francis Knollys who was still representing the town in Parliament in 1648 when he was 98. Henry founded the abbey in 1121, using stone from Caen and from the Roman site at Silchester, and was buried here in 1136 in a silver coffin which is now said to be under the playground of St James' school. Matilda, the Empress Maud, is nearby. King Stephen built a castle inside in 1150 but that was soon destroyed. John of Gaunt married Blanche here in 1359, Parliament met here in 1453 and 1464 and the oldest English song, *Summer is Icumen In*, used in Benjamin Britten's *Spring Symphony*, was written down here in 1240 by monk John Fornsete. Pilgrims came to see the hand of St James the Great. The abbey lasted 400 years and the adjacent church is one of the buildings to be constructed from the stones. Only tall sections of wall remain after the Dissolution. The Scottish baronial-style prison is where Oscar Wilde was imprisoned in 1896/7 for gross indecency, writing *De Profundis* here and *The Ballad of Reading Gaol* after his release. Toad of Toad Hall also did a stretch here.

St Mary the Virgin's church, Reading Minster, is partly 13th century. St Laurence's is where the future Archbishop Laud, the son of a local draper, was baptized in 1573 and has the grave of a railwayman killed in 1840 by a whirlwind.

The Maiwand Lion in the Forbury Gardens is a memorial to the 66th Berkshire Regiment soldiers killed in the 19th century Afghan Wars. By George Blackall Simonds, it is the largest lion sculpture in the world and one of the largest sculptures in cast iron. Simonds is said to have committed suicide after discovering that he had left out the tongue. The 1883 Museum of Reading in the Victorian town hall has a British copy of the Bayeux Tapestry and Silchester material including a Roman eagle. The Hexagon theatre opened its doors in 1977. Those born here include Mike Oldfield, Arthur Negus, Chris Tarrant, Kate Winslet and Sam Mendes and it is where the Beatles first performed in public. Underage Jane Austen was allowed to attend the Abbey School with her older sister.

Below Caversham Lock are View and Heron Islands, Better Boating and King's Meadow. The Danes beat Alfred here in 870. A Tesco Extra with moorings precedes Kennet Mouth where the River Kennet joins, bringing in the Devizes–Westminster canoe race from the Kennet & Avon Canal at Easter. The 1890s Horseshoe footbridge has high sides to stop horses seeing the drop, also closing out trains and gas holders.

The north bank returns to Oxfordshire while the south bank becomes Wokingham with the Wokingham Waterside Centre on Dreadnought Reach. Thames & Kennet Marina is in former gravel pits with the Redgrave Pinsent Rowing Lake for the GB squad and Oxford University rowers, rather less comprehensive than for use by rowers and canoeists in general, for which the planning application was made. Beyond is Caversham Park where the BBC have the satellite dishes of their world monitoring station.

Thames Valley Park, partly built on the site of the former **Earley** power station, has attracted Microsoft, Oracle and Cisco to make it a significant computing centre. There is also a Thames Valley Park nature reserve with adders.

Reading Blue Coat School is a red Victorian Gothic building of 1646 on the site of the Bishop of Salisbury's Sonning Palace. It is where Henry IV imprisoned the 12 year old widow Isabella of Valois after the death of Richard II and tried to get her to marry his own son. The school has been used for filming *The Hole* and *Inspector Morse*. Ricky Gervais was a pupil.

Sonning belonged to the Sunna clan. It is reached through Sonning Lock, where poet James Sadler was

The mill and Archimedes screw at Mapledurham House.

the lock keeper in the 19th century. The 1180 Norman church founded in Saxon times, adjoining St Sirac's chapel for the mentally ill, had pilgrims, the 14th century Bull Inn serving as lodgings for them. The Grade II Grove was owned by Prime Minister Henry Addington. The defeated Admiral Villeneuve stayed in it after Trafalgar and was visited by Pitt the Younger. General Eisenhower stayed before D-Day. Turpins belonged to the highwayman's aunt and was used after robberies on the Bath Road, the horse going into an underground stable while Turpin escaped over the river. The Acre is where Pre-Raphaelite founder William Holman Hunt painted *The Light of the World* in 1900. One of the most dramatic changes came in 1916 when a storm felled 26 large elms in a few minutes.

Caversham Heights, the expensive part of Reading.

Sonning Bridge of 1775 has 11 red brick arches with quite a steep summit on the site of a wooden Saxon bridge. It carries the B478 and is plagued by lorries using satnavs which have found that they are too large to go over and have difficulty reversing through the village's corners and hills to find somewhere to turn round. Sonning Mill, which supplied flour to Huntley & Palmer until 1950 and worked until 1969, is now a theatre and restaurant. The French Horn is on another backwater at Sonning Eye.

The 1901 Deaneries is in Arts & Crafts style by Lutyens for Edward Hudson on a site owned by the deans of Salisbury on the boundary between the Salisbury and Lincoln dioceses. A weathervane shows a dean preaching to empty pews. Gardens are by Gertrude Jekyll and it is owned by Jimmy Page. The Great House is a pre-Elizabethan hotel in 2ha and incorporating the Red House where Sir Terence Rattigan lived. The 15th century St Andrew's church, restored in the 19th century, contains some Saxon minster material including a Saxon coffin lid. It produced three successive Archbishops of Canterbury. Uri Geller is a local resident and was visited by Michael Jackson. Meadowsweet, scabious, ragwort, toadflax and willowherb are some of the plants to be found around Reading University's farm.

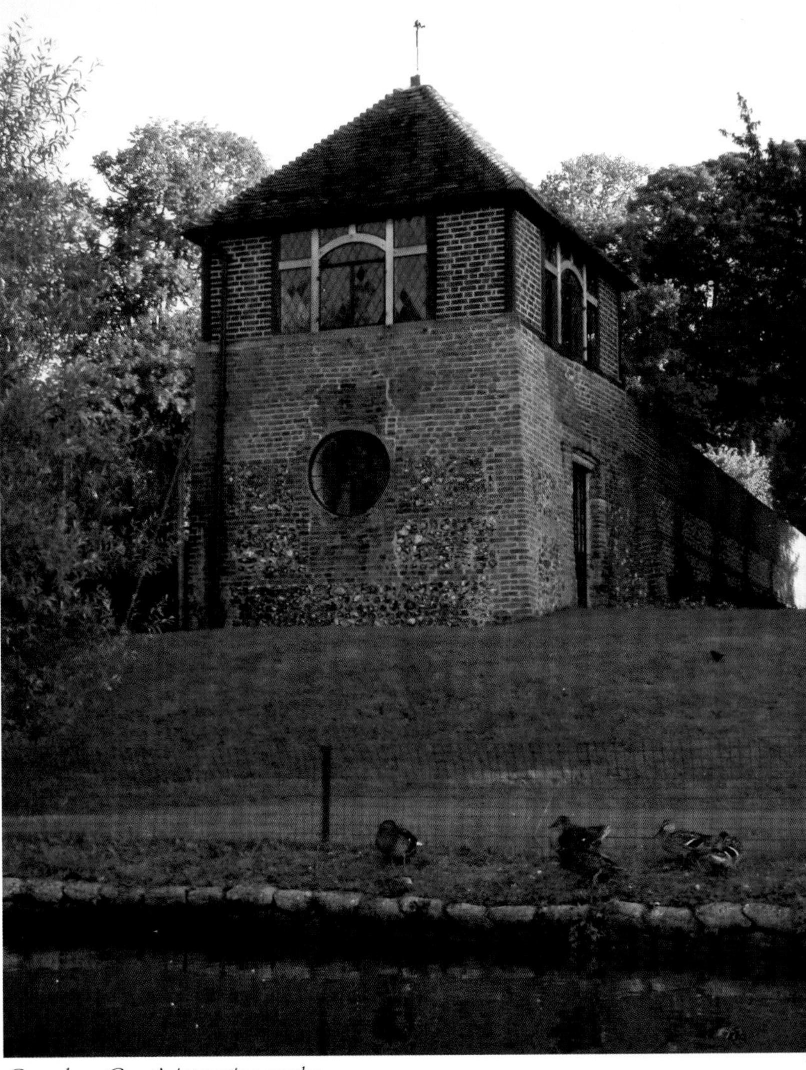

Caversham Court's interesting gazebo.

St Patrick's Stream leaves to meet the River Loddon and then return to the Thames. It has no weirs and bypasses Shiplake Lock so it has a decent flow while being narrow and twisting, making it an interesting run for small craft. It passes under a 5th century bridge by St Patrick.

The main river passes Buck and Hallsmead Aits and the Lynch. Shiplake was the sheep wash stream. The stone and flint church of Sts Peter & Paul is partly from 1140, restored in 1869 by George Street with a Jacobean pulpit from the Dorset Dorchester, a font copied from Iffley and medieval 15th century glass saved from St Bertin Abbey at St Omer during the French Revolution, buried and then brought here. There are also local chalk pillars. Tennyson married lawyer's daughter Emily Sellwood here in 1850, writing a poem in lieu of paying a fee. Shiplake Court of 1890 was used by the BBC during the Second World War. Shiplake College was founded in 1959 in a red Victorian Tudor building. Phillimore Island is named after Sir Robert Phillimore of Shiplake House, the mill being worked by descendant Colonel Robert Phillimore until 1984. Borough Lake joins from Borough Marsh and St Patrick's Stream. Ian Paice of Deep Purple is a local resident. The island at Shiplake Lock was bought in 1889 by the Corporation of London as a campsite for poor Eastenders.

Shiplake Railway Bridge, taking the Henley–Twyford line, was built in 1897 and leads to the course of the Wargrave & Shiplake Regatta which had already been running for 30 years by then. Attempts to close the line were blocked by some influential users from Henley.

Wargrave means weir grove. Bushnell's Thameside Marina is on this reach. Behind is St Mary's church which has an 1121 doorway and a 17th century brick tower. It has the grave of Thomas Day, author of *The History of Sandford & Merton*, who espoused Rousseau's philosophy of kindness and the simple life. Having failed to train an orphan as his wife, he was killed by a horse he had raised from a foal. Another unfortunate fatality was the Earl of Barrymore who bankrupted himself entertaining the Prince of Wales and then, at the age of 24, shot himself in the eye while escorting prisoners of war. In 1914 the church was subject to an arson attack by Emmeline Pankhurst and the Suffragettes because the marriage ceremony included the word 'obey'.

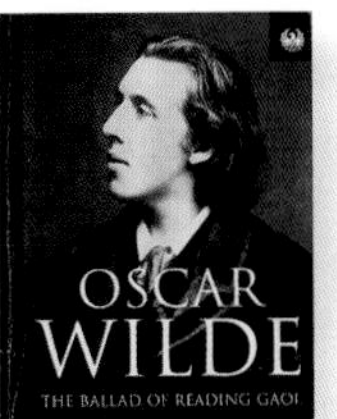

The Bull Inn has a ghost while the conspicuous George & Dragon's sign was painted by Royal Academy members George Leslie and Mr Hodgson, one side each. Dave Allen and Robert Morley lived here while Paul Daniels failed to come up with a trick to prevent himself from being flooded regularly by the river.

Sonning bridge looks less steep from the water than the road.

Coot's nest on a little-used runabout at Rod Island.

Wargrave Manor in its deer park, mentioned in *Domesday*, was owned by Queen Emma, the Fair Maid of Normandy, who married the Saxon Æthelred and then the Danish Cnut. It was later owned by Gertrude Jekyll's family and then by the Sultan of Oman.

After Val Wyatt Marine the Hennerton Backwater leaves through Fiddler's Bridge, no significant gradient this time but much smaller than the main river. This is where Harris disappeared with the beefsteak pie in *Three Men in a Boat*. Hennerton House farmed the backwater for eels in the 18th century.

Lower Shiplake makes better use of the river than Shiplake does with even Henley Sailing Club based here. Lashbrook chapel is in an old barn and the Doghouse is the recording studio of Barriemore Barlow of Jethro Tull. The Baskerville Arms are here, a safe distance from the hounds the family kept at Crowsley Park, and there is a polo ground. George Orwell lived at Roselawn when younger, his *Awake Young Men of England* being published before he left. Vince Hill, Terence Rattigan and Norman Hartnell have all been resident. One of the Edwardian houses has a narrow gauge railway but this is eclipsed by Thames-Side Court with a larger narrow gauge railway based on St Moritz in a 3ha garden for Swiss financier Urs Schwarzenbach.

This is where Harris was attacked by swans in *Three Men in a Boat*.

Temple Combe is the only British house designed by American architect Frank Lloyd Wright and has an 8m circle of megalithic stones shipped from Jersey by former Governor Henry Conway.

Happy Valley leads to Park Place, built in French Renaissance style in 1719 for the Duke of Hamilton. It was bought in 1738 by Frederick, Prince of Wales and had the first Lombardy poplars in England, a grotto, an amphitheatre and the spire from the lightning-damaged St Bride's church in London. Victoria considered buying it. The narrow Conway's Bridge by Humphrey Gainsborough has large stones which may have come from Reading Abbey.

A long footbridge crosses most of the width of the river to Marsh Lock and then runs back across the weirpool to avoid a brass foundry mill. Raymond Baxter, the Spitfire pilot and *Tomorrow's World* presenter, lived up the hill in one of the Edwardian mansions, his Dunkirk Little Ship *L'Orage* being moored below near the lock. There was also a corn mill here at one time.

Henley-on-Thames means at the high wood. Lower down, Rod Island has all its buildings on stilts because of flooding. The River & Rowing Museum was opened in 1998 in a building, by David Chipperfield, like an Oxfordshire barn, covering the Thames, rowing and *The Wind in the Willows*. Hobbs have a significant presence on the river, accompanied by the Sea Cadets' TS Guardian and the odd replica stern wheeler. Amongst the Tudor and Georgian houses are the Chocolate Theatre Café and Richard Way's nautical bookshop in an area which is Hartscombe in local writer John Mortimer's *Paradise Postponed*. The 18th century Angel on the Bridge uses a 14th century site and has a stone and flint arch in the cellar which was part of the medieval bridge and a piece of 1250 stained glass from Westminster Abbey chapter house when it was bombed in 1940. It faces the Royal Henley Regatta headquarters by Terry Farrell. Speaker's House in Hart Street was the birthplace of Speaker Lenthall, who stood up to the King on behalf of Parliament. Local MP Boris Johnson resigned his position in order to become Mayor of London.

Henley Bridge, carrying the A4130 back, was built in 1786 to replace a wooden bridge of 1774 which had been swept away. It has five stone arches with the mask of Isis facing upstream and of Thamesis downstream. A 14th

Superior riparian property in Lower Shiplake.

The Angel and the church by Henley Bridge.

century bridge had a chapel and other buildings and in the Civil War there were skirmishes around the bridge.

Henley was a 12th century port and an 18th century coaching town. A 15th century granary is now timber-framed cottages. Charles I stayed at the Red Lion Hotel in 1632 and 1642 and Prince Rupert stayed during the Civil War. Boswell and Johnson dined in the 1770s, Wellington and Blücher stayed after Waterloo, the Prince Regent ate 14 lamb cutlets at a sitting and the Duke of Marlborough had his own room. William Shenstone engraved a poem on a window. The 15th century Grade II Bull Bar & Brasserie and the 16th century former Bear Inn had baiting yards.

St Mary the Virgin's church was recorded in 1204 and supplied by Dorchester monks. It is mostly 14th century. The flint chequerwork Tudor tower may be by Cardinal Wolsey in about 1550 with Victorian stained glass, a monument to William Hayward who died in 1782, the grave of Richard Jennings, the chief builder of St Paul's, and a memorial to Dusty Springfield, Dusty Day being in April. The adjacent chantry house is from about 1400.

Brakspear's 1890s Georgian Henley Brewery traded until 2002, when it closed, but George Harrison was a successful campaigner against the closure of the Regal cinema. The 1805 Kenton Theatre is the fourth oldest still active in England.

Noncomformist minister Humphrey Gainsborough, builder of Conway's Bridge, invented a sundial for use at sea and a reversible tidemill wheel and beat James Watt to the invention of the steam engine. Other residents have been Jeremy Cross, George Cole and Rodney Bewes. Friar Park of 1895, by Sir Frank Crisp, had many unusual water features and a huge collection of gnomes, used by later resident George Harrison on the cover of *All Things Must Pass*. Harrison was attacked by an intruder in 1999 and took steps to make his property less open to the public.

The council offices are in the 18th century West Hill House while the 1900s town hall is in Queen Anne style. The Open Spaces Society is a local body. Henley Festival of Music & the Arts and the Rewind Festival are other town events.

The first Oxford and Cambridge boat race in 1829 was rowed from Hambleden Lock to Henley Bridge, including a restart after a collision. The losing Cambridge pink became the colour of the 1818 Leander Club, who have the best haul of Olympic and world championship medals, helped by being the world's oldest club and because members are elected for winning major races. Women have been admitted since 1998. Redgrave and Pinsent trained here. Henley Regatta has taken place since 1839, probably the world's first river regatta, under the royal patronage of Albert from 1851. There have been many arguments over excluding menial workers, considered professional as they worked for money. The regatta takes place in the first week of July, a social event with strict dress code, fireworks and, in the past, pugilists and fighting booths. The course is 2.1km from Temple Island to Phyllis Court and has two lanes so that other craft can still use the river alongside the course.

Barn Elms was the home of First World War pinup Gladys Cooper, the house later bought by Dr Walter Scott, who saw it while competing.

This Henley Reach, remote and dark in the small

Temple Island at the start of the Henley rowing course.

hours, exposed and heading into any wind with some north in it, is the one most likely to finish off ailing crews in the Devizes–Westminster Race.

The Thames Traditional Boat Rally takes place where the west bank changes to Buckinghamshire.

Fawley Court was built by Wren in 1683 with grounds by Capability Brown. It was sacked by the Royalists, rebuilt in the 1680s, visited by William III and IV and called Poland-on-Thames as it housed the sons of exiled Poles after 1953. There is a museum with Polish monarchy documents, military history and Middle Ages sculptures and paintings.

Remenham means village by the riverbank. The 13th century Norman church of St Nicholas has an 1836 tower and was restored in 1870 with iron gates from Sienna. Jenny Agutter was married here. The carved lych-gate has the grave of Caled Gould who was Hambleden lock keeper for 59 years, dying at 92. He was an ancestor of former Labour leadership contender Bryan Gould.

Temple Island has a 1771 temple by James Wyatt with the first English Etruscan interior, built as an angling lodge and to give a focal view from Fawley Court.

Greenlands was destroyed in 1644 by Parliamentary artillery across the Thames in the Civil War and rebuilt in 1853 in Italianate style. It was the home of Viscount Hambleden, W H Smith, the First Lord of the Admiralty and MP, mocked in HMS *Pinafore* and described by Jerome K Jerome as his newsagent. It is now Reading University's Henley Business School. Wildlife might include blackheaded gulls, Egyptian ducks and clubtailed dragonflies.

A long walkway crosses the top of the weir from Hambleden Lock to Hambleden Mill, where there was a mill in 1086. The current white weatherboarded structure is 16th century, used until 1957 and now apartments. It overlooks the large weirpool which has been used for whitewater canoeing events, the local Chalfont Park Canoe Club being allowed to adjust the sluices to produce the conditions required for different activities. The Manor House at Mill End may have a poltergeist and the yew walk to the pond has been exorcised. There was a Roman villa by the river here.

A slipway leads up to the Victorian Flower Pot Hotel at Aston, rebuilt in about 1890 and welcoming of boating parties. The Georgian Culham Court of 1770 had hot rolls brought from London by horse relay when George III was a guest. It was later owned by Lady Barber, who founded Birmingham's Barber Institute for Fine Arts, then by banker and arts patron Michael Behrans with a copy of Elizabeth Frink's *Striding Madonna* statue from Salisbury, set in a garden by Raymond Erith.

The south bank becomes Windsor & Maidenhead. The north bank at Medmenham has a monument which records an important legal case of 1899. Although the ferry was disused, a slip remains. Its use in 1678 by Charles II established a right of way. The lane leads to the Dog & Badger of 1390, which Nell Gwynn is said to have used. Marriage banns were read here before being read in church until 1899. The Norman church of Sts Peter & Paul was restored in the 19th century. In September 1935 a storm felled many trees so elephants from a travelling circus were used to clear the road.

The 1201 St Mary's Abbey for the Cistercians was much destroyed at the Dissolution. The 1595 abbey house was Elizabethan with more building in Georgian Gothic and Victorian. It was Chancellor of the Exchequer Sir Francis Dashwood's home from 1750 to 1774 and used for the early days of the scandalous Hellfire Club which included John Wilkes, Lord Sandwich and Frederick, Prince of Wales. It was later the home of RAF Signals Command and there is now a research centre.

Bolbec's Castle was an Iron Age hill fort but Danesfield got its name from a Danish fortification. Danesfield House was built in 1899 in Victorian Tudor by Romaine Walker for Robert William Hudson, the inventor of soap powder and the first person to use mass advertising. The house has since been an RAF camp, the headquarters of Carnation milk and now a hotel. The red brick Harleyford Manor was built in 1755 for MP Sir William Clayton by Sir Robert Taylor, providing more inspiration for Toad Hall. Chargers Paddock was used by a descendant to graze Waterloo horses.

Hurley, wood or clearing in a gap in the hills, had a Bronze Age settlement and a 6th century ford. The lock used to be a flash lock and there is still a capstan among the trees on the north bank which was used for winching up boats. The weirpool is now a popular freestyle site for canoeists. There is a slip and Hurley Lock Tea Shop caters for visitors. Peter Freebody & Co's boatyard has been established on the Thames since the 13th century, a workshop where the odours of wood shavings and varnish produce an instant Edwardian atmosphere.

St Birinus founded a church in about 635. Geoffrey de Mandeville added a Benedictine priory in 1056 for monks from Westminster Abbey. St Mary the Virgin's church has Saxon remains from 1086 beneath it and the grave of Princess Editha. Richard Lovelace built the Elizabethan Ladye Place on top of the dissolved building, used in 1688 to plot the Glorious Revolution under John Lovelace which forced James II abroad, allowing William and Mary to replace him. William later inspected the house, to be replaced in 1837 with an Edwardian building. A hawthorn tree planted by Admiral Kempenfelt died the night his ship, the *Royal George*, the world's largest, sank at Spithead in 1782 with the loss of over 800 lives. The Olde Bell from 1135 is England's oldest coaching inn, located in the priory guest house. There are also a 12th century tithe barn and dovecote and the 17th century Hurley House and almshouses. There is a marrow wassail festival in October and Steve Rider is a local. On the hill behind the house is the Grassland Research Station.

The longest hardwood bridge in Britain, at 46m, was installed in 1989 as the first footbridge for the Thames Path, several footbridges being needed to replace ferries which have closed down. The Knights Templars had a mill here, extended in 1710 for a copper foundry, making brass kettles, then pans, then brown paper. It had the largest wheel on the Thames until 1969, after which the marina was built. Temple Lock has twin chambers, one of which is disused.

Bisham Abbey Sailing & Navigation School draws attention to Bisham Abbey itself, brick and flint with mullioned windows, a great bell from 1260, a clocktower above the stables and threadbare flags which date from the Middle Ages. In the tower the ghost remains of Lady Elizabeth Hoby, trying to wash the blood off her hands. She locked her son William in the tower for blotting

Hambleden Mill overlooks the weirpool.

his copybook and then forgot about him for a week while she was at court, a blotted copybook being found subsequently. On the other hand, this left the estate to her illegitimate grandson, Peregrine Pinkney. The site was owned by the Knights Templars in 1139, was an Augustine priory from 1307, was used as a prison for the wife and daughter of Robert the Bruce and was the only monastery to be restored by Henry VIII after the Dissolution, for the Chertsey Benedictines to pray for Jane Seymour but only for six months. Abbot John Cordery placed a curse on it as he was taken away and this has held most of the time. It was given to Anne of Cleves as part of her divorce settlement and Elizabeth I stayed with the Hoby family for three years as protection from Mary Tudor. It has 15th century graves of the Nevilles, including, in 1471, Richard the Kingmaker, the Earl of Warwick, after the Battle of Barnet. It is now a national sports centre, used by the England football team.

Beside the river in Bisham is All Saints' church with its Norman tower and graves of the Hoby family.

Marlow, mere shore, was a Saxon market town which became fashionable in the 18th and 19th centuries. Many houses are 18th century Georgian but others are from the 14th century onwards and there are some by Wren.

St Mary's Abbey at Medmenham.

Danesfield House now a hotel above the river at Hurley.

Replacing a missing ferry for the Thames Path at Temple.

Bisham Abbey, now a sports centre.

All Saints' church by the river at Bisham.

Higginson Park provides open space with a Millennium Maze and a statue of quintuple Olympics gold medal winner Sir Steve Redgrave, who was born in the town. Marlow Town Regatta is a regular fixture and Marlow Rowing Club is next to the bridge. Marlow Bridge of 1832 is a white suspension bridge with arched towers and a 72m main span. It was started by John Millington and completed by William Tierney Clark, a precursor for his Budapest Szechenyl bridge. Earlier bridges had been opposite St Peter Street, where there is a slipway, including a bridge damaged by Parliamentary forces in 1642. The Roman Catholic St Peter's church by Pugin has the hand of St James from Reading Abbey.

The 14th century old parsonage is the oldest building in Marlow, with fine panelled rooms and Decorated windows. All Saints' church is the most conspicuous. The site was in use by 1070 and the church has 12th century foundations but these were damaged by flooding and the church was rebuilt in 1835 with a neo-Gothic spire. It contains the first publicly funded memorial, that of 1628 to MP Miles Hobart, the Speaker who closed the House of Commons door in the face of Black Rod because of a dispute. It also has the grave of E J Gregory.

A milestone in the market place recalls the Gout Track, built in the 18th century by the Cecils from Hatfield House to the Bath Road in Reading so that they could avoid the poor roads when going to take the waters in Bath.

Sir Evelyn Wrench, the editor of the *Spectator*, founded the English Speaking Union and the Royal Overseas League and lived in Marlow Mill, there having been three mills there in the 19th century, producing the first English brass thimbles. The Royal Military College was based in the town from 1799 to 1871. Thames Lawn was the home of Captain Morris, who commanded HMS *Colossus* at Trafalgar, and was the home of M in filming *On Her Majesty's Secret Service*. Dr William Battie had a 1760s mansion in Higginson Park and wrote the first mental health book, his name being adopted for a state of mind. T S Eliot is buried here. Thomas Love Peacock wrote *Nightmare Abbey* and Shelley wrote the *Revolt to Islam*. Following a short story writing competition between a group of friends in 1817, Mary Shelley was encouraged to expand her *Frankenstein* into a full length book. American theatre manager Charles Frohman was a regular visitor to the town. In 1999 the Macdonald Compleat Angler was the first restaurant outside London to be visited by the Queen.

The Cross Keys of 1935 is in mock Tudor. The Two Brewers, shown on two sides of a former pub sign, were Thomas Whethered and Samuel Whitbread, Whitbreads taking over Whethereds. It was where some of *Three Men in a Boat* was written. The Prince of Wales has a pub sign with a caricature of Prince Charles which is striking and unusual rather than flattering. The landlord of one of the lesser pubs, in a wind up, was once invited to ring the telephone number of an apparently dubious lady and ask for Liz. He took up the challenge and Buckingham Palace answered.

The long Marlow Weir leads to Marlow Lock. The A404 Marlow Bypass crosses at the start of Longridge, the Scout boating centre, now independent. Quarry Wood may have inspired the Wild Wood in *The Wind in the Willows* which Kenneth Grahame wrote in Cookham Dean. Dame Nellie Melba, the first singer on British radio, lived here and practised out of doors. Elton John also lived here. Known as Little Switzerland, its trees were badly damaged in 1987 and 1990. Above is Winter Hill terrace, popular with Dickens. Below is a castellated house and Woottens Boatyard.

Waterskiing takes place in former gravel pits to the north. Bourne End Reach has the Upper Thames Sailing Club, where the Thames A class compete in May for the 1893 Queen's Cup. Beyond a sewage works is Little Marlow, where the lane to the cemetery is marked as a no through road. The village has a 16th century manor, in 57ha of grounds, and the church of St John the Baptist, founded in the 12th century. The 1867 Victorian Spade Oak at Well End is a popular pub while the 12th century Benedictine nunnery was one of the smallest in the country. Saltings houses were former baker, butcher, blacksmith/farrier and slaughterhouse businesses.

There are Bronze Age burial mounds and the Cookham Stone and sarsen Tarry Stone megaliths, used for sports before 1507. Cock Marsh, used by the Saxons and Danes, is the best remaining site in the area for valley grassland and has sparrowhawks and redshanks. There has been common grazing since the 13th century and there

Another All Saints' church and Marlow Bridge.

is a golf course. Cock Marsh to Widbrook Common has been preserved with commoners' rights as these have been defended.

Bourne End Railway Bridge of 1894 takes the railway across three 30m spans. The section of line to High Wycombe has been lost so trains from Maidenhead now reverse at Bourne End for what was the spur to Marlow. This latter section of line used to be worked by the Marlow Donkey, a pannier tank operating with a single coach. There are Edwardian houses. Tom Stoppard was born here, Kenneth Connor lived here and Enid Blyton was in the Old Thatch. Louis Bleriot's house burned down in 1926.

The Saxon Witenagemot met at Cookham, cocc ham being hill village. It had an 8th century Saxon monastery and a 10th century Saxon palace. The 1140 flint Norman Holy Trinity church is on Saxon foundations, is where Susan George married and has a copy of Spencer's *The Last Supper*. The village is in Georgian and Victorian red brick with pubs from 1417 onwards although the Crown burnt down in the 1920s and 1930s despite having the fire station behind it.

Cookham Reach leads to Cookham Bridge, an 1867 Victorian iron structure carrying the A4094 with a toll house which appears in Spencer's *Swan Upping at Cookham*. Turk's boatyard is here, Turk being Swan Keeper to Her Majesty the Queen. Swan Upping, in colourful costumes, has been undertaken since the 1470s. Originally the Queen's swans were unmarked, the Dyers' had one nick to the beak and the Vintners' had two nicks, leading to the confused pub name of the swan with two necks. The cygnets are now ringed. This piece of pagentry has no practical purpose these days as swans are no longer eaten.

The Stanley Spencer Gallery is in the Victorian Wesleyan chapel. Spencer was born in the village in 1891 and commuted to the Slade School of Fine Art from 1908 to 1912. His wives were the artists Hilda Carline then Patricia Preece. His paintings were mostly portraits or scenes of Cookham, particularly religious episodes in local settings as he moved his paints around the village in a pram. His 1926 picture of *The Resurrection, Cookham* was set in the churchyard, *The Crucifixion* was in the High Street with locals as tormentors and his uncompleted *Christ Preaching at Cookham Regatta* was set by the ferry.

Noël Coward's *Hay Fever* was set here. Lillebrook Manor's owner had the first car in Cookham, which could have been further inspiration for Toad Hall and Mr Toad.

D B Marine stands at the start of the 1830 Cookham Cut, leading to Cookham Lock past crabapple bushes. The northern arm, the Hedsor Stream, was the original navigation channel and the Environment Agency successfully opposed an attempt to close it to navigation. Formosa Court was built in 1785 for Sir George Young, Formosa Island being 20ha in size. Alfred fortified Sashes Island. Wood pigeons, jays, green woodpeckers, kingfishers, longtailed tits and hobbies might be seen.

Cliveden, meaning steeply sloping wooded valley, is on an ancient trackway, surrounded by beeches and trees from around the world, and is considered to be the most beautiful reach on the Thames.

The house was first built in 1666 for George Villiers, who killed the 11th Earl of Shewsbury in a duel over his wife, the Countess, who watched, disguised as a pageboy. The 1850 house by Sir Charles Barry for the 2nd Duke of Sutherland followed the first two which had burned down in 1795 and 1849. On a chalk cliff 60m above the river, it has 1.5km^2 of Grade I gardens, an Italian garden, flower borders, topiary, water gardens with Japanese pagoda and maples, parterre, wooded and riverside walks, Greek and Italian statues, temples, balustrades, eight Roman sarcophagi and a helipad. In Italianate style, the house was one of the first stately homes to have central heating. It is run as a hotel which may be hired out but is not cheap as it has more staff than guests. Suits of armour are frequent. *Rule Britannia* was first performed here while the house was being hired out in 1739 by the Prince of Wales. Less happily, he was the first person to be fatally injured by a cricket ball after one hit his head here. The house was bought in 1893 by American multimillionaire William Waldorf Astor and was home to Nancy Astor who, in 1919, became the first female MP. Visitors included Canning, Garibaldi, John Evelyn, Henry James, Hilaire Belloc, Charlie Chaplin, G B Shaw, T E Lawrence, Oswald Mosley, Winston Churchill and most monarchs since George I. In 1936 the Cliveden Set with the Astors, German Ambassador Joachim von Ribbentrop and *Times* editor Geoffrey Dawson were accused of appeasing Nazi Germany.

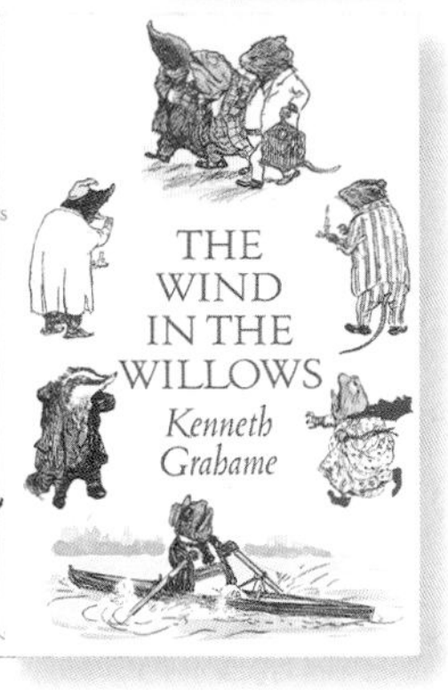

The riverside Spring Cottage of 1813 was enlarged in the 1870s and visited by Victoria. In 1961, during the Cold War, Secretary of State for War John Profumo and Soviet Naval Attaché Yevgeny Inanov were each sharing the attentions of Christine Keeler here with all that implied for the passing on of military secrets, resulting in

Enid Blyton's *Famous Five*

a major political crisis which came close to toppling the Government.

Open air theatre is still performed in the grounds, where Kenneth Branagh married Emma Thompson. Cliveden House was Lady Penelope's house in filming *Thunderbirds*, was used in filming *Sherlock Holmes*, *Carrington*, *Chaplin* and *Scandal* and was Buckingham Palace in filming *Help!* Islet Park House was used by Gerry Anderson for early puppet films including *Noddy* and Joyce Grenfell lived on the estate.

There are numerous channels around Cliveden Reach, the main one having been from Cookham via the Fleet Ditch (now built up) via Maidenhead, the York Stream and the Cut to Monkey Island. There are proposals to reopen a navigation route via the White Brook through the centre of Maidenhead.

The Jubilee River, the Maidenhead and Windsor flood relief channel, was opened in 2002 with the Environment Agency attempting to remove the automatic right to navigation but an administrative error during the signing of the legislation left the public right in place. Commandos managing to negotiate the Taplow Inlet Structure will still be faced with a wall of trees planted very close together, before the next launch point, and several weirs. The channel won numerous awards but was found to be under capacity and repairs for structural failure were needed within a couple of years of opening.

Ray Mill Island has a zoo, aviary and Eunice Goodman's Maiden with Swans sculpture. Richard Dimbleby lived here and harangued fast boats but the house is now owned by a former Olympic sprint kayak racer, who takes a more relaxed attitude. Boulter's Lock Hotel was the 1726 mill on the island, a boulter being a miller producing bolts of cloth. Boulter's Lock, the longest and deepest above Teddington, has handled up to 900 craft in a day. The lock was rebuilt in about 1910 and has an ornate stone bridge onto the island. Below the lock is the site of John Gregory's painting *Boulter's Lock – Sunday Afternoon 1895*, now in Port Sunlight Gallery.

Taplow was named after the Saxon Taeppa. It provides the name for the gravel Taplow or Fifty Foot Terrace of the Thames. There is a Saxon burial mound which produced a rich hoard when excavated in 1883. It was said to be the site of the last battle between the Romans and the incoming Saxons.

Cliveden is thought to be the best reach on the Thames.

Taplow Court was the home of the 1st Earl of Orkney, the first British Field Marshal. It was rebuilt in Tudor style in 1852. Later it was owned by William Grenfell, Lord Desborough, a member of the Oxford boat race crew and Thames punting champion who rowed the Channel, swam the Niagara rapids twice, climbed the Matterhorn three times, was president of the 1908 Olympic Games and was chairman of the Thames Conservancy for 32 years. It is now the headquarters of the Soka Gakkai Buddhists.

Taplow was the original terminus of the Great Western Railway, attracting people from London with Edwardian champagne and punting parties, drinking clubs in the Roaring Twenties and Gaiety Girls. Skindles Hotel, now demolished, was built in 1833, the centre of attention, used by the Prince of Wales with Lillie Langtree and by the top pop groups in the 1960s and 1970s. The Victorian Thames Hotel, River Bar, Thames Riviera Hotel and Blue River Café are a shadow of what went before.

There has been a bridge at **Maidenhead** since the 13th century. The current one, built in 1777 by Sir Robert Taylor in a style similar to his Swinford Bridge, is Grade I in Portland stone and balustraded. It is 140m long with 13 semicircular arches of up to 11m span, seven over the water, and carries the A4 Great West Road. Tolls ceased in 1903 following misuse of revenues.

The Saxon Elentone, Ellen's town, had become the Old English Maidenhythe, maiden's landing, by 1296, mai dun also meaning great hill. Maidenhead, priding itself as the Jewel of the Thames, was a coaching town, where Wellington's coffin fell off its hearse into the water during the floods of 1852, fortunately recovered or faces would have been even redder.

Maidenhead Rowing Club is based on the left beyond the bridge.

The river was the obstacle to extension of the GWR but Brunel cleared it in spectacular fashion. His 39m semi elliptical spans have 7.3m rise, the longest and flattest brick arches ever. Sceptics required the bridge to be propped but Brunel left the supports so that they were not touching the bridge. They subsequently fell down in a storm and were not replaced, the bridge now carrying far more than its original intended loads at much higher speeds. It was widened on each side in 1893 as true ellipses so there are discontinuities against Brunel's work. With electrification planned, it has been requested that overhead lines should not spoil the look of the bridge, third rails being used across it instead with all power units having dual collection systems, an idea not likely to be accepted. It has been claimed as the location for Turner's *Rain, Steam & Speed on the GWR* but that was probably at Hanwell instead. A good echo is obtained across the river from the towpath so it is also referred to as the Sounding Arch. In 1853 a 400m tall waterspout was seen near here.

Large houses on the banks of what is known as

Enid Blyton's *Noddy*

The Sounding Arch of Brunel's railway bridge at Maidenhead.

Millionaire's Row have attracted such residents as Rolf Harris, Michael Parkinson and Gerald Ratner.

The chalk gives way to the Reading beds and then London clay. Bray, which means mud, has black and white cottages. The flint tower of the 1293 church shows over the top. Buried in the graveyard is Simon Alwyn, the vicar who repeatedly changed denomination under monarchs from Henry VIII to Elizabeth I to retain his post although the song referred to a later vicar, Dr Francis Carswell in 1667. The church has a 16th century cottage over the lych-gate. Marriages here have included that of snooker player Steve Davies.

The Duke and Duchess of York dined at Michel Roux's Waterside Inn two days after announcing their separation but John MacCarthy and campaigner Jill Morrell dined elsewhere after seeing the prices. Top end prices are also available in Heston Blumenthal's Fat Duck and Hind's Head. The 17th century Jesus Hospital is back from the river.

Bray Lock has sloping lawns which, at first glance, make it look like a turf-sided lock.

The M4 crosses before Dorney Reach. Dorney means island of bees, honey still being made here. Monkey Island, perhaps from monk's eyot and owned by Merton Abbey, has the Monkey Island Hotel in which the restaurant has a Monkey Room with a domed ceiling painted in 1744 by Andien de Clermont with monkeys in costume as part of the 3rd Duke of Marlborough's angling lodge. The duke also built a temple incorporating an octagonal room with Wedgwood-style high relief plaster at the heart of the present conference centre. The buildings are founded on rubble from the fire of London in 1666. Peacocks roam the premises. Edward VII and family visited and Clara Butt and Nellie Melba entertained here. Rebecca West set *The Return of the Soldier* here and returned to meet H G Wells at times. It was also the location of the pineapple tin incident in *Three Men in a Boat*.

The Long White Cloud was the house where Elgar composed his violin concerto and was visited by Gilbert Fauré, Siegfried Sassoon, Walter Sickert and G B Shaw. Later it was the home of Stirling Moss. Gerry Anderson lived on the estate.

Dorney Court, built in 1500 on a site in use after the Conquest, is one of the finest Tudor manor houses in England, in brick and mortar with notable furniture. It was the home of Barbara Palmer, the Countess of Castlemaine, the favourite mistress of Charles II and mother of several of his children, where he was presented with the first pineapple grown in England by John Rose here in 1661. The house has a carved stone pineapple, a great chamber, a great hall, a Lely painting of the Countess and the ghost of a woman who used to point to a dark panel in the little room. It was used for filming *I'll be There* and was Syon in filming *Lady Jane*. The Norman St James the Less' church is 13th century.

James Hanratty abducted Valerie Storie and Michael Gregsten in 1961 and made them drive their car from a cornfield in the village to Bedfordshire where he carried out the A6 murder, rape and attempted murder, for which he was the last person in Britain to receive capital punishment.

The Cut emerges before Bray Marina. Queen's Eyot is owned by Eton College. The college opposed lord of the manor John Penn's Enclosure Bill, Dorney or Eton Wick Common remaining unenclosed with cranesbill, buttercups, meadowsweet and thistles.

Hammer Films' Bray Studios at Water Oakley are in Down Place of 1750, which was used by the Kit Cat Club. Films produced here included *Alien*, *The Rocky Horror Picture Show*, *The Curse of Frankenstein*, *Horror of Dracula* and *The Mummy's Shroud*. Oakley Court was built in Victorian Gothic in 1857 by an Englishman for his homesick French wife. During the Second World War it was the headquarters of the Résistance and Charles de Gaulle was a frequent visitor. It was used in *The Rocky Horror Picture Show* and has been the school in *The Wildcats of St Trinians*, the home of Tommy Steele in *Half a Sixpence*, the mansion in *Murder by Death* and a hotel. Windsor Marina follows.

Dorney Lake is Eton's 2.2km rowing regatta course in 1.8km^2 of park, sale of the excavated gravel assisting the construction costs nicely. It was used for the 2012 Olympic Games rowing and canoeing regatta.

Boveney has Tudor houses and a green. A pair of rampant stone lions guard the 15th century timber-framed Boveney Court in red brick, E shaped in plan, the property of **Burnham** Abbey. The redundant 12th century Grade I stone and flint chapel of St Mary Magdalene may be on a pre-Christian site. It has a timber-framed tower and a Norman window. There is no road access but Hammer Films managed to get there to use it.

Royal Windsor horse racecourse has a figure 8 track In June 1979 a tornado formed near Boveney Lock.

At Clewer Village, Mill House has housed Jimmy Page, Sir Michael Caine and Natalie Imbruglia. French Boats also have a base here. St Andrew's 11th century early Norman church is on a Saxon site and retains a Saxon font. William the Conqueror attended services here. It has the grave of Sir Daniel Gooch, the GWR's first mechanical engineer, who set up the Swindon works and laid the first transatlantic cable with the SS *Great Eastern*. Another grave is of Mary Ann Hull, better known as Nanny May to Victoria's children. There is a local history museum in the gatehouse. The 19th century House of Mercy is where Gladstone sent fallen women he found on the streets of London.

The Elizabeth Bridge of 1966 carries the A332 Windsor & Eton Bypass. Carrying the **Slough**–Windsor & Eton Central railway line is a skewed bowstring girder bridge, the world's oldest wrought iron bridge in regular use. With 28m span, it has triangular cross section tubular girders. It leads onto the Windsor Railway Viaduct of 1849 with the world's highest number of continuous brick arches, replacing a timber viaduct.

Brocas Meadows were known as Athens, where naked Eton pupils were required to get in the water or behind screens when boats containing ladies appeared. Feral ringed parakeets have made it this far up the Thames from Richmond.

The river is now entirely within Windsor & Maidenhead. The promenade along the south bank acts as the quayside from which trip boats operate. The scene on a summer evening is a far cry from January 1936, when the Thames was up to 1.5km wide, or 1895, when an ox was roasted on the ice. In a 1957 storm a woman was killed when a chimney was blown through the roof of the Harte & Garter Hotel and a 75 year old woman was trapped by a fallen tree at the Willows Riverside Park.

There was a wooden bridge at **Windsor** by at least 1172 and a flood took one in 1809. The current cast iron Windsor Bridge of 1824 is a Grade II structure by Charles Hollis, its central 18m span having a 2m rise, supported on granite piers. Tolls in the 18th century were 2d walking or 6/8 in a coffin. The tolls were stopped in 1898 after a three year court case and vehicles were stopped in 1970. Until 1990 Eton boys were not allowed to cross without collars and ties. There can be a standing wave up to a metre high under the bridge in times of spate.

St Mary Magdalen church at Boveney.

Bray church of varying denominations.

Windsor was named from the Old English windle sora, banks up which boats were winched, or from the Anglo-Saxon wyndesore, winding shore, or Hardy's Castle Royal. It has many Georgian and Victorian buildings. Sir Christopher Wren's house is here and Chariott's Charity Gothic almshouses.

The intentionally dominant building is Windsor Castle, the largest inhabited castle in the world and by far the world's longest continuously inhabited castle, with a royal presence for 900 years since Henry I. It occupies 5.3ha on a 30m upfold of chalk inlier above the river, the castle Norman with Stuart and Regency changes. Around the site have been found palaeolithic hand axes, neolithic flint picks, Bronze Age swords and spears and an Iron Age broach and amber glass. The site was much used by the Romans and Saxons. The castle was founded in 1170 by William the Conqueror, to be a day's march from the Tower of London. It has been rebuilt five times, the first stone buildings being by Henry II, who held Parliament here. Curtain walls with square towers from the 1170s surround the upper bailey while the gate is Norman. The Curfew Tower of 1227 has eight bells and medieval vaulted dungeons with secret passages in walls which are 4m thick. Another curtain wall with D plan towers was added round the lower bailey in the 13th century. More internal buildings date from the 14th century. The shell keep was doubled in height in the 19th century, the whole structure dominated by the 70m Round Tower. This is one of Britain's most visited attractions.

The Albert Memorial Chapel has a monument to Prince Albert in armour.

Pantry footmen in the castle had perpetual sore throats until 1844 when 50 full cesspits were found under the castle. The major 1992 fire destroyed only one painting; eerily, it was one which George III had wanted to burn. It did run up some unexpected expenses, however, such as doorknobs which the Queen was obliged to have made specially to match those destroyed, off the shelf items having the wrong diameter by a couple of millimetres. The State Apartments have a ceiling painted by Antonio Verrio and there are other paintings by top artists, tapestries, Henry VIII's armour, the bullet which killed Nelson, the Queen's Presents and the Royal Carriages. Queen Mary's Doll's House of 1923 by Sir

The Royal Standard flies above Windsor Castle.

Edwin Lutyens is 2.4m x 1.5m with books and paintings at 1:12 scale by leading writers and artists. The Royal Standard flies when the Queen is present.

Edward III was born here and founded the Order of the Garter here in 1348 when he picked up a garter dropped by Joan, Countess of Salisbury, and declared to the court 'Honi soit qui mal y pense,' shame to him who thinks evil of it, to avoid a scandal. The library has the ghost of Elizabeth I, George III looks out of a window, Henry VIII is here and it was used for filming *An American Werewolf in London*. With the First World War looming, George V decided to change the family name from Saxe-Coburg-Gotha to Windsor in 1917, a name also used for such familiar items as a brown soup, a tie knot and a form of chair.

St George's chapel was built from 1475 to 1528, the best Perpendicular architecture in England, late Gothic with fan vaulting, 16th century sculptures, a notable stained glass west window, banners of the Knights of the Garter and the graves of ten monarchs including Henry VIII, who was brought by boat and buried with Jane Seymour. The boat bringing the beheaded Charles I secretly from London in January 1649 had problems with icefloes. Ice of a different form made its impact in 1859 when there were hailstones the size of pigeons' eggs.

The Dungeons of Windsor and the Town & Crown Exhibition can be seen. Madame Tussaud's Royalty & Empire Exhibition is in Windsor & Eton Central station, which was provided in 1849 for Queen Victoria. It features the 1897 Diamond Jubilee, the Royal Train and a military parade. Combermere Barracks have the Household Cavalry Museum.

St John the Baptist's church, rebuilt in 1820 by Jeffry Wyatt on the site of an 1168 church, has the 4.6 x 4.3m painting of *The Last Supper* by Franz de Cleyn from St George's chapel and 16th century plate, the chancel has mosaics by Salviatti, the royal pew has carving by Grinling Gibbons and there is a brass rubbing centre. The Theatre Royal was founded in 1793, the present one built in 1910, one of the most beautiful Edwardian theatres in Britain. A bronze golden jubilee statue of Victoria was undertaken in 1887 by Sir Edmund Beohm. The 17th century Burford Lodge in the Royal Mews was built by Charles II for his mistress, the home of Nell Gwynn. The Three Tuns was built in 1518 as the guildhall, the Crooked House of Windsor tea room was built in 1687 from unseasoned timber and Queen Charlotte Street is Britain's shortest named road at 16m. The Guildhall of 1690 was by Sir Thomas Fitz and Sir Christopher Wren, who were forced by councillors to add central columns for safety. In fashion to be followed by Brunel, they stopped them 30mm short of the ceiling. It was used by Prince Charles to marry Camilla Parker-Bowles in 2005 and contains a museum of the town's history. The Grade II Sir Christopher Wren Hotel recalls 1688 when Wren was the local MP. The Windsor Castle Hotel was a Georgian coaching inn. H G Wells was apprenticed in Windsor as a draper, a theme he pursued in *Kipps* and *The History of Mr Polly*. The Crown Jewels of the World Museum has over 150 replica crowns from a dozen countries and the Old King's Head of 1648 had the warrant for the removal of it from Charles I. This is where Shakespeare is said to have written *The Merry Wives of Windsor* at the request of Elizabeth I, performed for her at the castle in 1593. Riverside station has ornate iron and glass, in Tudor style with another royal waiting room.

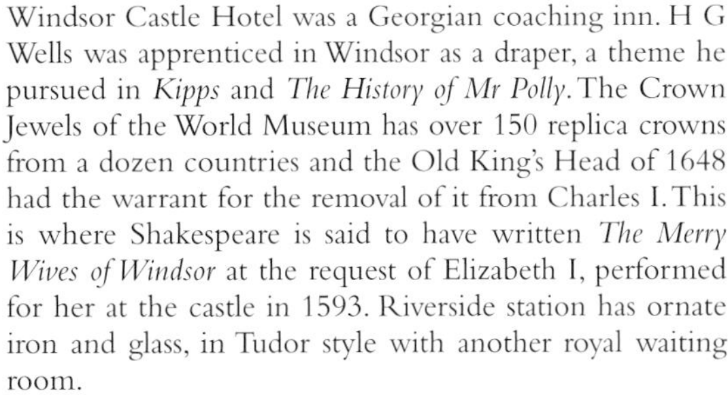

Thomas Sandby painted a watercolour of a UFO after he saw, with some eminent scientists, a lit spherical object under the clouds on 18th August 1783. It stopped, changed colour, divided, exploded and disappeared. The painting is now in the British Museum. It may be significant that the Montgolfier brothers had made the world's first balloon flight on 5th June and that the first recorded launching of a hydrogen balloon was to follow later that year. The world's first airmail flight landed here from Hendon in 1911.

Windsor hosts the Windsor Festival Spring Weekend, Windsor Festival and Fringe Festival in the autumn. The 100km^2 Home Park has the Royal Windsor Horse Show and Windsor Championship Dog Show.

Eton boathouses are for wet bobs. Rowing was forbidden before 1840 so boys who were doing so shirked by covering their faces with their arms when stopped by masters. Things have changed with the *Eton Boating Song* and a ceremony on June 4th below the House on the Bridge, in the Romney weirstream, where rowers stand up and shake flowers out of their boaters. The location is not ideal. In the 1970s the Thames Water Authority, now the Environment Agency, installed anti-scour weirs, which were known to be lethal, at a number of Thames locks. This is one of those which has killed since then. Romney Weir now supplies a third of Windsor Castle's power. A pumping station may contain a Victorian steam engine used to supply water to the castle.

Eton College was founded in 1440 by Henry VI in preparation for Cambridge. Pupils wear pinstripe trousers, wing collars and black tail coats in mourning for George III, a score of them having gone on to become prime ministers. The chapel, intended to be the choir of a building the size of a cathedral, is one of the three best Perpendicular buildings in existence, no worse for its 15th century miracle wall paintings. Eton's quad was used for filming *Chariots of Fire*. Wellington, an old Etonian, may have said that Waterloo was won on the playing fields of Eton while another former pupil, Thomas Gray, wrote his *Ode on a Distant Prospect of Eton College*. George Orwell was an old Etonian and fictional pupils included Bertie Wooster, Tarzan, Captain Hook and James Bond.

The Christopher Hotel was a coaching inn. The Cockpit Restaurant was used for cockfighting in the 17th and 18th centuries, Charles II being a spectator, with stocks and a Victorian postbox in front in the form of a Doric

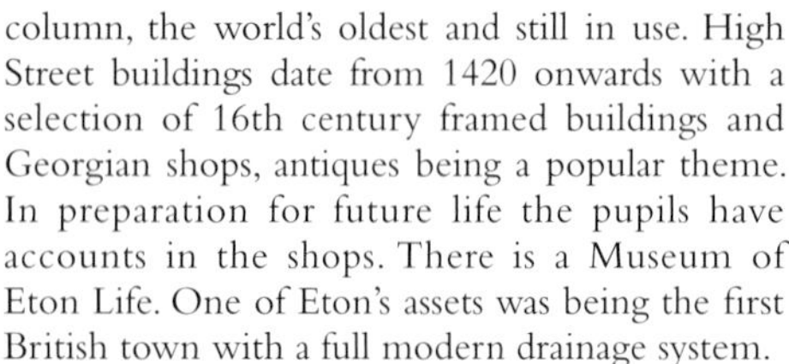

column, the world's oldest and still in use. High Street buildings date from 1420 onwards with a selection of 16th century framed buildings and Georgian shops, antiques being a popular theme. In preparation for future life the pupils have accounts in the shops. There is a Museum of Eton Life. One of Eton's assets was being the first British town with a full modern drainage system.

Swan Uppers drink a toast to the Queen while standing in their boats in Romney Lock.

Black Pott's railway bridge was built in 1849 by Sir Joseph Lock to carry the Windsor & Eton Riverside–Staines line, with decoration by Sir William Tite. An angling lodge was used by Isaak Walton and by Charles II near where the Jubilee River rejoins.

Herne's Oak near Victoria Bridge blew down in 1863. Herne or Cernunnos, the Celtic god of the underworld, has stag's antlers and rides a black horse. He appeared in 1962 after youths blew a hunting horn in the park. It is a criminal offence to land in Home Park, where the royal boathouse housed the Royal Barge until 1953.

Beyond a golf course and a house with a large water slide is the 1967 concrete Victoria Bridge, carrying the B470 on a site used in 1851. It forms a pair with the 1928 brick Albert Bridge carrying the B3201. Albert had these built in place of Datchet Bridge, which he had removed in 1848 because the councils could not agree on funding and the method of construction, the Berkshire end being in iron and the Buckinghamshire end in wood.

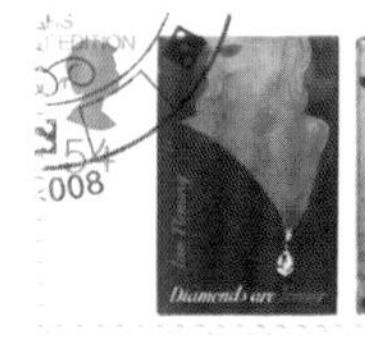

A **Datchet** housing estate has the graves of 30 cats in coffins, the whim of Lady Cholmondley. The church has a 13th century chancel and a more conventional memorial to Christopher Barker, Elizabeth I's printer. Herschal built the world's largest telescope here and, in 1895, Evelyn Ellis became the first Briton to own a car, a Panhard-Levassor, founding the RAC. There was a serious collision in 1881 between railway engines involved in snow clearance. The conspicuous transport forms of today are aircraft, the flight path from Heathrow being 6km away. Boaters may note Kris Cruisers. This is where Falstaff was thrown in the Thames in *The Merry Wives of Windsor*. Laura La Plante, Billie Whitelaw and Donald Pleasance have all been local residents.

Frogmore House, built in 1680 with Tuscan columns, was bought in 1792 for Queen Charlotte and was a favourite with both Victoria and Albert and George V and Mary. Earl Mountbatten of Burma was born here in 1900 and a 17th century mural was uncovered in the 20th century. The Royal Mausoleum where Victoria and Albert are buried has marble statues of them, a copper roof over granite and Portland stone, Raphael paintings and a granite sarcophagus. The Prince Consort's Home Farm is here, as are the Royal Gardens.

The New Cut was made in 1822, leaving Ham Island with sewage works and a bird sanctuary. At the far end of the cut is **Old Windsor** Lock. Friday Island is named from its footprint shape, the home of Dr Julius Grant, who invented Marmite and edible paper for secret agents and who showed that the *Hitler Diaries* were a forgery.

The 13th century Norman church of Sts Peter & Andrew is on the site of a Saxon minster. It has the grave of Mary Robinson, the mistress of the Prince Regent in 1779, who sat for Gainsborough, Romney and Reynolds and was known as the Fair Perdita from her part in *Florizel & Perdita*, based on *The Winter's Tale*. There is a monument to Thomas Sandby, the founder of the Royal Academy, who gave London Zoo its first hippopotamus. It is by the site of the wooden Anglo-Saxon palace of Edward the Confessor, where the synod of 1072 agreed that the Archbishop of Canterbury took precedence over

Windsor Castle seen across Home Park.

the Archbishop of York. It was a royal residence until 1110. King John had a royal hunting lodge here. As the name suggests, this was the original site of Windsor.

Wraysbury's gravel pits and reservoirs have 20% of the British wintering smew and a cormorant roost. Beryl Reid lived at Wraysbury's Honeypot Cottage and collected stray cats.

Friary Island is not obvious from the rest of the bank but the Bells of Ouzeley is conspicuous. Osney monks, fleeing the Dissolution on rafts, took the abbey bells with them and hid them in the ooze. They were never found. One of the first V2 rockets fell close to here in 1944.

The south bank now becomes Surrey. Pats Croft Eyot is followed by Lutyens' gatehouses at Runnymead-on-Thames. The John F Kennedy Memorial of 1965 in Portland stone is on 4,000m^2 of land given to the USA. Magna Carta Island, no longer an island, is where King John is thought to have signed this document, put to him in 1215. The American constitution was to be based upon it. One clause included removing all fish weirs from the Thames. Another possible venue was an island owned by Ankerwyke nunnery, under a yew tree up to 2,000 years old, badly damaged in the 1987 storm and also having been used by Henry VIII to court Anne Boleyn. The American Bar Association added a Magna Carta temple memorial in 1957. Four years earlier the 2.4ha Commonwealth Air Forces Memorial had been built with the names of 20,456 Allied airmen with no known graves.

Cooper's Hill had the East India Company's engineering school, taken over by the Royal Indian Engineering College to train engineers for the Government of India's Public Works Department with eminent staff until 1906. Later it became the home of Baroness Cheylesmore, the 1939 war headquarters for London County Council, a teacher training college then Brunel University. Fairhaven Lodges were also by Lutyens.

The river loops round the remains of a priory. Bell Weir Lock takes its name from former ferryman Charlie Bell. The current crossings come together next to the Colne Brook confluence. Ove Arup's balanced cantilever concrete bridge of 1980 for the M25 matches the lines of Lutyens' existing brick bridge for the A30, A30 carriageways now on each side outside the M25 for the crossing. In front of Queensmead Lake Reservoir, Holme Island hides Hollybrook Island, used by Edward VIII and Wallace Simpson. The river is now entirely in Surrey.

A glassfibre replica of the 1285 London Stone marks the start of the jurisdiction of the City of London. Richard I sold the navigation rights to the Corporation of London in 1197 to raise funds for his crusades. This was the tidal limit until 1812, when locks were built downstream. The original stone is in Staines' Flemish style Old Town Hall Arts Centre of 1880. Sir Walter Raleigh had been condemned for treason in 1603 in an earlier hall here when the court was moved out of London to avoid the plague. Church Island has St Mary's, built in 1828 by Inigo Jones on a 1631 tower base.

Staines-on-Thames takes its name from stones around Chertsey Abbey. The Roman Pontes took its name from its bridges, the road from Silchester to London crossing a bridge built here in about 43. A 1791 bridge in stone failed because of its shallow foundations and a cast iron single span of 1803 failed when its abutments moved apart. The current Grade II Staines Bridge by George Rennie, carrying the A308, has three segmental river arches of white Aberdeen granite, the centre one with a 23m span, and eight further spans. Many Anglo-Saxon kings were crowned in the town, which has Memorial Gardens.

The River Colne is the other river implied in the Two Rivers shopping centre, built on the site of the 1862 linoleum factory which closed in 1969, a bronze statue of two lino workers being sited in the High Street. Staines also had the Lagonda factory, winning Le Mans in 1935.

Amenities include Jimmy Spices, the Slug & Lettuce, the Swan Hotel and the Staines-upon-Thames. Staines Boat Club and Strodes College Boat Club precede Tims Boatyard. The three arched Staines Railway Bridge of 1856 carries the Reading–Waterloo line and is painted grey with yellow stripes so that swans can see it. St Peter's church of 1894 was by Sir Edward Clarke, the lawyer who built and lived in the adjacent house, now the vicarage.

Penton Hook Lock has an 1814 Regency lock cottage and cuts off a loop of the river which makes 20m progress in 800m. The loop was used in 1665 as a plague burial ground. Penton Hook Marina, by the loop, is the largest inland marina in Europe with 575 berths.

Laleham, named after twigs or willows, has Georgian houses. The 2nd Earl of Lucan built the neo-Classical Laleham House with Doric porch in 1803. The Barn was built in 1909 by Sir Edward Maufe for Marie Studholme and named after her music hall song *The Little Dutch Barn*. The 12th century All Saints' church has an 18th century brick tower. Matthew Arnold, born here, was buried in the churchyard with his father, Thomas. The Tudor Lucan chapel has the grave of the 3rd Lord Lucan, who ordered the Charge of the Light Brigade at Balaclava, wanted the large Norman pillars removed from the church and objected to the swans which fouled his 9ha of fields, threatening to shoot six a week until there were just six left. The 7th Lord Lucan disappeared in 1974 after the murder of his children's nanny. Gabrielle Anwar was born here. The golf course opposite adjoins an enclosure and screams carry across from Thorpe Park, Britain's first theme park in 1979. Some of the stone from Laleham Abbey was used for building Hampton Court but apartments are now sited here.

More gravel pits accompany the river as it approaches the M3 and is joined by the Abbey River, probably dug for Chertsey Abbey. Chertsey Lock was sited below the confluence so that it did not spoil Lord Lucan's view.

Chertsey Bridge was first built in 1410. The current one dates from 1785, Grade II by James Paine. There are five Purbeck stone segmental arches over the river, two towpath arches and four more buried, the main span being 13m. It featured in *Oliver Twist*.

Chersey, founded in 666, has a Sheila Mitchell bronze statue of Blanche Heriot, who held onto the church bell clapper to prevent it from striking while her lover, a soldier in the Wars of the Roses condemned to die when the curfew bell rang, waited for a messenger to return with a pardon from the king.

The river winds between a marina, duck houses and sets of powerlines to the Chertsey Meads ferry point. A large moat stands back from the river by Dumpsey Mead. Pharaoh's Island was given to Nelson after the Battle of the Nile, actor Ian Hendry later living here. The Thames Court pub follows.

The river braids at Shepperton Lock, below which the River Wey joins. Shepperton ferry has provided a connection to Weybridge since the time of Henry VI. Nauticalia, a source of boating gifts and oddities, is based here.

Sir Arthur Sullivan had his Ladye Place on D'Oyley Carte Island with its willows and it was here that Gilbert and Sullivan wrote *Tit Willow* for *The Mikado*.

The Desborough Cut of 1935 bypasses Shepperton. The natural course of the river loops past Desborough Sailing Club, the Warren Lodge Hotel and the Red Lion at Shepperton, meaning shepherd's farm. The 1614 church with its 1710 brick tower replaced an earlier church damaged by floods. It has the grave of Thomas Love Peacock following a library fire at Peacock House. Novelist George Meredith lived in Vine Cottage and carol writer J M Neale was brought up in the vicarage, often visited by Desiderius Erasmus. There is the ghost of a monk from Chertsey Abbey who left to live with a woman but was pursued and beheaded. The King's Head was used by Charles II and Nell Gwynn and the Anchor Hotel is used by Shepperton Studios film casts. Film director John Boorman was born here and writer J G Ballard lived here. Shepperton Manor had the longest lawn on the Thames until some of it was sold for a public park, where George Eliot wrote *Scenes from Clerical Life* and John Bright was a regular visitor, writing his speech opposing the Crimean War here. A medieval dugout was taken from the silt in the 1960s. George Meredith lived at Lower Halliford, holy ford. The Desborough Cut with its speed markers rejoins beyond a waterworks and has Embridge Canoe Club, one of the country's leading racing clubs.

Coway Stakes were causeway stakes, visible in the 7th century and possibly the remains of fish traps. This is where Caesar crossed the Thames in 674 and fought Cassivellaunus.

Walton Bridge was an ugly structure erected as a temporary measure in 1953, following war damage. It was finally replaced in 2013 by a thrust arch bridge with a 90m clear span for the A244. Earlier bridges here were painted by Canaletto and Turner. A slip follows with Walton and Shepperton Marinas, the Sea Cadets' TS Black Swan, the Anglers and the Swan Inn where Jerome Kern met the landlord's daughter, Eva, marrying her in St Mary's in 1910. The church has Saxon foundations, Norman pillars, a 15th century tower, a copy of a scold's bridle, the huge 1740s Louis Roubillac tomb of Viscount Shannon which blocked out light, a good sculpture of Sarah D'Oyley and the grave of cricketer Edward Lumpy Stevens whose accurate bowling resulted in the introduction of the central stump.

Walton-on-Thames was a serfs' farm. Hersham & Walton Motors built the HWM racing cars used in the 1950s by Stirling Moss. The 15th century manor house, which has been occupied by judge George Jeffreys and by John Bradshaw, who sentenced Charles I to death, has the ghost of a judge. Sir Arthur Sullivan lived in River House. Walton Reach is used by terrapins and for regattas. Julie Andrews was born in Walton.

Walton wharf sent timber to London in Tudor times and Wheatley's Ait was used for osiers until the 1880s, then had bachelor residents. To avoid the English Channel during the Second World War, petrol was taken to Avonmouth, delivered to a terminal here and then taken down the Thames by tanker to Fulham and Vauxhall.

Sunbury was Sunna's stronghold. On this reach are the Thames Valley Skiff Club, the Weir Hotel and the Cloven Barrow Bronze Age burial mound at a Bronze and Iron Age settlement. T Harrison Chaplin, the riparian service contractors, were founded in 1907 and pioneered environmentally friendly bank protection, becoming part of Greenham in 1998. Oliver Twist and Bill Sykes slept under the yew in the churchyard of the Victorian St Mary's with its Georgian tower and cupola before committing their Shepperton robbery.

The 1812 Regency lock cottage is at a former lock site. The current Sunbury Lock of 1927 has a mechanized chamber with an additional manual chamber which can be brought into use at peak times. The lock cottage here is mock Georgian. This is where Swan Upping starts.

The Walled Garden contains the 7.6m Sunbury Millennium Embroidery.

The Knight and Bessborough Reservoirs have a pumping station which still has a 1911 triple expansion steam engine. Molesey Reservoirs feed a waterworks with a battery of filter beds and a 2.6m diameter concrete tunnel to the Lea valley.

Kempton Park horse racecourse was opened in 1889. Monksbridge has a topiary teddybear by the Prince of Wales for his mistress, Freda, wife of his host, MP William Dudley Ward. Diana Dors danced on the tables when it became the Club de Clio in the 1950s. At the 1970s home of David Gilmour, the tennis court surround inspired *The Wall* for Pink Floyd. Aquarius Sailing Club is on this reach.

The City of London post indicates that coal arriving is subject to tax. The red and white Sunbury Court of about 1770 is now the Salvation Army Youth Centre.

West Molesey or mul's island is where Thorneycroft made float planes and plywood torpedo boats on Platt's Eyot.

Hampton was the farm on the great bend, where Hampton Ferry crossed, in use by 1519. Hampton Sailing Club acted as Ravensbeck police station in London Weekend TV's *Duck Patrol* series. The 1831 Gothic church is on a 14th century site. Next door is the house of Edward VI's childhood nurse, also used by *Radio Times* illustrator Eric Fraser. Garrick lived in Hampton House from 1714, remodelled by Robert Adam in a garden by Capability Brown, now Garrick's Villa apartments. Garrick's 1755 Temple was a tribute to Shakespeare and had a Roubillac bust of the bard, now in the British Museum. Garrick was painted here in 1762 by Zoffany and Garrick's Ait is one of the islands on this reach.

Fred Karno's 1913 houseboat *Astoria* became Vesta Victoria's then David Gilmour's recording studio, used for *On an Island*.

Bushy Park was established in the 16th century, covering 4.5km^2, and has fallow and red deer and a 1.4km Chestnut Avenue to Wren's Diana Fountain. After the Dissolution Henry VIII tried to link it to Windsor Forest as a continuous hunting ground. Hurst Park, on the south bank, had duelling, a fatal bare knuckle fight in 1816, early cricket and golf matches and horse races until 1910, the first Molesey lock keeper being killed by a racehorse. There is still a Bushy Park riding school.

Tagg's Island was named after a waterman with a boatyard. Fred Karno had a circus here, a music hall and a Karsino, attracting the famous including the Prince of Wales with Lillie Langtree and Alice Keppel and discovering many of the leading performers such as Charlie Chaplin, Stan Laurel, Will Hay, Max Miller and Flanagan and Allen, known as Karno's Army. Sarah Bernhardt lived here. The 1889 Swiss chalet was opposite and Molesey Boat Club is based in East Molesey.

St Mary's church was rebuilt in the 1860s with old toll bridge posts to deter bodysnatchers. The adjacent Bell dates from about 1450.

Hampton Court Bridge was built in 1933 by Lutyens with three concrete spans faced with red brick to match the palace. Carrying the A309, it is the fourth on the site. The first was the world's largest ever Chinoiserie bridge with its toll house in the Carlton Mitre Hotel, painted by Alfred Sisley.

Overlooking Albany Reach is the red brick Tudor Hampton Court Palace, converted in 1514 for Cardinal Wolsey from a Knights Hospitaller house. It was given to Henry VIII and Anne Boleyn in 1529 in exchange for Richmond Palace, perhaps not enthusiastically by Wolsey, who was beheaded the following year. It was England's largest house and the best secular building. Using stone from Chertsey Abbey after the Dissolution, it has 1,000 rooms, a great gatehouse, state apartments, a great hall with hammerbeam roof, all different chimneys, Tijous gates in 17th century wrought iron, a chapel and Tudor kitchens. The Tudor tennis courts were the world's oldest while the clocktower with Nicholas Oursian's 1540 astronomical clock includes the time of high water at London Bridge. The 1690 maze by William of Orange is the world's most famous maze, not least because of its description in *Three Men in a Boat*, the world's oldest surviving puzzle maze with the need to find the way out as well as in. It covers 1,300m^2 and has 800m of

Garick's Temple tribute to Shakespeare at Hampton.

paths, numerous copies having been made around the world. Twin 76mm diameter lead pipes of 1531 bring clean water under the Thames from Coombe Hill. The orangery has Raphael cartoons, which were priced so ludicrously that they introduced the current meaning of the word. This oldest Tudor palace in England has 3,000 weapons, arms, armour, tapestries, fine paintings and, on the king's staircase, Verrio paintings of all of Henry's chambermaid conquests. Some of the best gardens in England cover 24ha and include a 1924 knot garden in Elizabethan style with formal, woodland and wilderness gardens, avenues, mistletoe and the world's oldest and largest vine, the Great Vine planted in 1769 by Capability Brown, its girth 2.1m and its branches up to 35m long, all within the 2.8km^2 Hampton Court Park. Hampton Court Palace Flower Show, the world's largest horticultural show, has been run since 1990 and there is an annual Hampton Court Palace Festival.

Henry engaged Jane Seymour here in 1536 although she died the following year giving birth to Edward VI. Henry married and lived here with Catherine Parr. Queen Mary and Philip of Spain had their honeymoon here. James I's Hampton Court Conference of 1604 resulted in the *Authorized King James Bible*. Charles I lived here and was imprisoned here in 1647, escaping by Thames before being recaptured and executed. The palace was used by Cromwell after abolishing the monarchy. Charles II was given a pair of Venetian gondolas and four gondoliers. Shakespeare performed here. William of Orange used the palace during the Glorious Revolution and had a Baroque façade added by Sir Christopher Wren in 1689 as he wished to surpass Versailles. He died here in 1702 from injuries after his horse trod on a molehill. Anne held court here, as recorded by Pope in the *Rape of the Lock*. In the 1870s it was used by the Thames Conservancy to rear fish to release into the Thames.

There are ghosts here of Henry VIII, Edward VI's nurse Sybil Penn, Jane Seymour and Catherine Howard, the latter shrieking as she is led away. The palace was used in filming *A Man for All Seasons*. Author Captain W E Johns lived in Park House.

The shallop *The Lady Mayoress* is pulled down to Greenwich in the wake of Henry VIII to raise funds for the Philip Henman Foundation and with lady passengers because of the drowning of a Lady of the Bedchamber in a capsize near London Bridge in 1264.

The River Mole or Ember joins opposite the palace. Dittons Skiff & Punting Club and Harts Boatyard are at Thames Ditton, ditch farm, and AC Cars were here. Thames Ditton Island has timber houses. The 11th century St Nicholas' church has a small spire and the 13th century Olde Swan was used by Henry VIII.

In the park, the 1700 red brick Pavilion built by Wren as a summerhouse for William III was used by Cecil King of Daily Mirror Newspapers, who suggested a military coup under Mountbatten to replace the Wilson government. There is also a Hampton Court Palace Golf Club.

Devizes–Westminster Race support crews need extensive abilities, here route finding at Molesey Lock.

Surbiton was the southern homestead. Local residents have included anti-apartheid campaigner Donald Woods and first British astronaut Helen Sharman.

By Queen's Reach the Seething Wells were therapeutic springs. The Thames Sailing Club is on the bank before Raven's Ait, which was used in the BBC's *The Good Life*.

The Hogsmill River joins after being crossed by the 13th century Clattern Bridge. HMV's trademark dog, Nipper, was buried in 1895 in front of what is now Lloyds Bank. All Saint's church, part 13th century, has a 14th century pillar painting of St Blaise and was the setting for some of John Millais' paintings including *My First Sermon*. Holy Trinity chapel was built by the Shipman's Guild, later Trinity House, next to a Saxon church site.

Edward Lapidge's Kingston Bridge of 1828 takes the A308 back over the river on a seven arched structure of Portland stone, five of the arches over the river, the central arch an 18m span. A Roman ford site here was used by Caesar. The landlady of the Queen's Head was ducked

The ferry landing for Hampton Court.

here in 1745 for scolding, one of the last cases to get the punishment. The Bishop Out of Residence is on the site of a house used in the 14th century by William of Wykeham, Bishop of Winchester, when going to Southwark. There is an Italianate town hall and a golden statue of Queen Anne. This is where the *Three Men in a Boat* hired their skiff and where Twickenham Sea Cadets are based. On the other bank at Hampton Wick is the 1850 Italianate St Raphael's church.

The three arches of Kingston Railway Bridge carry the line from **New Malden** to Teddington.

Kingston upon Thames takes its name from Cyninges-tun, a Celtic king's manor, a royal town from 933. Charles I's charter forbids any other market within 11km. King Egbert held a Great Council in 838. The King or Coronation Stone, the earliest English throne, is in front of the Guildhall and was used to crown seven Anglo-Saxon kings from Eadweard the Elder in 901 to Æthelred the Unready in 979, whose investiture stone remains. Alfred had been crowned here in an attempt to unite Mercia and the Saxons against the Danes in St Mary's Saxon chapel, which collapsed because of grave digging in 1730, killing the sexton. It was next to the remaining Norman All Saints'. There has been a market here for 700 years at what was the lowest safe crossing point on the river for livestock. Born here were authors John Cleland and John Galsworthy, an early cinema photographer who proved that horses leave the ground when galloping, Donald Campbell, racing car driver John Cooper and actor Jonny Lee Miller.

Canbury Gardens promenade was known as Perfume Parade because of the smells from a fertilizer factory. Kingston Rowing Club and the Leander (Kingston) Sea Scout Group add to the activity on the river with Albany Park Canoe and Sailing Centre. The Tamesis Club sail A rated boats. On Trowlock Island is the Royal Canoe Club, founded in 1866 as the world's first canoe club, with the Prince of Wales as a member. It incorporates the Kingston Royals dragon boat racing crews.

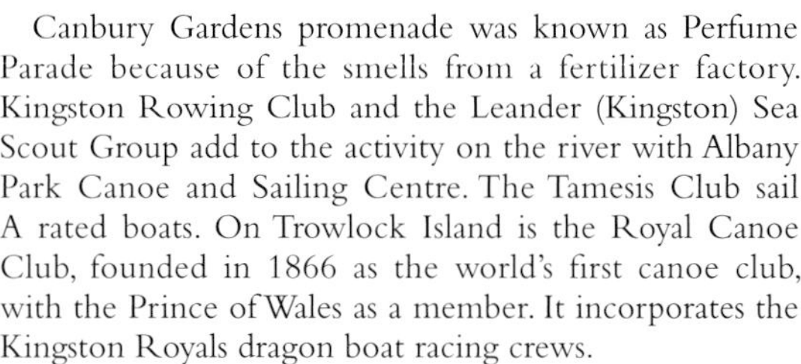

Broom Water is a natural creek which has been extended. By it is Teddington Hockey Club of 1871, which was the world's oldest and invented the rules, and the Shell sports ground.

Teddington was named after the 14th century Tuda's family. R D Blackmore used the royalties from *Lorna Doone*, written here, to attempt to fund an unsuccessful market gardening business.

Teddington Weir is the longest on the Thames, discharging an average 81m^3/s although it can reach 350m^3/s in the winter. The 1947 flood recorded 714m^3/s but water was pumped to flow upstream during the 1976 drought. Built in 1811, the weir was damaged in 1827 by ice and there were further breaches later in the century. A long suspended footbridge crosses the river above the locks. Teddington Lock was also built in 1811 but had to be rebuilt in 1858 as the removal of the Old London Bridge in 1848 had dropped the water level at the cill by 760mm although there was still enough for a tug to pass through in 1906 during a flood without having to open the gates. E M Forster may have been confused by this when he had Henry Wilcox taking shares in the lock in *Howards End*. From here the water is tidal but held over the lower part of the cycle by **Richmond** Half Tide

Leander Sea Scouts, a hive of activity in the summer.

Lock. Water has not been the only problem. In the early 19th century there were repeated attacks on the lock house so guns and a bayonet were supplied.

Next to the weir are Thames Television Studios, owned by Pinewood, having produced many comedy films and programmes including *The Avengers*, *This is Your Life*, *Opportunity Knocks* and *Pop Idol*. The Landmark Arts Centre is also here, as is the Haymarket Media Group, who are Britain's largest independent publishers. The Anglers public house backs onto the river with a 'No fishing' notice while the Tide End Cottage faces Ferry Lane and an area which can be used for unloading small craft although it often floods at high water. The Thames Path continues to the Thames Barrier, using both banks most of the way.

There are moorings below the weir and the British Motor Yacht Club have their base. A plaque recalls the 100 Little Ships assembled here in the Second World War by the former Toughs Boatyard with headquarters in the Tide End for Operation Dynamo to help rescue British and French troops from Dunkirk beaches.

St Mary with St Alban's church is based on Clermont-Ferrand cathedral after the vicar and churchwarden paid a visit in 1889 and wanted one like it. Its choristers have included Noël Coward.

The Boundary Stone of 1909 marks where Environment Agency control passes to the Port of **London** Authority.

Strawberry Hill was Horace Walpole's Gothic revival fantasy castle, spawning the Strawberry Hill Gothic style, where he wrote the first Gothic novel, *The Castle of Otranto*.

Former gravel pits have become Ham Local Nature Reserve, home of Thames Young Mariners, an active watersports centre. At dawn, or even before, on Easter Monday this is the start of the final leg of the staged section of the Devizes–Westminster canoe race. A water skiing area adds further activity at Cross Deep, off Swan Island or Chillingworth Ait.

Pope's Grotto is a set of tunnels under the A310 to connect his former house with his riverside gardens, the tunnels lined with geological specimens. Fielding wrote *Tom Jones* locally.

The Royal Canoe Club, the world's oldest.

Distance
225km from Cricklade to Teddington

Navigation Authority
Environment Agency

Navigation Society
River Thames Society
www.riverthamessociety.org.uk

OS 1:50,000 Sheets
163 Cheltenham & Cirencester
164 Oxford
(173 Swindon & Devizes)
174 Newbury & Wantage
175 Reading & Windsor
176 West London

Connections
Oxford Canal – see CoB p45
Kennet & Avon Canal – see CoB p106
Tidal River Thames – see RoB p213

45 River Wey Navigation

Placid but potentially explosive

When rivers were canalized in England, long ago,
For economic transporting of commerce to and fro,
The Wey stream's navigation was to Godalming begun,
And first became a water-way in 1651;
Connecting with the Basingstoke canal, now in decay,
And with the Wey and Arun one, long derelict today.
John Pitt

Godalming town bridge formerly carried the A3.

Capturing the headwaters of the Blackwater has strengthened the River Wey, in which the level can rise rapidly after rain and which has a moderate flow rate even in dry times. It winds its way northwards from Haslemere to the River Thames, cutting through the chalk North Downs at Guildford on its journey, running through the Surrey Hills AONB, and has a towpath throughout.

The Wey was improved from 1618 and made navigable for barges from 1653 after 14km of cut had been made. It was one of the earliest navigations and made use of pairs of rising gates to act as locks. The navigation takes barges to 80t. It was prosperous with peak traffic in 1838. The Godalming Navigation above Guildford was a separate business from the River Wey Navigation. The Basingstoke Canal increased traffic at the lower end from 1796. The navigation carried agricultural produce, timber and Farnham pottery to London, bringing back manufactured goods and grain. It came into the hands of the Stevens family of which Harry Stevens managed to hold motorized lighters at bay as he preferred horsedrawn barges and used them until 1960. He only used timber for bank protection and then only when absolutely necessary. Its major use now is as a cruising waterway, especially as it is mostly rural although close to London. The River Wey Navigation was given to the National Trust in 1964, followed by the Godalming Navigation in 1968. Commercial traffic ceased the following year. Jerome K Jerome said in *Three Men in a Boat* that he had intended to explore it but never got round to it.

Godalming Wharf, the most southerly point on the network.

Apart from the southern Stratford-upon-Avon Canal, this is the only waterway where the National Trust have been the navigation authority, not always happily as some serious allegations of mismanagement were put to the National Trust's AGMs in the 1990s.

The river is blocked at **Godalming** by the town bridge which carries the A3100, the A3 until 1934. This medieval bridge was rebuilt in 1782 to a similar design to those used for Cobham and Leatherhead, five red brick arches of 3.9–4.5m span, Portland stone string courses and capping, semicircular pedestrian refuges on stone trumpets and blind occuli near each end of the brickwork.

Godalming takes its Saxon name from the Old English Godhelm. In medieval times its industry was cloth, especially the Hampshire Kersies blue, of which it had the best colour in England. A knitwear factory has been a more recent version of the trade. A commuter base, it was formerly a Regency town with 16–18th century Tudor and Stuart half-timbered houses. It was a staging post on the Portsmouth–London road. Peter the Great stayed at the King's Arms & Royal Hotel in 1698, ate well and had a rowdy party with a score of friends but failed to pay the bill. Glasses and other objects are still mysteriously thrown about the room they used. Another Russian, Czar Alexander I, dined in more civilized manner in 1816.

The local General James Oglethorpe, who founded Georgia in 1732, brought back ten Yamacraw Indians, quite a topic of local conversation. It was claimed that the son of Sir Theophilus Oglethorpe of Westbrook Place was swapped for a stillborn son of Mary, wife of James II, who had many miscarriages and no other surviving child, this child going on to become the Old Pretender. A ghost in a brown cloak often seen in the twilight is said to be the Young Pretender, who met supporters here before the 1745 Rising. There is a Godalming Museum and a museum of local history in the octagonal pepperbox Old Town Hall of 1814, built on eight arches on a site which was in use by 1086.

The church of Sts Peter & Paul has two Saxon windows which were found blocked up in 1890. The town has a Phillips Memorial garden to the chief wireless telegraphist of the *Titanic*, one of the more noteworthy posts in maritime history.

Godalming Wharf is the most southerly point on the connected canal network, base for the horse-drawn trip boat *Iona*. The dock was filled in 1832 but the wharf remained commercial until 1950. The area is now surrounded by Sainsbury and other large stores.

Improvements below here had been made by Smeaton by 1763 for the Chilworth gunpowder trade although the banks were to burst in 1795. The river crosses water meadows edged by cow parsley, alders, willows and elders as is characteristic of leafy Surrey and used by mallards and swans.

Below Catteshall Lock and bridge are the moorings of Farncombe Boat House, which hires out narrowboats, rowing boats and canoes, and Hectors on the Wey bistro.

Ivy festoons Trowers bridge, an unusual design with a flat centre span joining two red brick approaches with low semicircular arches.

The Manor Inn faces Broadwater Park Golf Course. Hurdle weave protection edges the bank in places but yellow irises are much more extensive in season.

Godalming above a summer dawn mist, from Catteshall Lock.

Buttercup meadows occupy the land between the cut and the natural river channel and broom surrounds a pillbox, one of a number defending the line of the river against invasion.

Unstead Lock is in Peasmarsh where a railway bridge has been replaced by a cycle and footbridge.

Gun's Mouth is the confluence with the River Tillingham, from which gunpowder was carried in punts to Stonebridge Wharf, named Gunpowder Wharf from 1764 until 1920, sending it to Godalming for onward carriage to Portsmouth from 1780 to 1815. An alternative from 1816 was the Wey & Arun Junction Canal, closed in 1871 but being restored. The Wey - South Path follows the river to Guildford, lilies and Canada geese adding to its rural feel.

The lattice Broadford bridge takes the A248 away round the Parrot Inn. The heavy girder Shalford railway bridge, taking the Guildford–Redhill line, has two bosses which seem unnecessarily large as they project down and obstruct the navigation, needing to be protected by piles in the middle of the river.

Shalford, from shallow ford, has Tudor buildings and the 18th century timber framed Shalford Mill which ceased working in 1914. It is thought that Bunyan lived in Shalford, the Pilgrims' Way between Winchester and Canterbury gave him the title for *The Pilgrim's Progress* and this was the original Slough of Despond.

Beyond St Catherine's Lock the wooded ridge of the South Downs, steeper on its south side, rises ahead, to be cut by the river. Gorse adds colour as highland cattle relax by the river. A sharp corner has a post fitted with a roller to assist tow ropes, more to follow below Guildford, all in surprisingly good condition despite being unused for over half a century.

In 1864 a gunpowder boat exploded, killing its two crew and sinking the boat, heard 30km away in Pallingham. Gunpowder boats were not allowed to moor in Guildford but one had been moored there illegally two years earlier, 50m from a timberyard which was destroyed by fire. The operator had refused to go to it to take it away to safety and had been lucky on that occasion.

Moorhens rush away from rowers, who turn above St Catherine's footbridge, but crayfish are unseen. The bridge carries the Pilgrims' Way and its modern counterpart, the North Downs Way, replacing a former ferry although an earlier route may have taken pilgrims along the bank of the river for some distance. On top of the hill is St Catherine's chapel ruin while Pilgrim Cottage has a mosaic of St Christopher on the chimney.

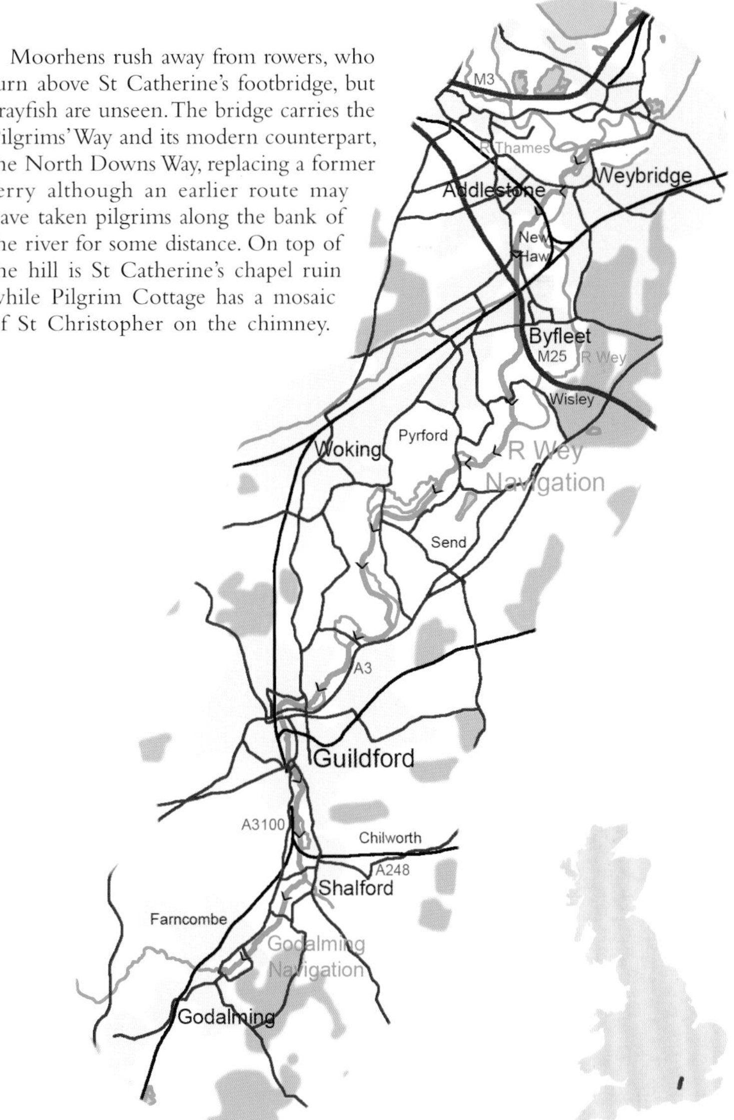

Ivy envelops Trowers bridge at Farncombe.

Scots pines near the Wey at Peasmarsh.

Piles protect a railway bridge projection at Shalford.

There were holy springs here with medicinal properties and a Victorian grotto. The golden sand spilling down the hillside could have given the gold ford, for **Guildford**, or the name could have come from the Old English gylde, marigold.

Large beech trees on the left are pale green in spring, darkening to rust-coloured in autumn, overlooking weeping willows which edge meadows of summer buttercups, in the past flooded in winter for skating.

Guildford Rowing Club and Quarry Hill footbridge begin the obviously built-up part of Guildford. The county town of Surrey, it was founded on wool but had not over-impressed Defoe.

What was known to generations as the Jolly Farmer is now the Boatman. Guildford Boathouse hires out narrowboats, rowing boats, punts and canoes. Opposite is a weirpool which has been used for canoe slaloms including, on the only occasion it has been held, the Oxford and Cambridge intervarsity event when Cambridge trounced Oxford.

Millmead Lock has old telegraph poles as balance beams.

The ruins of the three storey keep of the Plantagenet Guildford Castle for Henry II are now set in gardens. It was here that a disguised woodman told how his son had been drowned in the Silent Pool at Shere while trying to rescue his bathing teenage sister, who had also drowned trying to resist the advances of a stranger. John, the Prince Regent, said the murderer would be punished, forgetting that he was the perpetrator until evidence was produced in the castle. History does not say who witnessed the events at the pool. Noted for its acting by the river is the 1965 Yvonne Arnaud Theatre. A sculpture of Alice and the White Rabbit is a reminder that Lewis Carroll died here in 1898.

The White House is at the foot of the steep cobbled High Street on the other side of the river. Founded in 1507 was the Tudor Royal Grammar School, endowed in 1553 by Edward VI and with a chained library. The Tudor Abbot's Hospital with its Jacobean gatehouse, domed turrets and cupola, was founded in 1619 by local George Abbot, Archbishop of Canterbury for 22 years, and serves as almshouses for elderly residents. Formerly a courtroom and council chamber, the 16th century guildhall with 17th century façade has an ornate 1683 bracket clock with later works extending over the road, a hexagonal bell turret, civic plate and a set of standard weights presented by Elizabeth I, one of the few complete sets.

About January 27th two poor servant maids of good report not living in an inn or alehouse shake dice for the interest on £400 left in the 1674 will of John How.

St Catherine's Lock as the river cuts into the South Downs.

St Catherine's footbridge and the sandy hillside.

The first English bull baiting took place in Guildford in the 14th century, each member of the corporation in turn having to provide a bull and breakfast for the other members, a practice which died out in the 19th century. Guildford punk band the Stranglers have more recently provided their own kind of mayhem.

The Guildford House Gallery in a 1660 town house has an art gallery, a carved staircase, panelled rooms and decorated plasterwork. Guildford Museum, also in a 17th century house, covers local history, archaeology, Wealden ironwork, needlework and Lewis Carroll.

There is plenty of artwork along the river. A boatman with rope on the cobbled Guildford Wharf waits by the 18th century treadmill crane last used to unload barges in 1908 and restored and repositioned in 1972 to allow space for the A3100 roundabout which is the centre of Guildford's road network. The 6.1m crane, one of three left in the country, can lift 2t. The 19th century navigation offices were demolished in the late 1960s.

Guildford was a Saxon cemetery site and there has long been a town mill. A warehouse-like structure proclaims that it was the electricity works of 1913 and a number of brick canalside structures have been tastefully restored.

Guildford Cathedral has a commanding position on Stag Hill, the second new Anglican cathedral site in Britain since the Middle Ages. Built from 1936 to 1966, it is 111 x 12 x 21m high in red brick with a gold angel on a 55m tower and a honey-coloured sandstone interior in simplified Gothic Revival style but it is not universally loved. Despite being fairly well down the hillside on Stag Hill and having a tower rather than a spire, it is clearly visible from a large area of the surrounding Surrey countryside.

Guildford University was also completed in 1966 when Battersea College of Advanced Technology joined the decentralization boom. It hosts the biannual Guildford International Music Festival.

The Guildford–Effingham Junction railway crosses Dapdune bridge as it loops round Dapdune Wharf, the National Trust's canal centre flanked by the Sea Cadets' TS Queen Charlotte. In about 1901 there was an experiment with overhead wires between Guildford and Woodbridge, the wires 4.6m above the river, long before trolley buses used a similar system, electric boats being powered by a dynamo at Dapdune. Barges were built here until 1940. *Reliance*, built in the early 1930s, was sunk in the Thames after a collision in 1968, recovered from Leigh-on-Sea and brought back here for restoration in 1996. The last floating example, *Perseverance IV*, was built in 1935, worked until 1982 and was restored here in 1998. The other remaining Wey barge, *Speedwell*, is at Ellesmere Port.

Beyond the railway Woodbridge Meadows have been laid out as a riverside sculpture park with a number of exhibits in wood.

Buttercup meadow below St Catherine's chapel.

Guildford Wharf with man powered crane and sculpture.

Dapdune Wharf is the National Trust's canal centre.

A giant's eyebrows, nose, hands and feet beyond the plants in Woodbridge Meadows sculpture park.

A rope guide post above Stoke Lock, one of several to be found on the Wey.

Bowers Lock has a rural setting but within sound of the A3.

An industrial area is sited around the former Dennis works which turned out many fire engines, refuse lorries and buses before the river moves under the A3 Guildford bypass.

Houses remain on the left, almost every one with its own boat, it seems.

The navigation is well signposted and a fingerpost indicates where the navigation turns left. Stoke Park hosted the former Guilfest music festival.

A sewage works gives olfactory notice of arrival at Stoke Lock and return to the river. The route winds across watermeadows, alders on one side, pollard willows on the other, until turning right at the top of a weir to Bowers Lock and the 19th century mill which has been converted to a desirable residence, although nothing like Sutton Place which lies on the other side of the river.

Although it is not seen, the navigation completes a semicircle round it. It was built in the early 16th century by Sir Richard Weston, the promoter of the Wey Navigation, and has housed the art treasures of a more recent owner, Paul Getty, before passing into the hands of his junior.

After the A3 moves away for the last time the navigation passes a further attractive residence, Send Grove, with its own church.

A longer length of navigation through a nature conservation area ends with a return to the river at Triggs Lock. Although **Woking** is close, nothing is seen of it except for a single tower block over the trees. Worsfold Gates form a flood lock, normally left open. They are fitted with wooden sluice rods, levered up with a crowbar and held up by passing pins through. Once common, these are the last remaining examples of this system of operation.

The New Inn with its canalside garden welcomes users of the navigation.

Church near the water at Send Grove.

Statues watch Worsfold Gates, normally left open.

John Donne's summerhouse at Pyrford.

Papercourt Lock is completely surrounded by farmland with fine views in all directions. While not the first to have a high level discharge bypass channel, this one takes the form of a flight of wide weir steps with an awkward cross current just below the lock. The whole setting is most agreeable.

Back on the natural course, the route winds across watermeadows towards Newark Lock. Although the magnificent weatherboarded mill there was destroyed by fire in 1966, several other interesting buildings remain, enhanced by a display of restored agricultural equipment next to the navigation. A nearby weir is unusual in having a tiled roof over the sluice gates while across in the fields without a roof are the white stone remains of the 12th century Newark Priory. Once again it is a most rural and attractive area.

The route now breaks from the river for most of the remainder of its journey, passing through the floodgate at Walsham Gates. The remaining turf sides were only removed from working locks late in the 20th century with Walsham Gates still turf sided as they are normally left open.

A house on the left was John Donne's summerhouse with a roof of complex geometrical shape. Next to it is a house with fine gardens that come down to the river, stone lions on pillars and strategically placed floodlights, perhaps taking its influence from the Royal Horticultural Society's gardens at Wisley on the other side of the river.

The Anchor below Pyrford Lock proves popular with boaters, towpath users and motorists alike. Opposite it, Pyrford Marina is different from other boat areas in that it is off the navigation in a segregated lake.

The tranquillity comes to an end with the arrival of the M25 alongside at the southern end of a 2km straight but

The popular Anchor at Pyrford.

first it passes round West Hall, a red brick structure with the appearance of a school and with a venerable plane tree in the grounds, its spreading branches supported on large props.

The houses of the affluent **Byfleet** now back onto the navigation and must have received a rude awakening from the M25, newly arrived high above on the other bank. Byfleet Boat Club is surrounded by moorings for boats named with puns on Wey with monotonous regularity.

Bridges on this waterway usually have flat soffits but the notable exception is the round arched brick bridge carrying the railway over and breaking this long straight into two sections. Immediately between it and a power

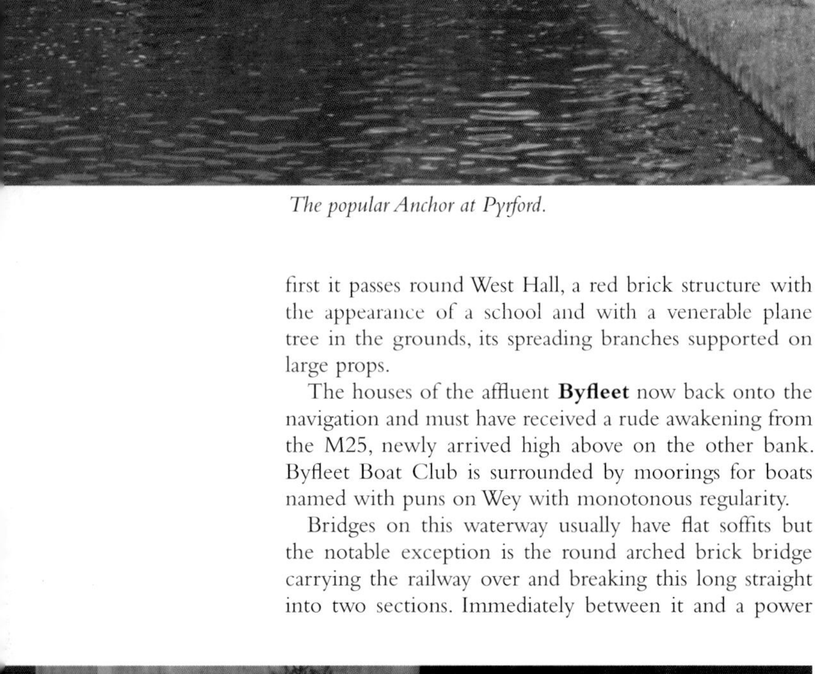

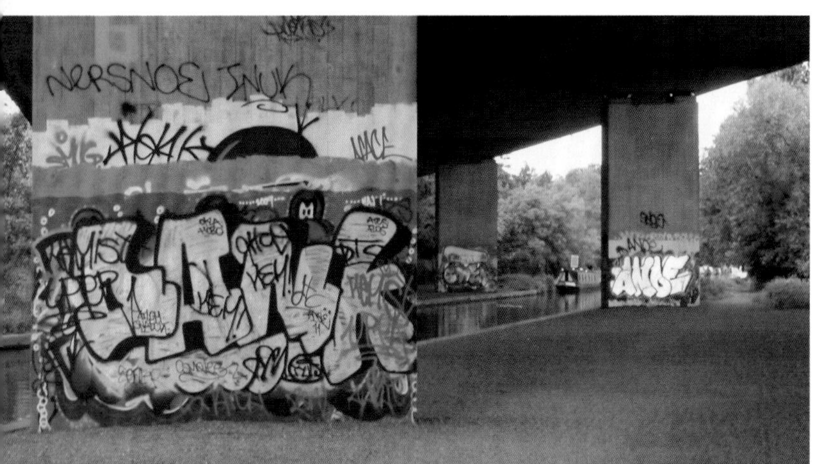

The M25 gives the graffiti merchants plenty of scope.

New Haw Lock was still turf sided in the 1980s.

A huge Coxes Mill complex at Addlestone.

station with low corrugated sided bridge over the navigation, the Basingstoke Canal joins on the left.

The M25 soars over on a viaduct of which the coloured graffiti is an artform in itself and more decorative than most.

Beyond the motorway is the former Brooklands car racing circuit, notable for its banked bend. It was 4.5km long, the fastest circuit in Britain from 1907 to 1939 with a record average lap speed of 200km/h, hosted the British Grand Prix and was used for setting the last track world speed record, Guinness's 215km/h in a Sunbeam in 1922. It also had an airfield, aircraft production displacing motor racing in 1939. Today some of the classics machines of car racing and flying are on display.

The oblique northern approach to Weybridge Town Lock.

New Haw Lock ends the straight and is overlooked by a lock keeper's delightful cottage. It also has a less common feature. The A318 bridge is so close to the lock that balance beams have had to be shortened and knotted ropes attached for pulling the lock gates shut. The White Hart is across the road.

Wildfowl abound on the large millpond above Coxes Lock. Coxes Mill is an eight storey brick structure which appears old despite its reinforced concrete extension at the rear yet it was completed in 1906. Closed in 1983, haunted and now used residentially, it looks over the high overflow discharge weir from the millpond, now operated as a wildlife area. It was supplied with grain from Tilbury by barge until 1969. In 1981 the barge traffic began again until the mill closed, the 70t barges showing a 70% fuel saving over the equivalent road transport costs.

Housing replaces the only ugly industrial area of the navigation which surrounded the Pelican at **Addlestone.** The church spire in **Weybridge** rises high above a sea of stockbroker Tudor in what is one of the most exclusive areas of Surrey, with the highest density of millionaires in the country. Residents have included E M Forster.

Weybridge Town Lock provides a problem for portable craft in that it is not easy to reach the water level on the downstream side because of the high walls and the proximity of a bridge. The problem is solved by portaging right into the weir stream and joining the river before it passes under the road to rejoin the navigation which still has woodland on one side.

Two successive channels weir off to the right.

The mill above Thames Lock was served by barge until the early 1960s despite the technical problems at this last lock. The 1653 turf sided structure was rebuilt in concrete in the 1930s, not without subsequent problems. There is only 900mm clearance over the bottom sill of the lock so an additional gate has been added 100m downstream. For boats with more than 800mm draught the extra gate has to be used to raise the bottom water level. Small boats need to portage to below the lower gate and make an awkward launch from the bottom of the wooded bank.

Thames Lock, the last on the Wey.

The lock keeper's cottage still serves its intended purpose, having been saved from demolition in 1975.

The river joins the River Thames between the Lincoln Arms and Shepperton Weir, site of numerous slaloms. To join the navigation of the River Thames below Shepperton Lock involves crossing the tail of the weirpool with the water still swirling and eddying by the time it reaches the far bank.

Shepperton Weir with its roofed controls in dry flow conditions. Often the whole of this area is white water. The Wey Navigation exits on the left with the main Thames on the right.

Distance
32km from Godalming to the River Thames

Navigation Authority
National Trust

OS 1:50,000 Sheets
176 West London
186 Aldershot & Guildford
187 Dorking & Reigate

Connection
Basingstoke Canal – *see CoB p105*

46 River Medway

Across the Garden of England

'Oppin' is all over,
Money is all spent,
Don't I wish I'd never
Come 'oppin dahn in Kent -
Wiv a tee-ay-ay, tee-ay-ay, tee-ay-ee-ay-O!
Anon

Leigh flood barrier is the official head of navigation.

The Medway Navigation has seen various changes during its life. Locks were first added in the 17th century and by the middle of the 19th century it was a thriving link between Tonbridge and the Thames estuary. In 1929/30 James Christie attempted a 10km extension to Penshurst, without success. In the early 1980s the Southern Water Authority (now the Environment Agency) partly succeeded where Christie failed. A new sluice was built just downstream of the A21 as part of a flood relief scheme and a cut was made, running along the north side of the railway.

Boating is not permitted by them upstream of the concrete footbridge below Leigh Sluice, now considered the head of navigation. It is surrounded by a battery of notices telling people to keep away.

There is very little cut, the navigation usually using the natural course of the River Medway, a chalkland river draining the Weald before carving through the North Downs beyond Maidstone. As it turns away from the Redhill railway line it rejoins the natural river course, a river which is lined with oaks more frequently than with any other tree. It is possible to follow the navigation all the way on foot but is not always cycle friendly, especially further down the navigation.

The railway line from Charing Cross passes over and the river divides round a 900m long island. The left fork winds round the back of a cricket pitch, surely unique for the number of lifebelts around its boundary. Towards the end there are public toilets. Hilden Brook enters, one of the maze of waterways which criss-cross this valley. The brook bounds one side of the ruined Norman castle largely hidden behind a high stone wall facing the river.

Great Bridge carries the A227, **Tonbridge**'s main street, the bridge acting as the physical limit of navigation for many larger craft. On its downstream side is the Castle public house facing Lyons Wharf.

Attractive modern buildings line the water. At Town Lock one of the SWA's controversial sluices was constructed. The lock itself is the top one of nine well-spaced broad beam locks on the navigation, in addition to Allington. The gates have a fussy design with no less than three separately controlled penstocks in each of the four gates and allowance for water to overtop them.

The navigation is quickly into open country with meadows on each side.

The first of many pillboxes lead down to Eldridge's Lock. At first the defence works seem to be near locks but they become more frequent as the river travels on. Hadlow Stair, near the lock, is pleasantly rural and includes a converted timber barn. There are many blackberry bushes lining the left bank of the river above and below the lock.

The flat land here is often known as the Garden of England and hopfields and orchards become more frequent. From Porter's Lock the first oast houses can be seen near Golden Green. The strangest structure to break the skyline is the thin tower of Hadlow Castle. This 46m folly was erected in 1835 by Walter Barton May who wished to have a view of the sea from his estate in the centre of Kent.

There was concern at the time of installation that the EA's sluices would kill, as they did. A canoe trail has now been designated. At East Lock a canoe chute has been installed beside a fish ladder, virtually unknown in this country but commonplace on the Continent, and beside a memorial. At Oak Weir Lock, the confluence with Hammer Dyke, the 1980s sluice in place of the popular Oak Weir has killed. Here a combined canoe chute and fish ladder has now been built.

Dredged gravel has been tipped on the banks. Below Sluice Weir Lock a corner of a steel barge is just visible in its final resting place below its tumulus of gravel.

M2
M20
Maidstone
Tovil
Wateringbury
Teston
E Farleigh
Nettlestead
Yalding
Hadlow
Hale Street
Golden Green
Hilden Park
A227
Tonbridge
R Medway
Leigh
A21

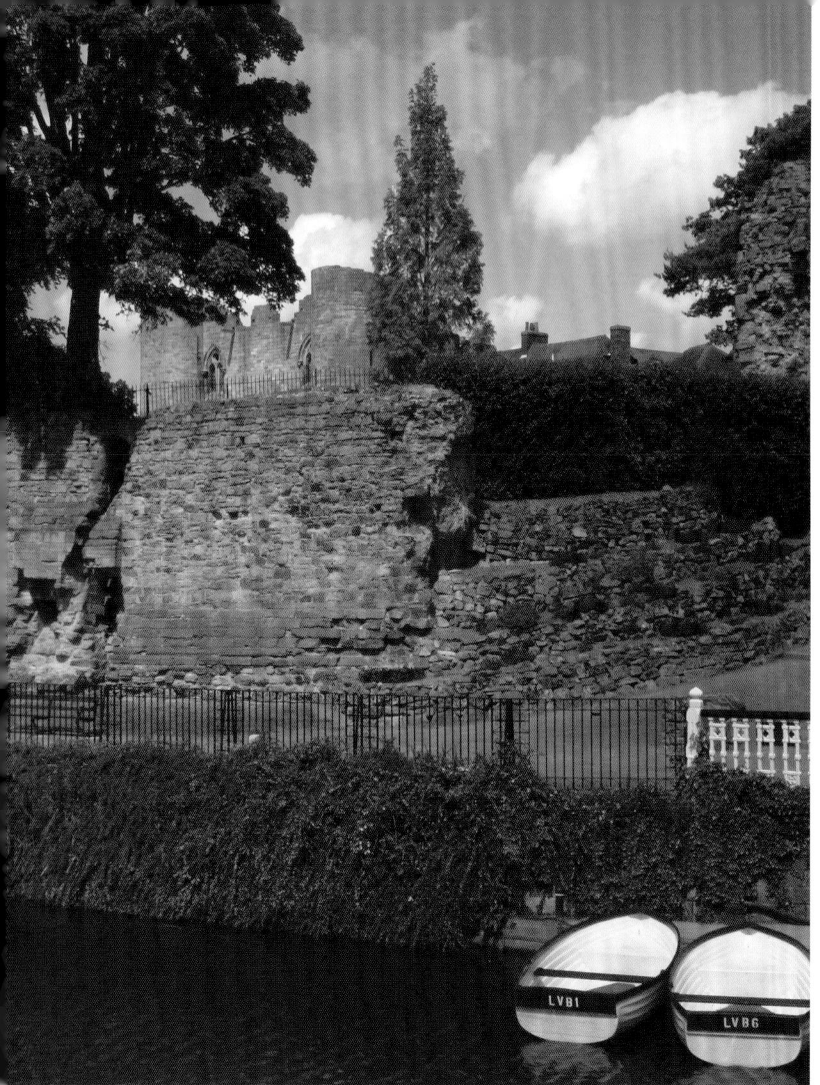

Tonbridge Castle next to the river.

Woodland downstream of Eldridge's Lock.

The twenty five 19th-century oast houses of Whitbread's Hop Farm are now a museum of hops, agriculture and shire horses with a high ropes course.

Beyond the railway bridge at Hale Street Stoneham Lock stands without gates, being one of three locks which were eliminated in 1915.

Orchards begin to flank the river and a set of magnificent oast houses at Yalding are right on the bank, described by Edmund Blunden in *The Hop Leaf.*

An exhibition of 3,500 teapots accompanies a potter on Teapot Island. The River Teise comes in at the top of Yalding Weir. A cut next to the partly thatched Anchor Inn and its drawbridge takes the navigation away from the river in a narrow section with sheet piled sides which enhance the waves thrown up by the cruising traffic. The EA have a depot which is in brick and shiplap timber. It is interesting just how many of the traditional canal maintenance buildings have survived around the country and are still being used without modification for their original purpose. Yalding Café is also on the cut. Hampstead Lock is surrounded by a group of factories and a marina but these are soon left as the cut rejoins the river, here overlooked by a hopfield.

Nettlestead introduces an even more potent plant than its name suggests, the giant hogweed.

Wateringbury is largely moorings plus a caravan site and Riverside Restaurant but its jewel is the delightful Grade II station, an absolute caricature of a Victorian railway station, tall and rickety with lofty chimneys and hexagonal panes in the leaded windows. The modern trains and colour light signals are wrong. It was made for semaphore signals and steam engines with small boilers and tall funnels and cabs.

At the far end of the moorings is a field of buttercups backed by a wood full of bluebells. On the opposite bank the field of hops has a backdrop of orchards of pink and white blossom. The Garden of England earns its title.

Teston Lock was overlooked by the remains of a linseed mill. Teston Bridge, below the lock, dates from medieval times and it is in ragstone with pedestrian refuges above the heavy cutwaters. The topography has become hilly by now and buildings as different as weatherboarded cottages and the solid block of Barham Court look down on the bridge from opposing sides of the valley.

East Farleigh must be the pride of the river, its church high on the hillside, its 14th century stone bridge leading across past a heavily timbered house and groupings of oast houses looking down over the lock.

Maidstone, the county town of Kent, is the major area of riverside buildings with houses first appearing

Oast houses near Golden Green.

on the left bank. Tovil has been the upstream terminus for commercial traffic on the navigation but wharves on the right bank now bear housing and the railway bridge carrying the freight line over the river to Tovil has been dismantled. Houseboats have been converted from old Thames sailing barges. An industrial estate remains and then large houses on the right have their grounds sweeping down to the river. The last of these, next to the church, is the Archbishop's Palace, a substantial structure mostly of stone right next to the river. A modern block opposite houses the law courts. A number of modern buildings represent what is pleasing in current architectural thinking by the river in the centre of Maidstone, a town once known for flint glass, and unused space has been landscaped to make best use of the river frontage.

The Restaurant Actief is moored opposite the gasworks. Sharp's toffee was produced here until 1998.

Anti tank blocks remain in place in front of a water intake on the right bank while a sewage works a little further down on the left has a particularly comprehensive set of Archimedes screw pumps outdoors where they can be seen spiralling their way upwards.

The Kings School Rochester boathouse has a striking structure reminiscent of a modern church with two steeply sloping sides and tall triangular ends, allowing boats to be stored vertically.

East Lock's fish ladder and canoe chute.

Beyond the railway crossing is the Kent Messenger Millennium Bridge, the world's first stress ribbon bridge cranked in plan. The catenary walkway is not quite self-supporting and requires a worryingly slim stainless

Riverside dwelling converted from oast houses at Yalding.

Yalding bridge on the natural river channel. The seat is one of several items in the area with such carving.

steel prop in the centre but would probably look more disconcerting with no prop, which it almost manages.

At the other end of the time scale is the 13th century moated Allington Castle, once owned by poet Sir Thomas Wyatt, now a conference centre.

The Malta Inn is a steakhouse and boasts a garden of children's playthings. The oast houses behind it house the Kent Life open air museum and this area may be the best vehicle access point for the downstream end of the navigation, even if space is at a premium.

Boats have been moored all down the bank.

Allington Lock is the bottom of the navigation and the tidal limit. Lack of water below the lock means that it is only in use from three hours before high tide to two hours after it.

Another historical bridge at Teston.

East Farleigh bridge with more oast houses beyond.

East Farleigh church on its hill above the river.

Distance
31km from Leigh to Allington

Navigation Authority
Environment Agency

OS 1:50,000 Sheets
(178 Thames Estuary) 188 Maidstone & Royal Tunbridge Wells

Connection
Tidal River Medway – see RoB p236

The Archbishop's Palace fronts the river at Maidstone.

47 River Rother

A river lost in the Edwardian era

And east till doubling Rother crawls
To find the fickle tide,
By dry and sea-forgotten walls,
Our ports of stranded pride.
Rudyard Kipling

Bodiam bridge was formerly vulnerable to naval attacks and also to settlement.

Rising near Rotherfield, the River Rother flows eastwards across East Sussex to Rye Bay. Previously called the Limen, it is sometimes known as the Eastern Rother to distinguish it from the tributary of the Arun. From the mid 16th century it was used for carrying iron from

Bodiam Castle is the best example of its type in the country.

Udiam and Bodiam. In 1800 it was proposed to develop it as the Medway & Rother Junction Canal to Rye. Rennie's plan of 1802 for a London–Portsmouth canal had the River Rother as one of its branches and in 1813 he carried out a survey for a canal between Mayfield and Bodiam. A popular motor cruise in Edwardian days was from Scots Float Sluice to Bodiam. Commercial navigation ceased about 1914.

The current width does not reflect the former commercial use. The head of navigation is by the Castle Inn at Bodiam bridge, which has settled badly at some stage in its history. There are levées for much of the length of the river, meaning that interesting features seen in the distance may never be seen again from the water. The water level may be kept low for land drainage interests but there is plenty of depth and the flow is fast and narrow to Newenden. Before Scots Float Sluice was built the river was tidal to Bodiam.

The Sussex Border Path follows the river, running along the levée above the nettles and springtime celandines.

There are three oast houses in the vicinity but the major structure is Bodiam Castle. Surprisingly, considering the size of the river today, it was built to protect the south coast from attack as the French could sail up the River Rother. It was built by Sir Edward Dalyngrigge with stone brought up the river and is the best example of its type in the country, its external walls being almost complete, spiral staircases, battlements and massive round stone towers rising vertically from a lily pond moat which formerly served his manor house. Lack of military action has helped preserve its good looks.

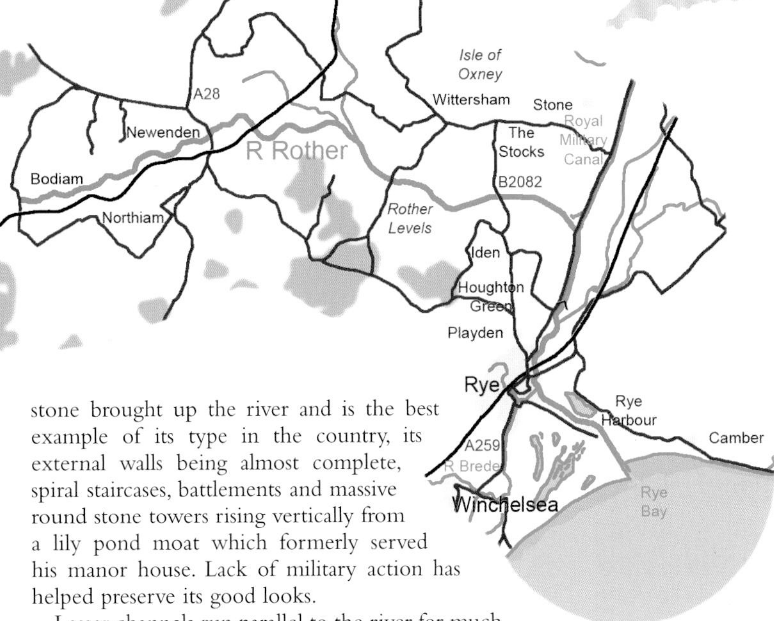

Lesser channels run parallel to the river for much

The old bridge carrying the A28 at Newenden.

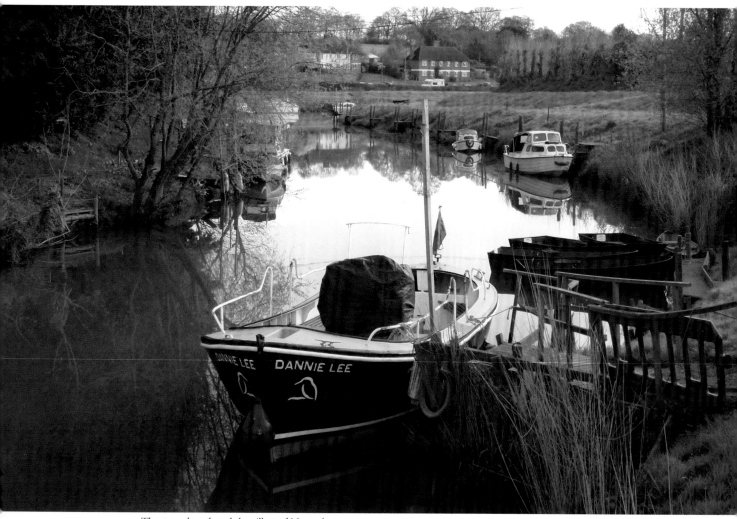

The steam launch and the village of Newenden.

One of the owl boxes at Iden.

of the way and occasional pumping stations on the banks are almost the only buildings seen as the river winds its way through open countryside. At intervals there are pairs of large owl boxes on long poles on top of the levées. These are for barn owls and are the most successful in the country. They are in pairs because the female kicks the male out when the young are being reared. The male owl often has the further indignity of finding the other box of the pair being used by kestrels as a nesting site. Sheep graze and skylarks sing above the fields.

Just before powerlines cross, the river is joined by the Kent Ditch on the left and the county boundary with Kent follows the river most of the way to Iden.

Dixter Wood rises up the hillside towards Great Dixter, a half-timbered manor house of 1460, restored by Sir Edwin Lutyens early in the 20th century and extended with a medieval house brought from Beneden. The great hall has an unusual roof and fine furniture and needlework inside while the gardens were planted in the style of Gertrude Jekyll with a formal topiary lawn, wild meadow garden and unusual plants grown by Christopher Lloyd. Also amongst Northiam's thatched and weatherboarded cottages is Brickwall, a 17th century half-timbered mansion with an 18th century bowling alley and a chess garden where shaped yews are still being grown to form the pieces. St Mary's church has a tall ironstone spire on a Norman lower tower, 14th century arcades in the nave and a chancel of 1837. John Frewin and his son, Thankful, were rectors for 102 years and Accepted Frewin became Archbishop of York in 1660. A century earlier, Elizabeth I changed her shoes in the village in 1573 on her way to Rye, the green silk shoes she took off being preserved here. The oak tree on the green may be a thousand years old but even older still was the 9th century 20m x 4.3m Danish ship found in the field by the river in 1822.

Bulrushes and greater reedmace edge the river at intervals and in the spring there is a spread of lady's smock at Newenden where a fine bridge of rounded weathered stone arches takes the A28 over. Beyond the hop fields to the south are more oast houses. A steam trip boat is moored in Newenden, the white weatherboarded houses of which face across the river at this former port. Cricket has been played here for about seven centuries.

Since the start the right bank has been closely followed by the Kent & East Sussex Steam Railway which now crosses. Opened in 1900 as the Rother Valley Railway, it was the world's first full size light railway. These days it has 17km of track with Victorian steam and commuter diesel

Old oast houses at Houghton Green.

engines and has a marked Edwardian flavour. The line is best known for its part in the TV filming of the *Darling Buds of May* but was also familiar to the many Londoners who used it to bring them down for the annual hop picking.

The river turns away from Brickhurst Wood and Great Knelle Farm with its wild boar towards New Barn where there is a wind turbine. Levées were formed from dredgings and upper levels back from the water are edged with sheet piling while the river eats away at the intermediate banks. A towpath follows most of the way and white angling pegs are also staked all along the bank.

In 1823 a 16th century 19m Dutch trading vessel was found, apparently covered with nearly 6m of deposited material.

Hexden Channel and Newmill Channel both enter from the north, separated by a former sluice. Meanwhile, the Otter Channel follows the right bank and is pumped in at Wittersham Bridge. There are still otters in the vicinity.

The river turns to follow the foot of a hill, skirting the Rother Levels and cutting through beds of soil containing shells. The Kent border moves off north across these levels and powerlines follow the river for 4km as a pumping station adds some more streams to the flow. North of the levels is the Isle of Oxney where there are a windmill and water tower at the Stocks, the isle ending at the surprisingly steep Stone Cliff.

Iden bridge carries the B2082 which descends through orchards surrounding the village of Iden. The house next to the bridge has a very neat weathervane with a sheep in outline and a solid crouching sheepdog to catch the wind. Moorings follow.

The next bridge carries the minor road following the Royal Military Canal which joins, there being plans to reopen the connection to let larger craft use the canal. The road now follows the River Rother which acts as an extension of the military fortifications. This is also the line of the Saxon Shore Way walk. Indeed, Appledore was a busy port until the course of the river changed in 1287.

Caravans accompany a set of moorings on the east bank, the river having now turned to flow south.

A house at Houghton Green incorporates a pair of truncated oast houses.

Scots Float Sluice, formerly Star Lock, is the present tidal limit, the current sluices built in the mid 1980s. EA rules forbid unpowered craft from approaching within 200m, meaning a portage down the road where the carriageway comes right up to the fence or a trudge through deep vegetation, again with no path.

It pays to relaunch at the top of the tide as the banks below the sluice are of steep silt and the channel almost empties. There is a concrete slipway on the right with a locked but climbable gate at the top. However, this also becomes a silt slope lower down.

Heavy training walls, partly collapsed, mark the entry of the Union Channel. To the east is a large windfarm. Banks collect areas of flotsam, mostly plastic, and the river passes through a designated water ski area, overlooked by white weatherboarded cottages at Playden. The slim spire is on a church of about 1190.

The Ashford–Hastings railway and the A259 pass over, a pillbox strategically sited between them. The change beyond the second bridge is immediate and dramatic as the moorings and associated shorebase of Rye's fishing fleet, the largest in the south, is met although only a

Below Scots Float Sluice at low tide with silt worth avoiding.

The Rye fishing fleet with the town itself on the hill behind.

The unusual town water reservoir outside St Mary's church.

The Land Gate, at one time protected by a portcullis and the only dry land approach to the town.

low wall divides the industry from a bowling green and a children's playground on the Town Salts where there were at least a hundred salt pans. Rye is the only harbour controlled by the EA.

Rye is the finest example of a small medieval hill town in Britain, the hill capped by the 12th century St Mary's church with Norman to Perpendicular styling, notable stained glass windows, carved mahogany altar and a turret clock still using the works made in **Winchelsea** in 1560 – a 5.5m pendulum and twin guilded cherub quarter boys outside to toll the quarter hours. In the corner of the churchyard, the highest point in Rye, is an oval brick tower 5.2m x 2.7m which projects through a brick arch roof, topped with tiling and a lead ridge like an upturned boat. Below is a 9.1m x 6.1m oval brick cistern which holds 91m^3 for the town's water supply and was fed from springs in the Ashdown sands, rising 24m though 50mm diameter elm pipes. At the foot of Conduit Hill are the remains of a 1718 horse gin pump.

Although now 3km inland, the town was formerly on an island and then was surrounded by sea except for the 14th century Land Gate which had a portcullis and drawbridge in the flint town wall. The Romans used the port to export lead. In 1030 the estate was given to the Abbot of Fécamp by Cnut. The port was captured by the French in 1216, attacked by them in 1339 and 1365 and rebuilt after they nearly destroyed the town in 1377. The Ypres Tower was built in 1250 for fortification, burnt by the French in 1377, bought by John de Ypres as a ruin in 1439, bought back by the corporation in 1518 for use as a courthouse and jail and now houses Rye Castle Museum of shipping, smuggling, military items, the Cinque Ports, dolls, toys, Rye pottery, sheep and the formation of Romney Marsh. The Gun Garden in front used to contain cannons to protect Rye although the three current guns were made in 1980 to commemorate the 80th birthday of the Queen Mother, the Warden of the Cinque Ports at the time. Rye became part of the expanded Cinque Ports & Two Ancient Towns in 1336, providing maritime defence before the navy was formed, giving the town and residents special privileges in return, including being an important supplier of fish to London. However, this did not stop the major French raid in 1377, when the church bells were stolen, being recovered by an expedition organized by the Bishop of Lewes the following year. As a result of the raid the townsfolk hanged and quartered their officials for negligence.

When Elizabeth I visited the town in 1573, following the shoe changing episode, she proclaimed it Royal Rye after the reception she received.

French attacks continued into the 15th century.

The town became a refuge for Hugenots who brought weaving skills and the town economy developed in the 18th century on wool, lace, brandy, gin, rum and tea smuggling, the 600 strong Hawkhurst Gang being notable proponents. They used the Mermaid Inn of about 1500 built over a vaulted 13th century cellar and the town had many cellars for contraband with interconnecting attic escape passages. On his visit in 1773 John Wesley expressed his disquiet about the smuggling.

The Town Hall contains a pillory and a cage holding the skull of a butcher who tried to murder the mayor in 1732 but killed his brother-in-law by mistake.

This town of steep cobbled streets, half-timbered buildings and medieval and Georgian buildings has attracted many writers. The playwright Fletcher lived here in a

The Ypres Tower looks over the estuary, the sea now only just visible on the horizon.

The sea reach with withies marking the fairway.

15th century house. Henry James lived in the Georgian mansion Lamb House (named after a former mayor) from 1898 to 1916 and wrote the best novels of his later period including *The Wings of a Dove* and *The Golden Bowl*. The house was later occupied by E F Benson, another mayor, who wrote the *Mapp & Lucia* books about Tilling, his name for Rye, the subsequent TV series being filmed in the town.

Rye Town Model Sound & Light Show charts seven centuries of Rye history at the Strand Quay.

The River Rother has made great changes, its mouth having moved from an earlier position near New Romney. In the 13th century a series of storms devastated the south coast, the Great Storm of 1287 moving the rivermouth in one night.

Silting problems have long been present. A 63-year project to build a new channel from Rye, sited on its sandstone rock, to the sea 3km west of the old harbour was completed in June 1787. Five months later it was abandoned because of the accumulation of sand and shingle.

Over the centuries there has been conflict between navigation and agricultural interests, the needs to maintain scouring of the riverbed and to control water. Construction of sluices on the Rother were said to obstruct navigation and resulted in the people of Rye rioting in 1817 and again in 1830, the Marines and cavalry being called in on the second occasion.

Today the main incidents are the Rye Arts Festival, Rye International Jazz Festival and the weekly sheep market. Stone is a regular import.

The River Brede enters from the right along the inappropriately named Rock Channel, used by pleasure craft.

Sea aster grows along the banks of the River Rother, introducing a more maritime feeling as seaweed floats up and down with the tide. Gravel workings along the banks add an industrial flavour.

Rye Harbour afforded shelter for George I from a storm in 1726. Opposite the William the Conqueror is a relatively new inshore rescue boat station. There was an offshore lifeboat until 1928 when the *Mary Stanford* was lost with her crew of 17, commemorated in a window in the church. This is the last road access point to the river.

Overlooking the final reach of the river is a Martello tower. Rather grander is Camber Castle, built 2km further west in the 1530s for Henry VIII. Tudor rose in plan to deflect cannon balls, it was intended to defend the estuary until the river changed its course. It was partially torn down in 1643 and is now occupied by sea birds.

To the west of the river the Rye Harbour Nature Reserve forms a major part of a 7km^2 SSSI with shingle ridges, saltmarsh, grazing marsh, arable fields and gravel pits. It has one of the finest examples of shingle vegetation in Britain and has 3,200 species including rare wild flowers, dragonflies and other insects including up to 90 species of moth, good winter wildfowl and breeding terns. Hides give views onto the estuary where blackheaded gulls, oystercatchers, turnstones and other species search the mud for food.

Rye Harbour's Martello tower.

The final reach is unusual in that it is marked at very close intervals with beacons and withies which form straight lines. Flows are outgoing from Dover high water. At low water the estuary nearly drains and ingoing flows start five hours twenty minutes before Dover high water at up to 9km/h, much more strongly than the ebb, strongest between two hours and one hour before high water. There are training walls at the end, the ingoing flow forming an eddy on the northeast side of the west training wall. Southwest winds cause the sea to break heavily on the bar and easterly winds cause clapotis off the west training wall. Tidal streams are weak in Rye Bay but numerous gill nets may be deployed.

A pillbox on the west side guards the entrance. Opposite, the golf course breaks up into dunes and then Camber Sands which run on past Camber, the bulks of the nuclear power stations in the distance marking Dungeness.

To the east the chalk cliffs at Fairlight give an unexpected vertical element to a largely horizontal landscape.

Distance
26km from Bodiham to Rye Bay

Navigation Authority
Environment Agency

OS 1:50,000 Sheets
(188 Maidstone & Royal Tunbridge Wells)
189 Ashford & Romney Marsh
199 Eastbourne & Hastings

The larger western training wall, seen from Rye Bay.

Index

Main coverage is listed in **bold** print.

Which book?

This visual index gives a quick guide to which waterways are included in each of the three books in this series.

Canals of Britain

British River Navigations

Rivers of Britain